Guide to
Namibia & Botswana

2nd Edition

Chris McIntyre
Simon Atkins

BRADT PUBLICATIONS

First published in 1991 by Bradt Publications, 41 Nortoft Rd, Chalfont St Peter, Bucks SL9 0LA, England.
  Distributed in Southern Africa by Media House Publications, PO Box 782395, Sandton 2146, South Africa.

British Library Cataloguing in Publication data
 A catalogue record for this book
 is available from the British Library

ISBN 1 898323 00 3

Cover photos: Sossusvlei (Namibia) and Okavango Delta (Botswana) by Chris McIntyre

Maps by Caroline Crump
Printed by the Guernsey Press, Channel Islands

The Authors

Simon Atkins and Chris McIntyre decided independently to write a travel guide on the region whilst they were both VSO science teachers in schools in rural Zimbabwe. Joining forces, they spent many months travelling throughout southern Africa.

Back in Britain, Simon is a documentary film maker concerned with social and developmental issues, currently based in London. Whenever possible, he tries to escape from 'the smoke' to go walking and climbing.

Chris now works from London, enjoying the good life in Notting Hill Gate. A frequent traveller and freelance writer promoting responsible tourism in southern Africa, he is also pursuing a professional career and finding time to play competitive racquet sports.

Major Contributors

Phil Deutshle (Information on Botswana and general travel information).
Phil taught mathematics in a village school in Mapoka, Botswana, for three years before setting out to cycle across the Kalahari. Following this, he was invited to feature in an episode of the television series *Classic Adventure*, where he and the presenter crossed the Namib desert on foot.

Dave Else (Information on Waterberg Plateau).
David has been working, trekking and travelling in Africa since 1983. He has written several guides for walkers and travellers in Africa, many of which are published by Bradt Publications.

Damien Lewis (Articles on the Okavango and Veterinary Cordon Fences).
An environmental research journalist, Damien specialises in detailed and original articles concerning conservation, development and the rights of indigenous peoples throughout the developing world.

Fritz Tallantire (Information throughout the book).
A seasoned traveller, Fritz has made many expeditions to southern Africa and helped both editions of this guide immensely, with information, suggestions and proof-reading. When not travelling, he lives in west London, drives a classic 1954 Citroen, and works successfully to increase the country's consumption of fine wine and spirits.

Gill Thomas (Drawings and illustrations).
An artist and teacher, Gill returned in 1990 from three years teaching with VSO, at Mposi, a rural Zimbabwean school. She now divides her time between drawing, walking, climbing, and working as a teacher in inner London.

Duncan White (Namibia information, especially Swakopmund).
Duncan lived in Africa for several years before delaying a canoe expedition down the Congo to help Chris with some final research in Namibia. His assistance, and his penchant for cold beers, were immeasurable.

Acknowledgements

In the course of our travels in Namibia and Botswana, we have received a great deal of help from various people, both in the form of hospitality and in the form of specialist information. We would particularly like to thank the following: the Blackie family; Shirley Cormack; Alan Elliot; Anne and Lennox Gibson; Alison Martin, for *that* hitch; Irene Johnstone; the late Louw Schoemann; the Sculphur family; Surveor General of Windhoek; Dr. Nigel Wilson; and finall the many people in Namibia and Botswana whose names we neve knew (or have forgotten), for their help and generosity.

Back at home, the following cannot go without a mention and thanks: Jabbar Al-Sadoon, for encouragement; Trevor Atkins, Simon's father; Pete Bagley and Gaynor Jenkins, who put Simon up at the start; Veronique Bovington; Maggie Boys, for the letters; Hilary Bradt, our publisher, for endless patience as we struggled to write everything up; Kylie Brown, Simon's mother; Michelle, for welcome distractions; Ginny Devonshire; Mr and Mrs Fritz; Jane Harley, our copy editor, who also provided extra travel information on Botswana; Anne-Marie McDermott, for putting up with Simon's constantly changing deadlines; Peter and Elizabeth McIntyre, Chris' parents, for the organisation which made these trips possible, and for much else besides; Jonnie Mogford; Alison North; Stuart Raeburn, for information and help at the very beginning; Iain Young, for his perspective; and last but not least Purba, Jeremy and Ocky, for their endless mugs of coffee, food, good company and unfaltering support.

Chris McIntyre and Simon Atkins, June 1991, Oxford

Acknowledgements to the second edition

In the course of extensive research for this second edition, I have received more help from many of those above, as well as assistance and much valuable update material from Tim Best; Andrew and Mary Bingham; Steve and Louise Braine; David Owen and Lucy Brock; Nigel Cantle; Diana Clement (U.K.); J.R.Corney (S.Africa); Jane Elliot; Hennie Fourie, Namibia's Director of Tourism and Resorts; Manfred Goldbeck; Wayne and Lise Hanssen; David Hatford (U.K.); Marie Holstenson; Janine and Uwe at Kessler; Solomon Khundu; Chris Lake; Chris MacIntyre; Susan Oatway; Jane Parrit; Rhodri Pazzi-Axworthy; Nigel Pearson; Mr Pimenta; Paul Reed; Dennis Rundle; Anette Faber and Terry Ryan; Amy Schoemann; Dr. Anne Skeldon; Cindi Smith (Canada); Rose Smith; Caroline Thom; Gavin and Val Thomson; and Keith Woosey.

A final thanks to my very tolerant flatmate, Sarah Stevenson, for her endless understanding and good cheer, and special notes of gratitude to Hilary Bradt, my publisher, and Jane Harley, my editor, for help, encouragement and patience throughout the time that it took to prepare this edition.

Chris McIntyre, March 1994, London

Contents

Part 2 : Namibia

7. In Namibia 81

8. Windhoek 95

9. Southern Namibia 109

10. Central Namibia 129

11. The Central Namib 137

Part 3 : Botswana

Introduction

Namibia and Botswana epitomise the magic of Africa, conjured up by views of vast game-covered plains under inky-blue skies, or harsh desert landscapes dotted with strange contorted plants – uncharted wilderness where you seem to be the first to tread.

People are few and far between since the region has one of the world's lowest population densities. This makes the scattered towns and villages all the more vibrant. Here is life at its most basic, a raw untapped energy in the land and its people.

Travelling in both countries is remarkably trouble-free, allowing the visitor a freedom, rarely found elsewhere in Africa, to explore at will. Communications are efficient, the towns modern, and both countries offer value-for-money. Neither however is 'cheap'. Botswana, in particular, can be expensive, but offers in return the chance to experience some of the world's top game parks, still little visited.

Your own vehicle will give you the greatest flexibility, allowing you to explore remote areas which would otherwise be impossible to reach. However, some spectacular destinations – such as the Okavango – are accessible using public transport or, of course, by hitching.

For the thrill of safari and perhaps your first sight of lion, Chobe and Moremi are unbeatable, whilst Etosha boasts vast herds of game amidst some of the region's most spectacular scenery. Visiting the Okavango Delta, you can leave your vehicle behind to relax in a dug-out canoe, gliding through lagoons and reeds, past islands teeming with birdlife.

Away from the parks and reserves, the naturalist will be fascinated by the unique flora and fauna which has evolved in the Namib, one of the world's oldest deserts. Here periodic fogs are the only source of moisture, sustaining the white beetles unique to this area and the prehistoric *Welwitschia* plants which can live for over a thousand years.

Intrepid anthropologists may also head for the deserts, seeking the mystical, isolated hills – Gcwihaba, Tsodilo, Brandberg and Aha – which have sheltered bushmen, and their paintings, for millennia.

The hiker has a chance to walk remote seldom-used trails through forbidding yet stunning scenery. These range from trekking along the Fish River Canyon – second in size only to the Grand Canyon – to stalking white rhino on the Waterberg Plateau.

Newly independent Namibia is fascinating for its diversity of peoples. Its constitution has been hailed as one of the world's most democratic. Botswana has the strongest economy in sub-Saharan Africa, based primarily on its enormous diamond wealth, but is facing growing environmental and social problems. Both countries have maintained a strong anti-apartheid stance, though have nevertheless been heavily reliant economically on their powerful southern neighbour. The coming first multi-racial elections in South Africa should finally put an end to this conflict.

How to use this guide

There are five main types of information contained in this guide.

Background Information to explain something of the history, people, language and environment of Namibia and Botswana (*Part 1,* Chapters 1, 2 and 3).

General Travel Information to help plan your trip, safeguard your health, and make the most of your trips into the bush (*Part 1,* Chapters 4, 5 and 6).

Specific Country Information with details of the individual countries to organise your time in the region. This is dealt with in Chapter 7, *In Namibia*, and Chapter 16, *In Botswana*.

Comprehensive Regional Travel Information to give up-to-date advice on all the main towns, national parks, and other places of interest. This specific information is arranged by region.

Special Interest Boxes which cover a range of topics from the details of Namibia's flora and fauna to the controversial issues surrounding conservation of the Okavango Delta and the Kalahari Desert.

Part 1
General
Information

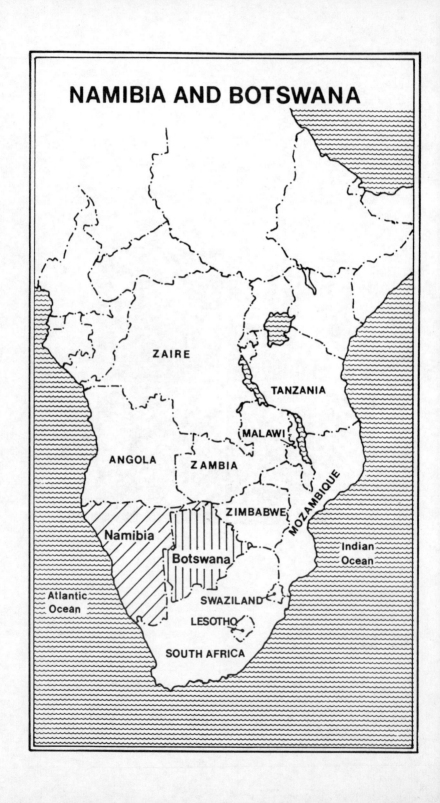

NAMIBIA AND BOTSWANA

ZAIRE

TANZANIA

MALAWI

ANGOLA

ZAMBIA

ZIMBABWE

MOZAMBIQUE

Namibia

Botswana

Indian Ocean

Atlantic Ocean

SWAZILAND

LESOTHO

SOUTH AFRICA

Chapter 1

Namibia and Botswana: an overview

FACTS AND FIGURES

Location

Namibia and Botswana are extensive and sparsely-populated countries, situated on the Tropic of Capricorn in the sub-tropical desert region of southern Africa. Namibia extends east into the sub-continent from the south Atlantic Ocean, abutting landlocked Botswana in central southern Africa. Between them they share the Kalahari Desert which dominates the east of Namibia, and most of Botswana.

Size

Namibia is the larger of the two countries at 824,290 square kilometres, compared to Botswana's 581,730 square kilometres. Together they have a land area almost six times that of Great Britain, yet only a tiny combined population of three million. The population density of both Botswana and Namibia is two inhabitants per square kilometre – roughly a hundred times smaller than Britain and one of the lowest in the world.

Topography

Namibia   Namibia can be conveniently split into three topographical areas: the Namib Desert in the west stretches for 1,600km along the Atlantic coast in a narrow strip of gravel flats and sand dunes, and is one of the driest places on earth; inland, a deeply incised escarpment climbs up from the coast to the central plateau at 2,000m; from here the interior plateau gently descends to the Kalahari Desert at about 1,000m, merging with Botswana.

Botswana   Botswana too can be divided into three distinct regions: the Kalahari Desert lies in the centre and south-west, covering two-thirds of the land area; the Okavango river basin in the northwest contains the Okavango Delta, an extensive area of swamp and marshland with a tropical climate; by contrast, the developed eastern strip of the country, bordering South Africa, is away from the Kalahari Desert and contains the railway and 80% of the population, with sufficient rainfall for crops.

Climate

Both Namibia and Botswana have a sub-tropical desert climate. Rainfall occurs in the hottest season – generally from December to March – and can be very heavy in northern Botswana, and north-eastern Namibia. The further south or west you go, the drier it gets, with many southern regions of the Kalahari and the whole of the coastal Namib Desert receiving no rainfall at all some years. 'Summer' temperatures can reach an unpleasantly hot (and humid in the north-east) 40°C. In the 'winter' (May to September), it's generally cool, pleasant and clear with day temperatures averaging around 25°C, and night-time temperatures much colder. Frost is possible in the higher areas and the deserts.

History

Namibia   Namibia was a German colony until 1915 when it was invaded by South African and British forces during the First World War. At the end of the war, South Africa received a League of Nations mandate to administer the territory, which it called South West Africa. Despite a UN vote to revoke the mandate in 1978 (Resolution 435), and increasing military pressure by the South West African People's Organisation (SWAPO) led by Sam Nujoma against the occupying South African troops, South Africa held onto the territory for another 10 years. Following extensive talks in 1988, UN Resolution 435 was implemented, and Namibia became independent on March 21 1990.

Botswana   From the 18th Century, the original Bushmen inhabitants of the whole region were gradually pushed into the central Kalahari and marginalised by the progressive expansions of Tswana, Ndebele and finally Boer peoples. The British made Botswana a protectorate in 1885 (calling it Bechuanaland), in order to keep it from German expansionism in Namibia and to keep open the north-south trade route. The protectorate was barely developed during the British administration, and remained very poor right up to independence in 1966. A year after independence, diamonds were discovered, and the country has developed rapidly since then.

Government

Namibia   The elected president, Sam Nujoma, heads a multi-party government with a SWAPO majority. The main opposition party is the pro-South African Democratic Turnhalle Alliance (DTA), which has 21 of the 72 seats in the Constituent Assembly.

Botswana   The Botswana Democratic Party (BDP), founded by Sir Seretse

Khama, has held power since independence in 1966, with Khama the first president. Dr Quett Masire succeeded Khama on his death in 1980, and has been president since then. Five of the 32 parliamentary seats are held by minority parties.

Economy

Namibia   Diamond mining is the mainstay of the Namibian economy, and there are important reserves of copper, uranium and other minerals. Fishing, cattle rearing and tourism also play an important role. Economically Namibia is very dependent on South Africa, sharing the same currency.

Botswana   Immediately after independence, Botswana was ranked in the bottom 20 poorest countries of the world, with cattle ranching the dominant industry and income earner. One year later, the world's second largest diamond pipe was discovered at Orapa and with diamond mining now accounting for up to 70% of export earnings, Botswana has one of the fastest-growing economies in the world. Beef exports to the EU rank second in importance, though there is growing concern at the damaging extent of over-grazing. The country also mines manganese, copper and nickel, and tourism is of increasing economic value.

Currency

Rates of exchange in March 1994:
£1   = N$5.30 (Namibia) = P3.80 (Botswana) = R5.30 (South Africa).
US$ = N$3.53 (Namibia) = P2.53 (Botswana) = R3.53 (South Africa).
Namibia's currency was changed in September 1993 from the South African Rand to the Namibian Dollar. This will be fixed at the same value as the Rand for the near future, though the banks will charge a small commission to convert from one currency to the other.

Namibia remains generally cheaper to visit than Botswana, though both economies are strong compared to their neighbours in central and east Africa – and therefore more expensive.

Population

Namibia   1,760,000 (1988). There are 11 ethnic groups, of which the largest are the Owambos which make up half the country's population. The Damaras and Hereros make up most of the remaining half. The population is densest in the north (near the Angolan border) and in the central plateau, where rainfall is heaviest.

Botswana   1,285,000 (1990). The Tswana ethnic group accounts for 90% of the population, although there are eight other separate tribes in the country. The Kalahari Desert is the last remaining refuge for the traditional hunter-gatherer existence of the Bushmen.

Language

Namibia   Before independence, the official languages were Afrikaans, English and German. Following independence the official language is now just English. The main ethnic language groups are Bantu and Khoi-San.

Botswana   English is the official language of government and business, and is taught at school. It's widely spoken in the main towns and tourist areas. Nearly everybody speaks Setswana – the language of the Batswana people. Other languages include Bakalanga (a Shona dialect) spoken in the north-east, and the Khoi (or 'click') language of the Kalahari Bushmen.

Religion

Namibia and Botswana   The main western religion is Christianity, although most people hold traditional African religions and beliefs.

Flora and Fauna

Despite their aridity, both Namibia and Botswana are full of game. The many national parks and game reserves are superb, and far, far away from the tourist hordes of East Africa. In addition, an extra dimension of interest is found in the extraordinary way that the plant, animal, and indeed human populations have adapted to survive in the harsh environment. Bushmen are the only people on earth who have learnt to survive in an environment devoid of any ground water. And strange, contorted plants live in the Namib Desert, with a nightly fog their only source of moisture.

NAMIBIA – A BRIEF HISTORY

Pre-Independence

On March 21 1990, Namibia finally gained its independence, after a bitter liberation struggle and diplomatic activity that stretched back for over 20 years. The legacy of colonialism that it shook off dates back hundreds of years to the European seafarers and explorers who first claimed this land as their own despite the indigenous people.

In the 15th Century, trade between Europe and the East opened up sea routes along the Namibian coast and around the Cape of Good Hope – the first Europeans to step on Namibian soil were the Portuguese in 1485. Diego Cão stopped briefly at Cape Cross on the Skeleton Coast and erected a Limestone cross. On 8th December 1487, Bartholomeu Diaz reached Walvis Bay and then continued south to what is now Lüderitz. However, the coast was so totally barren and uninviting that even though the Portuguese had already settled in Angola, and the Dutch in the Cape, little interest was shown in Namibia.

It was only in the latter half of the 18th Century when British, French and American whalers began to make use of the ports of Lüderitz and Walvis Bay, that the Dutch authorities in the Cape decided in 1793 to take possession of Walvis Bay — the only good deep water port on the coast. A few years later, France invaded Holland, prompting England to seize control of the Cape Colony and with this Walvis Bay. Very little was known about the interior, and it wasn't until the middle of the 19th Century that explorers, missionaries and traders started to venture inland, with Charles Andersson leading the way.

In 1884, a German merchant called Lüderitz started to buy land on the coast, and established the first permanent settlement in Namibia — the town that grew was named Lüderitz after him. (It was this act that finally prompted Britain to make Bechuanaland a protectorate.) Lüderitz was bought out a few years later by the newly formed German Colonial Company for South West Africa, and shortly after that the administration of the area was transferred directly to Germany's control. The Berlin Conference of 1900 saw Britain and Germany neatly partition their colonial conquests. Amongst many territorial dealings (mostly involving pen and ruler decisions on the map of Africa), a clearly defined border between Britain's new protectorate of Bechuanaland and Germany's South West Africa was established — and Britain ceded a narrow corridor of land to Germany. This was subsequently named after the German Chancellor, Count von Caprivi, as the Caprivi Strip.

During this time, the land was being progressively bought up, or simply taken from, the local inhabitants — leading to many skirmishes and uprisings which were brutally put down by the colonial troops. The last, and perhaps largest of these, was the Herero uprising of 1904, in which many of the Herero people were massacred at Waterberg. The survivors fled east into the Kalahari, some crossing the border into Bechuanaland.

At the onset of the First World War, Britain encouraged South Africa to wrest German South West Africa from the Germans and in July 1915, the German Colonial troops surrendered to South African forces at Khorab — a memorial now marks the spot. At the end of the war, Namibia became a League of Nations 'trust territory', assigned to the Union of South Africa as 'a sacred trust in the name of civilisation' to 'promote to the utmost the material and moral well-being of its inhabitants'. The Caprivi Strip was incorporated back into Bechuanaland (though it was returned 20 years later).

After overcoming their initial differences, South African Boers and the German colonists of Namibia soon discovered a common interest — the unabashed exploitation of the native population whose well-being they were supposed to be protecting. In 1947, after the Second World War, South Africa formally announced to the United Nations its intention to annex the territory. The UN — which had inherited responsibility for the League of Nations trust territories — opposed the plan, arguing that 'the African inhabitants of South West Africa have not yet achieved political autonomy'. Until 1961, the UN insisted on this point year after year and was systematically ignored by South Africa's regime.

Between 1961 and 1968, the UN tried to annul the trusteeship and establish

Namibia's independence. Legal pressure, however, was ineffective and some of the Namibian people led by the South West African People's Organisation (SWAPO) chose to fight for their freedom with arms. The first clashes occurred on August 26 1966.

In 1968, the UN finally declared the South African occupation of the country as illegal and changed its name to Namibia. Efforts by the majority of the UN General Assembly to enforce this condemnation with economic sanctions were routinely vetoed by the western powers of the security council – they had vested interests in the multinational companies in Namibia and would stand to lose from the implementation of sanctions.

The independence of Angola in 1975 affected Namibia's struggle for freedom, by providing SWAPO guerillas with a friendly rearguard. As a consequence the guerilla war was stepped up, resulting in increased *political* pressure on South Africa. But strong internal economic factors also played heavily in the political arena. Up to independence, the status quo had preserved internal inequalities and privileges. Black Africans – 90% of the population – consumed only 12.8% of the Gross Domestic Product (GDP). Meanwhile the inhabitants of European origin – 10% of the population – received 81.5% of the GDP. Three-quarters of the agricultural production was in the hands of white farmers. Although average per capita income was (and remains) one of the highest in Africa, whites earn on average over 17 times more than blacks. The white population clearly feared they had a great deal to lose if a majority government committed to addressing these racially-based inequalities came to power.

However, external South African economic factors had perhaps the greatest effect in blocking Namibian independence. South African and multinational companies dominated the Namibian economy and carried massive political influence. Prior to independence, the Consolidated Diamond Mines Company (a subsidiary of Anglo-American) contributed in taxes 40% of South Africa's administrative budget in Namibia. Multinationals benefited from extremely generous facilities granted to them by the South African administration in Namibia. According to one estimate, the independence of Namibia would represent costs for South Africa of $240 million in lost exports, and additional outlays of $144 million to import foreign products.

In South Africa the official government view stressed the danger that a SWAPO government might present to Namibia's minority tribes (since SWAPO membership is drawn almost exclusively from the Owambo ethnic group), whilst taking few serious steps towards a negotiated settlement for Namibian independence. These concerns were not allayed by the timely assassination of an important Herero leader.

On the military side, South Africa stepped up its campaign against SWAPO, even striking at bases in southern Angola. It also supported Jonas Savimbi's UNITA (National Union for the Total Independence of Angola) forces in their struggle against the Soviet/Cuban-backed MPLA (Popular Movement for the Liberation of Angola) government in Luanda. Meanwhile, Cuban troops poured into Angola and aggravated the situation further by threatening the South African forces in Namibia.

On the diplomatic front, a proposal put forward by the UN security council (Resolution 435) called for, amongst other things, the cessation of hostilities, the return of refugees, the repeal of discriminatory legislation and the holding of UN-supervised elections. South Africa blocked this by tying any such agreement to the withdrawal of Cuban troops from Angola, and demanding guarantees that its investments in Namibia would not be affected. SWAPO refused to agree to special benefits for the European population and other minority groups, nor would it accept predetermined limitations to constitutional change following independence.

By 1987, all the states involved in the conflict were showing clear signs of the need to call a halt to hostilities. After 14 years of uninterrupted war, Angola's economy was on the brink of collapse. (The war is calculated to have cost the country $13 billion.) On the other side, South Africa's permanent harassment of Angola, and occupation of Namibia were costing the regime dearly both economically and diplomatically.

In December 1988, after prolonged US-mediated negotiations, an agreement was reached between South Africa, Angola and Cuba for a phased withdrawal of Cuban troops from Angola to be linked to the withdrawal of South African troops from Namibia and the implementation of Resolution 435.

The independence process began on April 1 1989, and was achieved with the help of the United Nations Transition Assistance Group (UNTAG). This consisted of some 7,000 people from 110 countries who worked from nearly 200 locations within the country to ensure free and fair elections and as smooth a transition period to independence as was possible.

In November 1989, 710,000 Namibians (a 97% turn-out) voted in the members of the National Assembly which would draft the country's first constitution. SWAPO won decisively, but without the two-thirds majority it needed to write the nation's constitution single-handedly, thereby allaying the fears of the white and 'international' community. The 72 elected members (68 men and four women) of the Constituent Assembly, representing between them seven different political parties, soon reached agreement on a constitution for the new Namibia, which was subsequently hailed as one of the world's most democratic. Finally, at 12.20am on March 21 1990, watched by Pérez de Cuéllar, the UN Secretary-General, F.W. de Klerk, the South African President and Sam Nujoma, Namibia's first president, the Namibian flag replaced South Africa's over Windhoek.

Politics since Independence

Since independence, there has been every indication that Namibia is standing by its constitution and developing into a peaceful and prosperous state. Walvis Bay, previously disputed by South Africa, is being transferred to Windhoek's control, and relations with neighbouring countries are good.

Resources and Economy

Before independence, the South African administration controlled the economy along traditional colonial lines. The country produced what it did not consume and imported everything it needed, especially food. Namibia still exports maize, meat and fish, and imports rice and wheat. It exports minerals and raw materials and, since it has no industries, meets its needs for manufactured goods by importing 90% of its consumer goods from South Africa.

Multinational and South African economic concerns still have a great influence in Namibia, being dominant in the three main sectors of the economy – mining, agriculture and fishing. Mining is the most important industry and the most internationalised. Both livestock and fishing have declined in importance in recent years due to recurrent droughts in the interior, and the overfishing of the coastal waters. Foreign investments in mining have, however, increased – British, North American, German and South African companies control the industry which accounts for three-quarters of Namibia's export revenue.

Following independence, Namibia inherited a well-developed infrastructure, and has considerable remaining mineral wealth. The revenue and foreign exchange from mining is needed to provide the financial muscle for the new government's nation-building programme – in the short-term at least. And realistically, the government is likely to stay intimately involved with the South African economy for the time being – Namibia continues to use the South African Rand as its currency.

Although these are early days, the new government is developing structural changes to make the economy more equitable, to diversify its components and make it less vulnerable to the vagaries of international market prices. Better living conditions for the majority of Namibians might be realised by increasing the productivity of the subsistence areas, particularly in the populated north. By developing the 'informal' part of the economy, future problems of food production, urbanisation and unemployment might be avoided. With hopes for fully-fledged reform in South Africa, there is every reason for considerable optimism for Namibia's future as the world's newest independent state.

BOTSWANA – A BRIEF HISTORY

Pre-Independence

The early history of Botswana is the story of the Bushmen (also called *San*, and in Setswana called *Basarwa*). They had the area to themselves for 30,000 years, leading a sophisticated hunter-gatherer existence. Sometime around the 1400s, the first Bantus arrived. These Bakgalagadi quickly adapted to the desert environment, and lived like the Bushmen, intermarrying with them.

A century later, things began to change when the Batswana expanded into the region with their cattle and highly organised social structure. The chiefs established large communities in the south-east of the country. Disputes were often settled by communities splitting and following their leader-of-choice to another site. If the area was already occupied, a battle might ensue. Later, a chief would die or be assassinated, and the groups would recombine. This system allowed smaller minority groups to be (generally) peacefully subsumed under the larger Batswana umbrella — albeit as the lowest class citizens — and led to the more rapid growth of the Batswana, relative to the other major groups.

Meanwhile, the scramble for Africa was on. The Dutch, British, Portuguese, and Germans were staking out claims on all sides, but they balked at the Kalahari. Who wanted to administer 50 million hectares of sand? However the area did have great strategic importance; the British needed it to connect their valuable colonies to the north with the port of Cape Town, whilst the Portuguese saw advantage in uniting their colonies of Angola and Mozambique. And the Germans, acutely conscious of having largely missed out in the race for 'bagging' colonies in Africa, were increasing their presence to the west in present-day Namibia. Despite this, none of the imperialist powers were willing to take responsibility for Botswana.

In the 1800s, major land pressures arose. The Zulus led by Shaka the Great and then the Ndebeles led by Mzilikazi made repeated forays into the area, having been driven from their own lands in South Africa by the expansion of the Boers. However, the Boers too came at this time, searching for lands free from the expanding British influence around the Cape. They attacked the Batswana, taking control of their pastures and forcing them to work on Boer farms. All this prompted the chiefs to ask the British for protection. The British declined — there was still no profit to be made.

In 1884, after things had settled down, the Germans formally claimed Namibia. The British now terrified of having their trade route to the north cut off, announced to Germany the following year the formation of the Bechuanaland Protectorate. The Batswana received the news themselves after the event. The British quickly imposed a hut tax on the Batswana to pay for their own 'protection' and to try to offset the administrative burden they had found themselves with. Mafikeng became the administrative capital — a town outside the borders of the protectorate!

Then, just 10 years later, Cecil Rhodes asked the British government to incorporate Bechuanaland into his British South Africa Company (BSAC). Britain agreed — Rhodes was building a railway and he would administer and 'protect' the region without the British having to pay anything. Three of the Batswana chiefs (then called kings), who feared a reduction of their own power, travelled to Britain to protest. In London, they were told that the decision was final. Undaunted, the kings took their case to the people, with the backing of the London Missionary Society, and toured Britain spreading word of the evils of Rhodes's BSAC (already infamous in Rhodesia). A flurry of letters was written and the British government, fearing a loss of votes, agreed to keep Bechuanaland as a protectorate.

The British trusteeship prevented political absorption of Bechuanaland by

South Africa, through the Anglo-Boer War and two World Wars, but paved the way for Afrikaner economic supremacy. Although Botswana is largely semi-arid, it had come to be one of southern Africa's major exporters of cattle and meat. At the beginning of this century, 97% of the population lived in rural areas, with every family having at least two heads of cattle and the richest even having oxen to plough the land. But, in order to pay the taxes imposed on them by the colonial administration, many Batswana men had to migrate to South Africa to work on the mines, leaving the women to take over all agricultural work. Bechuanaland then began to decline in comparison to its two prosperous neighbours, South Africa and Rhodesia.

By the 1960s, 15% of the population had moved to the cities, and over 40% of the remaining rural population had lost their cattle. This concentration of land ownership enabled Afrikaners to control agricultural production, and to become the suppliers of 60% of all meat products and, therefore, export earnings. When the first nationalist movements arose, their main aim was to put an end both to this inequality and the constant threat of being annexed by South Africa.

In 1966, the British (who had never made any money out of all that sand) willingly granted independence, and the Bechuanaland Protectorate became Botswana. Seretse Khama, leader of the Botswana Democratic Party (BDP), became president, with the BDP polling 80% of the votes. He was knighted a year later by the British. Gaborone became the new capital – this time within the nation's borders.

Politics since Independence

Despite Botswana's economic dependence on South Africa, Seretse Khama managed to keep his distance on the political front by supporting the anti-apartheid movements of the region. Botswana became one of the 'Front Line' nations fighting apartheid (by giving diplomatic support to the Rhodesian and Namibian liberation struggles), and played an important role in the establishment of the Southern African Development Coordination Conference (SADCC) in 1979. The aim of SADCC, is for the member states to become regionally self-sufficient and independent of South Africa's economic domain. However the simultaneous anti-apartheid stance, and economic closeness to South Africa, was and still is an uncomfortable position for Botswana.

Seretse Khama died in mid 1980, and was succeeded by his vice President, Quett Masire, who made few changes to his predecessor's policies. Strong pressures were exerted on Masire by socialist groups to limit the concentration of good arable land in the hands of the whites, and to increase the area allocated to cooperatives, though change has been slow. (Following independence, the BDP pursued a conciliatory approach towards the European descendants who owned 80% of the country's economic resources at the time.) Rural farmers accused the large landowners of raising too much livestock on impoverished lands which would soon become barren if something were not done. A movement also arose demanding the nationalisation of the diamond, iron, copper and nickel mining industries, which are half owned by South African companies. However, Masire's administration openly favours a more capitalist approach and, with the economy in good shape, his party receives little serious opposition. In the 1984 general elections, Masire's BDP kept its huge majority, winning 29 of the 34 elected seats in the National Assembly.

Following Zimbabwe's independence and throughout the 1980's, South Africa used military, economic and diplomatic pressure on Botswana to end its anti-apartheid statements, recognise the 'independent homelands' in South Africa, expel ANC and SWAPO refugees, and sign a 'non-aggression treaty'. The treaty was withdrawn in 1985 following Masire's agreement to stop militant members of the ANC living along the border, or carrying out military activities in exile. But despite this, South Africa launched a surprise attack on Gaborone in June 1985, killing 12 people who had allegedly given refuge to ANC guerillas. This was strenuously refuted by President Masire. Renewed South African pressure was exerted in the first months of 1987, this time threatening to cut off road communication with Gaborone, Botswana's main connection with the outside world. Botswana did not give in to these pressures but maintained its political support of the ANC.

Resources and the Economy

At Independence, Botswana was one of the world's poorest nations, having inherited virtually no infrastructure or means of self-support from decades of British colonialism. Its prospects were dire indeed. Then remarkably, in 1967, the world's second largest diamond pipe was discovered at Orapa. Within a few years Botswana had become one of the world's major diamond producing countries, in partnership with the South African diamond cartel, De Beers. The world's third largest diamond pipe was discovered at Jwaneng several years later.

The BDP has focused on economic development and, due to financial necessity, stayed on cordial economic terms with South Africa – a difficult balancing act. A large number of Batswana citizens still work in South Africa, and Botswana is a member of the Southern African Customs Union which maintains free trade between South Africa, Namibia, Botswana, Swaziland and Lesotho. Diamonds, along with beef exports to the EU, have made the country financially secure with one of the fastest growing economies in the world (a record average 12% per annum growth rate between 1978 and 1988). The military budget is kept low, with education and development of the infrastructure given top priority. The government is acutely aware of the precariousness of its reliance on only two main export earners – diamonds and beef – and is committed to the diversification of the economy. The contentious development of the soda-ash plant on Sowa Spit in the Makgadikgadi Pans is one such example. Equally, it's all too aware of its dependency on South Africa for essential imports and as a major export market – almost all imports originate in South Africa or come through Cape Town, whilst 60% of its exports are purchased by South Africa. As a leading member of SADCC, Botswana is striving for regional self-reliance.

Despite the country's calm, problems exist. Immense tracts of land have been destroyed by the overgrazing of cattle, while frequent droughts (almost every seven years) make the small farmer dependent on governmental assistance. The gap between rich and poor widens with increasing rural depopulation and urbanisation – successful businessmen and government officials drive their Mercedes, while the impoverished and jobless put up shanties on the outskirts of town. Although Botswana's population is small, population growth runs at a large 3.4% per annum, threatening to outstrip job creation despite the rapid economic growth. Hard decisions (such as on population control) will have to be made, and the BDP government will need to remain flexible if it's to remain in power, but Botswana does have the resources to do well in the future. No doubt the current political re-orientation in South Africa will prove to have profound ramifications for Botswana (and the whole of the SADCC region) in due course.

Chapter 2

The people and languages of Namibia and Botswana

Namibia – General Impressions

Travelling around Namibia just after independence, you couldn't fail to sense the immense enthusiasm of most people towards the future. Even the Afrikaner whites were optimistic about 'building a new and better country'. They saw it as an opportunity to leave South Africa's racial problems behind and, most importantly, to free themselves of its sanctions. Finally, they had the chance to make a fresh start in a country with rich natural resources. The cultures of the Namibian people have been dominated by South Africa for some 70 years, and by colonial influences for much longer – at present it's very difficult to predict what will emerge as the formative cultural influences of the independent country.

Botswana – General Impressions

Citizens of Botswana are called *Batswana*, while a *Motswana* is a single individual. However the prefixes *Ba* and *Mo* before *any* of the ethnic group names in Botswana have the more specific meaning of several people, or one person, of that group. This dualism reflects the government's 'we're all Batswana' policy, adopted at independence in an effort to achieve national unity and curb tribal partisanism. School textbooks tell us about the languages that used to be spoken, but now 'we all speak Setswana' (the prefix *Se* implying both the language of the Tswana people, *and* the language of the country). Whilst this has led to the gradual loss of cultural identity of all other ethnic groups, in many ways the policy has been successful – Botswana has avoided the ethnic clashes that have brought disaster elsewhere in Africa. Perhaps Botswana's minority groups have been dominated by Tswana's and Europeans for so long that they've come to accept their lower status.

THE PEOPLES

It has long been a colonial legacy of the west to view the many peoples of
Africa in terms of a multitude of culturally and linguistically distinct *tribes*
(which were often portrayed as being culturally incompatible and in a state of
constant warfare with each other). Whilst of course there are an enormous
variety of different ethnic groups, many are closely related to others in
language, beliefs, and way of life. Over time there has been (and continues
to be) considerable intermixing of peoples and cultures. The Batswana, for
example, frequently incorporated other ethnic groups into their society, whilst
also splitting into smaller groups themselves as a peaceful way of resolving
disagreements.

When the colonial powers carved up their conquests in Africa, national
borders bore little relation to traditional areas and frequently cut across land
occupied by one ethnic group, splitting it into two or more parts. Many of the
ethnic groups described here are split between Botswana, Namibia or South
Africa, and are therefore arranged alphabetically rather than under country
headings.

Bakgalagadi, Bayei, Hambukushu and Subiya
(mostly in Botswana)

Like all African countries, Botswana has a multitude of minority tribes, each
with its own traditions and cultural heritage. Whilst being minorities in a
national sense, they may well be the *only* tribe in a given village and so, are
far from the minority at home.

The Bakgalagadi were the first Bantu-speakers to move into present-day
Botswana. They mixed and lived along with the Bushmen who were already
there. Presently, they occupy villages throughout the Kalahari Desert, where
they've become servants and herders at large cattle posts.

The Bayei, Hambukushu and Subiya, all live in the north-west of the
country, in and around the Okavango Delta. They catch fish, hunt game and
grow crops of sorghum, maize, and millet. Their dugout canoes (*mokoros*)
are poled or paddled throughout the waterways. If you travel into the Delta,
your poler will probably be a Yei.

Bakalanga
(Botswana and Zimbabwe)

The homeland of the Bakalanga is divided by the Botswana-Zimbabwe
border, though ties across the boundary remain strong. Their language is an
off-shoot of the Shona spoken in Zimbabwe. Most Bakalanga live in and
around Francistown, but there are significant numbers in all the large towns.

Traditional Kalangas do not congregate in densely-populated villages, nor
do they separate their homes, fields, and cattle into three sites like the
Batswana. Instead, they live in sprawling villages, with houses, crops and

cattle *kraals* all intermixed. The Kalangas are chiefly farmers, and their few cattle are used for ploughing and for paying the bride-price.

Bakalanga chiefs lead their people and settle disputes, but are not venerated to the degree that Batswana chiefs are. They serve their people, rather than being served. In some areas, due to the absence of missionary influence, oracles still exist who are intermediaries for contacting Mwali (The Almighty) to get advice and to request rain. The Kalanga are the only people in Botswana who continue to hold tribal rain dances.

Names

by Phil Deutschle

Obvious, Knowledge, Beauty, Naughty-Boy, and Precious are all names of people I know. Such exquisite names are often just English translations of common Kalanga names — Shathani means Rejoice, and Musani can be Arousement.

Almost everyone has at least three different names: a Kalanga name (for home), a Setswana name (for school), and an English name (for work). Add to this a plentitude of nicknames and you can be at a loss to know who you're talking about. This weekend, I was being told all about a certain 'Greg'. It was some time before I realised that it was someone who I already knew well, but by the name of 'Ringo'.

Parents are often called according to the names of their first-born children. So the mother of Shathani, who I know as Washule, is Maando at home but is now being called Mmashathani!

Students will give themselves new names as the fancy strikes them. Tom suddenly becomes Cool-Ruler, and Innocent switches to His Master's Voice.

As Botswana develops, new-borns are being given some bizarre names: Roadblock, Extension, or Spar (after a South African chain store). My favourite is the baby boy who was named 'Diploma' by his grandmother.

'His mother went away to school to get an education, to get her diploma,' explains the grandmother, bouncing her grandson. 'But *this* is what she came home with. So that's what I call him — Diploma!'

Baster

(Namibia)

The Basters are the descendants of indigenous Hottentot women and the Dutch settlers who first arrived at the Cape in the early 17th Century. The original 'coloured' or 'bastard' children found themselves rejected by both the white and black communities at the Cape, so keeping together they relocated themselves further north away from the colonialists. Proudly calling themselves 'Basters', they set up farming communities and developed their own distinct social and cultural structures.

During the 1860s, white settlers began to push into these areas so, to avoid confrontation, the Basters crossed the Orange River in 1868 and moved northwards once again. Trying to keep out of the way of the warring

Hereros and Namas, they founded Rehoboth in 1871 and set up their own system of government under a *Kaptein* (Headman) and a *Volksraad* (Legislative Council). Their support of the German colonial troops during the tribal uprisings brought them later protection and privileges.

Demands for self-rule and independence were repressed throughout this century until the *Rehoboth Gebiet* was granted the status of an independent state in the 1970s. This move by the South African administration was made with the aim of reinforcing racial divisions amongst the non-whites – rather like in the South African 'independent homelands'. Today, the country's 29,000 Basters have a strong sense of identity and make up about 2.5% of the population. Most still live in the good cattle-grazing land around Rehoboth.

Batswana
(Botswana and South Africa)

Altogether, ethnic Tswanas number some five million, though the majority are citizens of South Africa. Their language, Setswana, is closely related to the Sesotho spoken in Lesotho.

Batswana tend to live in large, closely-packed villages. Some have populations as high as 30,000 while still retaining a village atmosphere. The people often maintain three homes: one in the village, another at the lands (where crops are grown some distance from the village) and the third at the cattle post (where cattle are kept up to several hundred kilometres from their village home).

With this tradition of fragmentation, the Batswana have readily accepted having families scattered in distant towns by the search for jobs. A complete family of mother, father and children is a rarity. Often, the children are left with the grandmother while the mother stays in town and the father is off at the mines. Still, the village is considered home. The richer Batswana build expensive houses at their home villages, even though they might only stay there once a year, at Christmas time.

The Batswana of Botswana are divided into eight major tribes. The well-being of the chief is of paramount importance. A tribe judges its success by the affluence of its chief. The chief presides over traditional court (*kgotla*) meetings, where village matters are freely discussed by all concerned parties.

Ownership of cattle is linked to prestige and some of the largest herds are owned by government officials. Beef is a major export item, but historically the cattle also served as a back-up source of food and income during times of drought.

Bushmen/San
(Botswana, Namibia, Angola and South Africa)

The Bushmen are the oldest inhabitants of southern Africa and undoubtedly one of the most studied and documented ethnic groups in the world. They are, anthropologically, an intriguing group, as a few of them still maintain their traditional lifestyle and are among the world's last hunter-gatherers. Whilst this lifestyle has now almost died out, the Bushmen still exist as a linguistically and ethnically distinct group.

The Bushmen have no collective name for themselves, and all their popular names are in some sense derogatory. *Bushmen* is the most widely used term but has racist and sexist connotations. Many anthropologists and historians have more recently chosen the term *San*, but this refers to the language group, not culture, of the people and isn't used in southern Africa except in academic circles. *Basarwa*, the Setswana word for 'people from the uninhabited country', has negative connotations, and is disliked by the Bushmen themselves, as is the clinical abbreviation *RAD* (Remote Area Dweller) used by the Botswanan government in an effort at neutrality.

The Bushmen are often thought of as desert dwellers, though they used to occupy nearly all of southern Africa. For at least 25,000 years Bushmen have hunted and gathered on the subcontinent, probably spreading throughout much of sub-Saharan Africa. About 2,000 years ago *Bantu*-speaking farmers started migrating south from central west Africa in search of new land, and the Bushmen hunting and gathering areas became increasingly under pressure. The situation was accelerated by the arrival of the Boers at the Cape in the 17th Century. With the Boers taking land for farming in the south and the Bantus expanding to the north, the Bushmen had insufficient land to survive and were forced to take cattle from Bantu and Boer farmers. In retaliation Boer farmers shot the Bushmen as vermin, killing many thousands and resulting in their extinction at the Cape. However, most of the reduction of the Bushmen was not due to slaughter by whites, but caused by their assimilation into black farming communities, where they were often treated as little more than slaves. It was only in the most remote and inhospitable areas, like the central Kalahari, that their traditional way of life survived.

In Botswana, this assimilation has produced direct contradictions. While legally equal, the Bushmen are reviled by many Batswana as the lowest form of humanity – social pariahs. Paradoxically, a Bushmen's yellow skin on a 'real' person is considered beautiful. Bushmen women are especially attractive to Bantu men because of their small stature and pale, yellowish skins. Many Batswana have some obvious Bushmen physical traits – light skin, small size, lack of ear lobes. These people are thought comely, but to imply any hint of Bushman blood is a terrible insult.

Remote bands of Bushmen do still live a traditional lifestyle of hunting and gathering in the central Kalahari desert. Far from being a 'primitive' people who had failed to 'progress' to a sedentary way of life, the Bushmen had evolved a sophisticated and, to us, almost utopian existence with their environment. The sharing of all food and almost all possessions, communal decision making (there were no chiefs) and an all-embracing spiritual life which stressed the one-ness of the world, enabled them to survive where no other people could.

The 'traditional' Bushmen of the central Kalahari know exactly where to go when looking for foodplants, game, or water. Assorted roots, tubers, berries, seeds and nuts form the bulk of their diet – often up to 90%. These are collected by the women and children, while the man's business is to hunt. He sets snares, and hunts using arrows poisoned with beetle larva juice, taking only as much game as is needed. Hunting, and the distribution of meat following a kill, is as important socially as it is nutritionally, emphasising unification and sharing.

Bushmen are amongst the only people in the world who have learned to live with no permanent access to water. While there is no surface water in the Kalahari, there are sufficient amounts of water in other forms. Water is obtained from plants, tubers, melons and other water-storing vegetation, as well as being found underground in *sip wells*, reached by long thin grass straws. Once collected, water is stored underground in hollowed out ostrich eggs.

Of today's 50,000 Bushmen, many have settled into communities where they grow crops and keep livestock. Others work on isolated cattle posts, where they often get no wages, but only food. A few may receive livestock as payment, but they can't sell it without their 'Master's' consent. (Many Bushmen are called, and truly consider themselves to be, their 'Master's' 'subjects', and will regularly vote a 'Master' into elected office.) Poverty, unemployment, powerlessness and above all despair afflict most Bushmen, who are at the bottom of the social ladder in all the countries they inhabit. What most want is the land to combine an agricultural existence with more traditional hunting and gathering, but with the same health and schooling facilities available to their fellow citizens of other ethnic groups. They want to be a part of their country's development, *and* retain their own culture and sense of identity. In the same way that the Bushmen have no common term to call themselves, so also they have little sense of belonging to a common heritage, and very few Bushmen are collectively campaigning for their rights. This is left to individuals like Laurens van der Post and organisations such as Survival International, who have been campaigning on their behalf over the last few decades, if not always from the same perspective.

Damara
(Namibia)

Along with the Nama and the Bushmen, the Damara are presumed to be the original inhabitants of Namibia, speaking a similar 'Khoi' click language. Like the Nama, the Damara were primarily hunting people, who owned few cattle or goats. Traditionally enemies of the Nama and Herero, they supported the German colonial forces at Waterberg against the Herero uprisings and were awarded for their loyalty by an 'enlarged' homeland from the German authorities. Of the 80,000 Damara today, only a quarter manage to survive in this area adjacent to the Skeleton Coast park – the rest work on white-owned farms, in mines or as labourers in the towns. Damara women share the same 'Victorian' style of dress as the Herero and Nama women.

Herero
(Namibia & Botswana)

In 1904, the Herero and the Hottentots staged a massive uprising against the German colonial troops in South West Africa which ended in a bloody massacre of over half the total Herero population at the battle of Waterberg. The few Herero that survived fled into the Kalahari, some crossing into what is now Botswana. Today, the Herero constitute the third largest ethnic group in Namibia, after the Owambo and Kavango – about 8% of the present population. In Botswana, they are a 'minority' group inhabiting Ngamiland, south and west of the Okavango Delta.

Traditionally pastoralists, the Herero prefer raising cattle to growing crops – prestige and influence is dependent on the number of cattle possessed. Today, the majority of Namibian Hereros use their cattle-handling skills on white-owned farms.

The women wear very distinctive long, flowing Victorian gowns and headdresses. Multiple layers of petticoats made from over 12m of material give a voluminous look (two women walking side by side occupy the whole pavement!). This style of dress was introduced in the 1800s by missionaries who were appalled by the Hereros' semi-nakedness. Now the Hereros continue to wear these heavy costumes in their desert environment and it has become their traditional dress.

Himba
(Namibia)

The Himba share a common ethnic origin with the Herero people, having split from the main Herero group on the Namibia/Botswana border and moved west to present-day Kaokoland in search of available land. The land they found, however, is mountainous, sparsely vegetated and very arid. Cattle is central to their way of life, with the size of the herd an indication of wealth and prestige – but overgrazing of the poor lands is a major problem. The Himba are a minority group in Namibia (less than 1% of the population), and live almost entirely in their traditional areas in remote Kaokoland.

Kavango and Caprivian
(Namibia, Angola and Botswana)

The Kavango people share their name with the Okavango River, which forms the northern border of Namibia with Angola. Not surprisingly, they have based their traditional agricultural and fishing existence on the fertile land and good water supply afforded by this environment.

Many of the Kavango who used to live on the northern side of the Okavango River in Angola, fled south of the river into Namibia during the last 10-15 years, away from the civil war between South African-backed UNITA rebels and the Soviet/Cuban-backed MPLA regime – and away from the harassment of the regular incursions by South African troops into the south of Angola. As a consequence, the Kavango population more than doubled in size during the 1970s, and now forms the second largest ethnic group in Namibia, making up almost 10% of the population.

The Caprivi people traditionally live in the fertile, swampy land between the Chobe and Zambezi rivers – at the far end of the Caprivi Strip. Like the Kavango and the Owambo, they farm a variety of crops, raise livestock, and fish – the agricultural potential of the area is one of the highest in Namibia. However, this potential has been largely unrealised – before the war with Angola, and the heavy involvement of South African troops (which brought roads and infrastructure), the whole of the Kavango and Caprivi region was one of the least developed in Namibia.

Nama/Hottentot
(Namibia)

The Nama people are perhaps the closest in origin to the Bushmen, traditionally sharing a similar type of 'click' or Khoi language, the same light-coloured yellowy skin, and a hunter-gatherer way of life. One of the first peoples in Namibia, their tribal areas were traditionally communal property, as indeed was any item unless it was actually made by an individual. Basic differences in the perception of ownership of land and hunting-grounds, led in the past to frequent conflicts with the Herero people. The 50,000 or so Nama today, mostly live in Namaland, north of Keetmanshoop in the south of Namibia – mostly working on white farms. Nama women share the same 'Victorian' traditional dress as the Herero and Damara women.

Owambo
(Namibia and Angola)

The Owambo people (sometimes called Ovambo) are by far the largest group in Namibia and make up just over half the population. The great majority live in their traditional areas – Owamboland – away from the main transport arteries in the remote far north of the country, straddled on the border with Angola. The area receives one of the highest rainfalls in the country, and supports a range of traditional crops as well as allowing good grazing for the extensive cattle herds.

Before independence, the existence of half a million indigenous Namibians on the border with (socialist) Angola, seriously perturbed the South African administration. By investing some money into the region, the administration hoped to establish a protective buffer against Angola to protect the white areas in the interior. The policy back-fired – Owamboland became the heartland of SWAPO during the struggle for independence. With this, harassment by the South African Defence Force, and a rapid population increase (exacerbated by a large influx of refugees from Angola), have left the area over-pressurised and undeveloped. The new SWAPO government has pledged to redress this imbalance.

Whites and Coloureds
(Namibia and Botswana)

The first whites to settle in Namibia were the Germans who set up trading businesses around the port of Lüderitz in 1884. Within a few years, Namibia formally became a German colony, and German settlers began to arrive in ever increasing numbers. Meanwhile, white farmers of Dutch origin (the Boers, who first settled on the African continent at the Cape in 1652,), were moving northwards in search of land free from British interference, following the ceding of the Dutch Cape Colony to the British government. To avoid the Germans in Namibia, and encouraged by Rhodes's British South Africa Company, some Boer *trekkers* headed for Bechuanaland and settled in Ghanzi (in the central Kalahari of Botswana), and in the Tuli Block (land along the Limpopo River, on the border between Botswana and South Africa). Following the transfer of German Namibia to South African control after the First World War, Boers (Afrikaners) moved into Namibia, and soon significantly outnumbered the German settlers. Whites of British origin joined the Afrikaners in British Bechuanaland, and a few moved to Namibia and settled there. The Namibian whites collectively refer to themselves as 'Southwesters' after Namibia's colonial name of South West Africa.

The term 'Coloureds' is generally used in southern Africa to describe people of mixed (black-white) origin. The coloured people maintain a strong sense of identity and separateness from either blacks or whites – though they generally speak either Afrikaans or English (or frequently both) rather than an 'African' language.

NAMIBIAN LANGUAGES

Namibia's variety of languages reflects the country's great diversity of peoples – black and white. Amongst the indigenous languages there are two basic groups which bear no relation to each other – Bantu languages (such as of the Owambo and Herero people), and Khoi-San Languages (such as of the Bushmen and Nama peoples). Unlike Botswana, there is no one African language that is widespread enough to be useful as the *lingua franca*. Most black townspeople speak both Afrikaans and English in addition to their 'mother' language. In the more rural areas, Afrikaans tends to be more widely used than English (which may not be spoken at all) – despite the widespread enthusiasm felt for the latter. In some parts, notably in the farming areas of the central region, German is also commonly found.

Following independence, one of the new government's first actions was to make English Namibia's only official language – removing Afrikaans and German. This step sought to unite Namibia's great diversity of people's and languages under one common tongue ('the language of the liberation struggle'), leaving behind the oppressive and colonial overtones of Afrikaans and German. This choice will also help in international relations and with education – English-language materials are the most easily available.

For the purposes of this guide book, there is little point in giving a language guide to either the many African languages, or to Afrikaans and German. However, in your travels you are likely to come across a number of words – mostly Afrikaans – that have entered the common 'English-speaking' vocabulary of this part of southern Africa. Some of them (self-evidently) have racist connotations, but it is as well to be aware of them.

Southern African terms

baas	'master' (usually white)	mielie	corn, maize
		mieliepap	maize flour
bakkie	pick-up truck		porridge (shadza
beester	cattle		in Botswana)
bioscope	cinema	orlag	war
boerwors	sausage	pad	road, track
bokki	goat	pontok	'native' hut
braiivleis (braii)	barbecue	rivier	river
donga	small ravine	robot	traffic lights
finach	quick	rondavel	African hut
kanatschi	'native' child		(round)
klippe	stone	suppi	measure of
kloof	ravine		alcohol
kopje	rocky hill	tackies	running
kost	food		shoes/sneakers
kraal	cattle enclosure or African huts (Owambo)	veld	grassland
		werft	'native' settlement (Herero)
lecker	good, nice		

BOTSWANA LANGUAGE GUIDE

Compiled by Phil Deutschle

Setswana is the national language of Botswana, while English is the official language. Though many people speak other languages at home, most can converse in Setswana. English will be spoken by all who have been to school, or who have been outside the country. You should not expect to find English-speakers in rural or isolated areas (like the Okavango Delta). Even among the educated, trying to speak some Setswana will show a degree of respect and will open many doors. The largest 'minority' language is *Tjikalanga* (of the Bakalanga ethnic group), spoken in and around Francistown.

Setswana

Learning to speak Setswana is easy. Carry the most important phrases on a slip of paper and practice whenever you can.

Pronunciation

The only difficult sound is the g, pronounced like ch in the Scottish loch or German *Ich*. If you have trouble with that, just say the g like an ordinary h. The r is often rolled. Vowels are pronounced as follows:

a: like a in China   e: like ay in day   i: like ee in see
o: like o in go   u: like oo in too

Greetings

(words in brackets are optional)

English	Setswana
Greetings Sir/Madam. (Informally, 'Hello')	*Dumela Rra/Mma.*
(How) did you rise?	*O tsogile (jang)?*
I have risen (well).	*Ke tsogile (sentle).*
(How) did you spend the day?	*O tlhotse (jang)?*
I spent the day (well).	*Ke tlhotse (sentle).*
How are you? (Informal)	*O kae?*
I'm fine. (Literally, 'I'm here')	*Ke teng.*
It's OK.	*Go siame.*
I am going.	*Ke a tsamaya.*
Stay well. (Said to one staying)	*Sala sentle.*
Go well. (Said to one going)	*Tsamaya sentle.*
Sleep well.	*Robala sentle.*

Basic Phrases

What's your name? (Formal)	*Leina la gago ke mang?*
My name is _____.	*Leina la me ke _____.*
Who are you? (Informal)	*O mang?*
I'm _____.	*Ke _____.*
Where are you from? or Where are you coming from?	*O tswa kae?*
I'm (coming) from _____.	*Ke tswa kwa _____.*
Yes.	*Ee.*
No.	*Nnyaa.*
I don't know (Setswana).	*Ga ke itse (Setswana).*
What is this (in Setswana)?	*Se ke eng (ka Setswana)?*
How goes it?	*Wa reng?*

It goes OK.	*Ga ke bue.*
Thank you.	*Ke itumetse.*
What's the time?	*Nako ke mang?*
Excuse me!	*'Sorry!'*
I'm asking for money/tobacco.	*Ke kopa madi/motsoko.*
I have no money/tobacco.	*Ga ke na madi/motsoko.*

Shopping

English numbers are used.

Where's the shop?	*Shopo e kae?*
What do you want?	*O batla eng?*
I want _____.	*Ke batla/kopa _____.*
There is none.	*Ga go na.*
How much?	*Ke bokae?*
It's expensive/cheap.	*Go a tura/tshipi.*
sugar	*sukiri*
meali meal	*bupi*
tea/coffee	*tee/kofee*
meat	*fnama*
milk	*mashi*
water	*metse*

Travelling Phrases

Where are you going?	*O ya kae?*
I'm going to _____.	*Ke ya _____.*
Where are you coming from?	*O tswa kae?*
I'm coming from _____.	*Ke tswa kwa _____.*
far/near	*kgakala/gaufi*
I'm satisfied. (Regarding food)	*Ke kgotshe.*
It tastes good.	*Go monate.*
Men/Women (On toilets)	*Banna/Basadi*
What do you do? (Your job)	*O dira eng?*

Speaking Setswana

Make sentences with a pronoun and verb – eg *Ke reka borotho* (I buy bread); *O rabala* (You sleep); *Ke ithuta Setswana* (I learn Setswana).

Negatives: *Ga ke reke* (I don't buy); *Ga o robale* (You don't sleep).

Pronouns

I	*ke, nna*	we	*re*
you	*o, wena*	you plural	*lo*
she/he	*o*	they	*ba*

Verbs

apaya	cook	kwala	write
bala	read	duela	pay
batla	need	iwala	be sick
bina	dance	reka	buy
bolaya	kill	rekisa	sell
bona	see	robala	sleep
bua	speak	sala	remain, stay
dira/bereka	do/work	sega	cut
ithuta	learn	tsamaya	depart
itse	know	tsena	enter, come in
ja	eat	utlwa	hear
kopa	beg, ask for	ya	go

Other words

mang?	who?	eng?	what?
leng?	when?	kae?	where?
jang?	how?	pula	rain
moeti	traveller	tsotsi	thief/rascal
Mosarwa	Bushman	jalo	like that
Tla kwano	Come here	Tsaya	Take this
sentle	well, nicely	voetsak!	scram!
tsela	path, road	monate	nice
fela	only	gape	again
dikgomo	cattle	setulo	chair
ka moso	tomorrow	wa utlwa?	understand?
gompieno	today	bogobe	porridge

A Few Phrases of Tjikalanga

Greetings.	Dumelani.
(How) did you rise?	Ma muka (tjini)?
I rose (well).	Nda muka.
It's OK.	Kwaka lulwama.
Thanks.	Nda boka.

CULTURAL DOs AND DON'Ts

The following piece was written by Phil Deutschle from the point of view of a visitor to Botswana, but the basic ethos is just as relevant to travelling in Namibia – or anywhere in the world for that matter.

'I want to see this. I want to do that. I want to photograph you.' That's essentially what we say when we come travelling. We arrive as uninvited guests and we owe it to our hosts to be as unabrasive as possible, to try to fit in, to show respect for local attitudes.

One of the most important, and easiest, things to do is to learn something of the local language, Setswana. A simple *'Dumela, Mma'*, will bring a great smile to an old woman's face. We English-speakers are exceptionally lax about learning other people's languages, and this can rightfully be considered an insult.

Greetings are indispensable in Tswana society. One must greet everyone when arriving and departing (see page 23). Even in a shop, it is good manners to say *'Dumela, Mma'* to a woman or *'Dumela, Rra'* to a man before doing business. In an office, some sort of greeting (in Setswana or English) is vital to avoid being coldly ignored. The one arriving at a place usually greets first, but if no one greets you, take the initiative. People may not know what to say to you.

Everyone, young and old, shakes hands. Not a firm hand clasp; more of a caress. While shaking with your right hand, use your left hand to hold your own right elbow, as though you were supporting a heavy load. This, at times, can be accompanied by a little bow. Don't be surprised if friends, men or women, after shaking hands, want to continue holding hands while talking.

When giving or receiving anything, such as money or change in a shop, it is polite to use your right hand, and to at least touch your left hand to right elbow. Do this even if you see many Batswana are neglecting to do so. It's proper etiquette that is dying out in the towns. Accepting a gift, including food or a tinned drink, should be done with both hands.

Bidding farewell is as important as greeting. If you're leaving, say *Sala sentle* (Stay well) to the ones remaining. If you're staying, say *Tsamaya sentle* (Go well) to the ones leaving.

Batswana, unlike Europeans, are very casual when asking for things. You may often hear, 'Take me one photo', 'Buy me a drink', or 'Give me money'. This is not because you are a foreigner, so don't be cross. To ask for something is not shameful. In this part of the world, it's just natural to express your wants and needs openly. This giving and receiving forms bonds between people. At the same time, you are not insulting someone when you refuse a request. If you do give things, remember that a 'thank you' is not the cultural necessity that it is in the West, so don't be hurt by its absence.

Begging is another matter. Batswana will often give to an old man or woman who begs, but almost never to a child. What you do must be a personal choice. Kids who beg wearing proper clothes are usually school brats who have learned that a foreigner is an easy mark to get money for buying sweets. Kids in rags are honestly destitute, perhaps having no parents, living in the streets. Since gifts of money might be used for almost anything, giving food is better. Unfortunately, this too gives only temporary relief to a long-term problem.

The clothes worn in Botswana are becoming increasingly westernised. While you will see Batswana men in shorts, and women in trousers, they are viewed as people who don't know better, or youngsters trying to show off the latest fashions. Except in the bush, it is best to dress conservatively in long trousers and skirts – especially in small villages. Hats are not worn indoors or at formal occasions.

Water, perhaps obviously, has special significance to a desert people, and there are strict rules on how and where and in which containers water may be used. At a public water tap, do not let the water run. Do not wash your face, nor your body or clothes at a tap. You may wash your hands, and use your cupped hands to drink from a tap. If you need to wash anything else, fill a container and carry it far afield.

When staying in someone's home, be certain to ask specifically about water use. Don't just assume. Before eating, you will be given water to wash your hands. If the food comes first, wait for the water. Refrain from ever smelling your food, as doing so means that you think the food might be bad. Don't feel compelled to finish a portion of food – this may even imply that you weren't given enough. Two or more people will often share the same plate of food, and pass around a container of water or a calabash of traditional beer. However, a cup of tea or a tinned drink is not shared.

On a bus, people don't usually give their seats to the elderly or to women with babies. After paying, keep your ticket as you may be asked to surrender it when you get off. Do not step over someone's legs in the aisle (or anywhere). This is very rude. If you need someone to move, say 'Sorry, sorry, sorry'. It's the same for getting through a crowd. 'Sorry' is also used when you see someone having a minor accident, like dropping something, even if it has nothing to do with you.

Batswana are very strong supporters of the President's political party, the Botswana Democratic Party (BDP). While freedom of speech legally reigns, no one enjoys hearing criticism from a foreigner. If you want to discuss the apparent contradiction between Botswana's public rhetoric towards South Africa, and its economic policy towards the southern giant, be sure of your audience first. You don't have to be paranoid, but refrain from insulting the President. An expatriate was deported after referring to Botswana's 'Bushman President' in a bar.

Most Batswana enjoy being photographed, but it's polite to ask first.

Specific advice, like 'picking your nose is OK, but farting is frowned upon', can only be carried so far. There are thousands of cultural blunders that a foreigner can make. The best that you can do is to be hyper-aware, and to ask, ask, ask. An example: on my way to a funeral, I met my adopted brother, who looked aghast at my stately clothes of trousers and button-down shirt. 'What's wrong?' I asked. 'Where's your jacket? You have to wear a jacket.' 'My only jacket is bright red.' I had assumed red to be an inappropriate colour for a funeral. My brother looked puzzled. 'But red is all right,' he said. I had assumed wrong. The jacket was essential, and the colour didn't matter, so I returned for my crimson jacket.

Don't assume. Ask.

On the bus
by Phil Deutschle

We were a mix of twenty men, women, and children in the small combi-bus, heading south to Francistown. A dusty man on the side of the road flagged us down, and we stopped to pick him up.

The man got into the bus and asked how much it would cost to go to his brother's house. "That depends on where your brother;s home is," replied the driver, as he pulled the bus back onto the road. "Where does he live?"

"I will tell you when we get there. He lives just next to my sister."

"But you must pay now. Where do they stay?" asked the driver.

The man shrugged. "I've never taken the bus there before," he said. "I always walk. I go down the track and turn at the tree that hangs out like *this*." And he showed us how the tree hung to one side. As the bus sped along, he looked out of the window and shook his head. "I can't see the tree from here," he said. "It must be further along."

After some minutes and many miles, the driver tried again, asking, "Who else lives near your brother and sister?"

"Which brother and sister? I have many brothers and sisters," was the reply.

"The brother and sister that you are going to see now!" we all cried out.

"Oh! And you want to know who lives near them? On the far side is the man who works in the shop."

"Yes," said the driver, "and who is that?"

"What do you mean — 'who is that?' He's the one who works in the shop, the *Shopkeeper*."

"But what's his *name*?"

"The shopkeeper's name is Monamati. Everyone knows that, but we all call him Shopkeeper."

"Monamati? Monamati's shop is in Butale. That's in the *other* direction. You're going the wrong way!"

The driver slowed the bus and pulled to the side of the road. "Now, when you get out," he explained to the man, "You have to cross the road and try to get a ride going the other way. *That* way."

The man got out, and then, as we drove off, he called out, "But how much do I have to pay?"

Chapter 3

The natural environment

THE PHYSICAL ENVIRONMENT

Climate

Most of Namibia and Botswana is classified as an arid to semi-arid region (the line being crossed from semi-arid to arid when evaporation exceeds rainfall). In general, both countries experience a sub-tropical 'desert' climate, characterised by a wide range in temperature (from day to night and from summer to winter), and by low rainfall and humidity. The eastern area of Botswana and the northern strips of both countries (in which the greater part of their population) have much less severe climates.

Temperatures range widely from very hot to very cold, depending on the height of the land above sea level and whether it's 'summer' (October to April) or 'winter' (May to September). In 'mid-summer' (January), the average maximum temperature is around 35°C and the average minimum is around 18°C. In 'mid-winter' (July), the average maximum temperature is around 25°C and the average minimum is around 5°C. These averages, however, conceal peaks of 48°C in summer months, and temperatures as low as minus 10°C in the higher desert regions in winter (this is rare!). Nevertheless night frosts are not uncommon during the months of June, July and August.

Rainfall Most rain falls in the summer months, generally from December to March, and can be heavy and prolonged in northern Botswana and north-eastern Namibia. The further south or west you get, the drier it gets, with many southern regions of the Kalahari receiving no rainfall in some years.

The Namibian coast follows a different pattern. The climate here is largely determined by the interaction between warm dry winds from inland and the cold *Benguela* Current. The sea is too cold for much evaporation to take place and, consequently, rain-bearing clouds don't form over the coast. Most of the coast is classified as desert – rainfall is an extremely low 15mm per annum on average – in some years there may be none at all. However, when hot air from the desert mixes with the cold sea air, it produces a moist fog which 'hangs' over the coastal strip penetrating up to 60km inland. The existence of many species of animals and plants endemic to the Namib is the result of this specialised environment, where the only dependable source of moisture is a periodic morning fog.

Geology and Topography

Geologically, Namibia and Botswana form part of an extremely old region, with *Precambrian* granitic and metamorphic rocks dating back over two billion years. These *shield* or 'basement' rocks are usually covered by more recent sedimentary rocks, mostly deposited during the *Mesozoic* era (65 to 235 million years ago). *Tectonic activity* or movement in the earth's crust over the last 100 million years or so created a number of rifts through which magma was able to reach the surface (see section on diamond pipes below) and resulted in the uplifting of most of the area above sea level.

Kimberlite (diamond) pipes   Diamond is a crystalline form of ordinary carbon formed under conditions of extreme pressure and temperature. In nature, such conditions are only found deep below the earth's surface in the lower crust or upper mantle. Under certain circumstances in the past (usually associated with tectonic activity) the rock matrix in which diamonds occurred was subjected to such great pressure that it became 'fluid' and worked its way up to the earth's surface in the form of a volcanic pipe of *fluidised* material. The situation is similar to a conventional volcanic eruption, except that instead of basaltic magma being erupted through fissures in the crust, the volcanic material is a peculiar rock called *kimberlite* which contains a wide assortment of minerals (including diamond) in addition to often large chunks of other rocks which have been caught up in the whole process.

The pipes are correctly termed *kimberlite pipes*, and occur throughout southern Africa from the Cape to Zaire. However, only a small proportion of those discovered have proved to contain diamonds in sufficient abundance to be profitably worked. Botswana mines two kimberlite pipes for diamonds, one at Orapa and one at Jwaneng. Namibia's diamonds derive not from primary kimberlite pipes, but from secondary diamond deposits – areas where diamonds have been washed down and deposited by old rivers which have eroded kimberlite pipes in the interior on their way.

The topography of Namibia and Botswana today can be described in a number of broad regions, each in the past affected in a different way by the tectonic activity of the Mesozoic era. The highest region, at 2,000m, is the central plateau of Namibia which runs roughly north-south. To the west, toward the Atlantic Ocean, the land falls off in a steep escarpment (which is deeply incised by river action), to the narrow coastal strip of the Namib Desert region. To the east of the central plateau the land slopes off much more gradually, merging with the Kalahari Desert region – a plateau at 1,000m, spanning both Namibia and Botswana. North of the central Kalahari, in north-west Botswana, the Okavango river basin region contains the Okavango Delta, an extensive area of swamp and marshland. The great salt pans of Makgadikgadi and Nxai to the north-east of Botswana are an associated region, filling a huge shallow basin that was once a vast inland lake. Finally, the eastern margin of Botswana forms another distinct topographical region with the land dropping slightly to the Limpopo river basin straddling the border between Botswana and South Africa.

Sand dunes

Barchan dunes arise wherever sand-laden wind deposits sand on the windward (up-wind) slopes of a random patch on the ground. The mound grows in height until a 'slip-face' is established by sand avalanching down on the sheltered leeward (down-wind) side. The resulting dune is therefore in a state of constant (if slow) movement – sand is continuously being deposited and blown up the shallow windward slope and then falling down the steep leeward slope. This slow movement, or migration, is more rapid at the edges of the dune than in the centre (there is less wind resistance) which results in the characteristic 'tails' of a mature *barchan* or *crescentric* dune.

Fairly constant winds from the same direction are essential for the growth and stability of *barchan* dunes, which can migrate from anything up to six metres a year for high dunes to 15 metres a year for smaller dunes. Probably the best examples of *barchan* dunes occur in Namibia's Skeleton Coast, where some of the dune crests are highlighted by a purple dusting of garnet sand.

Seif dunes Where the prevailing wind is interrupted by cross-winds driving in sand from the sides, a long *seif* or *longitudinal* dune is formed, instead of a swarm of *barchans*. The shape of *seif* dunes is in the form of a long ridge with high crests, parallel to the direction of the prevailing wind. They commonly occur in long parallel ranges, such as those south of the Kuiseb river which show up so clearly on satellite photographs.

Sand sheets When the land surface is vegetated with grass and scrub, or is covered with rocks and pebbles, the force of the wind is broken and becomes more random. In such situations poorly developed *seif dunes* or irregular *barchans* form, and may often join together to some extent, making an undulating *sand sheet*. From this platform of coarser sand, more erratic dunes often rise.

Sand sheets, in one form or another, are the most common dune formation in southern Africa, since the 'text book' conditions needed to form perfect *barchan* or *seif* dunes are rare. However, the principles remain the same and 'imperfect' dunes of *barchan* or *seif* origin are widespread throughout the Kalahari and Namib deserts.

FLORA AND FAUNA

Regional Flora and Vegetation

The natural vegetation of the region varies from the dry deciduous forests of Chobe, to the vast marsh areas of the Okavango and the barren desert dunes of the Namib. In general it becomes drier toward the south and west and the vegetation cover becomes correspondingly more sparse – although rivers and mountain ranges give much local variation to this trend.

The Caprivi Strip, northern Chobe and northern Owamboland are lush and tropical during and shortly after the rains, but become dry and relatively barren by the middle of the dry season. Where the land isn't used for agriculture, there are deciduous forests of tall *comboretum* and *acacia* trees above thick bush undergrowth.

The Okavango and Linyanti swamps are a patchwork of reedbeds, islands and lagoons linked together by channels. The reedbeds contain dense stands of a number of reed species, while the islands are home to water-loving fig and palm trees. Colourful waterlilies are scattered throughout most of the waterways and in the lagoons.

Northern Kalahari – takes in a broad band across Namibia and Botswana from Etosha pan, through the Tsodilo Hills to Makgadikgadi and Nxai pans – is characterised by a tree and bush savannah, interspersed by patches of open grassland. The soil is a nutrient-poor sand or sand/gravel mix, on which the *mopane* tree grows particularly well. *Mopane* is easily identified by its characteristic paired leaves that have earned it the name 'butterfly tree'. *Mopane's* deep red wood burns well and its bark is home to a large white grub – *mopane worm*, larva of the moth *Gonimbrasia belina* – eaten as a delicacy by the local people. (Try them roasted!)

Namibia's central plateau runs north-south through the centre of the country, dominated by extensive plains of shrub and grass. This is Namibia's agricultural heartland, with the land being used mostly for livestock farming, especially cattle rearing.

The central and southern Kalahari covers the majority of the remaining surface area of Namibia and Botswana. Rolling, mostly stabilised, dunes are interspersed by gravel plains and clay pans. The dunes are often thinly covered with grasses, while the gravel plains sustain a variety of shrubs, grasses and even occasional trees. Perhaps the most remarkable of these, occurring on the Kalahari's edge in southern Namibia, is the very distinctive *Kokerboom (Aloe dichotoma)* which stands aloof on the most inhospitable of rocky hillsides.

The Namib Desert, unlike the Kalahari, appears to the visitor to be a 'proper' desert, consisting of only barren, unvegetated sand dunes. Elsewhere the Namib is a desert of huge gravel plains, often covered with a carpet of fragile and beautiful lichens. On these plains, plants grow slowly and may live for centuries – the strangely contorted *welwitschia mirabilis* can live for over a 1000 years. Winding through even the driest areas are occasional ribbons of green. These linear oases, along the lines of old river valleys, come as a surprise and are sustained by the constant (if small) underground flow of the rivers.

Fauna: Mammals and Birdlife

Namibia and Botswana are both well known for their diverse range of wildlife and birdlife. Most of the major African game species can be found, along with a number of species that are endemic to the region. Compared to the rest of Africa the game has been well protected from the scourge of poaching – both Botswana and Namibia have good wildlife conservation records and, in general, the political will to keep it that way (especially as tourism becomes an increasingly important source of income).

The mammals are typical of savannah areas throughout sub-saharan Africa. Since the climate is drier than the rest of the sub-continent, however, the land can only support a lower density of animals than is the norm elsewhere. But the infrequent permanent sources of water result in game becoming all the more concentrated by the drinking places that do exist during the dry season – a major bonus for the game viewer!

The region's wetlands (Okavango, Linyanti and Caprivi) are a bird-watcher's paradise throughout most of the year. However, the best time of year is undoubtedly from November to April when palaearctic migrants come south, adding to the numerous indigenous species already present. At this time of year many of the pans may partially fill with water and become home to huge flocks of birds overnight.

Whilst here don't overlook the reptiles, insects and smaller animals that abound. Many exhibit fascinating adaptations to their environment, such as the Namib's fog-basking beetles, and are at least as interesting as the larger game. Even the ants here are worth watching – look out for those which forage in columns, if disturbed they'll hiss at you. Descriptions of some of these interesting smaller beasties have been incorporated into the regional guide, many more will fascinate you if you take the time to look for them.

Summary of major game and birdlife areas

Each of the areas described below are dealt with in detail in their respective chapters in parts two and three of the book. However, for ease of seeing at a glance which are the best game or bird-watching areas (and at what time of year), we have included the following summary in alphabetical order:

Chobe Famous for the large herds of elephant that visit the Chobe river during the dry season. Savuti, in the centre of Chobe national park, is excellent for big game, especially lion and buffalo. When the Savuti channel flowed and supplied the Savuti marsh, this was considered to be one of Africa's top game spots.

Etosha In the dry season this is one of Africa's best game areas – don't miss it. As well as huge herds antelope, wildebeest, zebra etc. – and good numbers of cats – the rarities found here include black-faced impala, mountain zebras and red hartebeest. It's also probably your best chance to spot an elusive black rhino.
  Bird-watching is also good – Fisher's Pan is the best place for waders, often keeping its water longer than the main pan in the dry season. The large number of raptors include the black, or king, vulture. In the dry season, look out for the snake-eating secretary birds and the startling crimson-breasted shrike.

Kaokoveld Only fairly sparse populations of some of the big game species. Giraffe locally common, as are zebra, gemsbok and springbok but large predators are very scarce. The animals here are often very nervous and should not be approached too closely, even in a vehicle.

Kaudom Good for the quiet game spotter. Kaudom typically has less game than Etosha, but includes the uncommon roan antelope, tsessebe and reedbuck. All the big cats and even wild dog can be found here, but animals tend to be shy.

Khutse The game on the Khutse plains can be scarce and difficult to spot, so come for the experience of the Kalahari landscape more than glimpses of gemsbok! Animals are most plentiful following the rains when there is good grazing, typically from January to March.

Linyanti/Kwando The area is like a smaller version of the Okavango Delta from the point of view of bird-watching. It gets summer migrants, though not in quite the same numbers as the Okavango, and is especially good for cranes and egrets.

Mabuasehube A good reserve for quiet, undisturbed game viewing and probably best at the end of the rainy season, around March to May. Watch out for the Kalahari's 'black-maned' lions, and the entertaining troops of meerkats.

Mahango This is the single best area for bird-watching in Namibia, with over 300 species recorded. Since it's situated at the north-western edge of the Okavango (see below), many species are common to both areas.

Makgadikgadi   The presence of the Boteti river ensures game even in the dry season. Numbers are highly variable, however, with wildebeest, zebra and springbok usually in the most common. Look out also for red hartebeest and cheetah.

If the Makgadikgadi pans fill with water then, like Etosha, there's a chance they will be inundated by thousands of breeding flamingos. Don't miss it if you are in the country – although at other times there is much less to see.

Mamili and Mudumu   Sitatunga, red lechwe and the very rare puku are the main attractions here, though many species are represented. The bigger game includes elephant, sable, roan and reedbuck and even an occasional leopard or cheetah.

Moremi   Gradually building up an excellent reputation (perhaps taking on some of Savuti's mantle), this is the park in which to view the Okavango's big game. Dry season is best, and the copious game includes large numbers of buffalo and lion.

Namib-Naukluft   Scattered groups of gemsbok, springbok, mountain zebra and ostrich are often the only visible game here. Many other inhabitants are nocturnal – so come for the scenery and let any animals be a bonus.

Namibian coast   For bird-watching the lagoons around Walvis Bay and on the Lüderitz peninsula are frequent haunts for migrant waders, as are the occasional freshwater 'seeps' which occur along the length of the coast. Halifax island, near Lüderitz, has the region's only colony of jackass penguins, while the coast north of Swakopmund is home to the rare and endemic damara tern.

In Sandwich harbour large flocks of flamingos, pelicans and other residents are found, in the company of huge numbers of migrants at the right time of year. It is estimated that over 40,000 birds use these lagoons to overwinter every season.

Nxai   Timing is everything – visit at just the right time of year (somewhere between January and April!) and you'll witness the migration of large herds of springbok, wildebeest and zebra, along with attendant lion. In general the open nature of the country favours cheetah and plains species, rather than leopard, elephant or buffalo.

Okavango Delta   From a *mokoro* game-viewing is difficult – apart from spotting hippos and crocs! Walking on the islands is sometimes better, but make sure you have a guide who knows what he's doing.

However, for birds, the Okavango Delta is unequalled in the region. Whether you set off in a *mokoro* or aim to drive along the edge of Moremi, you're unlikely to be disappointed. If you're interested in a particular species, good local guides will help you find the best places.

Skeleton Coast   Not really a game park, but it does have fascinating populations of desert-adapted elephant and black rhino. The coast and river valleys are home to rare brown hyena, and visited by the odd lion. Further inland zebra, gemsbok, impala and ostrich can be found.

Waterberg   Notable as home to nucleus populations of reintroduced species, including roan, sable, tsessebe and white rhino. Existing game includes giraffe, eland, cheetah and leopard – though apparently no lion.

CONSERVATION AND DEVELOPMENT

A great deal has been written about conservation in Africa, much of which is over-simplistic and intentionally emotive. As a visitor, you are in a unique position to experience some of the many issues at first hand and ask the local people for their own perspectives. It's not so much a matter of balancing points of view, but of bringing out and smashing the various preconceptions and prejudices we all sub-consciously harbour – highlighting for once the complexity of the situation in all its detail. In this section we have tried to develop a few of the underlying ideas common to all areas where conservation is seen as being at odds with development. Specific conservation issues in Namibia and Botswana are discussed under their relevant sections in the book.

To start with, *conservation* must be taken in its widest sense – saving the animals, for example, is no use if it is done at the expense of peoples' livelihoods. Most people in 'developing' countries are deeply conscious of their fragile environment, but for many of them the day to day need to feed themselves, and purchase basic commodities, can often result in their environment's degradation. On a larger scale, governments may (understandably) put their nations development at a higher priority than conservation of their environment, seeing conservation as a luxury that only 'developed' countries can afford. There's no point in us sitting comfortably in the West proclaiming the wisdom of conservation, when it's not our livelihood or standard of living being affected.

Whilst there is clearly much that the 'developed' world can and should do to help the situation, any long-term solutions must rest in the approach and work undertaken by the local population and their government. And any such solution can only be in methods which preserve the natural environment as well as allowing continuing economic advance for the local people. In other words, sound ecology also means solving social problems – all too often the worst enemy of nature is simply poverty. In practice this means reconciling, and indeed integrating, the twin objectives of conservation and development – ultimately, anyhow, one cannot exist without the other. For both Namibia and Botswana, development is quite rightly a national priority – in the short as well as long terms. The problems only arise when development is clearly at the expense of conservation.

The *careful and planned* development of tourism is one possible way (of particular relevance to both Namibia and Botswana) in which conservation and development can be integrated. In simplistic terms, an area and its wildlife can be conserved if, by developing tourism, the conserved area can be made to *pay* for itself. If the financial returns from tourism are larger than any other (destructive) use that the area might be put to (for example, mining and cattle grazing), then the area has been safely conserved indefinitely. Any situation where a conserved area could be more profitably used is inevitably in an unstable situation – protective laws can always be changed.

For such a scenario to work, the development of tourism must necessarily be both sustainable and undamaging to the environment. Botswana's approach in its national parks and reserves has, since 1989, been one of high-cost/low-density tourism, together with a limited amount of licensed hunting. This aims to maintain (and even increase) the revenue from the conserved areas, whilst minimising the negative impact that tourists can have upon the environment. In essence it's a damage limitation exercise, but it's questionable if this will prove to be a long term solution. Geologists are presently prospecting for oil in the huge Central Kalahari Game Reserve, whilst the Okavango Delta (most of which is not protected in a conservation area) is under threat of having its valuable water drained for the Orapa diamond mine and agriculture.

Newly independent Namibia is still evolving its own wildlife policy, which often requires the needs of the wildlife to be balanced against those of the local people. All too often throughout the world, indigenous people have been thrown off their land to make way for the establishment of national parks or reserves, which fail to take into account the fact that people are as much part of the environment as flora and fauna.

One positive example is the government designated 'wilderness area' of Namibia's northern coast, where Himba people have lived and hunted animals for centuries. Now, by involving the local people with the controlled *development* of game viewing and tourism in the area, the Himba are able to generate an alternative income (from the safari operators) by becoming the *conservators* of the remaining wildlife. In this instance conservation and development have been successfully united, and the situation appears stable over the long term.

FIELD GUIDES

Many excellent guides to the flora and fauna of Southern Africa are published in South Africa. The following are all available from the Natural History Book Service, 2 Wills Rd. Totnes, Devon TQ9 5XN, England. Tel: (0803) 865913. Their catalogue also contains other natural history books pertaining to southern Africa and not listed here.

General
Nature of Botswana IUCN, Cambridge. £9.50. Of scientific interest only.

Fauna

Birds of Botswana, Kenneth Newman. Southern Books. £12.95. The first fully comprehensive guide to the avifauna of Botswana, describing and illustrating more than 550 species in colour, plus distribution maps.

The Illustrated Guide to the Birds of Southern Africa, Ian Sinclair. New Holland. £19.95. A new guide showing 250 species most commonly seen in the region.

Ian Sinclair's Field Guide to the Birds of Southern Africa, Ian Sinclair. Collins. £14.95. Illustrated by colour photos; 900 species identified.

Newman's Birds of Southern Africa, Kenneth Newman. Macmillan, £14.95. Considered by most to be the best of the field guides covering this region. 2000 illustrations.

Robert's Birds of Southern Africa, Gordon Maclean. New Holland, £29.99. The bible of serious birdwatchers; too heavy (848 pages) for most travellers.

A Field Guide to the Mammals of Southern Africa, C & T Stuart. New Holland, £12.95. Habitat, behaviour and a distribution map for each species. Illustrated with photos.

The Land Mammals of Southern Africa, R. Smithers. Macmillan, £14.95. An informative identification guide to the 200 species most likely to be seen. Illustrated with colour plates.

Predators of Southern Africa, Hans Grobler and others. Southern Books. £9.95. Describes behaviour, tracks, habitat and distribution of 36 species.

Field Guide to the Snakes and other Reptiles of Southern Africa, Bill Branch. New Holland (South Africa). £13.95. Full descriptions, colour photos and maps.

A Field Guide to the Butterflies of Southern Africa, Ivor Migdoll. New Holland, £13.99. 232 of the more commonly found species, illustrated with photos.

Flora

Flowers of Southern Africa, Auriol Batten. Southern Books. £36. 100 colour reproductions of outstanding paintings of flowers. Too big to be a field guide, but a beautiful souvenir.

Trees of Southern Africa, K. Coates. New Holland. A detailed work with over 1,000 pages and hundreds of colour pictures. Covers everything south of the Zambezi. £39.99.

Shell Field Guide to the Common Trees of the Okavango Delta and Moremi, Veronica Roodt. Shell Botswana. A readable guide which describes 32 common trees and their uses to people and animals. This is highly recommended and best bought in Botswana.

Mmilili's Day

by Phil Deutschle

Mmilili wakes at 5.30am as his sister, Opha, shouts, 'Mmilili, *muka!* get up!' He shares two blankets on the mud floor with his brother, Knowledge. He pulls on an old shirt and shorts. Then, shivering, he walks out of the compound into the surrounding bush that serves as the family toilet.

Back in the kitchen, he sits by the fire and waits for the water to heat up for washing himself. He carries the basin back to the children's hut and washes his hands and face. He empties the basin into the hedge and trades it in at the kitchen for a cold piece of yesterday's steam bread. Finally, he gets dressed in his blue and grey school uniform and starts off on his three-mile jaunt to school. Before long, he stops to wrench a branch from a thorn-bush. Students are required to bring a stick of firewood to school each day. The bell is rung at seven o'clock. First the classrooms have to be cleaned. Mmilili starts moving the desks to the back, so that the girls can sweep. he knows that he can't get into trouble with the teachers if he's moving desks. At assembly, after a song and a prayer, all the students not wearing full school uniform are told to remain behind. The offenders are going to be beaten.

His class's first subject is Setswana, the national language. Mmilili *hates* Setswana. The teacher calls them names if they can't answer her questions. And no matter how hard you work on an assignment it always comes back with a bad mark on it. Next comes Agriculture, his favourite subject. The teacher, who is from Swaziland, never beats them and they sometimes have a lot of fun in the garden.

Break is over before it really begins. Coming all the way from the garden, they are among the last in line to get their bowl of sweetened milk tea and one thick slice of bread. The last four periods are not so busy. The class still has no Social Studies teacher, whilst in English they are told to go away and 'study hard.' The maths teacher unexpectedly collects the assignment, which Mmilili luckily did during the time they were supposed to have had Social Studies.

Lunch is the highpoint. Tuesday's fare is *samp* (boiled maize kernels) and soup. Mmilili eats with his fingers, washes his bowl and then puts it away in the locker that he shares with Simisani.

He's sitting and rocking on the edge of the open locker door, when the teacher comes in and shouts, 'Is that a chair?' Mmilili jumps up scared, not knowing what to do. The teacher looks down at Mmilili. 'Do you have a chair at home?'

'Yes,' answers Mmilili in a whisper.

'You have a *chair*?'

'No,' stutters Mmilili, too flustered to think. Everyone is looking at him and he just wants to cry. The teacher shakes his head and walks away.

Throughout afternoon studies, Mmilili tries to do his homework, but he is still upset. The schoolwork is hard enough as it is, being all in English or Setswana. He has never seen a single book in his own language, Kalanga.

Sports-time is spent kicking a ball around with the other boys who are not on the soccer team. Supper is a bowl of soft porridge. Evening studies gives him a chance to finally do his work, but he is already dreading the long, dark walk home. The lights of the school are nice, even magic. The school also has water, right in the tap, and bread every day, toilets, and you have your own chair. Not like home.

At 7.30pm the final bell is rung. Mmilili, Jabulani, Filbert, Moses and Simisani start the trek to their homes. They talk loudly to chase away the fear of the dark. The last section, Mmilili has to walk alone.

Opha has saved some *shadza* (maize porridge) for him. Then he crawls under the blankets with Knowledge and quickly shivers himself to sleep.

Chapter 4

Planning and preparations

GETTING THERE

By Air

There are several airlines flying into Namibia and Botswana, some are direct, and all are reliable. Most fly overnight, so you can fall asleep on the plane in London, and wake in southern Africa with no jet-lag at all.

British Airways (International Reservations (UK) Tel: 081-897 4000.) flies twice a week to Gaborone directly from London, with discounted tickets from £599. At the time of writing, the best alternative flight to Gaborone is via Harare, with Air Zimbabwe, at £679. This allows for one free stop-over. Air France also flies to Gaborone from Paris, but discounted tickets are harder to find.

If you decide to fly directly to Windhoek, then your cheapest option from Europe will probably be via Frankfurt with Lufthansa (as low as £529 from London). South African Airways fly via Johannesburg every day except Friday, and cost about £539, while Air Namibia operates an excellent direct service from London three times per week.

You may find it cheaper to fly to the 'gateway' countries of Zimbabwe or South Africa — which you might manage for as little as £450 — and then go overland by rail, bus or hitch. Whilst Botswana is easily accessible from both Zimbabwe and South Africa, reaching Namibia is only practical from South Africa.

Finding cheap tickets is an art in itself — so rather than give specific information here, which will be quickly out of date, your best bet is to visit one of the specialist travel agents with a specific interest in Africa. These will also often be able to help you with tours, advice, insurance and even vaccinations.

London Flight Centre 47 Notting Hill Gate, London W11 3JSO. Tel: 071-727 4290. A very professional travel agent, specialising in finding good, cheap flights.

Africa Travel Centre 4 Medway Court, Leigh St, London WC1H 9QX. Tel: 071-387 1211. A small set-up, catering specially for the independent traveller, with the latest cheap flight deals and reliable advice.

Trailfinders 42-48 Earls Court Rd, London W8 6EJ. Tel: 071-938 3366. Another specialist outfit, Trailfinders also offers advice on overland trips backed up by an extensive library and a vaccination centre.

STA HQ at 117 Euston Rd, London NW1 2SX. Tel: 071-465 0486. One of the most popular agents for good flight deals, with branches in Britain's main cities, as well as in the USA and Australia. STA has a specific 'Africa Desk', and both the advantages and disadvantages of a large company.

By Land

Botswana has fast and direct road and rail links with Zimbabwe and South Africa. Crossing between Botswana and Namibia is slow and laborious — only for those with their own vehicle, or lots of spare hitching time.

Namibia has fast and direct links with South Africa — good tarred roads and a railway service.

For full details on air, rail and road transport into and out of the region, check the *In Namibia* and *In Botswana* chapters (pages 81 and 233).

Crossing Borders

Namibia-Botswana Between Namibia and Botswana there are three border crossings: Buitepos, on the Gobabis-Ghanzi road (open from 7.30am until 5pm); Ngoma Bridge, between Eastern Caprivi and Kasane (open from 8am until 4pm); and Mohembo, between Popa Falls and Shakawe (should be open from 8am until 6pm, but it's not a well established post and so don't rely too heavily on these times).

Namibia-South Africa Coming into Namibia from South Africa there are two main posts: Nakop, between Upington and Karasburg; and Noordoewer, on the main B1 between Keetmanshoop and Cape Town. These are open from 8am until 6pm.

Botswana-Zimbabwe Ramokwebana on the Francistown-Bulawayo road (open from 6am to 6pm daily); Kazungula Road, on the route from Kasane to Victoria Falls (open 6am to 6pm daily).

Botswana-South Africa There are numerous border crossings between those two countries all the way along the border. The main crossing is Ramatlabama, on the Gaborone-Mafikeng road (open 7am to 8pm).

Botswana-Zambia The Kazungula ferry across the Chobe River (6am to 6pm daily).

VISAS AND ENTRY REQUIREMENTS
Namibia

Citizens of the following countries do not need a visa to enter Namibia:
Angola, Austria, Botswana, Canada, France, Germany, Italy, Japan,
Mozambique, Scandinavian countries, Tanzania, UK, USA, Zambia and
Zimbabwe. It is best to check, since the situation is likely to change as
Namibia finds its feet in the international community. Pre-independence
Namibia was represented abroad by South Africa — this has now largely
changed, and Namibian embassies/high commissions are being
established. If there is no Namibian representative near you then Zambian
High Commissions are sometimes empowered to issue Namibian visas.

The maximum tourist stay is 60 days, but this can be easily extended
by application in Windhoek. You may be required to show proof of the
'means to leave' — ie onward air ticket, credit card, sufficient funds, vehicle
etc — though so far we have not come across anyone having difficulty at a
Namibian border.

Botswana

Citizens of the following countries do not need a visa: Australia, Austria,
Belgium, Canada, Cyprus, Denmark, Caribbean States, France, Finland,
Gambia, Greece, Guyana, Hong Kong, Iceland, Ireland, Italy, Kenya,
S.Korea, Lesotho, Luxembourg, Malawi, Malaysia, Malta, Netherlands,
N.Zealand, Norway, Sierra Leone, Singapore, S.Africa, Sweden,
Switzerland, Tanzania, Uganda, USA, UK, Zambia, Zimbabwe. All other
countries require a visa.

Like Namibia, you may be required to show a ticket home and sufficient
funds to cover your costs in the country. The maximum allowed stay for a
tourist is three months in the year, though only a one-month stamp is
usually issued at first. You can fairly easily renew your entry stamp at a
local Department of Immigration office.

UK Telephone Numbers

Namibia High Commission, Tel: 071-636 6244
Botswana High Commission, Tel: 071-499 0031
South African Embassy, Tel: 071-930 4488

WHEN TO GO

There really isn't a bad time to visit Namibia or Botswana, but there are
times when some attractions are better than others. You must decide what
you are primarily interested in and then, using the specific information in
the following relevant chapters, choose accordingly. However, the weather
and South African school holidays do provide broad constraints on the best
time to go.

Weather

Weather follows a southern hemisphere sub-tropical pattern: mid-May to mid August, 'winter', cool (very cold at night, 0°C-5°C on average) and very dry with clear skies; mid-August to November, 'spring', warming quickly to top temperatures (35°C-40°C on average), no rain but clouds building up; November to mid-March, 'summer', hot and humid, 'rainy' season; mid-March to mid-May, 'autumn', limited rain, temperatures dropping. You are very unlikely to encounter prolonged heavy rain anywhere except in the extreme north of the region.

The game in specific areas varies with the season — in general, the drier parks are best just after the rains (February - April), whilst those with permanent surface water are better toward the end of the dry season (August - October).

South African School Holidays

The South African school holiday periods are times to avoid — Namibia particularly is a popular holiday destination for South Africans. Holiday periods do vary, but lie within the following times: the last two weeks of March and the first two of April; the last week of June and the first two of July; the last week of September and the first of October; the last three weeks of December and the first two weeks of January.

MONEY

Budgeting

Neither of these countries are cheap, but costs can be kept to reasonable levels depending on how you choose to travel. To do even a rough budget, decide on the following main factors (refer to the relevant sections in this chapter and in the *In Namibia* and *In Botswana* chapters): hiring a vehicle or not; hotels/camps or camping; how you visit the Okavango Delta; and how much time you wish to spend in Botswana's game parks.

How to Take your Money

Many travellers take their money mostly as Sterling or US Dollars travellers cheques, with just a hundred or so Pula (and/or Namibian Dollars) for when they first arrive. Banks in the cities will cash any travellers cheques, but American Express and Barclays Visa seem to be particularly well recognised. American Express has a reputation for issuing prompt replacements if they are stolen, and by carrying them you are eligible to use their customer mail-drop facilities in Windhoek and Gaborone — so by choice, these are best. Having said that, the major credit cards (Visa, Mastercard, American Express and Diners Club) are widely accepted — and have the advantage that your bills will take time to filter home through the system. Taking out money at the banks from credit cards is very easy, and you only have to change money as you need it.

WHAT TO BRING

This is an impossible question to answer fully, as it depends upon how you travel and where you go. If you plan to do a lot of hitching or backpacking, then you should plan carefully what you take in an attempt to keep things as light as possible. If you have a vehicle for your whole trip, then weight and bulk will not be such a problem.

Clothing

For most of your time during the day all you will really want is light, loose-fitting cotton clothing. Cotton (or a cotton-rich mix) is cooler and more absorbent than synthetic fibres, making it much more comfortable. For men shorts (long ones) are usually OK, but long trousers are more socially acceptable in towns and especially in rural settlements and villages. For women a knee-length skirt or culottes is the ideal. Botswana and Namibia have a generally conservative dress code — 'revealing' or scruffy clothing isn't respected or appreciated by most Batswana or Namibians, especially outside their capital cities.

. For the evenings, or those chilling rides in the back of open-top safari vehicles, you will need something warm. Night-time temperatures in the winter months can be very low, especially in desert areas. If possible, dress in layers — taking along a light sweater and a long sleeved jacket, or a track suit, and a light but waterproof anorak. Note that some excellent cotton safari-wear is produced and sold locally. Try the larger department stores in Windhoek or Gaborone, or the curio shops in the larger towns.

Camping Equipment

Tent Mosquito netting and good ventilation is essential, as is a tent that isn't too small. A small tent at home may feel cosy and warm, but is likely to be unbearably hot and claustrophobic in the desert.

Mat A ground mat of some sort is essential for warmth at night, protection of the tent's ground sheet from rough stony ground (put it underneath the tent), and comfort. The ubiquitous closed cell foam mats are good and readily available. Genuine Karrimats and Therm-a-Rest (a combination air-mattress/foam mat) are quite expensive, but much stronger and more durable — worth the investment.

Sleeping Bag A three-season down bag is an ideal choice, being the lightest bag that is still warm enough for the cold winter nights, and yet small and light to carry. Synthetic bag fillings are cheaper, but for the same warmth are heavier and much more bulky. They do have the advantage that they keep their warmth when wet, unlike down, but clearly this is not an important consideration in the Kalahari!

Sheet Sleeping Bag Thin cotton sheet sleeping bags (eg YHA design), are good protection for your main sleeping bag, keeping it cleaner. They can, of course, be used on their own when your main bag is too hot.

Stove 'Trangia'-type stoves which burn methylated spirits are simple to use, light, and cheap to run. They come complete with a set of light aluminium pans and a very useful all-purpose handle. Often you'll be able to cook on a fire with the pans, but it's nice to have the option of making a brew in a few minutes while you set up camp. Canisters for gas stoves are available in the main towns if you prefer to use these, but are expensive and bulky. Petrol- and kerosene-burning stoves are undoubtedly efficient on fuel and powerful — but invariably temperamental, messy, and unreliable in the dusty desert.

Torch (flashlight) Find one that's small and tough — preferably water and sand-proof. Head-mounted torches leave your hands free — very useful when you are cooking over a campfire or mending the car — but some people find them bulky. The new range of small super-strong and super-bright torches (such as Maglites) are good, but have unusual (and expensive) bulbs — bring several spares with you.

Water Containers If you're thinking of hiking, you should bring a strong, collapsible water-bag for times when you will be away from a close source of water. 10 litres is a useful size, and probably the most you'll ever consider carrying on top of your normal kit. (10 litres of water weighs 10kg.) Large plastic containers for the car can be bought when you arrive. For everyday use, a small one-litre water bottle is invaluable.

Other Useful Items

Obviously no list can be comprehensive, or reflect everyone's likes and dislikes. The following items are just intended as ideas and memory joggers: A roll of insulating tape — for taping parcels and general repairs; plenty of 'sunblock' or high factor sun lotion and lipsalve; sunglasses — preferably strong, dark and with high U-V absorption; nylon cord — buy 20m or so, for emergencies and washing lines; a Swiss Army knife — how does anyone survive without one?; a couple of short paperback novels — essential for hitchhikers; large plastic bags to line your pack and protect your belongings from dust (bin-liners — garbage bags — are good); a light pair of binoculars — essential for game spotting; a plastic bowl, mug and set of cutlery; several disposable lighters; long-life candles; compass and whistle; cheap, waterproof watch; concentrated, biodegradable washing detergent; universal plug; basic sewing kit (with good strong thread suitable for backpacks — dental floss works well); a magnifying glass for a closer look at nature's wonders (eg page 166).

MAPS

A good selection of maps is available in Europe and the USA from specialised outlets. The Michelin map of East and Southern Africa (sheet 995) is probably the best for both Namibia and Botswana; the newly published Freytag & Berndt map of Namibia also looks good.

Imported maps are obtainable in Europe from Stanfords, London (Tel: 071-836 1321) or Geocenter, Stuttgart, Germany (Tel: 711 788 9340). In the USP try Map Link, Santa Barbara, California (Tel: 805 965 4402).

It is cheaper to delay your map buying until you arrive in Namibia or Botswana. If you are venturing into the bush you will need more detailed regional maps, or aerial photographs which may prove a lot more useful for areas where a map can show no more than a massive expanse of sand of bush. Aerial pictures may take a week or more to order.

Namibia   The standard visitor's map is published by the DNC and available free at most tourist centres and information offices. It has useful distance tables as well as street maps of Windhoek and Swakopmund on the back.

Regional maps and aerial photos are available from the Surveyor General's office in Windhoek, to the right of the Post Office on Independence Way.

Botswana   The deceptively simple Shell Oil map is all that most people need; it has handy maps of the main national parks and reserves on the back. Detailed maps of Moremi, Chobe and Nxai Pan are usually available from book shops or national park offices.

Large scale maps and aerial photos may be bought from the Department of Surveys and Lands in Gaborone, east of the train station and also (a limited selection) from the Department's offices in Maun, Francistown and Selebi-Phikwe. Mail-order catalogues can be obtained from Private Bag 0037, Gaborone. Tel: 53251.

PHOTOGRAPHY

Cameras

35mm SLR cameras with interchangeable lenses offer you the greatest flexibility. For general photography, a mid-range zoom lens (eg 28-70mm) is recommended — it is much more useful than the 'standard' (50mm) lens. For wildlife photography, you will need at least a 200mm lens to allow you to see the animal close in. Alternatively (or in addition), compact cameras take up little space and are excellent to have handy for quick shots of people or scenes — though they are of no use for game.

Film

Film is expensive in both Namibia and Botswana, and the choice is limited. Print films are readily available in main towns, but slide films are less common and rarely process-paid. Kodachrome used to be unobtainable in Namibia as a result of sanctions, but this is changing.

Bring a range of film speeds depending on what type of photography you are most interested in. For most landscape shots, where you will have plenty of light, a 'slow' film (100ASA or less) will give the best results. For wildlife photography, you will need a 'faster' film (400ASA) to enable you to use your telephoto lens without fear of camera-shake. Films, especially when exposed, can deteriorate very quickly in the heat. Keep all films (and therefore your loaded camera) away from direct sunlight, preferably in a cool box. Pictures taken at dusk or dawn will have the richest, deepest colours, whilst those taken during the middle of the day often seem pale and washed-out in comparison. Beware of the very deep shadows and high contrast so typical of tropical countries. Film cannot 'see' the huge range from black to white that your eye can. If you want to take pictures of people (or any showing full shadow details) in very bright conditions, then it's worth investing some time learning how to deal with these situations. By restricting your photography to mornings and evenings, you will encounter fewer problems.

Camera equipment should be very carefully protected from dust and sand — use plastic bags if necessary. You should bring some lens tissues and a blower brush to clean the dust from your lenses — and it is a good idea to use the brush to clean any dust from the back pressure-plate of your camera each time you change a film — particles caught here can easily cause long straight scratches along the entire length of your film.

CAR HIRE

Many of Namibia and Botswana's attractions are game reserves and wilderness areas, which are sparsely populated, not well served by public transport, and difficult to get to. To reach them, the visitor must rely on unpredictable lifts, or hire a vehicle.

What kind of vehicle to hire, and where to get it from, should be thought about well before arriving in the country — and if you have arranged a small group to travel with, then it can be worth organising the car hire itself in advance as there are often special deals available outside the country, either through overseas branches of the hire companies or via the airlines. If you are flying into the region, do check these out before you buy your flights.

Avis   International Reservations and Information (UK).   Tel: 081-848 8733.
Budget International Reservations and Information (UK).   Tel: 0800-181181.
Hertz International Reservations and Information (UK).   Tel: 081-679 1799.

Choosing the right vehicle to hire will depend largely upon where you intend to visit, and how much money you have. The best for rough roads, and the only ones for some terrain, are high-clearance four-wheel drive (4WD) vehicles — though they are expensive to hire and run. That said, most of Namibia's sights can be seen using an ordinary 2WD saloon car (the exceptions being Kaudum, the Linyanti Area and the northern parts of the Kaokoveld) so hiring a 2WD for Namibia can work well. Botswana is different — only the roads between the few main towns are accessible by 2WD, in addition to a few parts of northern Chobe and the Makgadikgadi Game Reserve. A trip here really needs a 4WD to get deep into the parks, remote areas and the Kalahari desert. (See also Chapter 6, *Driving and Camping in the Bush*.)

Wherever you hire your vehicle, you must read the fine print of your hire agreement very carefully. The *insurance* and the *collision damage waiver* (CDW) clauses are worth studying particularly closely. These spell out the 'excess' that you will pay in the (all too common) event of an accident. These CDW excesses vary widely, and often explain the difference between cheap rental deals and better but more costly options. If you are unfortunate enough to have an accident, a high CDW could mean paying over N$50,000 in repair bills.

Hiring a Saloon Car

Firstly, where you hire is important, as it can affect the price and the conditions of hire. Because South Africa, Botswana and Namibia belong to the same South African customs union, hired cars can normally move freely across their mutual borders. This allows a regional trip to be planned which takes advantage of the large differences in car-hire rates between various locations. Prices do vary from city to city, with South Africa generally being the cheapest. Botswana and Namibia are more expensive, have more restrictions and their rates differ more widely between towns. You seem to get less favourable deals as you go north — but while searching for the cheapest rates, beware of excessive drop-off charges on some one-way hires.

The three big hire companies within the region are **Avis**, **Budget** rent-a-car, and **Imperial**. Of these Avis is easily the largest and has the best network of offices (including some in Botswana). Locally, their prices tend to b similar, even if the conditions vary. Imperial is associated with Hertz — so an international booking done through Hertz will be with Imperial. Typical on-the road prices per day from any of these three, based upon unlimited mileage during a three-week rental period are:

	Basic VW Golf (air conditioned)	4-door saloon	Toyota Twin-Cab (4WD)
South Africa	R150(£28/$42)	R275(£52/$78)	R375(£71/$107)
Windhoek (Namibia)	N$220(£42/$63)	N$330(£62/$93)	N$430(£81/$122)
Maun (Botswana)	P191(£50/$75)	P250(£66/$99)	P320(£84/$126)

Figures in brackets are in pounds sterling/US dollars, based on the current exchange rates (see page 3), and should give you a good indication of the relative costs between hiring vehicles in the three countries. Bear in mind that a cheaper deal can often be had from smaller local companies, though you may not have the same back-up.

If time is not in short supply but money is, consider just hiring for a few days at a time (on a time and mileage basis) to see specific sights. Then, for example, a basic VW Golf in Namibia would cost N$140 (£26/39) per day plus 85c per kilometre — which might not be too expensive if you are planning on sitting by water-holes in Etosha all day. Similarly, weekend hire from Avis in Kasane for a few days in Victoria Falls can cost as little as P240 (£63/$95) for three days.

Hiring a 4WD Vehicle

This requires both money and planning, but having a four-wheel drive (4WD) at your disposal opens up endless possibilities, and gives you the chance to mount an expedition into the wilder parts of the sub-continent. Whilst they are available at some car hire offices, 4WD vehicles are much less numerous and will usually need to be booked in advance and returned by a specified date. The only places where you will find much choice are Maun and Windhoek — or possibly in South Africa.

Of the two, Maun tends to be more expensive, but is arguably more central to the area in which you need such a vehicle. Perhaps the town's best bargain is Island Safari Lodge's chauffeur-driven 4WD for P280 (£74/$111) per day plus fuel (l00km per day free, then P1.15 per kilometre), especially for a short trip into Moremi or Chobe's Savuti.

Windhoek is home to the region's only specialists in 4WD vehicles of quality — *Kessler 4x4 Hire* (see page 105). Found on the corner of Curt von Francois and Tal St, they have a variety of different types of 4WD — including the twin-cab Toyota Hilux, which seats four in comfort, and various Land Rovers. Costs vary from around the N$350 (£70/105) upwards, depending upon the model, but unlike the international companies, Kessler aims to hire out vehicles for long trips into the wilds. Equally unusual is a willingness to let vehicles go into Zimbabwe — which most other firms are just beginning to match. See page 105 for more details of Windhoek's other car hire firms, but **beware** — there are a plethora of cheaper firms, many of whom have less experience and use older, less reliable vehicles.

The only drawback if you hire from here is that the car needs to be returned as well, necessitating a circular route — which is not always easy to plan. (A couple of such routes are given under *Suggested Itineraries*, below.)

Note that for circular trips from either Maun and Windhoek you can hire all the camping kit that you will need, and a lot more besides, at Kalahari Kanvas or Gav's Camping Hire respectively.

SUGGESTED ITINERARIES

If you choose to hire a vehicle, your time will probably be limited by money, and you will need to plan carefully to make the most of your trip. These suggested itineraries are intended as a framework only, and the time spent at places is the minimum which is reasonable — if you have less time, then cut places out rather than try to quicken the pace of your trip. When planning your own itinerary, try to intersperse the longer drives between more restful days and avoid spending each night in a new place if you can — shifting camp can be become very tedious. When touring Namibia, do book (permits, accommodation etc.) as much in advance as you can through Windhoek's DNC. To allow for this, we've included more detail in the itineraries with sections in Namibia, where advanced booking is sometimes a necessity.

Distances given are necessarily approximate. and are based on the minimum distances between two destinations by the shortest reasonable route. The distances do not allow for game driving or general exploration, which you must allow for yourself.

Etosha - Namib Tour, Windhoek round trip

2WD, Namibia, minimum of 2½ weeks, approx. 2,500km
Day   1:   Leave Windhoek for Waterberg. 286km.
Day   2:   Waterberg Plateau.
Day   3:   Buy food at Otavi, eat at Lake Otjikoto, arrive at Namutoni before sunset. 383km.
Day   4:   Game viewing around Namutoni.
Day   5:   Game viewing around Namutoni.
Day   6:   Long lunch at Halali, if open, then to Okaukuejo. 123km.
Day   7:   Game viewing around Okaukuejo.
Day   8:   Late lunch at Outjo — buy supplies — then to Khorixas. 250km.
Day   9:   Visit the burnt mountain, organ pipes, Twyfelfontein and the petrified forest; camp out at Brandberg (no facilities!). 271km.
Day 10:   Look around Brandberg; then to Swakopmund via Henties Bay. 232km.
Day 11:   Relax and replenish supplies in Swakopmund.
Day 12:   Explore the Namib Park; camp at Homeb or Mirabib. 158km.
Day 13:   Leisurely drive to Sesriem, via the Gaub Pass and Solitaire. 259km.
Day 14:   Pre-dawn drive/walk to Sossusvlei; Sesriem Canyon later. 120km.
Day 15:   Short drive to Naukluft, afternoon there. 108km.
Day 16:   A longer hike around Naukluft.
Day 17:   Return to Windhoek to eat out and relax. 249km.

Okavango — Etosha Tour, Gaborone to Windhoek

2WD/4WD*, Namibia and Botswana, min. of 2½ weeks, approx. 3,200km.

Day   1:   Start from Gaborone, buy supplies; sleep at Francistown. 433km.
Day   2:   Drive to Makgadikgadi Game Reserve via Nata. Camp in reserve. 360km.
Day   3:   Explore Makgadikgadi Game Reserve and drive to Maun. 145km
Day   4:   Okavango Delta trip. (Must be pre-arranged, or it takes longer).
Day   5:   Okavango Delta trip.
Day   6:   Okavango Delta trip.
Day   7:   Return from Okavango Delta trip.
*Day   8:   Leave Maun on long drive to Kasane, via Nata. 616km
Day   9:   Early game drive into northern Chobe, stay at Serondela or Kasane.
Day   10:   Cross into Namibia via Ngoma Bridge; buy food at Katima Mulilo and spend the night there. 114km
Day   11:   A rough day's drive to Popa Falls. 313km.
Day   12:   Look around Popa and Mahango; afternoon drive to Rundu. 219km.
Day   13:   Long drive to Namutoni, Etosha. 415km.
Day   14:   Game viewing around Namutoni.
Day   15:   Leisurely lunch at Halali, if open, then onto Okaukuejo. 123km.
Day   16:   Game viewing around Okaukuejo.
Day   17:   Game viewing around Okaukuejo.
Day   18:   Long drive to end tour at Windhoek. 435km.

*4WD alternative: spend day 8 driving to Lake Ngami (95km), days 9 and 10 at the Tsodilo Hills (approx. 320km), and continue to Popa via Shakawe on the Okavango's southern bank (approx. 120km).

Botswana Parks Tour, Maun Round Trip

One self-sufficient 4WD, min. of 2 weeks, approx. 1,500km.

Day   1:   Leave Maun for Nxai Pan National Park. 185km.
Day   2:   Explore Nxai Pan National Park.
Day   3:   Kudiakam Pan and Baines' Baobabs
Day   4:   Drive to Makgadikgadi Pans Game Reserve. 100km.
Day   5:   Explore Makgadikgadi Pans Game Reserve.
Day   6:   Drive to Sowa Pan via main Maun-Nata road. 235km.
Day   7:   Explore Sowa Pan and Kubu Island; drive to Nata Lodge. 110km.
Day   8:   Drive to Serondela via Kasane; relax by Chobe river in evening. 320km.
Day   9:   Head into Chobe National Park.
Day   10:   Arrive at Savuti by evening. 180km from Serondela.
Day   11:   Game viewing at Savuti.
Day   12:   Drive south into Moremi Wildlife Reserve.
Day   13:   Exploring Moremi.
Day   14:   Leave Moremi to arrive Maun by evening. 335km including 'grand tour' of Moremi from Savuti.

Okavango - Linyanti Tour, Maun Round Trip

One self-sufficient 4WD. Botswana and Namibia, min. of 2 weeks, approx. 1,500km.

Day 1: Leave Maun for Lake Ngami, camping by the lake. 95km.
Day 2: Early start for the Tsodilo Hills. approx. 320km.
Day 3: Whole day exploring the hills.
Day 4: North into Namibia via Shakawe, staying at Popa. 120km.
Day 5: Day to explore Mahango and Popa.
Day 6: East across the Caprivi Strip, into the Mudumu and Mamili
         Parks. 310km.
Day 7: Explore Mudumu / Mamili area.
Day 8: Explore Mudumu / Mamili area.
Day 9: Back into Botswana; replenish supplies and stay at Kasane. 114km.
Day 10: Into Chobe, camping at Serondela. 30km.
Day 11: Drive to Savuti: stay at campsite. 180km.
Day 12: Whole day spent exploring the Savuti area.
Day 13: A day game viewing, en route to Moremi Wildlife Reserve.
Day 14: Day in Moremi, returning to Maun by the evening. 245km.

'Grand Tour', Windhoek Round Trip

One self-sufficient 4WD, Namibia and Botswana, min. of 3 weeks, approx. 3,800km.

Day 1: Leave Windhoek on the C26, go north to Gaga after crossing the
         Kuiseb, then left and right via Hotsas onto the C28 to Swakopmund.
         370km.
Day 2: Day at Sandwich Harbour; stay at Swakopmund. 160km.
Day 3: Via the coast to Brandberg; camp there. 235km.
Day 4: Aim for Palmwag, via Twyfelfontein, the organ pipes and the
         petrified forest. 287km.
Day 5: Slowly explore the Concession Area near Palmwag.
Day 6: Cross-country to Okaukuejo. 302km.
Day 7: Long lunch at Halali, if open, then to Namutoni. 123km.
Day 8: Game viewing around Namutoni.
Day 9: Leave after lunch to get supplies and stay at Grootfontein. 167km.
Day 10: Full day to reach Popa Falls. 465km.
Day 11: Day trip from Popa to explore Mahango. 80km.
Day 12: Early start south; lunch by the Okavango then to Tsodilo Hills.
         120km.
Day 13: Whole day at Tsodilo Hills.
Day 14: Make an early start to reach Maun late afternoon. 355km.
Day 15: Replenish supplies and head out to Moremi Wildlife Reserve in the
         late afternoon. Approx. 1000km
Day 16: Explore Moremi.
Day 17: Explore Moremi.
Day 18: Leave early for Lake Ngami. 200km.
Day 19: Drive to Ghanzi, leaving time to look around in the evening. 215km.
Day 20: Very long drive from Ghanzi to Windhoek via Gobabis. 525km
         (last 205km on tar!).

Namibian Bush Tour, Windhoek round trip

Two self-sufficient 4WDs, min. of 3½ weeks, approx. 4,100km.

Day   1: Leave Windhoek for Sesriem, via the C24's Remhoogte Pass.
            322km

Day   2: Pre-dawn drive to Sossusvlei; Sesriem Canyon in the afternoon.
            140km.

Day   3: Into the Namib Park; camp at Ganab. 221km.

Day   4: More time in the Namib; to Swakopmund in the afternoon. 140km.

Day   5: Buy supplies and relax in Swakopmund, perhaps see
            Welwitschia Drive.

Day   6: Whole day trip to Sandwich Harbour. 160km.

Day   7: Leave Swakopmund by the coast road; camp at Brandburg.
            235km.

Day   8: Aim for Palmwag, via Twyfelfontein, the organ pipes and the
            petrified forest. 287km.

Day   9: Slowly explore the Concession Area near Palmwag.

Day   10: Leave for Sesfontein — camp in the bush near there. 115km.

Day   11: Visit Kaoko Otavi and Opuwo, then camp en route to Kamanjab.
            160km.

Day   12: Finish off the journey to Okaukuejo. 400km.

Day   13: Game viewing around Okaukuejo — after-dinner drinks at the
            floodlit water-hole.

Day   14: Long lunch at Halali, if open, then to Namutoni. 123km.

Day   15: Game viewing around Namutoni.

Day   16: Short drive to Grootfontein; replenish supplies. 167km.

Day   17: Full day to reach Popa Falls. 465km.

Day   18: Day trip from Popa to explore Mahango. 80km.

Day   19: Northern Kaudum via Katere; explore Kaudum *omuramba* itself.
            147km.

Day   20: A slow trip south to Sikereti camp for the night. 75km.

Day   21: Further exploration of Kaudum, based at Sikereti.

Day   22: Early start for Grootfontein, visiting Tsumkwe en route. 350km.

Day   23: Back to Windhoek. 452km.

IN-COUNTRY TOURS AND SAFARIS

If you do intend to book a package within either Namibia or Botswana then
there will be no shortage of choice. Often there is a 10% discount if you
book within the country, and residents of southern Africa sometimes get
more. Similarly, if you are booking off-season, or at short notice, then you
should get a bargain — but don't expect miracles! Balanced against these
advantages is the risk that you will not get what you want in the peak
seasons.

Generally, if you are flexible about time and are coming in the off-
season then look around and book in the country — if your time is limited
or you are here when it is busy, then book well before you arrive. The
centres for booking are Maun and Windhoek — though Gaborone,
Swakopmund and Kasane all have agencies for a variety of trips, and of

course Victoria Falls in Zimbabwe (just over the border from Kasane) is a major regional centre for travellers.

Details of how to book are given in *Part 2* and *Part 3*, together with specific information on some of the better deals available.

UK-BASED TOUR OPERATORS

If you only have a few weeks' holiday you may prefer the security of booking a tour in England (or your home country). The following are some of the smaller reputable tour operators who run trips to Namibia and/or Botswana:

Okavango Tours and Safaris (see page 306) 28 Bisham Gardens, London N6 6DD, England. Tel: 081-341 9442.

Okavango Explorations (see page 305) Regency House, 1/4 Warwick St, London W1R 5WB. Tel: 071-287 9672.

Naturetrek — Birding and Botanical tours. 40 The Dean, Alresfold, Hants. SO24 9AZ. Tel: 0962 733051

Safariland Holidays 3 Crescent Stables, 139 Upper Richmond Rd, Putney, London SW15 2TN. Tel: 081-780 0030.

Grass Roots, 8 Lindsay Rd, Hampton Hill, Middx TW12 1DR. Tel: 081-941 5753.

Art of Travel 268 Lavender Hill, London SW11 1LJ. Tel: 071-738 2038.

African Explorations 36 Kirtons Farm, Pingewood, Reading, Berks RG3 3UN. Tel: 0734 500146.

Explore Worldwide 1 Frederick St, Aldershot, Hants GU11 1LQ. Tel: 0252 319448.

Cox and Kings St James Court, 45 Buckingham Gate, London SW1E 6AF. Tel: 071-834 7472.

THE NEXT EDITION

Our readers play a vital part in updating books for the next edition. If you have found changes, or new exciting places, or have a story to share do write. The most helpful contributions will receive a free book. Write to:
"Namibia and Botswana", Bradt Publications, 41 Nortoft Road,
Chalfont St. Peter, Bucks, SL9 0LA, UK.

Building a mud hut
by Phil Deutschle

Even a small child can recognise the type of soil needed for a mud hut — there is something about the colour, containing a specific amount of clay and vegetable matter. When it came time to build a new kitchen in our compound, we were fortunate to have the proper mud-making soil just behind the proposed site. The children were set to work digging, while the women drew the floorplan — a large circle. They checked the size by sitting down with their backs to the soon-to-be-built walls and with their feet stretched out towards the imaginary fireplace. A foundation was dug by scratching a shallow groove in the ground, and next came the mud, called *vu*.

The dirt that the children dug up had to be mixed with the correct proportions of water and sand. The women formed the mixture into bowling-ball sized wads, and kneaded it thoroughly, like bread. I offered to help, but was told, "You don't know how to make *vu*. We will do it."

After kneading, a loaf of mud was rolled into a fat sausage and dropped from hip height onto the ground. This flattened it on one side. Then it was turned over and dropped from a lower height, creating a slab to be used something like a brick. Kopano, the construction forewoman, would take a slab and put it in position on its long edge, pat it into place, and smooth out the back end, forming a parallelogram-shaped brick. The women continued like this, around the circle, completing two layers, totalling a foot and a half high. More than this could not be built in a single day, as any higher layers would squash the lower ones.

Next day, the previous day's now-hard layers were spread inside and out with fresh *vu*, acting as both mortar and plaster. Again, I tried to help, but was rebuked with, "No, you can't do this. Your hands are too big." After the spreading of fresh mud, two more rows of bricks were constructed. The process continued the following day — first spreading mud on the previous day's work and then building two additional rows. After five days it stood at eye level.

While we waited the two weeks needed to get the poles to make the roof, heavy rains knocked down a third of what had been built. No one seemed concerned. Mud huts got washed away all the time. The broken walls just had to be rebuilt.

Roofing poles arrived from the bush, and the construction was done by two hired men. I didn't even suggest that I might help. I'd had enough rejections. They dug nine poles into the ground around the periphery of the kitchen, and on top of that they built a conical framework to hold the grass.

By this point, Kopano had begun conducting rituals to sanctify and protect the new kitchen. Each night she lit a small fire in the centre of the unfinished building and burnt herbs to safeguard the health of her children.

Now came the grass for the roof. It had to be tied into thick mats, each six yards long. These long mats were rolled up and lifted onto the roof supports. Unrolling the mats onto the framework was an easy job, and here I was certain that my great height would be appreciated. Yet again, I was wrong. "Leave it," instructed Kopano, "We will do it." They rolled out the grass in an ever-shrinking spiral and tied it all fast.

Lastly, I watched Kopano struggling to hammer together a wooden door. She gave me a scornful look, but I said nothing. Only much later did I learn the traditions of building — the women work with the mud and grass exclusively, while the men are expected to do all the building using poles and wood. I wish they'd told me!

Chapter 5

Health and safety

Some Initial Comments

There's always a great danger in writing about health and safety for the uninitiated visitor: it's all too easy to become paranoid about the Pandora's box of exotic diseases he/she may catch; and it's all too easy to start distrusting everyone you meet as a potential thief – falling into an unfounded 'us-and-them' attitude toward the people of the country you are visiting.

As a comparison, imagine an equivalent section in a guide book to a western country – there would be a list of possible diseases and, most relevantly, advice on the risk of theft and mugging in many major western cities would have to be given. Many western cities are dangerous – but with time we learn how to deal with them, accepting almost unconsciously what we can and cannot do.

It's very important to strike the right balance – avoid being either too cautious or too over-relaxed about both your health and safety. In time, you will find the balance that best fits you and the country you are visiting.

Namibia and Botswana stand out in Africa as being particularly healthy and safe. With good preparation and common sense, you should stay healthy and unharassed while here. Windhoek and Gaborone are certainly amongst the safest cities I know, and with most of your time spent outdoors, and plenty of healthy sunshine, you will probably find yourself returning home fitter than when you left.

BEFORE YOU GO

Travel Insurance

Full medical insurance is essential – and you should check that it covers repatriation to your home country if this is required for medical reasons. There are a number of relatively cheap specific travel insurance packages available, which will fully cover you for medical expenses, as well as providing useful cover against theft, lost baggage, and even flight cancellations. Most of these are perfectly adequate on the medical side, but check the exclusions and conditions for loss and theft of your possessions carefully. In particular be sure of the maximum amount you can claim, and the limit for 'valuable items', especially cameras. Often, you won't be able to claim more than about £250 maximum for a lost or stolen camera. If you have your possessions insured at home, you may find that the policy covers you abroad for a limited time – usually 30-60 days a year.

ISIS travel insurance (available from Endsleigh Insurance brokers, or the ubiquitous STA Travel Agents), is one of the most popular and cheapest policies around, but you should check the small print for the exclusions – it may not suit you. AMEX does its own very good, year-round policy that's worth investigating if you have an American Express card, while Avon insurance also comes highly recommended as providing a very good policy.

Planning Ahead

Having a full set of **inoculations** takes time, normally at least six weeks, though sometimes 'cocktails' of inoculations are available which reduce this time drastically. See your doctor early on, or one of the travel health centres listed, to establish an inoculation time-table (see also under inoculations). Equally it's worth allowing time to have a **dental check-up** before you go – you could be several painful days from the nearest dentist. If you wear glasses, bring a spare pair, or at the very least your **glasses prescription**. The same goes for **contact-lens** wearers – do bring some spare glasses in case the all-pervasive sand and dust proves too much for the lenses and your eyes. If you take **regular medication** (including contraceptive pills), bring a good supply with you – it may not always be readily available.

Vaccination Centres in London

British Airways Medical Department, 75 Regent Street, London, W1. Tel: 071-439 9584
MASTA, Bureau of Hygiene and Tropical Diseases, Keppel St, London WC1E 7HT. Tel: 0891 244100.
Thomas Cook Vaccination Centre, 45 Berkeley Square, London W1. Tel: 071-499 4000.
Trailfinders Immunisation Centre, 194 Kensington High Street, London W8 7RG. Tel: 071-938 3999.

Inoculations

Legal requirements   No inoculations are required by law for entry into either Namibia or Botswana if you have come straight from the West. However, a yellow fever vaccination certificate may be necessary if you have come from an area where the disease is endemic – eg East Africa or Zambia. The vaccine is very safe, effective and lasts ten years – so it might be a worthwhile investment, even if you don't legally need it.

Recommended precautions You should carefully check that you are protected against polio and tetanus – it's worth being covered for these whether you are at home or travelling abroad. Vaccinations against cholera and typhoid may be recommended by your doctor, though most now regard the cholera vaccination as ineffective, unpleasant, and only worth having if you need the certificate to enter the country you are visiting – you don't for Namibia, Botswana, Zimbabwe or South Africa. Some protection against hepatitis A can be had from a gamma-globulin jab, but you are unlikely to get this disease in Namibia or Botswana unless you live and travel in very rural populated areas. A better alternative is the new HAVRIX vaccine which gives several years of protection.

Malaria Prophylaxis (Prevention)

Malaria is the most dangerous disease in Africa, and much of the tropical world. Although the risk in Namibia and Botswana is small (least risk in desert areas and those over 1,500m in altitude), it is still worth taking malaria pills if you will be travelling into areas of much greater risk – the northern areas of the two countries, and around the Okavango Delta.

Currently recommended pills include: proguanil (Paludrine) – two tablets (200mg base each) every day (after food), and chloroquine (Nivaquine) – two tablets (300mg base each) at the same time every week. The two drugs are usually taken in combination. Some people find that the pills make them feel nauseous – this can be lessened by taking the pills last thing at night and sleeping through the worst! Chloroquine tastes disgusting (it defines bitterness) – so get hold of the sugar-coated varieties, or else develop an impressively fast swallowing technique. It's important to remember to start taking the tablets at least a week before you arrive in a malarial zone, and continue taking them for six weeks afterwards.

Prophylaxis doesn't stop you catching malaria – only stopping the mosquitos biting you will do that (see below) – but it drastically reduces your chances of fully developing the disease and, if it does develop, it will certainly lessen its severity. Falciparum (cerebral) malaria is the most common type in Africa, and must be guarded against – when left untreated it is usually fatal. Fortunately chloroquine-resistant strains are not yet a problem in these two countries – so prophylaxis is effective and treatment is not difficult. However, the situation is always changing so get the latest advice from the Malaria Reference Laboratory (London), tel. 071-636 7921 for a tape recording of up to date prophylaxis advice. Despite all these precautions you could still get malaria. See page 59 for advice in this situation.

Americans also have a source of free information at the Center for Disease Control in Atlanta, Georgia. By phoning (404) 332 4559 you can find out the latest recommended malaria prophylaxis, inoculation requirements and outbreaks of dangerous diseases in various parts of the world.

Medical Kit

Pharmacies in Namibia and Botswana are well stocked with over-the-counter medicines and general supplies – so it's not worth taking too much with you. A basic kit should include most of the following: antiseptic cream, sticking plasters (the roll which you cut to size is much more versatile than the pre-shaped band-aids), micropore tape (for closing small cuts and wounds, and preventing blisters), scissors, sterile bandage, lint and safety pins, aspirins, paracetamol, diarrhoea pills, malaria pills (prophylaxis and emergency treatment), vaseline or lanolin cream for cracked skin, 'lip salve' for dry and cracked lips (the best ones include a sunscreen), eye drops.

STAYING HEALTHY – HEALTH TIPS

Prevention is always better than cure – most of the ailments that afflict travellers or visitors are easily preventable. Keep up your resistance to diseases by eating and sleeping well – for many people, travelling quickly becomes a nightmare marathon of sporadic meals and even more sporadic night's sleep. Your hygiene standards shouldn't suffer when you travel either – be sensible about what you eat and drink, and how you prepare food.

Food and Storage

Most health problems encountered by travellers the world over are contracted by eating contaminated food or drinking unclean water. While Botswana and Namibia are no worse than most western countries, it is still worth being careful – avoid undercooked food and remember that the heat can turn foods inedible very quickly. Cool boxes can help, but it is still not a good idea to keep any animal products for more than a day or two. Instead travel with tins, packets, and fresh green vegetables when you can find them, as these are unlikely to cause food poisoning.

Water and Purification

The piped water available in the towns of both countries is usually safe to drink, so water quality only becomes an issue in the wilds. Here, if you are on a short visit, then your rule should be to purify all the water used for drinking or washing food. To purify water, first filter out any suspended solids – passing it through a piece of closely woven cloth will do fine – then either boil it for 10 minutes, or sterilise it chemically (boiling is more effective, and doesn't fill your system up with unwanted toxins).

The tablets sold for purification (puritabs, sterotabs, et al) are adequate, and based on either chlorine or iodine – simply follow the manufacturer's instructions. Iodine is the more effective, especially against amoebic cysts, and if you are travelling for a long period then it is cheaper to take a small bottle of medical quality 'Tincture of Iodine' (2% solution), and a small eyedropper. Use two to four drops of the solution to purify one litre of water (depending on how contaminated it is), leaving it to stand for 15 minutes (more if it is very cold) before use. The solution can also be used as a general external antiseptic. It stains a deep purple if spilt – so seal the container well.

If you are working in Namibia or Botswana, or on a very long trip, then there is a case for gradually allowing your stomach to get used to drinking unpurified (but still clean) water from natural sources. The Okavango and the rivers of the Kaokoveld are good examples. If attempting this, then ensure your source is crystal clear, running, and not downstream of human settlements. Then introduce yourself very slowly to it, gradually allowing your system to acclimatise. This is possible to do here because of the lack of population; it is not something that I would be happy doing in more crowded African countries.

Heat and the Sun

Heat stroke, heat exhaustion and sunburn are sometimes problems for newly-arrived travellers to Africa, despite being easy to prevent. That said, both Botswana and Namibia have dry climates where the heat is rarely the sticky, oppressive kind that causes most of the trouble. To avoid problems, just remember that your body is under stress and so make allowances for it. Firstly, take things gently – you are on holiday after all. Next, keep your fluid and salt levels high: lots of soft drinks and brews of tea, but go easy on the coffee and alcohol. Thirdly, dress to keep cool, with loose fitting, thin garments – preferably of cotton or silk.

Finally, beware of the sun. Hats and long-sleeved shirts are essential kit. If you must expose your skin to the sun then use sun-blocks and high-factor sun-screens (the sun's so strong that you'll still get a tan!).

Avoiding Insects – Repellents and Mosquito Nets

Research has shown that using a mosquito net and covering up exposed skin (by wearing long-sleeved shirts and tucking trousers into socks) in the evening and at night is the most effective way of preventing malaria. However, I have known mosquitos to bite through clothes, including my new light-weight *Rohan* trousers. Mosquito coils and insect repellents work to some extent. DEET is the active ingredient in repellents, so the greater percentage of DEET, the stronger the effect. Some people swear by repellents, particularly for keeping irritating insects off during the day. I find many of the concoctions so clearly toxic and smelly, that I am reluctant to put any on, especially when washing facilities are limited. Using a moderate strength repellent (eg 50% DEET) is a fair compromise. 'Jungle Formula' have introduced a combination repellent and sunscreen gel which works well.

Bringing a mosquito net with you is strongly recommended. It's worth thinking carefully about the design – some hang from a convenient branch or the ceiling of a room and tuck under the mattress, whilst others are built more like a tent and are perhaps more suitable for camping (without a tent). It's essential that your tent has mosquito netting built in – if it doesn't, consider buying some netting and doing the necessary modifications yourself.

Snakes, Spiders and Scorpions...

Encounters with aggressive snakes or vindictive scorpions are really more common in horror movies than in Africa. Most snakes will flee at the mere vibrations of a human step, whilst you will have to seek out scorpions to see one, and spiders are far more interested in flies than people. If you are careful about where you place your hands and feet – especially after dark – then there should be no problems (see Chapter 6).

Snakes do bite occasionally though, and then it's worth knowing the standard first aid treatment. Firstly, and most importantly, *don't panic*. Remember that only a tiny minority of bites – even by highly poisonous species – inject enough venom to be dangerous. Even in the worst of these cases, the victim has hours or days to get to help, and not a matter of minutes. He/she should be kept calm, with no exertions which would pump venom around the blood system, whilst being taken rapidly to the nearest medical help. The bitten limb should be immobilised and Paracetamol used as a painkiller. (*Never* use aspirin to kill the pain of a snakebite as it may cause internal bleeding.) *Do not* use a tourniquet; this may do more harm to the limb than good, and when released produce a surge of venom into the blood. If the bite is both serious and venomous, tightly (but not over-tight) wrap a bandage over the entire length of the limb which has been bitten.

Forget cutting out the wound, sucking and spitting, or any of the commercial anti-snakebite kits – which vary from being a waste of time to being positively dangerous. The only real treatment is for a specific antivenom to be medically administered. Identification of the snake is very helpful, so killing it and taking it along with you is a good idea if at all possible (!). When deep in the bush, heading for the nearest large farm may be quicker than going to a town – it may have a supply of antivenom, or facilities to radio for help by plane.

DISEASES – AND WHEN TO SEE A DOCTOR

Traveller's Diarrhoea

There are almost as many names for this affliction as there are traveller's tales on the subject. The truth is that in Namibia and Botswana you are unlikely to have any problems at all. Firstly, do resist the temptation to reach for the medical kit as soon as your stomach turns a little fluid. Most cases of traveller's diarrhoea will resolve themselves within 24 to 48 hours without any treatment at all. To speed this process of acclimatisation up, eat well but simply – avoiding fats in favour of starches and, most importantly, keeping your fluid intake high. Bananas and papaya fruit are often claimed to be helpful. If you urgently need to stop the symptoms, for a long bus ride for example, then Lomotil, Imodium or another of the commercial anti-diarrhoea preparations will do the trick – but they will not cure the problem.

When severe diarrhoea gets continually worse, or the stools contain blood or pus, or it lasts for more than 10 days, you should seek medical advice. There are almost as many possible treatments as there are probable causes, and a proper diagnosis involves microscopic analysis of a stool sample – so get yourself back to a town and go straight to the nearest hospital. The most important thing, especially in this climate, is to keep your fluid intake up, preferably with the addition of some dissolved salts and sugars – doctors recommend eight level teaspoons of sugar, and a teaspoon of salt, to one litre of water. If you are really unlikely to be able to reach help within a few days, then come equipped with a good health manual and the selection of antibiotics which it recommends. *Traveller's Health* by Dr. Richard Dawood (see end of this section) is excellent for this purpose – though rather detailed for the normal visitor.

Malaria
You can still catch malaria even if you are taking anti-malarial drugs. Classic symptoms include headache, chills and sweating, abdominal pains, aching joints and fever – some or all of which may come in waves, often starting in the evening. It varies tremendously, but often starts like a bad case of flu. If anything like this happens, your first response should be to suspect malaria – and seek medical help immediately.

If (and only if) this is not possible, then treat yourself by taking two quinine tablets (600mg) eight hourly for up to seven days, until the fever abates. Quinine is a strong drug and its side-effects are disorientating (nausea, buzzing in the ears) and unpleasant – so administering this on your own is not advisable. After the quinine, and if you still have a fever, take a single dose of three Fansidar tablets. Alternatively, for areas where the malaria parasite is still chloroquine-sensitive, instead of the quinine treatment, you can take four ordinary chloroquine tablets (600mg) at once, then two tablets six hours later, then two tablets twice daily for two days.

These drugs are very powerful and taking them in high doses, without medical supervision, is dangerous – at the very least you'll find their side-effects highly unpleasant. Do get to a doctor as quickly as possible. Another complication of treating yourself is that once started, it is much more difficult for a doctor to make a correct diagnosis.

Finally, don't worry about those people on other courses of prophylaxis, there are many possible options – but do stick rigidly to whatever is yours. The vast majority of malaria cases occur because people were not keeping to their regular tablet-taking regime.

AIDS

AIDS is spread in exactly the same way in Africa as it is at home – through body secretions, blood and blood products. This means that it can be spread through close physical contact, such as sexual intercourse, through blood transfusions using infected blood, or through unsterilised needles which have been used on an infected person.

In Namibia or Botswana, there is no special AIDS risk from medical treatment or blood products – all blood is screened for the AIDS virus. Your biggest chance of getting AIDS is through unprotected sexual intercourse. The greater the number of sexual partners, the greater the risk – prostitutes are a particularly high risk group. Practice 'safe sex' – abstain or avoid multiple partners, and always use a condom.

Hepatitis

This is group of viral diseases which generally start with coca-cola coloured urine and light coloured stools, before progressing to fevers, weakness, jaundice (yellow skin and eyeballs) and abdominal pains caused by a severe inflammation of the liver. There are several forms, of which the two most common are typical of the rest: type A (formerly infectious hepatitis) and B (formerly viral hepatitis).

Type A is spread by the faecal-oral route, that is by ingesting food or drink contaminated by excrement or urine. It is avoided as you would avoid any stomach problems, by careful preparation of food and by only drinking clean water. In contrast, the more serious but rarer **type B** is spread in the same way as AIDS (blood or body secretions), and is avoided the same way that one avoids AIDS.

There are no cures for hepatitis, but with lots of bed rest and a good low-fat, no-alcohol diet most people recover within six months. If you are unlucky enough to contract any form of hepatitis, consider using your travel insurance to fly straight home!

Rabies

Rabies is normally contracted when the skin is broken and the wound infected by the rabies virus, which is present in the saliva of infected animals. The disease is almost invariably fatal when fully developed, but fortunately there are now very good post-exposure vaccines which can prevent this. It is possible (if expensive) to be immunised against the disease, but not really worthwhile unless you are working with animals – and even then it's standard practice to treat all cases of possible exposure.

Rabies is rarely a problem for visitors, but the small risks are further minimised by steering well clear of dogs in the cities and small carnivores in the bush. If you are bitten or scratched then clean and disinfect the wound thoroughly and seek medical advice immediately. The early stages of the disease are characterised by itching around the bite, followed by headaches, fevers, spasms, personality changes and hydrophobia (fear of water). Thus animals acting strangely – be they strange dogs in the cities, or unusually friendly jackals in the bush, should be given an especially wide berth.

Bilharzia or Schistosomiasis

Bilharzia is an insidious disease, contracted by coming into contact with infected water, caused by an infestation of parasitic worms which damage the bladder or intestine. Often the parasites are present in the local population who have built up an immunity over time, but the visitor who becomes infected may develop a severe fever some weeks afterwards. A common indication of an infection is a localised itchy rash – where the parasites have burrowed through the skin. Bilharzia is readily treated by medication, and only serious if undetected (the symptoms may be confused with malaria) and untreated.

The life-cycle of the parasites starts when they are urinated into a body of water. Here they infect certain species of water-snails, grow and multiply and finally become free-swimming. At this stage they leave the snails to look for a human, or primate, host. After burrowing through the skin of someone coming into contact with the water, they migrate to the person's bladder or intestine where they remain – producing a large number of eggs which are passed every day in the urine, so continuing the cycle.

To only way to completely avoid risk of Bilharzia infection is to stay well clear of any bodies of freshwater – not even allowing splashes on your skin. Obviously this is very restrictive and could stop you enjoying your trip. More pragmatic advice is to avoid slow-moving or sluggish water, and ask local opinion on the Bilharzia risk – not all water is infected. Generally fast-flowing rivers are free from infection (a bad environment for the snails), as is the Okavango (away from settlements), while dams and standing water are usually heavily infected. If you think you may have been infected, get a test done on your return.

Sleeping Sickness or Trypanosomiasis

This is really a disease of cattle, which may be caught by people on rare occasions. It is spread exclusively by bites from the *tsetse fly*, which is about the size of a house fly, but has pointed mouthparts (designed for sucking blood). They are easily spotted as they bite during the day and have distinctive wings which cross into a scissor shape when resting. Prevention is much easier than cure, so avoid being bitten if you can by covering up and listening for the tell-tale buzz around you. Chemical repellents may be helpful also, but they are far from perfect.

Tsetse bites are quite nasty, so expect them to swell up a little and turn red – that is a normal allergic reaction to any bite. The vast majority of tsetse bites will do no more than this. If, however, a boil-like swelling develops after five or more days in the place you were bitten, and a fever two or three weeks later, then you should seek treatment from a good doctor immediately to avert permanent damage to your central nervous system.

Some Africans view the fly positively – referring to it as 'the guardian of wild Africa' – as fear of the disease's effect on cattle has prevented farming, and hence settlement, from encroaching on many areas of wild bush country. Given Botswana's and Namibia's dependence on cattle for export earnings, the tsetse fly and its eradication are emotive issues. In recent years the tsetse fly has been the subject of relentless spaying programmes over much of the sub-continent, removing the last natural barriers to cattle farming. This is currently happening in the Okavango Delta – the main concentration of tsetse fly in the region – which some believe heralds the end of the Okavango as a cattle-free wildlife sanctuary.

WHEN YOU RETURN HOME

Many tropical diseases have a long incubation period, and it is possible to develop symptoms weeks after returning home from abroad. (This is why, for example, it is important to keep taking the anti-malarial pills for six weeks following your return.) If you do get ill after you return home, make sure you tell your doctor where you have been – and alert him/her to any diseases that you have been exposed to. If problems persist, get yourself a check-up at one of the hospitals for tropical diseases. Several people die from malaria each year in the UK as their doctors are just not used to the symptoms. Note that to visit a hospital for tropical diseases in the UK you need a letter of referral from your doctor.

For further advice or help contact the London Hospital for Tropical Diseases, 4 St Pancras Way, London, NW1. Tel: 071-387 441. The staff here are excellent and are frequently world authorities when it comes to research, treatment and advice on tropical diseases – despite the run down and under-funded appearance of the premises and administration.

Useful Books

Traveller's Health by Dr Richard Dawood.
OUP, £6.95. This has become virtually the standard reference for travellers, including just about everything you might possibly catch – depressing (but gripping) reading!

Health Manual – A Self Help Guide by Dr Veronica Moss.
Lion Publishing, £4.95. The emphasis of this book is on basic, practical advice – which is easy to find in a hurry. The book starts rather helpfully with a section 'Where Does it Hurt?'

THEFT

Theft is really not a problem here unless you are careless. Namibia and Botswana are both very safe and the worst that the traveller is likely to encounter is a pickpocket in one of the major cities. Violent robbery is virtually unknown and most thefts occur because travellers become so lax about their property that they leave it lying around.

How to Avoid it

Be sensible. Keep your passport, credit cards and most of your cash in a money belt, neck pouch or secret pocket – and don't flash this around in public more than necessary. For general use, keep a day's supply of cash handy in a more accessible place. If you are driving, remember to lock the car whenever you leave it, and if you are hitching don't forget to get out of the lift with all your belongings.

Reporting to the Police

The police in both countries are at least as reliable and honest as those at home and will often go out of their way to help a foreigner. They are also surprisingly efficient; I know of one traveller who had his wallet stolen, only to have it returned to him in England by the police by post three months later, completely intact except for the cash. If you need a copy of a crime report for insurance purposes then do explain this carefully to the officer when you begin to report the crime, and try not to be too impatient.

SAFETY

Arrest

To get arrested in Namibia or Botswana you need to try quite hard. Taking photographs of 'sensitive areas' (bridges, government buildings, etc) may be one way, smuggling drugs another, and evading park fees is also a possibility. Perhaps the best way is to argue with a policeman or a soldier – and get angry into the bargain – this will almost certainly get you arrested!

If you are careless enough to be arrested, you will often only be asked a few questions. If the police are suspicious of you, then how you handle the situation will determine whether you are kept for a matter of hours or of days. Be patient, helpful, good-humoured, and as truthful as possible. *Never lose your temper* – it will only aggravate the situation – and avoid any hint of arrogance. If things are going badly after half a day or so, then start firmly to insist on seeing someone in higher authority – and as a last resort you do (in theory) have the right to contact your embassy or consulate, though the finer points of your civil liberties may end up being overlooked by an irate local police chief!

Bribery

Neither of the authors has ever encountered a situation in the region when bribery was demanded or even expected. Offering a bribe to a policeman may, however, be another excellent way to get yourself immediately arrested!

Chapter 6

Driving and camping in the bush

DRIVING

Vehicle Equipment and Preparations

Driving in the bush can present many problems to the uninitiated, but once mastered becomes both safe and great fun. You should prepare yourself well before you start to drive – if you are picking up a hired car then check that there's an accessible spare wheel (or two if you are driving on rough ground), a working foot pump and jack, and suitable basic tools (including a spanner and screwdriver set). Don't forget to bring spare oil and brake and clutch fluid. If you are going into rough 4WD country, then you should also take a more extensive tool kit, spare parts and a maintenance manual for the model of vehicle (plus sufficient personal knowledge and experience to be able to use it!).

Good fuel and water containers are a necessity – how large depends upon the type of environment through which you want to travel. As a general guide, two 20-litre water containers, and about 1,000 km worth of spare fuel in jerry cans, is about right for four people going into the wilds. You can easily and cheaply pick up large plastic containers to carry the water, but never carry fuel in these, however strong they seem. Plastic stretches, expands and can crack in the heat – and the tops are rarely strong enough, allowing lethal fuel vapour to escape.

Other useful items are: a spade to dig yourself out of sand; a large polythene sheet to lie on when doing vehicle repairs; a tow rope; and a light for working on the vehicle at night – those which can be connected to the vehicle battery are probably the most useful.

4WD Driving

It is beyond the scope of this section to explain the ins-and-outs of using a four-wheel drive (4WD vehicle). Whilst there is nothing particularly difficult about using a 4WD – even though using one well takes years of experience – you should make a concerted effort to familiarise yourself fully with the operation and limitations of your chosen vehicle. There are, in reality, several different basic varieties of 4WDs which differ markedly in their performance, and the use of their transmission and gear box. In particular, check whether your vehicle has switchable fixed/free-wheeling hubs and how they work – not understanding how these are used can cause many problems and seriously damage the transmission. If by now you are feeling apprehensive (and you can't understand the instruction manual), get hold of a copy of one of the many good books on the subject.

General Driving Advice

Road types   Gravel roads can be very deceiving – although relatively smooth, flat and fast, they still do not give you much traction, and you will frequently skid. With practice (at slower speeds!) you will learn how to deal with skids and treat them as normal. However, there will always be the unexpected – an animal wanders into the road, or there's suddenly a massive pothole ahead – so it's very unwise to ever drive over 100kph on these roads. In general it's safer to stick to 80kph. Dust roads should be treated with particular caution after rains – the surface can quickly become muddy and as slippery as ice.

Slowing down   Slow down if in any doubt about what lies ahead – road surfaces can vary enormously. Concentrate on looking out for potholes, ruts or patches of soft sand which can put you into an unexpected slide. When passing other vehicles travelling in the opposite direction, always slow down to minimise both the chances of chippings damaging the windscreen, and the danger from a lack of visibility as you enter the other vehicle's dustcloud. Using your headlights or horn can help alert other vehicles of your presence.

Animals and driving at night   Wild and domestic animals frequently hang around on the side of the road, and may suddenly take fright and dash into the centre – beware. A high-speed collision with even a small animal (such as a goat), will not only kill it, but will also cause surprisingly severe damage to your vehicle, and possibly fatal consequences for you and your passengers. Driving at night is particularly dangerous in this regard and in general should be avoided.

Using your gears   It's generally better to slow your vehicle down using a combination of gears and brakes on non-tarred roads than to use the brakes alone. You are much less likely to skid. Equally, use gears and not your brakes to slow down for a corner. A consequence of using low-ratio gears (ie first or second) more than usual is increased fuel consumption. Take this into account when planning fuel requirements. Air-conditioning units also use a significant amount of fuel – turn them off if you feel you are running short.

Driving in sand   Lowering your tyre pressures until there is a distinct bulge in the tyre walls – having first made sure that your hand pump is working –

greatly helps traction but increases wear. Pump them up before you drive again on hard surfaces (particularly tar), or they will be badly damaged. Don't fight the steering-wheel if there are clear, deep-rutted tracks – relax and let your vehicle largely steer itself. Driving in the cool of the morning is easier than later in the day – when cool, the sand is more compact and firmer. (When hot, the pockets of air between the sand grains expand and loosen the sand up.)

If you do get stuck, despite these precautions, don't panic. Dig a shallow ramp out in front of all the wheels – reinforcing it with pieces of wood or branches to give the wheels better traction. Lighten the vehicle load (passengers out) and push, keeping the engine revs high as you slowly engage your lowest ratio gear – using your clutch to ensure that the wheels don't spin wildly and dig themselves further into the sand.

Rocky terrain Have your tyre pressures higher than normal and move very slowly. If necessary have any passengers guide you along the track to avoid scraping the undercarriage on the ground.

Crossing rivers The first thing to do is to *stop* and check the river. Wade through the water, and assess the depth, substrate and current flow, to determine the best route to drive along. Before you cross, select your lowest ratio gear, and then progress through the water at a slow but steady rate. It's not worth taking risks – a flooded river will often subside to much safer levels by the next morning.

Grass seeds In grasslands (especially Makgadikgadi, Bushmanland and the approaches to Tsodilo Hills) keep a close watch on the water temperature gauge. Grass stems and seeds get caught up in the radiator grill and block the flow of air, causing overheating and the danger of the grass catching fire. You should stop and remove the grass seeds every few kilometres or so, depending on the conditions. If the engine has overheated, the only option is to stop and turn the engine off – don't open the radiator cap to refill until the radiator is no longer hot to touch.

BUSH CAMPING

The opportunity to be able spontaneously to camp where and when you like in the wilds of Botswana or Namibia, is one of these countries' greatest appeals for the visitor. For most travellers with a vehicle, bush camping is the norm rather than the exception, and when preparing for your trip you should take this into account from the point of view of both budget and equipment. When camping, it takes a little time to develop a system that best suits you – and to work out what you wish you had and what you could do without – but you will soon adapt to the lifestyle and slip into the routine. Don't forget that bush camping in Namibia and Botswana is an entirely different proposition from the cold and wet experience of 'northern climes'.

Where you can camp

Botswana   The vast majority of the land in Botswana is not privately owned, and you are more or less free to camp anywhere. If you are near to a village or settlement, then it is polite to ask the chief's permission – perhaps asking him to suggest a suitable spot. Remember that even if the land looks wild, it is likely to be used by someone, and invariably you'll have inquisitive visitors to share your fire with. Some large tracts of land, particularly in the Eastern Corridor, are privately owned – mostly by white farmers in the Tuli Block – and you are not free to camp in these areas without express permission.

Namibia   In Namibia, the situation is a bit different. Land was divided up in the early colonial days between white farmers (who took half the land), and nine different 'homelands' for the different ethnic groups (who had 40%, with the remainder taken by national parks and mining areas). This apportionment effectively exists today. As in Botswana, in white farming areas you are not free to camp anywhere, whilst in the ex-'homelands' you can generally camp anywhere you like, but should ask permission from the local chief first.

National Parks   The national parks of both countries have their own specific rules for camping, and almost all have designated campsites.

Choosing a campsite

Never camp on what looks like a path through the bush, however indistinct. It is may be a well-used game trail.

Beware of camping in dry river beds – flash floods are very dangerous and can arrive with little or no warning.

Camp a respectable distance away from any isolated source of water – or you may block animals from their only source of water, causing both you and them disturbance. This is not applicable to the Okavango area, where there is of course plenty of water everywhere.

In a marshy or damp area (eg the Okavango), camp on higher ground to avoid cold mists at night. In a dry desert area, it is warmer to camp on lower ground, in the less-exposed sites.

Camp-fires

Camp-fires can add a great atmosphere to a campsite and can warm you on a chilly desert night, but they can also be very damaging to the environment and leave unsightly piles of ash and blackened stones. Dead wood for burning is very limited in desert areas – where vegetation grows very slowly – and by burning dead vegetation you are removing it from the local ecosystem, further depleting the area. On the same note, use only dead wood – never use any living vegetation. Don't be tempted to make huge destructive fires – these are, anyhow, impractical for cooking.

Beware of bush fires. Restrict your fire to a small circle, ringed with stones, that you can control. Always have water handy and never leave the fire unattended.

A fire at night can help keep smaller raiding animals away from the campsite, but is certainly not a foolproof guard against most big game. Animals that are used to being around campsites (eg hyenas at Savuti and lions in parts of Moremi) will often disregard unattended fires to an alarming degree. There is little point in trying to keep a raging fire going all night.

Keep one or two bundles of firewood in the back of your vehicle for camping where wood is scarce or non-existent.

Using a tent (or not)

To use a tent or to sleep in the open is a personal choice, dependent upon where you are. In Chobe or Moremi, or at any well-used campsite in a game area, you should *always* sleep completely inside a tent – a protruding leg can look like a tasty snack to a hungry hyena or curious lion. Away from such well-used sites, the same type of animals are not a problem although it is better to err on the side of caution. Most big animals will avoid an unfamiliar campsite.

Outside obvious game areas you will be fine either in just a sleeping bag or preferably under a mosquito net – with the deep, blue-black skies of Africa overhead. Sleeping beneath a tree will help reduce morning dew on your sleeping bag.

If your vehicle has a large flat roof, sleeping on this will provide you with good protection from animals. You will probably see 4WDs with purpose-built tents on their roof-racks.

Animal dangers for campers

Scorpions can be a problem as you set up and clear a camp – they are often found underneath rocks or branches. Always move rocks with caution, and avoid collecting wood in the dark. Shake out your shoes in the morning before you put them on.

Although snakes will invariably attempt to escape from human 'intruders', they may be caught by surprise and pose a threat if you set up camp in areas of long grass (eg Okavango islands). Be noisy, and give them a chance to move away. When sleeping in the open, it is not unknown for snakes to lie next to you for the warmth. Don't panic, and you won't be bitten – just gently move away without any sudden movements. This is one argument for at least using a mosquito net at night!

In a game area carefully store away – either in your tent, or preferably in your vehicle – anything that can be carried off by an animal. Be particularly careful about putting food away – especially citrus fruits, a delicacy that elephants will do anything for! Needless to say, food is better in your vehicle than your tent.

MINIMUM IMPACT

When you visit, drive through, or camp in an area with *minimum impact*, that area is left in the same condition – or better – than when you entered it. Whilst most visitors would view minimum impact as being clearly desirable, it's worth considering the number of ways that we contribute to environmental degradation, and how these can be avoided.

Driving

Use you vehicle responsibly. Don't go off the road or track if the environment will clearly suffer, or better don't go off the tracks at all. In desert areas, the tracks left by one vehicle can remain scarring the landscape for decades. Desert plants – especially the dry-looking lichens on gravel plains – are easy to kill, and very slow to regrow. Don't disregard the country's regulations – there are usually good reasons for permits being required to enter certain areas.

Hygiene

Human excrement should be well buried away from paths or rivers, and the tissue burnt before it is covered up. This is especially important in desert areas where the tissue won't rot, but may be unearthed only to blow about in the wind.

If you use a river to wash, then soap yourself on the bank (do bring bio-degradable soap) and take a pan for scooping water – make sure that no soap finds its way back into the water. Sand makes an excellent pan scrub, even if you have no water to spare.

Rubbish

Bring along some plastic bags with which to remove all your rubbish and dump it at the next town. Even 'biodegradable' rubbish will look very unsightly and spoil the place for those who come after you.

Burying rubbish – particularly containers and cans – is *not* a solution. Animals will always find these and dig them up.

Empty tin cans can be 'cleaned' and made easier to carry away, if you burn them in your fire overnight, then squash them flat.

Host communities

Whilst the rules for reducing impact on the environment have been understood and followed by responsible travellers for many years, the effects of tourism on local people have only recently been considered. Many tourists consider it their right, for example, to take intrusive photos of people, and are angry if the person does not co-operate. They refer to higher prices being charged to tourists as "a rip-off" without considering the hand-to-mouth existence of those selling their products or services. They deplore child beggars, then hand out sweets or pens to kids that crowd around their vehicle.

Our behaviour towards "the locals" needs to be looked at in terms of their culture, with the knowledge that we are the uninvited visitors. Read Phil Deutschle's *Cultural Do's and Don'ts* and aim to leave the local people unchanged by your visit - this is the best present you can give them.

ANIMAL ENCOUNTERS

Whether you are on an organised foot-safari, on your own hike, or just walking from the car to your tent in the bush, it is not unlikely that you will come across some of Africa's larger animals at close quarters. Invariably, the actual danger of the situation is much less than imagined, and a few basic guidelines will enable you to know how to deal with these situations and even enjoy them!

Animals are not normally interested in people – you are not their normal food, or their predator, and so provided you take precautions not to annoy or threaten them, you will be largely left alone. Remember that it is their environment not yours – they are designed for it and their senses are far better attuned to it. To be on less unequal terms, always stay alert in the bush and try to spot animals from a distance. This gives you the option of approaching carefully, or staying well clear.

Bush walking

It's assumed here that you are walking with the intention of maximising your chances of seeing animals, whilst still remaining cautious to potential danger.

Do not walk at all if the vegetation is too thick, you should have a bare minimum of 20m visibility all around you.

Don't walk in large groups – four is a good number, certainly not above eight.

Single file and no chatting may seem strict, but it makes sense. Stay as quiet as you can and stop if you want to whisper something.

Wear dark colours, not light ones, earth tones are best.

Do take your time: rush and you will miss the points of interest and walk unknowingly into problems.

Make the most of the small things that you observe; insect life can be at least as interesting as the big cats at times.

Use your ears and nose as well as your eyes – any strange smells or noises should attract your attention immediately.

If there is a wind, consider your scent. Walking into the wind will help to hide this and thus give animals less warning of you – but you are then in danger of frightening them with a surprise discovery.

Beware: No wild animals are completely safe – even a gemsbok's graceful horns can kill – so keep your distance.

Lion Tracks
by Phil Deutschle

All night long we heard the deep-throated *wouu wouu* of distant lions. At first light, my Wei companion, Obi, and I left the safety of our small island. Obi poled the *mokoro* through the reeds of the Okavango Delta and in a half hour we arrived near to where the lions must be. I jumped barefoot into the water and pulled the *mokoro* half-way onto the bank. A quick search revealed the spoor of lion, but we could have easily found the spot by smell alone. The carcass of a Cape buffalo lay under an acacia tree. The tracks showed that the lions had wandered off into a region of tall grass, where it would be foolish to follow them.

Eight days previously we had begun our trip with no more goal than to see what there was to see. For me it had become an intensive course in the art of tracking and stalking African game. Slowly, I was learning to identify the different species from their prints and droppings and, by observing Obi, I was also discovering how to read the age of the track by the sharpness of the imprint, the occurrence of game across the track, or by faint differences in the colour of the soil.

Together, Obi and I had crawled beneath miles of thorn bushes, waded through waist-deep stretches of water, and sheltered behind innumerable termite mounds, always staying downwind, trying to get ever closer to a reedbuck or a jackal. Each type of beast reacted in a different way when they spotted us. Impala and zebra would passively continue to graze, while giraffe would flee at first sight. Warthog would stay concealed in the grass and bolt away when you were nearly on top of them. Cape buffalo also ran at the last moment, but they were more likely to run over *you* than to run away. We shunned buffalo.

Next morning we left the *mokoro* on the bank of yet another island, and found lion tracks that were several days old. Following a game trail through heavy bush, we emerged at the edge of a large lagoon and cautiously skirted it looking for more tracks. After 300 yards we both stopped. Before us were gigantic prints. 'Now, now' whispered Obi, as he examined the spoor. 'Now, now.' Even I could see how fresh the prints were. The lion had planted its feet in the shoreline to drink, and the water was still seeping into the pug marks. Obi had explained what to do when facing a lion. We were to 'stand quiet and look...the lion looks to us and then goes'. This sounded fine, but what if the lion didn't want to just go away?! The lions of the Okavango can and do break down the doors of huts to drag out the screaming victim inside. Our only protection was Obi's axe, my German knife, and mankind's warped sense of dominance.

The tracks led us back into the bush eventually Obi gave up. The tracks were everywhere. We didn't know where the lion was, and we were becoming apprehensive, figuring that the lion knew exactly where *we* were. I had the feeling that the lion was now behind us, along the way that we had first come, so I took the lead. We cut back thought the tangle of low trees and scrub. We couldn't see more than ten yards ahead of us, and I kept gripping the knife in my pocket, wishing it was something more formidable, like a spear.

Suddenly, we came to the original game trail that we had followed into the bush. There were our tracks, made only minutes before, and there *on top of our tracks* were the lion's huge prints. The lion was now stalking *us*! Obi and I looked at each other, and then without discussion, we quickly and silently left the area. We didn't see our lion, but we would at least still be around to try again another day.

Unexpected or unwelcome face to face encounters

Don't panic! The animal is probably as frightened as you are and also as anxious to remove itself from danger – but some animals will attack if they feel overly threatened. In most cases, back off very slowly – facing the animal – and take care not to trip or make sudden (threatening) movements. Don't just turn around and run.

There are a few exceptions to this basic rule, which require you to have a greater understanding of the animal facing you:

Buffalo   To hikers this is probably the continent's most dangerous animal. Short-sighted, but with an excellent sense of smell, they can charge without provocation if they fear that something is sneaking up on them. Avoid a charge by quickly climbing the nearest tree, or by sidestepping at the last minute. If adopting the latter technique, stand very still until the last possible moment as the buffalo may well miss you anyhow!

Black Rhino   Like buffalo, these are short-sighted, fairly stupid, and frequently bad-tempered. Similar tactics of tree-climbing or dodging are employed.

Elephant   A major problem only if you disturb a mother and calf, so keep well away from these. Lone bulls can usually be approached quite closely, and will mock-charge (ears flapping, head up, noisy) as a warning before they do it for real (ears down, head down, full speed ahead!). Testing this out is not for the faint-hearted – so steer well clear.

Lion   A major problem as they are so well camouflaged that you can be next to one before you know it. If you had been listening you would probably have heard a warning growl already! Back off slowly, showing as little terror as you can – but if a lion starts to show too much interest in you then, as a last line of defence, make loud, deep confident noises – shout at it!

Hyena   Not so much a problem when walking, though often met at popular campsites at night, where they make raids for anything they can pick up. Show aggression and confidence and you should have no problems.

Hippo   Surprisingly account for many deaths in Africa, with a bite that can split a boat in half. Treat with respect in and out of the water. Don't go swimming if there are hippos about! If you are in a boat, never cut off a hippo in shallow water from its escape route to deeper water or it will panic. If necessary, stop paddling and tap loudly several times on the boat to warn the hippos of your presence – they will then all head for the safety of the deeper water, leaving a shallower route by the bank for you to use. Likewise on land, never get between a hippo and the water.

Crocodiles   Dangerous only in the larger rivers and the Okavango. Check for tell-tale signs of eyes and nostrils just above the water before going for a swim or even washing on the bank. Ask local people which areas are safe — crocodiles are territorial, and generally only hang around one or two deep pools of water in a given stretch of water. Bathe with someone keeping a look out.

Snakes   These really are not the great danger that people imagine. Most will flee when they feel the vibrations of your footfalls, though a few — like the puff adder — will stay still, puffing themselves up as a warning, and for this reason you should always watch where you place your feet. Similarly, there are a couple of arboreal (tree) species which may be taken by surprise if you carelessly grab at vegetation as you walk, requiring you to watch where you place your hands.

Eat a Worm

by Phil Deutschle

Anyone who travels will encounter dubious-looking dishes. Be it duck embryos, blood sausage, or fish eggs, one is caught in a dilemma between the desire to be part-of-the-gang and the fear of being sick in public.

I find it best not to know what I am eating until I am finished — in Botswana this is made easier when eating in a dark and smoky kitchen. Unable to see the food, I just grope into it with my fingers and chew. I try to keep in mind that if everyone else is eating it, it must be OK. That's the essential truth — the food is O.K. It's just our individual biases that are sometimes out of line.

Worms, or to be accurate, the larvae of various insects, are eaten all over Africa. In Botswana they are just common fare, eaten like french fries. The local "worm" is the caterpillar of a large moth, the *gonimbrasia belina*. The caterpillar grows to the size of a finger, and lives solely on the mopane tree, thus its common name, the mopane worm. They are collected in the summer and can be dried for long-term storage. Some educated Batswana, trying to emulate Western Whites, scorn mopane worms, though the majority happily munch mopanes while sipping traditional beer.

After coming to Botswana, and slowly sliding into local society, I began wondering how, or if, I could convince myself to take the plunge and bite into a worm. One day some children presented me with a live mopane that they'd picked up by the side of the path. It was glossy black with iridescent markings of blue and green. Taking it home to be photographed, I soon got culinary ideas. I dropped the beast into boiling water, which caused it to swell to ever larger proportions. After a few minutes came the frying in hot oil laced with a pinch of salt. By then it had lost its colour and no longer resembled a worm, but reminded me of a grilled Vienna sausage. My ministrations with pot and pan had added to the impression that this was now something to *eat*. It felt only natural to bite into it. The taste was like crispy scrambled eggs.

Part 2
Namibia

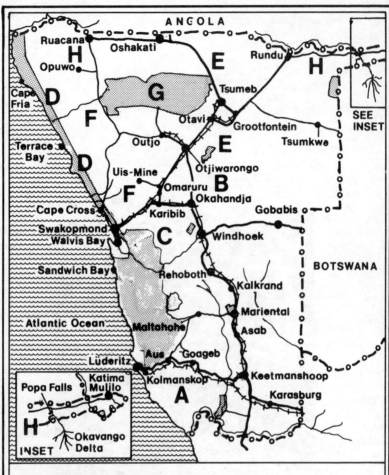

Namibia Regions

A **Southern Nambia** - Chapter 9
B **Central Namibia** - Chapter 10
C **The Central Namib** - Chapter 11
D **The Skeleton Coast** - Chapter 12
E **North Central Namibia** - Chapter 13
F **The Kaokoveld** - Chapter 14
G **Etosha** - Chapter 15
H **The Northern Strip** - Chapter 16

National Parks

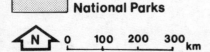

N   0   100   200   300 km

Chapter 7

In Namibia

TOURISM IN NAMIBIA

Until recently most of Namibia's tourists were from South Africa. They came, usually in their own vehicles, for the sea fishing and the game parks — both of which have well organised facilities. Now, following independence, there are a greater number of visitors from overseas, though the infrastructure and facilities developed for the South Africans remains. Namibia's attractions are generally well signposted and the national parks and reserves have a centralised booking system — based at the Department of Nature and Conservation (DNC) in Windhoek — which can be a great help if you make the effort to use it.

Tourism in Namibia remains on a small scale, although since independence numbers have been growing slowly. You will still find campsites where you are the only people for miles around, while many of the fascinating areas outside the official reserves are hardly visited at all.

COST OF LIVING/TRAVELLING

I am often asked if Namibia is expensive — the answer depends very much on where you come from, where you go, and how you wish to travel. If you are coming from Central or East Africa, then food and accommodation in Namibia will seem very costly — there is no network of cheap hotels for travellers here. If you arrive direct from Europe, the same things will probably strike you as cheap, with reasonable hotels at half the cost or less of those on the Continent.

Few, if any, of Namibia's attractions are intrinsically expensive — the vast majority being within national parks which charge very reasonable fees. Only the DNC's Terrace Bay and the northern section of the Skeleton Coast (private fly-in safaris only) are really expensive places to go, but their prices reflect their isolation and the cost of getting there.

Obviously the style in which you travel will affect your costs greatly. Probably the best way is with your own 4WD vehicle and camping equipment. This is not the cheapest form of travel but it does allow you to camp in most places and cook your own meals — reducing your costs to only food, camping and park fees and the cost of the car. Four people in a vehicle would be ideal — then food, camping and park fees could average about N$50 (£9/$14) per person per day — with vehicle costs from N$35 (£7/$10) each per day, depending upon what you rent, and where you rent it from. (See *Planning and Preparations*, Chapter 4, for more detailed information.)

Currency

In September 1993 the Namibian currency was changed from the South African Namibian Dollars (R) to the Namibian Dollar (N$), which is divided into 100 cents. This is freely convertible for the visitor so there's no black market and no customs regulations applicable to moving it across borders.

To maintain confidence in the new currency, it will remain tied to the Rand (ie N$1 = R1) for the near future. Note that overseas banks will sometimes only know of an exchange rate for the Rand, and find it difficult to quote a rate for the Namibian Dollar.

If the Rand does suddenly lose value, perhaps as the result of negative developments in the South African peace process, then Windhoek will probably take full control of the currency. The value of the Namibian Dollar would then float free, independent of the Rand. Check the latest situation with one of the bigger banks before you leave.

The last few years have seen the Rand become progressively weaker against sterling and the US dollar. Thus travel in Namibia for the western visitor has become even better value. In March 1994 the **exchange rates** are £1 = N$5.30 = R5.30 and US$1 = N$3.53 = R3.53.

Banks

Changing money at any of the commercial banks is usually easy and often, but not always, quick. Standard banking hours are 0830 to 1530 weekdays and sometimes 0830 to 1100 Saturdays, depending upon the place. These will cash travellers cheques or give cash advances on credit cards. Elsewhere Visa, Mastercard and American Express cards are often accepted, but travellers cheques which are not in Namibian Dollars or Namibian Dollars can be difficult to use. In the remoter areas cash is essential, and wherever you are, petrol stations always require cash. Note that at the end of the month, when many government employees are paid, the queue at the bank can be several hours long.

TRANSPORT

Air

International flights There are regular flights from J G Strijdom Airport to Maun (single N$510) with connections to Victoria Falls; Lusaka (single

N$903); Johannesburg (single N$640) and Cape Town (single N$679). While not a major centre for international flights, Namibia now has direct links with Germany and the UK, as well as Lusaka, Harare, Cape Town and Johannesburg. The airlines to watch for the latest developments are British Airways, South African Airways (SAA), Lufthansa, Air France and of course Air Namibia.

Internal flights   Because of its size, Namibia has a good network of internal flights which link the outlying towns to the hub of Eros Airport, 3km from Windhoek's town centre. Typical prices for one-way flights are: Swakopmund (N$257); Tsumeb (N$357); Rundu (N$485); M'pacha for Katima Mulilo (N$748); Keetmanshoop (N$351); and Lüderitz (N$618).

The main carriers are Air Namibia and SAA, but there are several smaller companies and hundreds of other bush airstrips. Many of the more remote safari camps and guest farms will transfer guests using their own air transport.

For the more adventurous, there's a 'Hire and Fly' in Windhoek if you've a private pilot's licence — and the skies are marvellously open and free of hassles.

Rail

There is a good rail network connecting the main towns with South Africa. The trains are pleasant and rarely full, but they do, however, tend to be very slow and stop frequently; travelling by train is not for those in a hurry and most travellers prefer hitchhiking to taking the train.

The carriages are divided into 1st, 2nd and 3rd classes, of which 1st and 2nd have sleeping bunks while 3rd simply has benches. The only advantage of 1st class is that there are only four persons per compartment, rather than six in 2nd class. There is no food or drink available in any class except on the trains between Windhoek and South Africa (when sweets and drinks are available — a very basic service).

1st and 2nd class must be reserved in advance through the Windhoek booking office Tel: 2982032), though any station will telegraph for you.

	Windhoek-Tsumeb	
	Fri/Sun (arrives Sat/Mon)	
Windhoek	2100	
Okahandja	2228	
Karibib	0200	
Omaruru	0435	
Otjiwarongo	0803a	
	1030d	1050d
Otavi	1225	1315
Grootfontein	—	1615
Tsumeb	1445	—

Tsumeb-Windhoek
Sun/Fri

Tsumeb	1130	—
Grootfontein	—	1050
Otavi	1305	1315
Otjiwarongo	1545a	1615a
		1830d
Omaruru		2135
Karibib		0045
Okahandja		0332
Windhoek		0522

	Windhoek-Walvis Bay	Walvis Bay-Windhoek
	Tues/Fri/Sun	*Tues/Fri/Sun*
Windhoek	2000	0637
Okahandja	2128	0453
Karibib	0040	0205
Usakos	0155	0040
Swakopmund	0516	1957
Walvis Bay	0705	1835

	Keetmanshoop-Lüderitz		Lüderitz-Keet.	
	Fri	*Sun*	*Sat*	*Sun*
Keetmanshoop	1800	1400	1030	2330
Goageb	1910	1510	0910	2210
Aus	2100	1700	0715	2015
Lüderitz	2230	1830	0600	1900

	Otjiwarongo-Outjo			Outjo-Otjiwarongo		
	Mon	*Wed*	*Fri*	*Mon*	*Wed*	*Fri*
Otjiwarongo	0830	1630	1700	0830	1400	1400
Outjo	0930	1730	1800	0730	1300	1300

Windhoek-De Aar (South Africa)

	Wed	*Fri/Sun*
Windhoek	1100	2030
Rehoboth	1320	2250
Kalkrand	1510	0032
Mariental	1658	0240
Keetmanshoop	2220a	0700
	2300d	
Grünau	0300	
Karasburg	0359	
Upington (RSA)	0120a	
	0952d	
De Aar (RSA)	2033	

	De Aar (South Africa)-Windhoek	
	Fri	*Sun*
De Aar (RSA)	0055	
Upington (RSA)	0930a	
	1000d	
Karasburg	1645	
Grünau	1820	
Keetmanshoop	2210a	
	2300d	2000d
Mariental	0325	0010
Kalkrand	0545	0215
Rehoboth	0740	0410
Windhoek	1000	1630

Notes

1. De Aar, in South Africa, is the terminus for Namibian trains. From here you can get a South African Railways connection to or from Cape Town or Johannesburg.
2. Where appropriate, arrival times are indicated with **a** and departure times with **d**.
3. These timetables are not comprehensive, the trains stop at far more places than are named here.

Sample fares in Namibian Dollars (prices are worked out on a per kilometre basis, and can be easily calculated)

	1st	2nd	3rd
From Windhoek to			
Keetmanshoop	105	77	43
Grootfontein	139	102	56
Swakopmund	81	59	33
Cape Town	463	326	191
Johannesburg	448	317	184
From Keetmanshoop to			
Lüderitz	N/A	N/A	32

Bus

Namibia is one of the few African countries with no cheap local buses — or equivalent — that the traveller can use. Small Volkswagen combies (minibuses) will ferry people from one town to the next, providing a good fast service at about N$20 per 100km, but more usually the local people just seem to hitch, often taking several days for a journey. There is one coach operator, Intercape Mainliner, which runs luxury vehicles on long distance routes, complete with food, music, videos and air conditioning. However, on the Cape Town and Johannesburg routes they may not let you travel just within Namibia (e.g. from Windhoek to Mariental), sometimes they insist that you go at least as far as South Africa with them. Note that in South Africa there are many more stops than indicated here.

Mainliner Coaches

Note that times and fares do change very regularly, so use those included here as a rough guide only.

Timetable	Windhoek-Walvis Bay Mon/Wed/Fri/Sat	Walvis Bay-Windhoek Mon/Wed/Fri/Sun
Windhoek	0700	1715
Okahandja	0745	1615
Karibib	0900	1500
Usakos	0915	1445
Swakopmund	1045	1315
Walvis Bay	1115	1300

Fares

	Swakopmund	Usakos	Karibib	Okahandja	Windhoek
Okahandja					40
Karibib				50	60
Usakos			40	55	65
Swakopmund		55	60	75	80
Walvis Bay	40	60	65	75	80

	Windhoek-Tsumeb Mon/Wed/Fri/Sat	Tsumeb-Windhoek Mon/Wed/Fri/Sun
Windhoek	0700	1730
Okahandja	0745	1635
Otjiwarongo	0930	1500
Otavi	1045	1345
Tsumeb	1130	1300

Fares

	Otavi	Otjiwarongo	Okahandja	Windhoek
Okahandja				40
Otjiwarongo			40	60
Otavi		40	60	75
Tsumeb	40	60	75	85

	Windhoek-Cape Town Mon/Wed/Fri/Sun (arrives next day)	Cape Town-Windhoek Sun/Tues/Thurs/Fri (arrives next day)
Windhoek	1900	0600
Rehoboth	2000	0500
Mariental	2145	0315
Keetmanshoop	2400	0115
Grünau	0145	2330
Cape Town	1100	1400

	Windhoek-Upington Mon/Wed/Fri/Sun (arrives next day)	Upington-Windhoek Mon/Wed/Fri/Sun (arrives next day)
Windhoek	1900	0600
Rehoboth	2000	0500
Mariental	2145	0315
Keetmanshoop	2400	0115
Grünau	0130	2330
Upington	0500	1945

	Upington-Cape Town *Tues/Thurs/Fri/Sun*	**Cape Town-Upington** *Sun/Mon/Wed/Fri*
Depart	1945	1900
Arrive	0600	0530

	Upington-Jo'burg *Mon/Tues/Thurs/Sat*	**Jo'burg-Upington** *Tues/Thurs/Fri/Sun*
Depart	0530	1100
Arrive	1400	1945

Fares	Windhoek	Reho.	Mari.	Keet.	Grünau	Karas.	Uping.
Upington	170	150	130	110	90	65	
Cape Town	285	265	245	225	205	180	115
Johannesburg	300	280	260	240	220	195	130

Bookings To book Mainliner, you can either phone their reservations office in Windhoek, Tel: (061) 227847, Fax: (061) 228285, or visit one of their agents:

Okahandja: Buro Rasch. Tel: (06221) 2494.
Karibib: Ströblhof Hotel Tel: (062252) 81.
Swakopmund: Trip Travel. Tel: (0641) 4031.
Walvis Bay: Flamingo Hotel. (0642) 3011.
Otjiwarongo: Kotze Reis (0651) 2382
Tsumeb: Tsumeb Aviation Services. Tel: (0671) 20520.
Johannesburg: Intercape Tel: (011) 333-5231
Cape Town: Intercape Tel: (021) 934-4400

Taxis

Taxis do operate in Windhoek but tend to be expensive, with the exception of those serving the routes between the townships and the centre which carry a very full load of passengers. See Chapter 8, *Windhoek*, for details.

Driving

Almost all of Namibia's major highways are tarred. They are usually wide and well signed, and the small amount of traffic makes them very pleasant to travel on. Less important roads are often gravel, but even these tend to be well maintained and easily passable. Most of the sights, with the exception of Sandwich Harbour, are accessible with an ordinary saloon car (referred to as 2WD in this book). Only those going off the beaten track — into Kaudum, Bushmanland or the Kaokoveld — really need a 4WD. (See Chapters 4 and 6 for full details.)

Get yourself an International Driving Permit before you arrive in Namibia — technically they are required if you wish to drive here. With a British licence they can be obtained at any Automobile Association office (in the UK) for £5, or from Triple A in the USA.

Hitchhiking

Without a vehicle, hitching is probably the best way to travel independently around Namibia, provided that you're patient and don't have a tight schedule to keep. It is certainly one of the best ways to meet people, and can be very speedy and cheap at times. How fast you get lifts is determined by how much traffic goes your way, where you stand, and how you dress. Some of the gravel roads have very little traffic, and people wait days for even a single car to pass — the important part is to set off with enough food and (especially) water to be able to wait for this long.

For the sake of courtesy, and those who come after you, it's important not to abuse people's kindness. Offer to help with the cost of fuel (most people will refuse anyhow) or pay for some cold drinks on the way. Listen patiently to your host's views and if you choose to differ, do so courteously — after all, you came to Namibia to learn about a different country.

Maps

See page 47.

ACCOMMODATION

Hotels

The hotels here are without exception fairly clean and safe, so forget the stories of rats, bats and crawling beasties — just be prepared with your wallet, as few are cheap. We've grouped the hotels into three categories, A, B and C, based both on their price and their merits. Generally you'll get what you pay for, and only in Windhoek and Swakopmund will you find a real choice.

Category A hotels should provide excellent rooms with en-suite bath and toilet, as well as a bar and restaurant. You'll normally find the service in these is excellent — equivalent perhaps to a three or four star hotel in England.

Category B hotels are generally comfortable and efficient. Although they appear less plush or lack the style of category A, they are considerably cheaper.

Category C hotels can vary from incredibly bare, to basic but pleasant. Though you'll probably have to share a bathroom and may have to go out to eat, there are no grounds for dreading them.

Guest Farms

These are private ranches which admit small numbers of guests, usually arranged in advance. They are often very personal and you'll eat all your meals with the hosts and be taken on excursions by them during the day.

Many have game animals on their land and conduct their own photographic or hunting safaris, while one or two have interesting rock formations or cave paintings to attract the visitor.

Although their prices are rarely less than N$150 per person — and usually nearer N$250 — they generally include full board and even day trips. Details of some are included in the relevant sections, but for more specific information consult the current *Accommodation Guide for Tourists*, published by the DNC, which lists all the Guest Farms, their addresses and charges.

Camping

Wherever you are In Namibia, you can almost always find somewhere to camp — either there will be a campsite nearby, or you will be so far from a settlement that you can just camp by the side of the road. The official campsites which are dotted all over the country have *ablution* blocks which vary from a concrete shed with toilets and cold shower, to an immaculately fitted out set of changing rooms with toilets and hot showers. These plusher ablutions will often also have facilities where you can wash clothes and occasionally even have washing machines.

Prices are frequently per site, which theoretically allows for 'a maximum of eight persons, two vehicles and one caravan/tent'. In practice, if you've a couple of small tents you will not usually be charged for two sites — so travelling in a small group can cut costs considerably.

FOOD AND DRINK

Food

Namibia has not developed its own cuisine for visitors and the food served at restaurants tends to be European in style, with a bias towards German dishes and seafood. It is at least as hygienically prepared as in Europe so don't worry about stomach upsets. We've used the cost of the ubiquitous — and often excellent — steaks as a guide to a restaurant's price.

All this shouldn't alarm vegetarians unduly. Like Botswana, Namibia is a very meat-orientated society. However, there's usually a vegetarian alternative in most restaurants, and if you eat seafood the choice is widened further. If you're camping then you'll be buying and cooking your own food anyway.

In the supermarkets you'll find pre-wrapped fresh fruit and vegetables (though the more remote you go, the smaller your choice), and plenty of canned foods, pasta, rice, bread, etc. Most of this is imported from South Africa and you'll probably be familiar with many of the brand names.

Alcohol

Because of a strong German brewing tradition the lagers are good, the Hansa draught being a particular favourite. In cans, Windhoek Export is one of a number to provide a welcome change from the Lion and Castle which dominate the rest of the subcontinent.

The wine available is mainly South African in origin, with very little imported from elsewhere. At their best, the vineyards of the Cape match the best that California or Australia has to offer, and at considerably lower prices. You can get a bottle of something drinkable from a *drankwinkel* (off license) for N$4, or a good bottle of vintage estate wine for N$8.

Soft drinks

Canned soft drinks, from diet coke to sparkling apple juice, are available ice cold from just about anywhere — which is fortunate, considering the amount that you'll need to drink in this climate. They cost about 50c each and can be kept cold in insulating boxes made to hold six cans. These polystyrene containers are invaluable if you have a vehicle. They cost only N$5 and are available from most hardware stores.

Water

All water in the towns is generally safe to drink, though it may taste a little metallic if it has been piped for miles. Natural sources should usually be purified, though water from underground springs — occasionally found flowing in dry river beds — seldom causes any problems. (See Chapter 5, pages 60-61, for more detailed comments.)

Tipping

Service charges are seldom included on restaurant bills and so a 10% tip usually meets with appreciation. Hotel porters and other attendants should also be tipped — a couple of Dollars is usually expected. National parks staff, except perhaps the lodge attendants, do not expect tips.

HANDICRAFTS AND WHAT TO BUY

With rich deposits of natural minerals, Namibia can be a good place for the enthusiast to buy crystals and gems — but don't expect many bargains as the industry is far too organised! For the amateur, the desert roses — sand naturally compressed into forms like flowers — are very unusual and great value at around N$10, while iridescent Tiger's Eye is rare elsewhere and very attractive. For the enthusiast, forget the agates on sale and look for the unusual crystals — in Windhoek the *House of Gems* is a must.

In Kavango and Caprivi you'll find some good local woodcarvings of masks, figures and animals, often sold by the side of the road on small stalls. In the Kalahari regions, Bushmen crafts are some of the most original and unusual available on the continent, often using ostrich eggshell beads with very fine workmanship. These can be difficult to find in Namibia, outside a few expensive shops in the major towns — so try Ghanzi in Botswana or possibly hunt around Tsumkwe in Bushmanland.

ORGANISING AND BOOKING

Public holidays
New Year's Day - January 1
Good Friday, Easter Monday
Independence Day - March 21
Worker's Day - May 1
Cassinga Day - May 4
Africa Day - May 25
Ascension Day (40 days after Easter Sunday)
Heroes Day - August 26
Human Rights Day - December 10
Christmas Day - December 25
Family Day - December 26

National parks
The Department of Nature and Conservation (the DNC) — sometimes called the Directorate of Nature Conservation and Recreation Resorts — is the government department responsible for all the National Parks and is efficient, if rather pedantic in its bureaucracy. The difficulty with its well organised system is that booking accommodation in advance must be done through the Windhoek office or not at all. There's really no substitute for going along there (on Independence Way, next to John Meinert Street) in person with the dates of your trip, and checking the availability of accommodation as you book it.

You can, theoretically, reserve accommodation by post — though paying for it in advance from overseas could cause problems. Try writing to the Directorate of Nature Conservation and Recreation Resorts, RESERVATIONS, Private Bag 13267, Windhoek. Tel: information section (061) 33875, reservations (061) 36975, or telex NATSWA Windhoek 0908-3180.

Entry permits for most parks are available at the gates, provided you're there before they close and there's space left. There are two main exceptions: permits to stay at Naukluft, Terrace Bay and Torra Bay can only be obtained from Windhoek DNC; permits to drive through the Namib section of the Namib-Naukluft Park are available at most tourist offices.

COMMUNICATIONS

Post
The post is efficient and reliable. An airmail letter or post card costs 35c and takes about a week to get to Europe. For larger items, sending them by sea is much cheaper (R4.65 to register and post a 1kg packet), but may take up to three months and isn't recommended for fragile items.

Telephone and fax

The telephone system is linked into the South African system, enabling you to dial direct internationally, without going through the operator, from any public phone box — provided you've enough coins. You can then arrange to be called back, which is a lot cheaper than reversing the charges. To phone out of the country, dial 00 and then the country code, eg 00 (44) for the UK.

The international access code for Namibia from abroad is 264, eg dial 010 (264) from the UK. If you are trying to phone a number outside Windhoek then be patient, you will probably speak to an operator first who will put you through. If faxing from abroad then always dial the number yourself, with your fax machine set to manual. Wait until you are properly connected (listen for a high-pitched tone), and then try to send your fax.

MISCELLANEOUS

Electricity

Sockets supplying power at 220/240V and 50Hz, taking the standard British three pin plug, are available in all the towns — and even at the campsites in Etosha.

Embassies and High Commissions

Angolan Embassy, 3rd floor, Angola House. Tel: (061) 220302

Botswana High Commission, 22 Curt von Francois St, PO Box 20359. Tel: (061) 221941

British High Commission, 116 Leutwein St, PO Box 22202. Tel: (061) 223022

Royal Danish Embassy, Sanlam Centre, Independence Avenue, P.0.Box 20126, Tel: (061) 229956

Egyptian Embassy, 6 Stein St, Klein Windhoek, PO Box 11853. Tel: (061) 222408

French Embassy, 1 Goeth St. Tel: (061) 22 9021

German Embassy, 11 Uhland St, PO Box 231. Tel: (061) 229217

Kenyan High Commission, Kenya House, Leutwein St. Tel: (061) 226836

Malawi High Commission, 56 Bismark St, PO Box 23384. Tel: (061) 52856

Nigerian High Commission, 4 Omuramba Rd, Eros, PO Box 23541. Tel: (061) 32103

Royal Norwegian Embassy, 73 Gevers St, Ludwigsdorf. Tel: (061) 51836

Portuguese Mission, 28 Garden St. Tel: (061) 28736

South African Embassy, Corner of Jan Jonker and Klein Windhoek Rds, PO Box 23100. Tel: (061) 227771

Swedish Embassy, 10 Stein St, Klein Windhoek, PO Box 23087. Tel: (061) 51284

Swiss Consul-General, 10 von Eckenbrecher St, Klein Windhoek, PO Box 22287. Tel: (061) 222359

USA Liaison Office. Tel: (061) 9199

Zambian Embassy, 22 Curt von Francois, Corner Republic Rd, PO Box 22882. Tel: (061) 37610
Zimbabwean High Commission, 398 Independence Way, PO Box 23056. Tel: (061) 227738

Hospitals, dentists and pharmacies

Should you need one, the main hospitals are of a good standard and will treat you first and ask for money later! The hospital in Windhoek is on Florence Nightingale Rd, off Pasteur St, in the north-west of the city. Dentists are also available in the main towns. When travelling outside the cities you could be many miles from even a basic clinic, let alone a good hospital, so carrying your own comprehensive medical kit is an absolute necessity in case of accident. (See Chapter 5, page 60, for just the basics of a kit.)

Pharmacies in Windhoek stock a full range of medicines, though specific brands are sometimes unavailable. However, do bring with you all that you need, as well as a repeat prescription for anything that you may lose or run out of just in case. A few of the larger towns also have good pharmacies, but don't rely on getting anything out of the ordinary away from the capital.

Imports and exports

Being a member of the Southern African Customs Union (SACU) means that there are few restrictions between Namibia and either Botswana or South Africa. If you wish to export any animal products, including skins or legally culled ivory, make sure you obtain a certificate confirming the origin of every item which you buy. Remember that even with these many countries will not allow skins or particularly ivory to be imported — check the current regulations before you leave.

Newspapers, radio and TV

There are no press restrictions in Namibia, though the government-sponsored Namibia Broadcasting Corporation (NBC) accounts for the radio and TV stations. Out of Windhoek the radio can be difficult to receive, while the TV maintains a restricted sunrise to the major areas. In Windhoek there is a choice of newspapers, but *The Namibian* — with its usually patriotic flavour — is dominant.

94

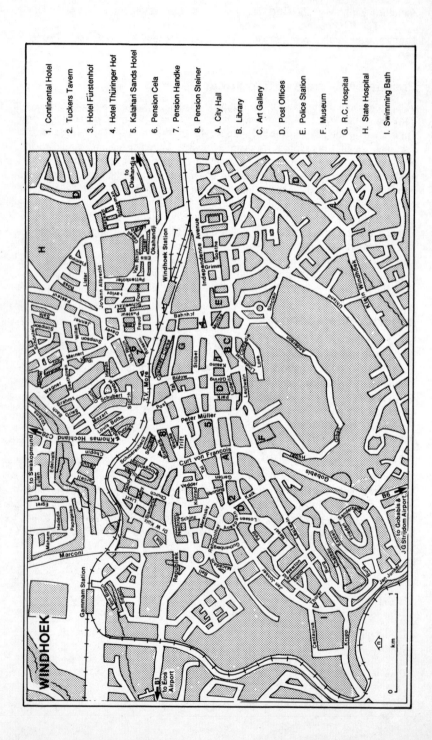

1. Continental Hotel
2. Tuckers Tavern
3. Hotel Fürstenhof
4. Hotel Thüringer Hof
5. Kalahari Sands Hotel
6. Pension Cela
7. Pension Handke
8. Pension Steiner
A. City Hall
B. Library
C. Art Gallery
D. Post Offices
E. Police Station
F. Museum
G. R.C. Hospital
H. State Hospital
I. Swimming Bath

Chapter 8

Windhoek

Namibia's capital spreads out in a wide valley between bush-covered hills and appears, at first sight, to be quite small. Driving from the international airport, you pass quickly through the suburbs and, reaching the crest of a suburban hill, find yourself suddenly descending into the very centre of the city.

Strolling through the city's centre, the cafes on pavements and balconies, and picturesque old German architecture conspire to give an airy, European feel, whilst basket sellers remind you that you that this is an African capital. Above, the office blocks are tall, but not sky scraping; below the pace is busy, but not as frantic as western capitals seem to be.

Next to Independence Way, the city's main street, is the Post Street Mall — a new shopping complex where cars, parked under cover, deliver their occupants to air-conditioned department stores under bright, pastel coloured roofs. Look inside the mall and, between the fast-food joints and fashion shops, you find street sellers setting out their jewellery on blankets, crouching with a smile amongst rows of carved figures and smoothly sanded salad bowls.

Windhoek is a very pleasant city, but it has few, if any, major attractions. Having said that, if you need an embassy, or to receive a bank transfer, or simply to catch a plane, then Windhoek is usually an efficient place to be. For those who plan to hire their own vehicle, this is by far the best place to get organised and obtain food, supplies, and book National Park permits and accommodation. It is also one of the few places where you meet other independent travellers and have a chance to compare notes.

Getting there

As well as its intercontinental air links, Windhoek is well linked to the other cities in the region by air, rail, and coach services (see Chapter 7, *In Namibia* , page 83).

Air Windhoek has two airports. Both are small, modern and very pleasant — at least as airports go. Eros airport, near the Safari Hotel, caters for most internal flights and local light aircraft, while J.G.Strijdom is the international airport.

J.G.Strijdom is 42km out of town, along the B6 towards Gobabis. Some of the car hire companies have their own offices at the airport, and the others will meet you there on request, so picking up a hired car on arrival is very straightforward. If you don't plan to have your own vehicle then there is a scheduled shuttle bus service which links up with flight arrivals and departures. To find out details, contact the information desk at the airport, the Air Namibia office in the city, Tel: (061) 298 2552/1111, or Trip Travel in the Trip Arcade on Independence Way, Tel: (061) 36880, Fax: (061) 225430. The city's terminus is opposite the SAA office on Independence Way, so there is often a timetable displayed on that bus stop.

Alternatively, the Kalahari Sands and Safari hotels run courtesy buses between the city and the airport for their guests, so talk to their reception desks.

Where to stay

Windhoek has a range of different hotels to suit different budgets. None are run down, as can be the case in other capitals, so you're very unlikely to find yourself in a hole, wherever you stay. Prices range from about N$75 to N$300+ per person, sharing a double room.

Category A
Kalahari Sands PO Box 2254, Windhoek. Tel: (061) 36900. Fax: (061) 222260. This is Windhoek's large, central international hotel with rooms which are very well-kept and equipped, although its character is like that of a Sheraton — rather unexciting.

Hard to miss on Independence Way, the Kalahari Sands is one of Windhoek's taller buildings. Its entrance is in the first floor of the shopping arcade below the hotel, and its prices are usually the most expensive around, with singles from N$225, and doubles from N$275, including breakfast. Breakfast for non-residents is N$26, and dinner or lunch buffets are N$38.

Hotel Safari PO Box 3900, Windhoek. Tel: (061) 222300. Fax: (061) 222260. About 3km from the centre of town, on the road to Rehoboth, the Hotel Safari covers several acres and includes a large pool set in the grounds. A large new wing has recently been added, and all the hotel's rooms are of a very good standard, with en-suite facilities, telephones and tea/coffee machines. Singles are N$170, doubles N$230, including breakfast. If you've no transport, then the complementary minibus is convenient for trips into and out of town. It leaves from opposite the Kalahari Sands, on Independence Way.

Hotel Fürstenhof PO Box 316, Windhoek. Tel: (061) 37380. Fax: (061) 228751. Less than 1km west of centre, the Fürstenhof is perched slightly above the city on Romberg St. It is small and personal, with a slightly German feel and a hint of old-world style about it. It has neither the facilities nor the monotony of the more modern hotels, but it possesses an excellent restaurant (see page 99). Costs are about N$195 for singles and N$290 for doubles, including breakfast.

Category B
Hotel Thüringer Hof PO Box 112, Windhoek. Tel/Fax: (061) 226031. Towards the north end of Independence Way, near Bahnhof St, this is the only Namib Sun Hotel within the city. It is very close to the DNC, in the centre of town, and across the road from the main police station. Its rooms are well furnished, although a little smaller than the Kalahari Sands. Singles cost around N$200, doubles N$300, including breakfast. At the back there is a lively beer garden which serves snacks for N$6 - N$12.

Continental Hotel PO Box 977, Windhoek. Tel: (061) 37293. Fax: (061) 31539. Very central, tucked away opposite the MODEL store on Independence Way, this hotel has recently been refurbished, and is similar in character to the Thüringer Hof, though its bar is small and unremarkable in comparison. Singles cost N$130, while doubles are around N$260. Note that there are a few rooms available with shared toilets for N$100.

Tucker's Tavern PO Box 5374. Tel: (061) 223249. At the southern end of Independence Way, by a roundabout, Tucker's has been under new ownership for the last few years and has improved greatly. The large public bar at the front (now with security guards) gets busy, while the back bar has the atmosphere of a western saloon bar in a small, quiet town.

Accommodation, in rooms which open onto the car park at the back of the hotel, is clean and simple. Singles with a bath (or shower) are N$126, without N$103, doubles with a bath (or shower) N$190, without N$161. There is also a family room (4-beds, no facilities) for N$190, and a room suitable for people using wheelchairs. All prices include a continental breakfast, and if you are not eating at the nearby restaurants then the back bar serves soup for N$6 and simple meals for N$15.

Aris Hotel Tel: (161) 36006. 25km south of the city, the Aris Hotel is really a *country restaurant* with half a dozen rooms for those who don't want to drive after dinner. Excellent food is served in the large dining-room: the normal main courses from a mouth-watering menu are below N$30 (excluding seafood), and a full meal, with wine, will probably cost you about N$60.

Booking is essential for the hotel, and advisable for the restaurant. Rooms cost N$75 for a single and N$140 for a double and, if you stay, then don't miss the full English breakfast for N$15 extra.

Category C

Hotel-Pension Handke PO Box 20831, Windhoek. Tel: (061) 34904. Fax: (061) 225660. Just out of the centre, on Rossini St, this quirky guest house is run by an idiosyncratic German woman notable for her acerbic comments. Typical was her concise retort to a traveller's complaint that the only milk available on the breakfast table was powdered. 'Dry country. Dry milk.'

Handke is clean, cheap, sometimes cheerful, and often full. Singles are N$100, doubles N$140, including a German breakfast of cold meats, cheeses and coffee. Great value, especially if you get along well with the owner.

Hotel-Pension Cela 82 Bülow Str. PO Box 1947, Windhoek. Tel: (061) 226295/94. Fax: (061) 226246. This suburban pension is very close to Handke and has large airy rooms which house solid wooden beds, en suite facilities and even mini-bars. Singles are N$137, doubles N$215, including breakfast.

Cela has a leafy swimming pool and a separate TV lounge, though neither are used much. This is just the place, if you need to clean up and recover from a long camping expedition in the bush, but book early as it is often full.

Hotel-Pension Steiner 11 Wecke Str. PO Box 20481, Windhoek. Tel: (061) 222898. Fax: (061) 224234. This new hotel, just off Peter Müller Str, has singles for N$125 and doubles for N$200.

South West Star Hotel PO Box 10319, Khomasdal. Tel: (061) 213205. The South West Star is about 4km out of town, in Khomasdal (what used to be the 'coloured' township). Its costs N$45 for a single and N$80 for a double, but it is run down and cannot be recommended.

Hotel Kapps Farm 20km east of the city on the Gobabis Rd, this appeared closed when I last visited — although it seldom seemed different when it was open. If it is still operating then singles are N$90, doubles N$120, with breakfast N$15 extra. This hotel is not recommended.

Backpacker's Lodge Mr H.L. Sachse, 25 Best St, Brachbrecht P.O. Box 8541, Windhoek. Tel: (061)228355. Fax: (061)36561. In a residential suburb 2km north of the city, this private house uses converted outbuildings as dormitories and N$25 buys you a dorm bed and use of a shower, a fridge and a small kitchen. The owners prefer you to vacate the place between 10am and 4pm, but are flexible if you really need to stay. It is rarely full, but to book in advance drop them a note at the above address.

Camping There used to be a campsite situated just behind the Safari Hotel, just off the road to Rehoboth. However, since mid 1993 this site closed to make way for the expansion of the hotel. So far, no other has opened up. Practical campers might take the philosophical view that they can camp anywhere else in this country, so sleeping in a hotel should make a pleasant change.

Where to eat

With about a dozen restaurants to choose from, you should have no problems finding somewhere to eat. Most of these serve fairly international fare, often with a slight German bias, though there are Italian, Chinese and even Korean specialists. Several of the restaurants are of a very high standard, and none are expensive in European or American terms.

For coffee or a snack, the two cafes in the Trip Arcade, the **Schneider** and the **Central**, are ideal, and great places to watch the world go by. Buy a local paper from the street sellers around there to find out what's really going on. For dinner, the more memorable restaurants include:

Hotel Fürstenhof West of the centre, on Romberg St., this is Windhoek's best restaurant. Its quiet atmosphere is almost formal. For men, a jacket and tie isn't out of place. The chef, Jürgen Raith, has won awards, and your taste-buds will appreciate why.

The food is classical French / German style, varying from seafood through to game and a daily vegetarian dish. The wine list is about the best around, though not inspired or outstanding value. Costs are about N$9 - N$14 for a starter, N$20 - N$35 for a main course, and N$10 - N$12 for a sweet.

Gathemans This must have the best position of the capital's restaurants, on a first floor balcony, opposite the park, with commanding views over Independence Way. The traditional German cuisine (with a bias towards game) is excellent and although not quite the Fürstenhof's equal, it does cost a few Dollars less. The wine list is extensive, and therefore good in parts.

Sam's About 2.5km from the centre, Sam's is on the left of Gobabis Rd, about 100m past the junction with Klein Windhoek. Its atmosphere is relaxed, with starters N$4-N$7, vegetarian meals or pasta N$10-N$12, steaks N$24, sweets N$4. On Saturday afternoons, there is a band in the courtyard, encouraging a young, trendy clientele.

Seoul House Restaurant This Korean restaurant on Rehoboth Road (just opposite Tucker's Tavern) has been upgraded in the last few years and is now a gaining a good reputation for its food and service. It opens seven days a week from 6 - 10pm and costs about N$30 for a good meal.

Spurs Situated above street level on Independence Way, opposite the Bank of Windhoek, Spurs concentrates on American burgers, steaks, a host of side orders and has the city's best serve-yourself salad bar. The atmosphere is lively, similar to a Hard Rock Cafe, and the prices are around N$20 for a main course. Recommended.

El Toro Steak-House Situated by the roundabout, near Tucker's Tavern, El Toro is very similar in price and atmosphere to Spurs. It opens for lunch from 12-3pm during the week, and from 7pm until late every day except Sunday.

Viva Espania Windhoek's only tapas bar, situated in the plush surroundings of the Kalahari Sands hotel. It opens from 7pm - 11pm all week except Sunday. At over N$30 for a meal it isn't one of the best value restaurants around, but if you have a craving for some tapas ...

Marco Polo Central, in the Kaiserkrone Centre, on the Post Str. Mall. It serves reasonable pizzas and pasta dishes for around N$15-N$25 in the evening, after masquerading as a lively cafe during the day.

Yang Tse A large, efficient restaurant, preparing probably the best Chinese food in town. Its first floor windows overlook the junction of Gobabis Rd and Klein Windhoek. Better suited to a business lunch than a relaxing dinner.

Aris Hotel Finally, if you've transport then consider a trip out of town to the Aris Hotel. Its a 50km round trip, but if you feel like a drive the food is very good. (See *Where to stay*, page 97.)

Getting around

In and around the city it's usually best to walk as everything is close together. If you need a taxi then **Windhoek Radio Taxis,** at 452 Independence Avenue, is the main taxi company. Tel: 37070. Alternatively **Namibia Radio Taxis** is based in Khomasdal, Tel: 211116 or 225222.

What to see and do

Around town

Behind the Library, near Lüderitz St, is the city's small **museum** with a good cafe/restaurant — the Alte Festa. Entry is free and there are some interesting displays on different types of desert, ethnic groups, *karakuls* and an unusual 'touch room' which is open only on Mondays. Nearby the **Art Gallery** is a small building on the corner of Leutwein and John Meinert St., which usually hosts a one-room exhibition. These are often of interest, so glance in as you are passing.

The **Namib Craft Centre**, at 40 Tal St (near Garten Str.) is an indoor market with a number of stalls for sellers of small arts and crafts. There are paintings, sculptures, designs in copper, hand-painted fabrics and much else. It opens 9am - 5.30pm from Monday to Friday, and from 9am - 1pm on Saturday. The shop selling hand-painted T-shirts for around N$55 was a favourite, as was the designer who sold individually coloured silk scarves.

Night-life
Windhoek is not famous for its night-life. Most visitors choose to go to a restaurant for a leisurely dinner and perhaps a drink, and then retire for an early start the following day. If you feel more lively, there are two cinemas, and some night-clubs for later on. Note that Friday is usually the best night of the week, being far more lively than Saturday night.

Cinemas   Windhoek isn't the place to keep up with Holywood's latest releases, but for recent popular films try the **Kine 300** on Klein Windhoek, close to Kuiseb Rd and the post office. Tel: 34155 for their programme, or look in the paper for details.

There's also a **drive-in** cinema near the stadium, about 3km from the centre. Take the B1 south to Rehoboth, and the signposted turn left shortly after the Safari Hotel. This can be a magical place, with the surrounding hills painted red in the sunset. However, it tends to screen an eclectic range of movies, which do not always reach the standard of the setting. Check the papers to find out what is showing.

Bars   In most traditional cultures in southern Africa, a respectable woman would not normally be seen in a bar. This attitude is gradually changing in the cities, where some hotel bars and night clubs have a lively mix of the sexes.

Many hotel bars, like the Continental's, are devoid of atmosphere, whilst some, like the front bar at Tucker's Tavern, seem too loud and aggressive for a quiet evening's drink. The best of Windhoek's hotel bars are probably the large beer garden of the **Thüringer Hof**, and the formal **Fürstenhof's**, which is small, but can be fun for a group.

Joe's Beerhouse is like an oasis in this desert. Joe's is opposite the Zimbabwean High Commission on Grimme Str., the third right off Independence Way, after the Thüringer Hof, heading away from town. It feels like a pub, has bags of character, a good choice of beer, and even generous portions of bar food. It opens from 5pm - 2am from Monday to Friday, and from 10am - 2am on Saturdays. There is a small garden at the back, but I remain uncertain why the thin, tin ashtrays are nailed down to their wooden tables.

Night-clubs   As in most cities, night-clubs go in and out of fashion in a matter of months, so anything written here is bound to be out of date. Windhoek normally has two or three clubs up and running at any one time — which can be cosmopolitan and excellent fun. Your best plan is to ask people that you meet during the day for their advice on the latest venues.

Perhaps quiz the staff in one of the restaurants. At the time of writing, the best night-spots are:

Casablanca's Tel: 32639. On Gobabis Road near its corner with Klein Windhoek, Casablanca's is just in front of Sam's restaurant. It serves cocktails and snacks with music which rocks until 5am. The entry charge is N$10 and avoid jeans.

Rock-a-fella's has a younger crowd (18 - 25) and is more of a disco. Again, avoid jeans.

Getting organised and shopping

Most of Namibia's consumer goods, and much of its food, is produced in South Africa, while high-tech goods are usually imported from Europe or Japan. Hence, food, clothes and the basics are normally cheaper than in Europe, whilst electronics and most luxuries are more expensive.

Souvenirs and Curios

Windhoek's best buys are probably **rocks and gems**, but don't buy to invest unless you know exactly what you are doing. There are good souvenirs to be had, but few great bargains. One of the larger shops sells a lot of imported Brazilian agates, simply because visitors expect these to be cheap here and so they buy them.

For **minerals**, the obvious supplier is Rocks, Gems and Minerals, on Independence Way, near the Trip Arcade. An eye-catching shop which seems overpriced. A better alternative is the House of Gems. Tucked away at 131 Stübel St., near John Meinert Str., and run by Sid Peters, this is a real collector's place stuffed full of original bits and pieces. Even if you're not buying, it is worth visiting. The stones are mostly from Sid's own Tourmaline mines (claimed to produce the world's best Tourmaline), and you can see them sorted, cut, faceted and polished on the premises.

Another good buy is **leather work**, especially ostrich, game and karakul products. Again there are few give-aways, but if you know what you want then there are good deals to be had. The standard of work varies greatly and you will find some local production work of a very high standard, aiming at export markets, while other work is of a much lower quality. As with anywhere, shop around. The best sources for leather are the shops in the centre of town, near the main Post Office and one on the adjacent Göring Str. has a good selection of belts.

For more traditional **African curios**, the prices offered by street sellers are hard to beat. Wander down the Post Str. Mall and you'll find wooden carvings, sculptures, basketware, crochet work and a variety of other crafts. You can bargain for these as you would at a market in the UK, but don't try to drive too hard a deal. Most of the sellers will either have produced the work themselves, or be selling it for friends or relatives and will price it at around the level they expect to receive. The exceptions to this rule are the occasional sharp characters who approach you with statues to sell. Be more wary of these dealers.

Bushmen crafts make some of the region's most interesting and unusual souvenirs. Traditional skills are used to fashion beads made from ostrich eggshells into bracelets, necklaces and even aprons. If you are passing through Ghanzi in Botswana (east of Gobabis), then wait until you get there to buy some of these. You will find a far greater range there, and at cheaper prices. Failing that, some of Windhoek's curio shops sell occasional pieces, so keep a look out.

Food and Drink
If you are heading off in your own vehicle, then you will need to take food and other supplies with you. Plan how much you will need (this could be a long list) and then drive to one of the town's big supermarkets: either the Model 7-day Store on Independence Way, opposite the Continental Hotel, or, better still, the big Woolworth's supermarket at the north end of the Post Str. Mall. This latter has a covered car park adjacent to it, reached from Tal Str.

Both stores have good fresh meat and vegetable sections, though with the country's high temperatures, do not expect meat or dairy products to last more than a day. Use tinned food for the rest of the time, supplemented initially by robust fresh vegetables. Aim to buy all your dry foods and tins here in Windhoek, where they are cheapest, and top-up with perishables at smaller towns on the way.

In addition to food, invest in at least one cool-box. These are invaluable to keep both food, drinks and film cool while on the road. Even if you are travelling from hotel to hotel, buy a couple of the expanded polystyrene ones, designed for six-packs. You will be grateful later, when you are sitting next to a water-hole under the merciless sun.

These supermarkets also have a good range of packaged foods for campers: good quality dried milk powder, rice, pasta and the Toppers range of dried soya bean mince meals, which make excellent lightweight food for backpacking.

For wines and beers of any sort, and ice to pack the larger cool-boxes, Keurwyn has a better choice than the supermarkets. Find them at 123 Tal Str., near the railway station. If you are a wine lover, then bring the latest *South African Wine Guide* (see *Bibliography*) with you. Almost all of the wine here is from South Africa, and there are real bargains to be had.

Other Supplies
If you need camping kit, or spares, then remember that South African equipment makes up the majority of what's available, and often you will not be able to find any European or American equivalent. The best place is probably Cymot, at 74 Tal Str. Tel: (061) 34131. Fax: (061) 34921. This is certainly the best shop for cycle spares in town.

Alternatively Gorelick's Motors Tel: (061) 37700, opposite the open parking at 119 Independence Way, comes highly recommended and may have what you are looking for, or Gav's Camping Hire, at 49 John Meinert Str. Tel: (061) 38745 may be able to help you.

Information and useful addresses

When trying to accomplish anything in Windhoek, remember the phone book. If you are looking for something unusual, try phoning rather than walking, it's much quicker. If you need an address then look here first. The whole country is covered by one rather slim volume, including all the international codes, a town by town directory, and a yellow pages section that covers the whole country, and even separate fax and telex directories.

AMEX Woker Travel Services, PO Box 211, Windhoek 9000. Tel: (061) 37946. Fax: (061) 225932. Woker Travel Services are the local American Express agent, found at 6 Peter Müller St, just down from Independence Avenue. They're an excellent travel agent and, if you have either an American Express card or AMEX travellers cheques, they can be used as an efficient address to have your mail sent to you. Mail should be addressed: c/o American Express Client Mail, at the above address. However, note that this office will not cash any travellers cheques themselves.

Automobile Association For advice about road conditions, contact the AA at 15 Carl List House, Independence Avenue, Box 61. Tel: (061) 224201. Fax: (061) 222446. Their 24-hour breakdown contact line is (061) 224201 ... but don't expect miracles.

Banks

The centre of town has several large, major banks. These are generally efficient and speedy, though to withdraw cash on a credit card requires the bank to make an international call, which takes time. You will find it quicker to use these rather than the smaller branches. Certainly if you need anything complex, like an international money transfer, go to the largest branch possible. In either event, remember to bring along your passport. The best banks are:

First National Bank (which used to be Barclays Bank), is in the centre, on Independence Avenue. Tel: (061) 229616. This is the best for VISA transactions.

The Bank of Windhoek is at 262 Independence Avenue, Tel: (061) 31850

Post Office In the centre of Independence Way, the large GPO has an efficient Post Restante facility, and a place to make international phone calls or send faxes. It's cheap and easy to send packages overseas from here. At the counter to the right of the main hall, a registered package of under 1kg costs N$4.65 to send by sea mail (complete with dripping sealing wax) but you'll need your own string to tie it up. It will take about two months to reach Europe.

Gav's Camping Hire 49 John Meinert Str., PO Box 80157. Tel: (061) 38745. Fax: (061) 230722. Gav's have a good range of equipment, and their business has expanded a lot in the last few years. This is the place to hire all your equipment for a trip into the bush. Items are hired on a cost per day basis, and can be paid for by cash or credit card. If cash is used then a deposit of 50% of the rental cost is asked. Typical daily costs are: 3m x 3m igloo tent - N$13; mattress N$1; two-ring gas cooker N$2.80; 20l water container N$1.00; 20-litre petrol Jerry can N$1.50; 30l cool-box N$1.50; plates/bowls/mugs about N$0.30; mosquito net N$1.50.

Car Hire Firms

For an overview of your options, and a general comparison of the services and prices available, see the section on hiring your own vehicle (pages 48 - 50). Of the firms below, Kessler/Budget, AVIS and Imperial all have offices at J.G.Strijdom airport. The others are all new, only have offices in Windhoek, and should be used with great caution — see the section mentioned above. The companies' main offices are:

Kessler Car Hire for 4WDs, are found at 72 Tal St. The only company to allow vehicles to be taken into Botswana, South Africa and Zimbabwe, they are excellent and keep their vehicles in first class condition. Contact by writing to PO Box 20274, Windhoek or Tel: (061) 33451 or 227638. Fax: (061) 224551. Telex: 50-908-3359.

Budget Rent-a-car This international franchise is held by Kessler, and although the businesses are separate they can be contacted directly at Kessler's office, as above. Alternatively you can book through your local country office at home.

AVIS can be found on Jean Str., next to the entrance to the Safari Hotel, just off Rehoboth road. This is the most international of the firms, and you may get a different deal if you book them from your local office back home. Contact them here directly by writing to PO Box 2057, Windhoek, or Tel: (061) 33166. Fax: (061) 223072. Telex: 0-908-3183.

Imperial Car Rental have a small network throughout Namibia, and South Africa. They can be found at 43 Stübel Str. Contact at PO Box 1387 or Tel: (061) 227103. Fax: (061) 222721.

Pegasus Car and Camper Hire is run by Ms Elisabeth Kuhlmann from PO Box 21104, Windhoek. Tel/Fax: (061) 223423.

Namib 4x4 Hire have offices in Windhoek and Swakopmund. Their Windhoek office is at the La Pardiz Centre, 90 Gobabis Rd. Tel: (061) 220604. Fax: (061) 220605.

Tempest Car Hire is new to Namibia, but one of a network of offices throughout South Africa. Visit them at 49 John Meinert Str. Based at Gav's Camping Hire, Tel/Fax: (061) 51526.

Adventure 4 Hire is yet another new car hire company — contacted via PO Box 9544, Windhoek. Tel: (061) 226188. Fax: (061) 224926.

Camping Car Hire (Pty) Ltd is a very recent addition to the market, and hires out a full range of camping equipment as well as VW Golfs and Toyota 4WDs. Find them at the corner of Edison and Republic Rd, or PO Box 5526, Windhoek. Tel: (061) 37756. Fax: (061) 37757.

Booking Agencies and Operators

If you want to book a tour from Windhoek, then contact one of the following:

Namib Travel Shop 34 Omuramba Road, Eros, PO Box 6850, Windhoek. Tel: (061) 225178 or 226174. Fax: (061) 33332. This large, efficient agent is also the base for Namib Wilderness Safaris.

Top Travel Information PO Box 80205, Windhoek. Tel (016) 51975. This small agent gives a very personal service, and can organise short tours around the city. They are closely involved with hiking trails near the Fish River, and Epupa Camp, on the Kunene River.

Kaokohimba Safaris 11 Satre St., Academia, PO Box 30828, Windhoek. Tel: (061) 42633. Fax: (061) 42933. Specialising in trips into the Kaokoveld.

African Extravaganza PO Box 22028, Windhoek. Tel: (061) 63086/7/8. Fax: (061) 215356.

Ritz Reise United Building, 250 Independence Way, PO Box 23113, Windhoek. Tel: (061) 36670/229780/229781. Fax: (061) 227575.

TransNamib Travel Gustav Voigts Centre, PO Box 415, Windhoek. Tel: (061) 34821. Fax: (061) 223056.

Trip Travel Trip Centre, Independence Way, PO Box 100, Windhoek. Tel: (061) 36880. Fax: (061)225430.

Toko Safaris 5th Floor, CDM Centre, Bülow St., PO Box 5017, Windhoek. Tel: (061)225539.

Oryx Tours 11 Van der Bijl St., North Industrial Area, PO Box 2058, Windhoek. Tel: (061) 217454. Fax: (061) 63417.

Encounter Namibia 116 Carl List Building, Independence Way, Windhoek. Tel: (061) 228474.

Excursions - Daan Viljoen Game Park

2WD. Entrance fees: N$5 per person, N$5 per car.
This small game park, some 20km east of the city, is well provided for in terms of facilities. It is a popular weekend retreat for those in the capital, and accommodation needs to be booked in advance at the DNC. It also makes an easy day trip, but if you have not booked to stay then ring the wardens for permission to visit for the day. Tel: (061) 226806.

During the middle of the week the rest camp is much quieter. Spend a few hours walking around this rugged little park and you have a fair chance of spotting some game. Mountain zebras and klipspringers occur here, as you would expect from the hilly terrain, as well as hartebeest, wildebeest and even eland. There is a circular drive, but if you have the energy then walk around instead.

The park encompasses some of the hills of the Khomas Hochland and, with its thorn trees and scrub vegetation, the environment is typical of the plateau area around Windhoek.

Getting there

Take Curt von Francois Str. east onto Khomas Hochland, and then follow the signs onto the C28 towards Swakopmund. The park is well signposted.

Where to stay

Bungalows N$46 for two people, complete with hot plates, fridges, bedding and towels. They only have wash basins though the showers and toilets are shared. Camping is N$25 per site.

There's a restaurant which opens for meals from 7.30am to 9.00pm, noon to 1.30pm and 7.00pm to 8.30pm, a small kiosk, and even a swimming pool — all on the shores of a veritable oasis named the Augeigas Dam. There is no petrol station though, or shop, so don't rely on buying anything here.

Hiking

The Game Park excludes potentially dangerous elephant, buffalo and the large cats, so you can safely walk alone on the short game trails. There are two prescribed routes, one of 3km and the other of about 7km. Ask at the Park's office for full details. Alternatively you can just follow the wild game trails anywhere within the Park's boundaries. You are unlikely to get lost unless you really try to. Before you set off walking, see if the Park's office has left any of its guides to the local birdlife. This excellent little booklet identifies the main bird species found here, and gives short descriptions of the habitats found in the park.

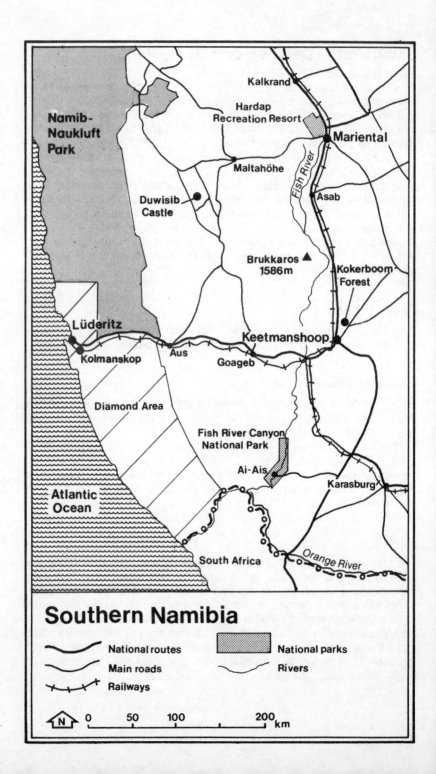

Southern Namibia

- ⌇⌇⌇ National routes
- ⌇ Main roads
- ×—×—× Railways
- ▨ National parks
- ⌇○⌇ Rivers

N 0   50   100   200 km

Chapter 9

Southern Namibia

If you have journeyed north from South Africa's vast parched plateau, the Karoo, or come out of the Kalahari from the east, the arid landscapes and widely separated towns of Southern Namibia will come as no surprise as you arrive here for the first time. Like the towns, the main attractions of the region are far apart – but special enough to be worth the effort that is needed to reach them.

The Fish River Canyon, perhaps the country's most awe-inspiring sight, is easy to find, hard to forget and invariably empty of the crowds that can spoil the most spectacular places elsewhere in the world. On the coast, Lüderitz is visually less stunning though none the less fascinating for its architecture – while the town's isolated position adds to the almost tangible feeling of history here.

The towns and main attractions are ordered roughly from south to north.

Karasburg

Within easy reach of the South African border, Karasburg is a popular stop-over. There are several garages, a good Spar supermarket, and a Sentra hardware shop. Both First National and Bank of Windhoek have branches here open normal hours, 8.30am to 3.30pm and also Saturday mornings.

Where to stay and eat
Category C

The hotels in the town are both well run by the same man and signposted from the centre of this small town. The **Kalkfontain** – PO Box 205. Tel: (06342)172 – is slightly the better as all its rooms are air-conditioned and it serves meals. Costs singles N$90-N$100, doubles N$140-N$150, triples N$170, 4-beds N$200 – inclusive of breakfast.

The rooms at the **Van Reibeck** – PO Box 87. Tel: (06342)23 – are about N$5 cheaper, but some are without air-conditioning and there's no food available. Guests are asked to eat at the Kalkfontain!

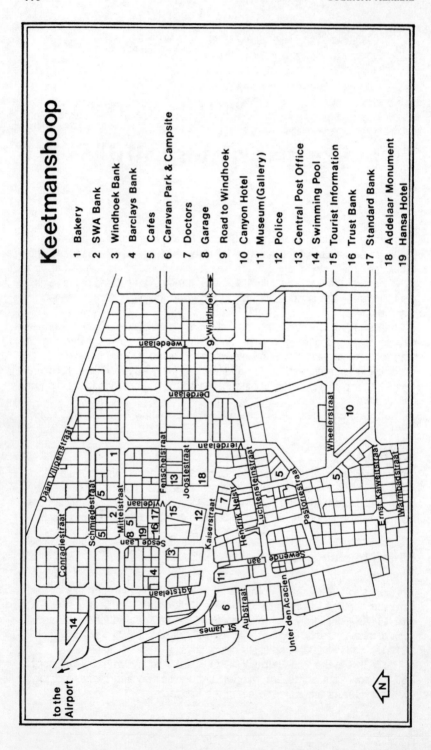

Keetmanshoop

1 Bakery
2 SWA Bank
3 Windhoek Bank
4 Barclays Bank
5 Cafes
6 Caravan Park & Campsite
7 Doctors
8 Garage
9 Road to Windhoek
10 Canyon Hotel
11 Museum (Gallery)
12 Police
13 Central Post Office
14 Swimming Pool
15 Tourist Information
16 Trust Bank
17 Standard Bank
18 Addelaar Monument
19 Hansa Hotel

KEETMANSHOOP

Keetmanshoop, often pronounced 'Keetmansverp', lies about 482km south of Windhoek at an altitude of 1,000m. Originally a Nama settlement on the banks of a seasonal river, the Swartmodder, it is named after the German industrialist Johann Keetman who provided the funds to found a mission there in the 1860s. Now Keetmanshoop is the largest town south of the capital and, being centrally located, makes a good base from which to explore the region.

Getting there

Keetmanshoop is at the hub of the region's road network. The main B1 conveniently skirts the east of the town, which is just north of the turn off to Lüderitz. Hitchers should have few problems. On the railway, the town is the terminus for the Lüderitz trains, and a major stop on the line into South Africa (see Chapter 7 for details).

Where to stay

Category A

Canyon Hotel PO Box 950, Keetmanshoop. Tel: (0631)3361. Singles N$184, doubles N$290; full breakfast N$15, continental N$12.50. Comfortable – if a bit impersonal, with air-conditioning and all facilities, including a pool. The Canyon is not very central, however, and is found on the southern side of town by following the signs from the B1 (see map).

Category B

Travel Inn PO Box 141, Keetmanshoop. Tel: (0631)3344. On Sesdelaan, between streets Mittel and Fenschel. Rooms: single sharing bath N$82, single with own bath N$115, double N$160; all prices include full breakfast. Centrally located with good air-con rooms, and a pleasant, if somewhat seedy, bar.

Municipal camp site. On Agtstelaan and Aub St just off Kaiser St, this costs N$7 per site, N$5 per person. Camp on the grass around the excellent ablutions, not on the gravel areas. There are washing machines for N$1 per load – this must be one of the country's best sites! Tel:(0631)3316.

Where to eat

Both the **Travel Inn** and **Canyon** hotels serve good food, though the former is definitely overpriced. Probably the best food, and certainly the liveliest bar, are at **Schutzen Haus** – about 400m south of the campsite on Agtstelaan. The restaurant has an intimate atmosphere and steaks for around N$19, while the adjacent bar has a good choice of beers and an L-shaped pool table!

What to see and do

If you've a spare half hour, the **museum**, near the campsite on the corner of Sewendelaan and Kaiser St, is worth a visit. Built in 1895, as a church – to replace the original one which was washed away by a flood – it now houses an interesting collection of local memorabilia, including a selection of early cameras. Open weekdays 8.00am to 12.00am, 4.00pm to 6.00pm. Saturdays 8.00am to 12.00am. If you're not going to the Kokerboom forest (see below) then don't miss the few small specimens in the museum garden!

Recently an **art and craft centre** has opened up on the corner of Sesdelaan and Pastorie St. Despite the number of plastic toys and athena prints there, it does have some good locally produced items and is worth a visit.

Getting organised

Keetmanshoop has few obvious attractions, though it's a pleasant town to wander around and a good one in which to visit banks and supermarkets. Entering the town on Kaiser St, from the B1 turn-off, the main shopping area is to be found one block to your right on Fenschel St. In many ways, this is really the main street of town, and here you will find the banks – Barclays, Standard, Trust and the Bank of Windhoek – as well as a couple of supermarkets and shops.

Your next stop should be the useful tourist information centre, opposite the main post office on the central square. This has all the standard maps and tourist guides and is run by a woman who has excellent local knowledge. For those interested in local history, the building itself – which also houses the Namib Air office – was built in 1910 and recently declared a national monument.

Kokerboom Trees

The Kokerboom *(Aloe Dichotoma)* occurs sporadically over a large area of southern Namibia, usually on steep, rocky slopes. Its English name, quiver tree, refers to its use by the Bushmen for making arrow quivers - the inside of a dead branch consists of only a light fibrous heart which is easily gouged out leaving a hollow tube.

The Kokerboom is specially adapted to survive in extremely arid conditions: the fibrous branches and a fibrous trunk are used by the tree for water storage, as are thick succulent leaves, whilst water loss through transpiration is reduced by waxy coatings on the tree's outside surfaces. Additionally, in common with most flora adapted for such harsh conditions, the kokerboom has a very slow growth rate.

Excursions from Keetmanshoop

The Kokerboom Forest

Although it doesn't seem like a forest, this is probably the thickest stand of trees in the region. Here *Kokerbooms*, which sport bright yellow flowers in June and July, cover the hillsides in their hundreds, creating, especially at dusk, a weird and fascinating landscape.

Getting there It's well signposted and about 14km north-west of the city, on the way to Koës. If hitching, walk out on the B1 about 2km from the town to the turning to Koës and try from there – it should be easy to get there and back in a day at most. Alternatively, the farmer there has recently set up a small campsite, with basic showers and toilets.

Brukkaros

Rising to 650m, the volcanic crater of Brukkaros towers over the expanse of the bare plains which surround it. In the 1930s a solar observation station was built here, on the crater's western side, to take advantage of the clear air in the region – and though the observatory is not used any longer the air seems as clear as ever!

Despite having no water or facilities at all, if you're well equipped, Brukkaros makes an unbeatable place at which to sleep out under the stars – and you will almost never meet another camper. The crater also provides some challenging scrambles around its rim, and the opportunity just to sit and watch dust-devils twist their way for miles around as the sun goes down.

Getting there From Keetmanshoop take the B1 north about 70km, then route 98 west towards Berseba. (Here there are a couple of shops, open in the morning and late afternoon, and one petrol pump.) About 500m before the town is a turn-off north, marked D3904, which eventually rises up to the crater rim, becoming a steep and rocky track. Negotiable all the way with a 4WD, we got to within 1.5km of the top with a 2WD and walked the rest. Don't even think about trying to hitch your way here – you'll have to walk from Berseba, and that is farther than it appears!

Karakul farm

Whilst travelling around this region, people are often surprised to see sheep on the dry pasture of local farms. These are in fact an unusual type of Central Asian sheep known as *karakuls*, which are well adapted to such shrivelled lands, although they do need a daily drink of water!

The original karakul were brought here in the early 1900s by a German fur trader, Paul Thorer, after an unsuccessful attempt to introduce them to the damper climes of Europe. Since then, they have been selectively bred and

their pelts marketed under the name of *swakara* (from 'SWA' and 'KARAkul')
sometimes known as Persian Lamb.

Prices for pelts depend upon their colour, pattern, and hair quality as well
as the fluctuating world market. The most sought after colour is white, which
occurs only on this sub-continent, followed by black, grey and brown, all of
which are farmed in the USSR and Afghanistan as well as here. The lambs
are slaughtered when only 36 hours old (the fur is said to be at its softest)
and subsequently the pelts are sold by auction in London.

If you wish to know more, then the head of the government research
station, Mr Kotze, will usually be happy to see visitors – though there's no
formal guided tour available as yet.

Getting there Take Kaiser St out of town, towards the airport, and then turn
left when the airport is in sight. Follow the signs to *Gellap ost karakul* farm.

FISH RIVER CANYON

At 161km long, up to 27km wide and almost 550m deep, it ranks second in
size only to Arizona's Grand Canyon, and must be one of Africa's least
known natural wonders. This means that you are very unlikely to have a visit
here spoiled by coach-loads of tourists, or leave with the feeling that the
place is over commercialised. In fact, if you visit outside the holidays, you
may not see anyone else here at all.

Formation The canyon probably started to form about 500 million years ago
when fractures in the earth's crust created a deep, steep-sided valley, which
was then further deepened by glacial erosion during the ice ages. Later faults
and more erosion added to the effect, creating canyons within each other,
until a mere 50 million years ago when the river started to cut its meandering
path along the floor of the valley.

Getting there

Car If you're driving from Keetmanshoop, take the B4 south-west for about
44km before turning off left onto the C12, then continue 77km before taking
a right and following the signs to *Vis Rivier* Canyon. This final part of the
approach is across undulating ridges and spectacular semi-desert plains,
leaving the visitor guessing until the very last moment about the spectacle
ahead.

Hitching This can be exceedingly difficult, although getting to the C12 turn-off
shouldn't be a problem. If your visit coincides with the start of the South
African school holidays, or if you're coming from the south, then it's worth
trying an alternative approach starting from the route 316 turn-off on the main
B1, about 260km south of Keetmanshoop and 37km north of the South
African border.

The Conservation Area

The whole area around the Fish River Canyon has been designated as a conservation area, and a few days spent here – perhaps staying at Hobas – can be very peaceful and pleasant indeed. Keep your eyes open for wildlife, as even on the most barren of plains you will find ostrich and springbok, whilst on the more rocky parts you may see baboon, klipspringer, or even Hartmann's mountain zebra.

After leaving the main observation point, which overlooks the spectacular Hell's Bend, it's worth taking the tracks to the Palm Springs viewpoint, and the opposite one to Hiker's Point, even if they are a bit rough – the views are different, and equally stunning.

Where to stay

The **Hobas Rest Camp** is situated in a slight valley, about 10km from the main viewing point. It has shady campsites with communal facilities, a kiosk for basic supplies, and a pool – and costs N$25 per site. It only opens from the second Friday in March to 31 October (the same as Ai-Ais), and though it is best booked at the DNC in Windhoek, you can often find a free site by just turning up. The camp is within the conservation area and whilst we were last there several flocks of ostriches picked their way across the very bare plain around the camp.

Whilst the camp is very pleasant, it is not luxurious and can get very hot, so if you need more comfort – stay at Ai-Ais (see below)!

Hiking

For the physically fit, the Fish River, so called for being Namibia's only river permanent enough to support fish, marks the route for a classic hike. Starting from Hiker's Point, on the north of the main view point, the trail descends to the river itself and follows it 86km to Ai-Ais in the south. It takes four or five days. En route there are hot springs, wind-carved rocks, and glimpses of the shy wildlife, as well as a lot of boulders to clamber over. Fishing is permitted, so you could bring a hook and line with you in addition to your normal kit and a food supply for about six days (neither Ai-Ais or Hobas has good hiking food).

The only way to organise this hike is by booking well in advance at the DNC in Windhoek, and you must have transport to and from the canyon for yourselves. It is best to camp at Hobas on the night before you start, and here you must show a certificate of medical fitness (obtained within the last 40 days) and sign an indemnity form. The hike costs N$25 per person, for a group with a minimum size of three. It has been possible for some hikers to join existing groups at fairly short notice, and thus avoid transport problems by sharing costs – talk to the DNC in Windhoek.

Beware: the day temperatures on the floor of the canyon are usually hot, even by Namibian standards, so don't carry any unnecessary weight, or try to rush through the deep sand at the bottom of the canyon – you are on your own, so enjoy it and take your time.

Ai-Ais Hot Springs

2WD. Entrance fees: N$5.00 for vehicles, N$5.00 per adult children
Ai-Ais, meaning 'burning water' in the local language, refers to the sulphurous springs which well up from the ground here. It's very much a spar, with an outdoor pool, private hot tubs, shop, filling station, and even a restaurant.

Getting there

Ai-Ais lies toward the southern end of the Fish River Canyon conservation area and is approached by taking the C10 west from the main B1, south of Grünau. Alternatively, route 324 from just east of Hobas provides some excellent, if distant, views as it meanders southwards parallel to the canyon. This then joins the C10 for the last few km before Ai-Ais which are steep, winding and quite amazing in their own right.

Where to stay

Accommodation is N$64 for a four-person hut with communal ablutions, N$105 for a four-person flat including bath, shower and toilet. Both include hotplates, fridges and bedding. Camping costs N$25 per site. Note that, as for Hobas, Ai-Ais is open only during the winter from the second Friday in March to the 31 October.

The Road to Lüderitz

Travelling from Keetmanshoop to Lüderitz is about 334km, mostly tar, and best done early in the day to avoid a powerful, late afternoon sun from the west. After leaving Keetmanshoop, look out for a mountain on the north known locally as *Kaiserkrone* – the Kaiser's crown – for its unusual conical shape. 106km west of Keetmanshoop you'll pass through **Goageb**, before hitting the gravel section of the road. This lasts for 102km until the **Aus** turn-off, after which the surface is again tar.

To the west of Aus, the road gradually descends onto an increasingly dry gravel plain, circled by distant jagged mountains. Look out around here for the world's only **desert horses** – a herd of around 170 horses which have adapted themselves to the Namib, using a waterhole at Garub as their only drinking point. Once, as we passed them in early March, they were all to be seen grazing photogenically on a thin, green sea of freshly sprouted grass.

Incongruously, half way across this parched plain, someone has created a **picnic site** – complete with tables, chairs, and nine well-watered trees for shade. The opportunity to stop at somewhere so spectacular definitely shouldn't be missed – this could be the continent's most solitary picnic site!

Continuing towards Lüderitz requires care, especially at night – watch for the marching dunes which constantly try to submerge the road in sand,

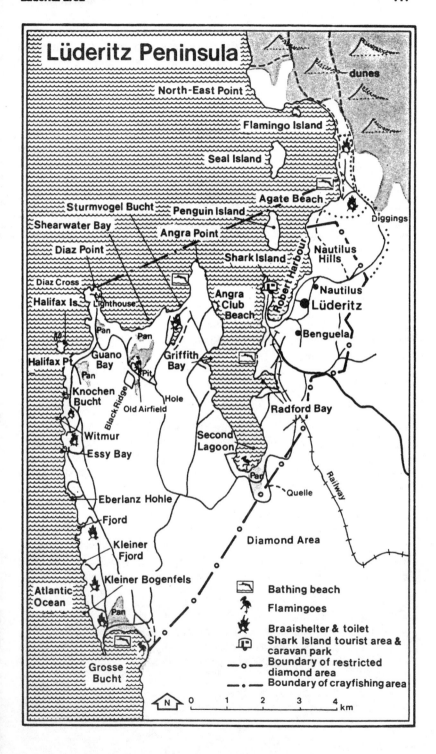

building up into dangerous ramps and mounds as they do so. **Take care**: these do not feel at all soft if you meet them at speed, so slow right down to about 20kph and also keep watch for the bulldozers which fight a constant battle to clear them from the road.

Goageb

This is a is a good place to stop and refuel. There's a simple shop and a small *category C* hotel, the **Konkiep**. Tel: (06362)3321. Here singles are N$20 and doubles N$35 – it's basic but clean!

Aus

Aus was the site of a South African prisoner of war camp during the First World War. It's now a fairly quiet town with one small (*category C*) hotel, the **Bahnhof**. Tel: (063332)44. Single rooms are N$50-N$60 and doubles N$100-N$120. Breakfast is N$15. Two of the ten rooms do have air-conditioning if the heat is really getting to you!

We have heard that the C13, south of Aus, is in navigable condition and can be followed through Rosh Pinah, along the banks of the Orange River, and to Noordoewer on the South African border. This would make a very interesting route indeed if you're going south, though its viability would need to be checked locally!

LÜDERITZ

Trapped between the desiccating sands of the Namib and the freezing waters of the *Benguela* current, Lüderitz struck us as a fascinating old German town, rich in history and full of character. These days its precarious prosperity is based mainly on the seasonal crayfish harvest and, increasingly, on tourists from both home and abroad. Because of its location, Lüderitz is not somewhere to 'drop in on' – you need to make a special journey to reach it – which perhaps gives rise to its sleepy atmosphere.

Unlike much of Namibia, its weather is moderated by the ocean and hence generally mild, though with the occasional morning fogs and strong breezes from August to January. If you do decide to visit, base yourself here for a few days – and don't forget your bathing suit for those bracing afternoon dips!

Getting there

Air   Air Namibia flies from Windhoek's Eros airport, via Swakopmund, to Lüderitz four times per week, for N$618 one-way. Unfortunately, there is no regular air service from Keetmanshoop to Lüderitz.

Train   There are overnight trains which leave Keetmanshoop at 1800 on Friday and 1400 on Sunday, and arrive at 2230 and 1830 respectively. From

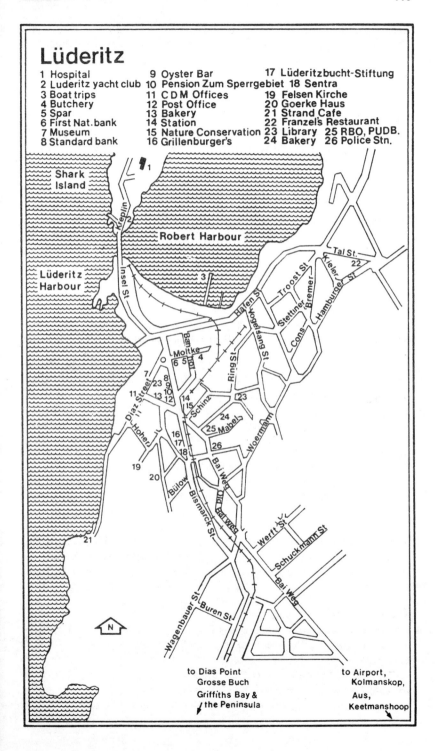

Lüderitz

1 Hospital
2 Luderitz yacht club
3 Boat trips
4 Butchery
5 Spar
6 First Nat.bank
7 Museum
8 Standard bank
9 Oyster Bar
10 Pension Zum Sperrgebiet
11 C D M Offices
12 Post Office
13 Bakery
14 Station
15 Nature Conservation
16 Grillenburger's
17 Lüderitzbucht-Stiftung
18 Sentra
19 Felsen Kirche
20 Goerke Haus
21 Strand Cafe
22 Franzel's Restaurant
23 Library   25 RBO, PUDB.
24 Bakery   26 Police Stn.

Lüderitz to Keetmanshoop the return journeys leave at 0600 on Saturday and 1900 on Sunday, and also take four and a half hours to return. The cost is N$32, and only third class accommodation seems to be available.

Car   See *The road to Lüderitz* section above.

Hitching is fairly easy both into and out of the town, but start as early in the morning as you can. It should be fine to accept lifts which only go as far as Goageb or Aus – as unless it is very late in the day you will probably pick up another, and it is not a problem to stay in either town.

Where to stay

Category B
Bay View Hotel. PO Box 100. Tel: (06331)2288. Near the bottom of Bay road (*Bai weg*). The town's most expensive hotel. It has a small pool and pleasant, well-kept rooms arranged around a courtyard. Like the Kapps, it's owned by the Lüderitz family! Singles N$116, doubles N$170, full breakfast N$9.

Kapps Hotel. PO Box 100. Tel: (06331)2701. Also found on Bay road, this is the oldest of Lüderitz's hotels – and gives that impression too! Singles N$80 without bath, N$100 with, doubles N$140, full breakfast N$10.

Zum Sperrgebiet Hotel. PO Box 373. Tel: (06331)2856. Despite its unimpressive front on Bismark St, Zum's clean and spacious rooms made this our favourite hotel. Shared facilities: singles N$77, doubles N$120. *En suite* facilities: singles N$88, doubles N$140, triples N$170, four-beds N$200. An excellent breakfast costs N$8.80, and you don't need to be a resident.

Category C
Strand Bungalows. These are small holiday chalets on a hillside behind the Strand Cafe (see map) and right above the town's only real bathing spot. They are individually priced, depending on whether or not they have cookers, fridges, and *en suite* facilities. Doubles N$30, four-beds N$50-N$140.

Shark Island Campsite. A true island until 1908, this spit of land is now just a picturesque, if windblown, campsite. Costs N$10 per site. *Take care*: It's worth pitching your tent firmly, to withstand heavy breezes!

Where to eat

Lüderitz is definitely the place to eat if you're into crayfish in a big way. It won't be cheap (unless you caught it yourself), but at least here it is guaranteed to be fresh and will probably be well prepared.

The **Kapps** and **Bay View** Hotels do have restaurants, although they often won't serve non-residents without prior notice.

Instead try the **Strand Cafe**, open all day for snacks and from 7.30pm to

10pm as a restaurant – it's lively and a good meeting point, though not the place for a romantic meal à *deux*. Crayfish N$32 (for a good portion), steaks N$19, wine N$11.

Franzels restaurant, on Tal St, can be recommended for authentic German food as well as seafood. A quieter atmosphere than the Strand.

What to see and do

The main attraction in the town itself is the large number of magnificent old buildings, built mostly in the German Imperial and Art Nouveau styles. A **walking tour** is an excellent way to spend an afternoon, and you could also visit the small **museum**, open on Tuesdays, Thursdays, and Saturdays from 4pm to 6pm. To this end there are walking guides available containing details of the local history and points of interest – ask at the museum or the DNC offices on Schinz St. Do include a wander up **Nautilus hill**, just above the town, which makes a pleasant detour with some great views.

From the harbour, the yachts *Sagitta* and *Sedina* run trips lasting a few hours to **Diaz Point** and **Halifax Island** (a jackass penguin colony). Costs N$25 and can be booked at the agent next to Hotel Zum, or directly with the boats in the harbour. On a hot day these are excellent, and the best (only!) way to get a good look at the penguins.

Visits to the **crayfish processing plants** can be arranged during the season between November and April, as can tours of the **karakul carpet weaving factory**, or the **oyster farm**, all year around. Enquire of the travel agents in town for arrangements and bear in mind that they'll probably be fairly informal affairs.

Finally, no visit would be complete without a dip in the Southern Atlantic, but beware – it's cold!

Excursions from Lüderitz

Agate beach

A beautiful and unusual beach of almost black sand, sprinkled with tiny shining fragments of mica. It may not be white coral sand, but it's pleasant and quiet to lie on or wander along beachcombing – just don't go expecting to find too many agates! There's a good road here – signposted from the corner of Tal and Hamburger St.

Kolmanskop

This boom-town, 9km east of Lüderitz, was abandoned over 30 years ago, and is now preserved to give a fascinating insight into the life of a diamond mining community during the early part of the century. Parts of it, like the old casino, have been specially restored, and there's a fascinating guide on duty who remembers it all as it was at its peak.

With the desert dunes fast encroaching on many buildings, there's a real ghost-town feeling about the place and it's certainly worth visiting on your way out of Lüderitz. To do that, however, you must first obtain a permit from the CDM (Consolidated Diamond Mines of South Africa) offices on Diaz St. These cost N$3 and you won't be admitted without one, so stop at the CDM before you leave Lüderitz!

The Lüderitz peninsula

South-west of the town lies the Lüderitz peninsula, surrounded by sea on three sides and yet a desert within. Around its coast are many beaches; some rocky, one or two sandy, all deserted and worth exploring if you've a car. (Whilst driving 2WD cars here, be careful not to follow the tracks across soft sand made by 4WD vehicles – otherwise, like a group we helped, you'll need one to tow you out!). To get there simply take Lüderitz St – the continuation of Bismark St – south, keeping the railway on your left.

Stopping places

Griffith bay gives excellent views of the town on its barren coastline, as well as some crystal clear rock pools to dabble in.

Diaz point, reached by a short wooden bridge, has a marble cross commemorating Bartholomeu Diaz, the first European to enter the bay, who sheltered here in the late 14th Century and called the bay, rather unimaginatively, *Angra Pequena* or 'little bay'.

Going south of Diaz point, into the area where you can legally collect crayfish, there's a reminder of the coast's forbidding nature in the form of a grave marked: 'George Pond of London, died here of hunger and thirst 1906.'

Following the road further south along the peninsula, Halifax Island comes into view with its jackass penguin and cormorant colonies. Further still, *Eberlanz Höhle* is a cave cut deeply into the rock about ten minutes walk from the road. Just keep to the left of the pinnacle before following the path down.

Frequent turn-offs for fishing spots and *braii* sites are passed as you continue until Grosse Bucht is reached, a long sandy bay good for crayfishing. From here you can cut across the neck of the peninsula and back to Lüderitz.

Warning   The second lagoon is noted for having stranded motorists on it, as well as flamingos, so don't try to drive across it!

Asab

This small group of buildings 124km north of Keetmanshoop, and 97km south of Mariental is notable mainly for being just to the west of what used to be one of the country's most unusual landmarks – the 'Finger of God.' The pleasant little **Asab Hotel** has singles for N$40-N$60, doubles for N$60-N$80 and breakfast at N$6.50.

Crayfish or Lobster?

The terms *crayfish* and *lobster* are often incorrectly used by many people — including most restaurant managers! Crayfish and lobsters are different animals both in their appearance and habitat, though they do both belong to the crustacean order *decapod*. While lobsters are marine animals, nearly all crayfish species live in freshwater.

Crayfish are normally found in freshwater streams and lakes. They spend the day concealed under rocks or logs, and come out at night to feed on insect larvae, worms and snails — some even eat vegetation. They are characterised by: a jointed head and thorax and a segmented body; a sharp snout, with eyes on movable stalks; and five pairs of legs, of which the front are a powerful pair of claws. They can live for up to 20 years, and the largest species — from Tasmania — can weigh up to 3.5kg.

Lobsters can be split up into four families: true lobsters; spiny lobsters (or 'sea crayfish' — hence the confusion); slipper or shovel lobsters; and deep-sea lobsters. All are marine and *benthic* (bottom-dwelling), feeding mainly by scavenging for dead animals, but also taking live fish and seaweed. Of these four families, only the true and spiny families are of commercial importance.

True lobsters are distinguished by having claws on their first three pairs of legs, with the first pair being larger and uneven in size. Spiny lobsters do not have such large claws, but have very spiny bodies instead for protection. The rock lobster, *Jacks lanandei*, is a spiny lobster and accounts for most of the 'crayfish' that gets eaten in Namibian restaurants.

Lobster fishing is an important industry in Namibia (especially in Lüderitz) and there are strict legal controls to prevent overfishing. It's illegal to catch animals with a carapace length of below 650mm — ie before they are about 7 years old — and fishing is only permitted within season — from 1st November to 30th April.

The current lobstering fleet is composed of about 20 motherships, which each carrying eight row boats. A further half dozen craft ferry between the shorebound factories and the fishing vessels. The fleet operates along the Namibian coast, from the Orange River to the southern border of the Namib-Naukluft Park (around 100 miles north of Lüderitz) and the industry as a whole employs over 1000 people. Almost all of the catch is processed into frozen lobster products, of which 97% are sold to Japan; the rest — as lobster tails — are sold to the USA.

Mukorob, or the **Finger of God** as it was more widely known, was a huge rock pinnacle which had resisted erosion for centuries – balancing some 34m above the surrounding plain, held by only a narrow neck of rock. Unfortunately it collapsed around the 8th December 1988, and now can be seen standing only on local postcards!

The cause of its fall has been the object of intense speculation, especially as local legends linked it with divine approval. At first, it was claimed as evidence that God was displeased with contemporary developments in the Independence process, while later it was suggested that right-wing political extremists might have been to blame – rather than divine intervention!

Subsequent theories have linked it with seismic activity and, in particular, the shock waves from the Armenian earthquake – which occurred on the 7th December at 11.41 local time.

MARIENTAL

Though a pleasant and very central town, there's remarkably little to do here. Most visitors stopping in this region shop here and then head out to Hardap, 20km north-west of the town (see below).

The town itself is just to the east of the main B1, and split into two by a railway running parallel to the road. On the western side is an excellent Central Bottle Stall, a good Spar supermarket, a Standard Bank, a Bank of Windhoek, both of the town's hotels, and most of its garages.

The First National Bank is immediately on the other side, while to reach the Post Office you must cross the railway, take a left along Orieboom St, then bend right onto Ernst Stumpfeweg, and another left at the Top Store.

Where to stay

There's no official campsite – most visitors stay at Hardap. In case of necessity there are two hotels, very different in character, within a few yards of each other just north of the Spar on the town's main street.

Category B
Mariental Hotel PO Box 671. Tel: (0661)856. Lively bar, quiet TV lounge, spotless rooms, very friendly and helpful staff – though often booked up! Singles N$120 (some with facilities, others without), doubles N$160, breakfast N$8.80.

Category C
Sandberg Hotel PO Box 12. Tel: (0661)2291. A seedy and run down place, with a very unhelpful owner and rooms priced individually. Singles range from N$100, doubles from N$140. We found the bar to be well worth avoiding and before even ordering a drink we were hassled – generally a rarity in Namibia!

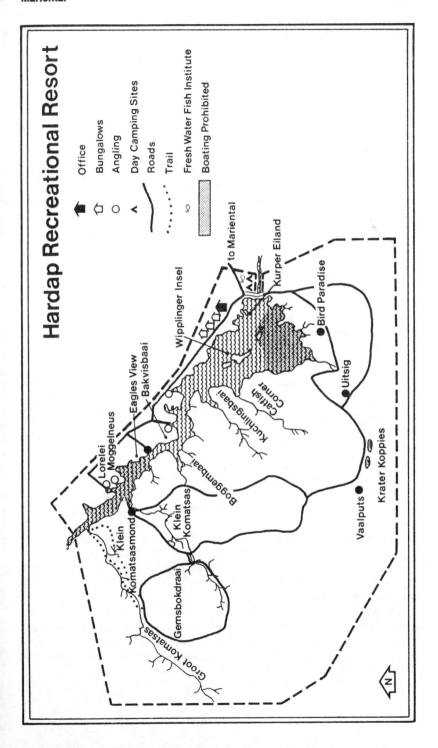

Hardap Recreational Resort

2WD. Entrance fees: N$5 per person and N$5 per car (one-off charge).

254km south of Windhoek and 24km from Mariental, lies Namibia's largest man-made lake. It's a popular place for local watersports, and a good place to stop for a night or two.

Where to stay

The self-contained bungalows here are well maintained and good value, while the camping sites can be exposed and windy! 5-bed bungalow N$104, 2-bed bungalow N$50, 2-bed room N$30, camping N$25 per site. Accommodation should be booked in advance at the DNC in Windhoek, but out of season you're quite likely to find space available.

Amenities

There is a shop which stocks basic foods, alcohol, gifts and postcards; a marvellously large pool with a small kiosk adjacent for soft drinks; a bar which, though it is small and shuts at 9.30pm, is good when open; and a restaurant which is inexpensive (N$15 for a main course) but uninspiring. Fish is your best bet here, and with it check out the extensive range of *Simonsig* estate wines.

What to see and do

A large section on the southern side has been designated as a **game park**, with ostrich, kudu, mountain zebra, gemsbok and even eland as the highlights. There are two walking trails through the area (of 9 and 15km), which are best done early in the morning to escape the heat, and over 80km of game drives.

For ornithologists, **the lake** is an important refuge for many water birds, including ospreys, fish eagles, and several species of heron. On an island amid the lake is one of the country's largest breeding colonies of great white pelicans – binoculars are invaluable!

Near Hardap's entrance is the **Freshwater Fish Institute**, which is at the centre of efforts to preserve Namibia's (understandably!) few indigenous species of fish. Again, there's no 'tourist tour' but if you're interested then call by. We found the staff to be enthusiastic and informative, and their breeding programme fascinating.

For less dedicated fish-watchers, the reception office has an interesting small aquarium, exhibiting various Namibian fish in several large, well-kept tanks, as well as a very useful noticeboard displaying, amongst other things, the **latest road information**. These notices should not be missed, especially if you're heading off the tar during the rainy season!

Maltahöhe

This small town is conveniently placed off the main north-south route, close to Duwisib Castle, the Namib-Naukluft National Park, Sossusvlei and Sesriem (see Chapter 10). There is a fairly comprehensive general store and fuel available.

Where to stay
Category C

Maltahöhe Hotel PO Box 20. Tel: (06632) 13. Run by Mr von Fischer, this has singles for N$65, doubles for N$95, and breakfast at N$7.50. In the evening, there is even a restaurant available. Mr von Fischer will take parties out on trips to Sossusvlei in his Land Rover – a possible way of visiting the Namib-Naukluft area for those without vehicles.

Duwisib Castle

A marvellous castle, built of sandstone and containing some fascinating German furnishings and antiques. Originally constructed for Captain von Wolff around 1909, it is currently owned by the DNC and undergoing some changes – so see them before you visit, to check that it's open.

Getting there   It's situated about 81km south-west of Maltahöhe. To reach it, take the C14 south for 38km and then turn a right onto the D824. 12km later, turn left onto the D831, then 16km later right onto the D826. After about 15km the entrance gate is on your right. It can be conveniently approached via the D826 direct from Sesriem.

Kalkrand

A small town 75km north of Mariental, on the B1 to Windhoek. There's a First National Bank on Maltahöhe Rd, but it only opens on Tuesday, Thursday, and Saturday from 9.30am until noon. The town has only one hotel, called – surprisingly – the **Kalkrand Hotel** PO Box 5. Tel: (06672)29. (*Category C*) It is reasonably clean and the manager will cook food on request, even if there's no menu! Singles N$55-N$60, doubles N$75-N$80.

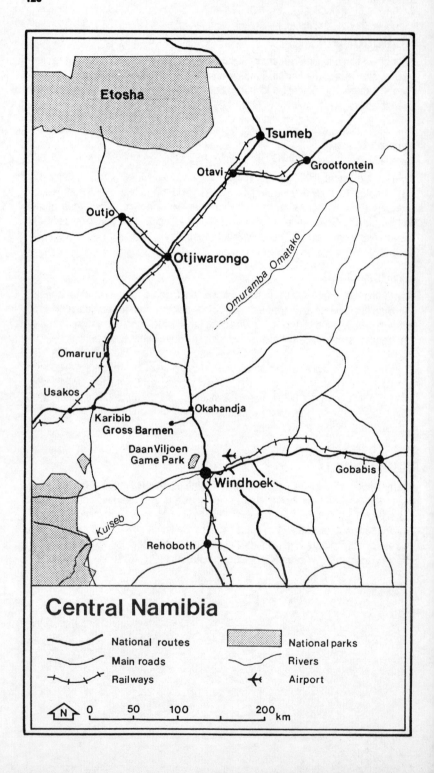

Central Namibia

Etosha · Tsumeb · Otavi · Grootfontein · Outjo · Otjiwarongo · Omuramba Omatako · Omaruru · Usakos · Karibib · Gross Barmen · Okahandja · Daan Viljoen Game Park · Kuiseb · Windhoek · Gobabis · Rehoboth

National routes	National parks
Main roads	Rivers
Railways	Airport

N   0   50   100   200 km

Chapter 10

Central Namibia

Despite Windhoek's dominance of the country's central region, remember that it only occupies a small area. The city doesn't sprawl for miles. Drive just 10km in any direction and you will be on an open highway — whichever direction you choose. Here lies this area's appeal for me, as some of the quieter roads are truly breath-taking.

The C26 route to Swakopmund takes a good six hours to drive — being very steep and winding in places — but the scenery is continually spectacular from the mountain views of the Gamsberg Pass to the deep fissures of the Kuiseb Canyon. The roads leading to Solitaire and the Naukluft mountains are attractions in their own right, while the Bosua Pass on the C28 from Windhoek to Swakopmund is beautiful but very steep. Whichever routes take — allow plenty of time for safety's sake and to appreciate them all more.

Windhoek has been covered in Chapter 9, and the other towns and places of interest are arranged below, from south to north.

Rehoboth

Just north of the Tropic of Capricorn and south of Windhoek, Rehoboth is the centre of the country's Baster community (see Chapter 2, pages 15-16).

Where to stay

Category C
The Rio Monte PO Box 3097. Tel: (06272)161. This is the only hotel in the centre of town with singles for N$35 and doubles for N$40. It's above a noisy bar and the rooms are exceedingly bare.
Reho Spa Well signposted on the south-west side of town. There's a memorable jacuzzi of thermal spring water the size of a swimming pool as well as an outdoor pool and some very good bungalow accommodation. Bungalows cost N$58 for 4-beds, N$70 for 5-beds and N$104 for 6-beds — all have fridges, cookers etc. The place can be marvellously empty if you avoid the weekends and holidays.

What to see and do

Museum   Located just behind the post office. It's small, but has an excellent section on bank notes (!) as well as some good local history exhibits on the origins of the Baster community.

Oanab Dam

A few kilometres to the west of Rehoboth, this is one of the country's newest dams. There is a display at the lookout point showing 'before' and 'after' photos of the dam's construction, as well as some of the technical drawings used. It's an amazing thought that such a small body of water as this is has a catchment area of about 2700 square kilometres.

Gobabis

This busy town, standing at the centre of an important cattle farming area on the western edges of the Kalahari, forms Namibia's gateway into Botswana via the Buitepos border post. It's an ideal place to use the banks, fill up fuel or get supplies before heading east towards Ghanzi, where most goods aren't so easily available.

Where to stay and eat

Category C
There are two hotels in town, the **Central** (PO Box 233. Tel: (0681) 2094/5 Fax: (0681) 2092) and the **Gobabis** (PO Box 474. Tel: (0681) 2568/3068 Fax: (0681) 2703). Both charge N$70-N$80 for a single and N$100-N$110 a double. The Central, which is marginally better includes morning coffee in the price, while breakfast at either is around N$12.

For snacks during the day there is a great little cafe, complete with menu in German, at the back of the general store — just to the right of the Municipal Offices on the main street.

Crossing the border into Botswana

Car   Bear in mind that while the Namibian road to Buitepos is in reasonable condition, the road on the other side of the border is exceedingly sandy and rutted. It will usually require at least a high-clearance vehicle and preferably a 4WD — so do not attempt to cross into Botswana this way in a normal saloon car without getting reliable advice first.

Hitching   This is the best town and route into Botswana, with many trucks passing through. try to get a lift at least as far as the border post — and ignore vehicles which aren't 4WD as they won't be going much past it. Don't forget to carry plenty of food and water!

Okahandja

This small town is 71km north of Windhoek. It has some good shops, a couple of banks, 24-hour fuel, an excellent open market for curios and quite a lot of history — if you've the time to stop.

History Okahandja is the administrative centre for the Herero people, despite being considerably south-west of their traditional land. The area was first reached by missionaries in the late 1820s, but it wasn't until 1849 that the first of them, Friedrich Kolbe, settled here. He remained for less than a year, driven away by the attacks of the Namas, under Jonker Afrikaner. He fled with good reason as, on 23 August of the following year, about 700 men, women and children were killed by the Namas at the aptly named Blood Hill. It is said that after the massacre, the women's arms and legs were chopped off in order to take their copper bangles.

The small *kopje* of Blood Hill can be seen just to the east of the main Windhoek-Swakopmund road, while Jonker Afrikaner lies peacefully in his grave, next to several Herero chiefs, opposite the church on Kerk Str. The most recent burial here was Chief Hosea Kutako — after his assassination in 1978. He was the Democratic Turnhalle Alliance's first president, and one of the first to petition the United Nations for Namibian independence.

Where to stay and eat

Category C
Okahandja Hotel PO Box 770. Tel: (06221) 3024. Situated on Hoof Str, this is the town's only hotel, and it offers fairly simple singles for N$45-N$70 and doubles for N$70-N$100, breakfast not included. Its restaurant is rather like a cafe though, serving toasties for N$5, burgers N$10, and steaks N$22.

As an alternative venue for simple meals, try the cafe on the corner of Franck Waldo and Ossmann Weg.

What to do

The town's small **information centre** is on Hoof Str, south of its corner with Van Riebeck Road. This has the usual glossy brochures and an interesting, if brief, leaflet to guide you around the town's historical sites.

By the side of the railway line, on Voortrekker Str, is a large open-air curio market. This is one of the best in the country, and the sculptors here specialise in large wooden carvings. These included some beautiful thin, wooden giraffes (a 7-foot high one costs N$350), huge "tribal" heads, cute flexible snakes, and wide selections of more ordinary carved hippos and bowls. About 1km out of the city, on the eastern side of the road to Otjiwarongo, is the city's small zoo park.

If you need a bank then there is a branch of Standard Bank on Main Str, and the Post Office is almost opposite the town's pharmacy on Hoof Str. The local grocery shops are known for having some of the best fresh vegetables available in the country.

Gross Barmen Hot Springs

2WD. Entrance fees: N$5 per person and N$5 for a car.

This popular resort for locals has a restaurant, tennis courts, mineral baths and several swimming pools fed by the hot thermal springs. It is built around a dam about 25km south-west of Okahandja, and there is a filling station here if you need to refuel.

Where to stay

A two-bed bungalow is N$46, and a camping is N$20 per site. Booking is done through the DNC in Windhoek, and day visitors must phone (06221) 2091 in advance, to arrange their visits.

Von Bach Recreational Resort

2WD. Entrance fees: N$5 per person and N$5 for a car.

This dam supplies the majority of the capital's water, and has a nature reserve around it. The environment is very hilly, and the game includes the expected kudu, baboon and leopard, as well as zebra, springbok and even eland. However, with only one road through the park they are all very difficult to spot. Don't come here for the game, but if you are camping (N$20 per site) then it is a nice quiet place to stay for a night. There are also two-bed huts available (N$35 per night), which are basic: no bedding is supplied and you must use the communal ablution blocks.

Karibib

For nearly 90 years, this small town on the railway line from Windhoek to Swakopmund has been known for the very hard, high quality marble which is quarried nearby. Now it could be set to expand rapidly as gold has been found on a nearby farm.

What to see and do

On the main street there's a Namib **information centre** which doubles as a curio shop, with a large selection of carvings and gems. If you have time to kill here, there are several historic buildings dating from the early 1900s which have changed little since then, so ask for details.

Where to stay and eat

Category C

Hotel Erongoblick PO Box 67 Tel: (062252) 9. Situated on Park Str, the quality of the rooms varies considerably here. Singles are from N$45-80, and doubles N$80-150, and there is a small restaurant and a pool to cool off in. Note that none of the rooms have telephones.

Hotel Stroblhof PO Box 164 Tel: (062252) 81 Fax: (062252) 240. This is the better, and the more expensive, of the town's two hotels with singles at N\$65-72 and doubles for N\$110-130. Situated on the east side of town, this comfortable hotel has a simple restaurant, a pool and its rooms have telephones and air-conditioning.

Nearby Guest farms

Tsaobis-Leopard Nature Park PO Box 143 Tel: (062252) 1304. Fax: (062252) 1034. This is a small private game reserve in beautifully hilly country west of the C32, just south of the Swakop River. The animals here include cheetah, wild dog, caracal, zebra and gemsbok — most of which are in large enclosures. They can be seen by either walking around, or taking a pre-arranged tour. This is a good game ranch for hiking, as there are several trails, and two-way radios are available for safety. Self-catering bungalows cost N\$85-N\$125 for two people, N\$105-N\$145 for three and N\$125-N\$165 for four. Alternatively food and accommodation can be supplied for N\$150-N\$180 per person, but this must be arranged well in advance. Note that there is neither fuel nor supplies here.

Usakos

This small town used to be the centre of the country's railway industry, though now it's little more than a stop on the line, with banks and fuel to tempt those who might pass right through. If you linger here then the old station is worth a brief look, and the Namib information office is useful if you're planning to do much exploration of the local area.

Where to stay and eat

Category C
The Usakos Hotel PO Box 129. Tel: (062242) 259. This is the only place in town, with singles for N\$50-N\$64, doubles N\$100-N\$I20. It's plain, but clean and family run. The food is simple, a good lunch costs around N\$15.

If you've no transport then you can arrange trips from here with the owner to **Spitzkoppe** (see Chapter 14, page 186) which can be visited in a day or even further afield — they often suggest overnight stops at the Desert Lodge (a guest farm).

Ameib rock paintings

This guest farm has some excellent rock paintings, many in Phillip's Cave which was made famous by Abbé Breuil's book of the same name (see *Bibliography*). There are also unusual rock formations, like *the Bull's Party* — a group of large rounded boulders which look like a collection of bulls talking together. Ameib Ranch (Tel: (062242) 1111, Fax: (061) 35742) offers good accommodation, at N\$220 per person full board, and camping at N\$25 per person.

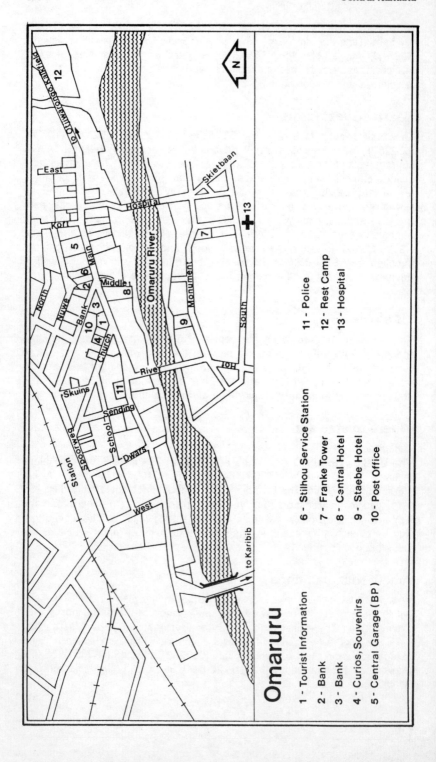

Omaruru

1 - Tourist Information
2 - Bank
3 - Bank
4 - Curios, Souvenirs
5 - Central Garage (BP)

6 - Stilhou Service Station
7 - Franke Tower
8 - Central Hotel
9 - Staebe Hotel
10 - Post Office

11 - Police
12 - Rest Camp
13 - Hospital

Omaruru

This green and picturesque town is set astride the river of the same name and surrounded by an area full of sculptured rocks and bushman paintings.

Where to Stay

Category C

Hotel Steabe PO Box 92. Tel: (062232) 35, Fax: (062232) 339. The hotel, situated on Monument Street to the south of the river, is well furnished and almost cosy, though with a distinct German atmosphere. Singles are N$105, doubles N$145, including breakfast.

The Central Hotel PO Box 29. Tel: (062232) 30. Located on the other side of the river, on the main street, this smaller hotel is less well furnished with singles for N$72 and doubles N$95. Breakfast is N$14 extra per person.

Where to eat

Both hotels have restaurants — the only ones in town — and will cook to order, despite not having menus! Expect to pay around N$12 for an omelette, N$20 for steak. Better still, if you are passing through, there's a good cafe/bakery opposite the shell garage on the main street.

What to see and do

There's a reasonable Namib information office opposite the Central Hotel on Main St, and the mediocre curio shop next to the post office is worth a visit. Otherwise the town's only attraction is **Franke Tower**. This is a monument to Captain Victor Franke who is said to have heroically relieved the garrison here, after they were besieged by the Herero in 1904. The achievement earned him Germany's highest military honour and this monument — built by grateful German settlers in 1908. It's normally locked, but to climb up it just ask at either hotel for a set of keys.

One of the largest collections of rock paintings in the country, and some interesting artefacts, is situated on the **Anibib Guest Farm**, which is 50km west of Omaruru, (almost in Damaraland) just off the D2315. Their guided tours for day visitors make a good introduction to bushman art. Tel: (62232) 1711 to make arrangements for a visit.

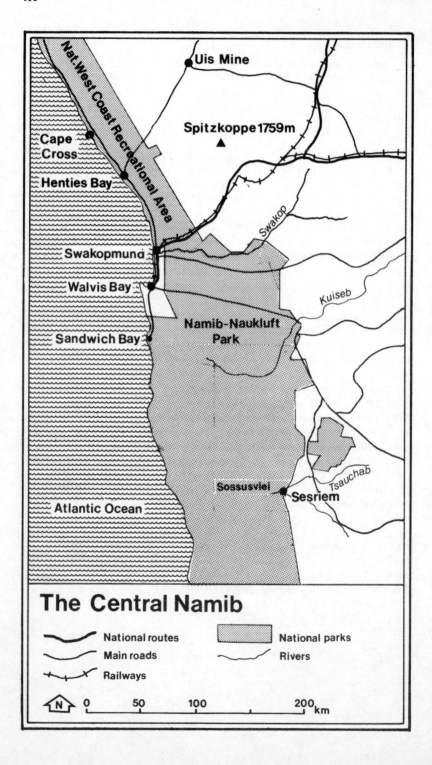

The Central Namib

National routes
Main roads
Railways
National parks
Rivers

N   0   50   100   200 km

Chapter 11

The Central Namib

This region encompasses the heart of the Namib Desert, the Namib-Naukluft Desert Park, and the two main coastal towns, Swakopmund and Walvis Bay. To visit the desert you need to be fairly self-sufficient, at least in terms of transport, while Swakopmund – as a major centre for local tourism – is easy to reach by bus or rail and is well prepared for visitors.

The Namib Desert stretches in a narrow band, seldom more than about 200km wide, along the whole coast of Namibia and into both South Africa and Angola. Its western border is the Atlantic and its eastern border, though not so clearly defined, is usually taken at the line of 100mm rainfall – which generally occurs at around 1,000m on the escarpment. Much of it is effectively protected, either within one of the diamond concession areas, one of the parks, or simply by being inaccessible for all practical purposes.

The Namib-Naukluft Park is one of the largest protected areas in Africa and gives us, as visitors, our best chance actually to spend time in the desert, camp, and get to know a little about it – without facing the difficulties of a long and potentially hazardous trip into one of its more remote corners. Here, where the band of desert is at its widest, there is the opportunity to explore many different desert environments and their associated ecosystems, occurring within short distances of each other.

The two towns in this area, Swakopmund and Walvis Bay, are close together and form a busy nucleus for this largely unpopulated section of the country. Outside these, there are no hotel facilities at all – so if you wish to explore, you must be able to take advantage of the excellent camping facilities provided throughout the region.

Getting around the region

Both Swakopmund and Walvis Bay are linked into the air, rail and coach networks, with three bus and three train services to and from Windhoek every week (see *In Namibia*, Chapter 7, page 84).

Hitching is quite easy between the main centres, and even to some of the less obvious places provided that you go fully self-sufficient with the

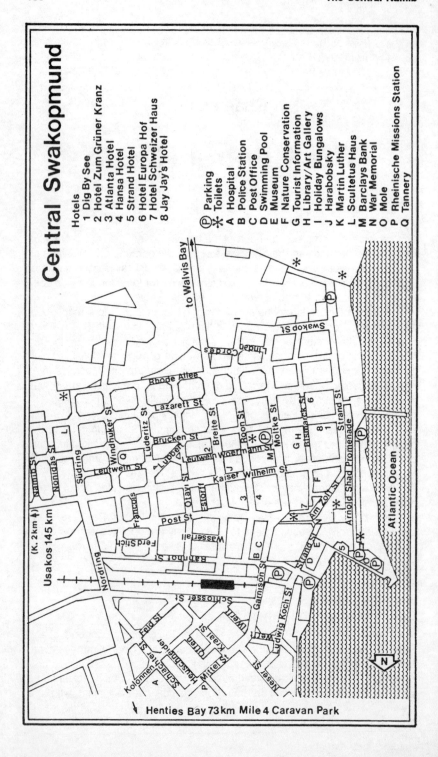

Central Swakopmund

Hotels
1 Dig By See
2 Hotel Zum Grüner Kranz
3 Atlanta Hotel
4 Hansa Hotel
5 Strand Hotel
6 Hotel Europa Hof
7 Hotel Schweizer Haus
8 Jay Jay's Hotel

Ⓟ Parking
✳ Toilets
A Hospital
B Police Station
C Post Office
D Swimming Pool
E Museum
F Nature Conservation
G Tourist Information
H Library/Art Gallery
I Holiday Bungalows
J Harabobsky
K Martin Luther
L Scultetus Haus
M Barclays Bank
N War Memorial
O Mole
P Rheinische Missions Station
Q Tannery

to Walvis Bay

Swakop St
Linden
Cordes St
Rhode Allee
Lazarett St
Windhuker St
Lüderitz St
Brucken St
Breite St
Boon St
Bismarck St
Strand St
Leutwein St
Leutwein St
Woermann St
Molke St
Kaiser Wilhelm St
Francois
Post St
Wasserfall
Ferd Stich
Bahnhof St
Olav
Am Zoll St
Arnold Shad Promenade
Atlantic Ocean
Nonidas St
Nama St
Südring
Nordring
Garnison St
Schlosser St
Ludwig Koch St
Werft
Kraal St
Mittel St
Neser St
Kolonnen St
Schlachter St
Feld St
Hensamschneider St
Quer St

(K. 2 km ↓)
Usakos 145 km

N

↓ Henties Bay 73 km Mile 4 Caravan Park

necessities of life. Often you'll get really helpful lifts visiting the very places that you aimed at, but sometimes you'll sit by a road junction for days and you must be prepared for this. There are very few shops in this area – and none in the National Park – so don't expect to buy food along the way.

SWAKOPMUND

Often considered to be Namibia's only real 'holiday resort', this old German town stands by the mouth of the usually dry Swakop River, and spreads out from the shore onto the flat desert plain which surrounds it. Climatically more temperate than the interior, the palm-lined streets, immaculate old buildings and well-kept gardens give it a feel all of its own, making a pleasant oasis in which to spend a few days.

Unlike much of Namibia, Swakopmund is used to visitors and has a good choice of places to stay, eat, and even tours into the desert itself.

History

In 1884, the whole of present-day Namibia was declared a protectorate of Germany, whilst the region's only large natural harbour, Walvis Bay, remained under British control. Thus, in order to develop their interests in the area, the German authorities decided to make their own harbour on the northern banks of the Swakop River, and in 1892 two beacons were planted – where the Mole is today – to mark the spot (see page 142).

Following this, there were several largely unsuccessful attempts to develop landing facilities. A quay was built, although it subsequently silted up, followed by a wooden, and later an iron, jetty. Finally in 1915, German control of the country was surrendered to South Africa and all ocean trading returned to Walvis Bay. During the South African administration of Namibia before Independence, Swakopmund remained undeveloped as an alternative port to Walvis Bay, which remained part of South Africa until February 1994.

Where to stay
Category A

Hansa Hotel PO Box 44. Tel: (0641)311. Centrally positioned on Roon St, beautifully furnished and somewhat colonial in atmosphere, this is the town's top hotel. Singles N$210, doubles N$320, including breakfast. Its restaurant is of similar calibre with fresh oysters at N$15 for half a dozen!

Strand Hotel PO Box 20. Tel: (0641)315. With an excellent sea-front location, right next to the Mole, this hotel can be quite expensive. Singles are about N$180, doubles N$230, including breakfast. Some have a balcony, some don't. The restaurant has fish dishes for around N$25 and steaks for N$30, though there's a popular coffee shop overlooking the beach which is a ideal for writing postcards or just relaxing in the sea breeze.

Hotel Europa Hof PO Box 1333. Tel: (0641)5061. Situated to the south of Bismark St, and by far the most modern of the hotels. Singles for N$110, doubles for N$170, including breakfast. Its posh restaurant has a good selection of seafood, with a good meal of prawns for N$32.

Category B
Hotel-Pension Prinzessin-Rupprecht-Heim PO Box 124. Tel: (0641)2231. This old hospital on Lazarett St, just west of Bismark St, has recently been refurbished and can be strongly recommended for its spacious and well-furnished rooms. Singles are around N$50, doubles N$80, including breakfast. It has no menu as yet, but snacks can be arranged.

Hotel-Pension Schweizer Haus PO Box 445. Tel: (0641)331. A comfortable hotel, overlooking the sea, to the north of Bismark St, this has a distinctly German feel to it and an exceedingly trendy cafe below known as Cafe Anton. Singles are N$40-85, doubles N$140, including breakfast.

Hotel Grüner Kranz PO Box 211. Tel: (0641)2039. On the north side of Breite St, this could be the place for you if you're missing the bright lights! Each room has a television and there are three videos shown nightly, as well as a lively music bar on the first floor. The rooms are reasonable value with singles at N$90 and doubles for N$140, including breakfast. The restaurant is fairly plain with steaks for N$20-N$25.

Category C
Hotel Jay Jay's PO Box 835. Tel: (0641)2909. Found at the western end of Brücken St, Namibian hotels don't come any cheaper than this. It's basic but very good value – singles N$16-25, doubles N$33-45, without breakfast. The informal restaurant here serves a memorable curry for N$10 and steaks for N$18, while the bar is often the liveliest place in town.

Hotel-Pension Dig By See PO Box 1530. Tel: (0641)4130. Next to Jay Jay's, this small family-run hotel has singles for N$55 and doubles for N$100, including breakfast.

Chalets   At the far, southern end of Roon St stands a conspicuous complex of holiday bungalows which belong to the municipality. While lacking a bit in individuality, they are excellent value and have useful laundry facilities nearby, though bear in mind that they're often booked up over the weekends and holiday periods.

All have at least a basic stove, a fridge, shower/toilet, and a sink. A two-bed bungalow costs N$28; four-beds (bunk beds) cost N$30; a six-bed split-level A-frame chalet is N$70; a luxury flat for six is N$100; and a VIP bungalow for six (complete with cutlery, crockery and even a barbecue) is N$140.

Camping   With fairly cheap accommodation in town, we wouldn't recommend camping here because of the awkward and exposed location of the sites. However, if you must, then there are plenty of sites available.

The least inconvenient is probably **Langstrand** PO Box 86. Tel: (0642)5981. It is situated within South Africa(!), on the coast road, about half way between Swakopmund and Walvis Bay. Here sites are N$10 and there are some tidal pools to swim in. The restaurant is well known throughout the area for its steaks, and hitching to and from the towns is especially easy.

Failing that, there are camp/caravan sites at four and 14 miles north of town as you go towards Henties Bay, as well as some much further into the National West Coast Recreational Area. These are mainly used by fishing groups and consist of little more than pegged out areas of the sand next to the shore. The charge is N$10 per site, though water is extra at 10c for a litre (if you haven't brought your own), and hot showers cost N$1 each.

Where to eat

There is no shortage of choice, but ask around to find out where the current 'in' places are; you'll probably find a very lively crowd. Here are some perennial favourites:

Garfields on the corner of Brücken and Roon St, is always busy with its pizzas and pastas at around N$17.

Atlanta Hotel restaurant opposite the Hansa on Roon St, is excellent value for money: their steaks start from N$15.

Kücki's Pub with its spit-and-sawdust atmosphere, is not only a popular watering hole but also a reasonable place to eat with steaks for N$20-25 and crayfish for N$45 if you really want to splash out.

For more special occasions try the subterranean delights of the cosy **Sea Food Haven**, also opposite the Hansa, or the reputedly excellent **Erich's** on Post Street. Then of course there's always the hotels.

What to see and do

A friend of mine, new in town, went along to the tourist information office a few years ago to ask what there was to do in Swakopmund. The reply from the woman behind the counter was succinct: 'There's nothing to do in Swakopmund.'

Should you not want to believe this, try some of the following:

The Museum next to the Strand, is open from 10am to 12.30pm and 3pm until 5.30. It costs N$3 (N$1 for children) to enter, and has an extensive display of rocks and minerals and some fascinating equipment used in the not-so-distant past by doctors and dentists.

Swimming   Opposite the museum there's an olympic-size swimming pool, entry N$2. There are also saunas for which a day pass costs N$7.50. Masochists shouldn't miss the opportunity to use these and then run straight into the cold surf!

The Mole   With a little time to spare, it's worth wandering down to the 'Mole'. This was to be a harbour wall when first built, but the ocean currents continually shifted the sandbanks and effectively blocked the harbour before it was even completed. A similar 'longshore drift' effect can be seen all along the coast – especially at inlets like Sandwich Harbour. Partially because of this sandbank's protection, the beach by the Mole is pleasant and safe to swim in, if a little busy at times.

ENOC centre   Near the corner of Mittel and Nordring St, this small business centre houses a souvenir gem shop, a small art gallery and a carpet weaving co-operative selling some excellent value rugs – don't miss it.

Hansa Brewery   A look around this is fairly easy to arrange by phoning them on (0641)5021, with as much advance notice as possible. The beer is brewed, we're told, according to the most rigorous German standards – but it's distressing to find out just how many of its ingredients are imported.

Historical Buildings   As you might expect, this town is full of amazing old German architecture in perfect condition. If you want a guide to the individual buildings then get in touch with Frau Flamm at Historical Sightseeing Tours, on (0461) 61647. Alternatively, the handout from the municipality itself, or the short book entitled *Swakopmund – A Chronicle of the Town's People, Places and Progress*, available at the museum, both give descriptions and brief histories for some of the buildings.

Nightlife

The Grüner Kranz's first floor bar and Jay Jay's bar with its pool table are usually among the best places during the week, however there's sometimes a 'public' party on the beach on Saturday nights – just bring your own drink and food to the *braii* (barbecue). If that's not on then check to see if the local football club is holding one of its weekend discos, which we're told can be very entertaining.

Getting organised

There are three main operators here, all offering a variety of short trips into the local area, jaunts to Sesriem and Naukluft, and longer expeditions into Damaraland and Kaokoland. These longer trips are usually done using combinations of light aircraft and 4WD vehicles, costing in the region of N$250 per person per day including food and accommodation. They generally require organising well in advance with a group of least four people.

The local day trips don't require any notice, they set off regardless of numbers and we felt they were well worth doing as an introduction to the various aspects of the desert.

Charly's Desert Tours PO Box 1400. Tel: (0641)4341. From the office at 11 Kaiser Wilhelm St, they offer the widest range of daily tours, typically costing N$60 for half a day and N$80 for full-day trips, which venture as far as Sandwich Harbour, Cape Cross and even Spitzkoppe.

Desert Adventure Safaris, found next to the passage by the Hansa hotel. PO Box 339. Tel: (0641)4072/4459. Usually slightly cheaper than Charly's, DAS charge N$55 for a half day and N$75 for full-day trips. They are probably the best people to go into Damaraland with as they have a home base at Palmwag lodge.

DAS do very occasionally run trips into Damaraland and Kaokoland in conjunction with The Endangered Wildlife Trust, guided by Garth Owen-Smith. He's a local conservationist, highly respected internationally, involved in projects working with the indigenous peoples of these areas. If you have a chance to go on one of these, don't miss it at any cost!

See Africa Tours PO Box 4123. Tel: (0641)4311. Fax: (0641) 4203. Based, not surprisingly, at the See Africa Safari Shop which is also just by the Hansa hotel. They do daily tours into the nearby desert, but seem to specialise in more costly trips further afield to virtually anywhere in the country.

Excursions

Camel Farm You might think there would be more of these in Namibia, but this does seem to be the only one. It's found on the D1901 about 12km out of town, and the usual 15 minute camel ride, starting at 3pm, costs N$12.50. There's even the chance to dress 'Arabian' if you like! With a small party you could organise longer, overnight, rides into the desert – though they don't do these very often. To book, talk to Desert Gems opposite the Hansa Hotel.

If camels are a little too adventurous (or uncomfortable) for you then how about **horse riding** in the desert? It can sometimes be arranged through Frau Doris Herholdt at Blatt Shoe Store, across from Charly's.

Fishing trips Heinz Göthje will hire out his boat, 'Bronzy', and himself as skipper, for about N$400 per day. The boat will take up to eight people. Contact him on (0641)2357 or at PO Box 153, Swakopmund.

Alternatively, try Sunrise Fishing Trips at 17 Dunen Rd, run by H.D. Herzig who can be reached by phoning (0641)4923/4214.

Information and useful addresses

Namibia Tourist Information Office. This is by the corner of Bismark and Kaiser Wilhelm St. and the staff are quite helpful. The book *Swakopmund –*

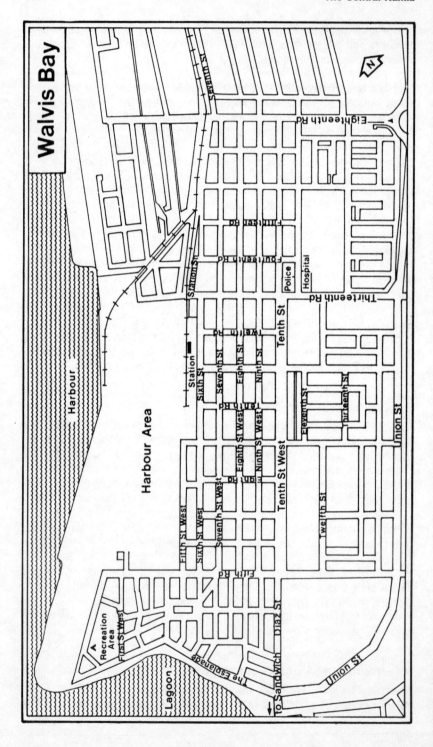

A *Chronicle of the Town's People, Places and Progress* produced by the municipality is well worth getting as an additional source of information.

DNC. For the permits to pass through the Namib-Naukluft Park, or to go north of the Ugab River (but not to stop overnight there), see the DNC on the corner of Kaiser Wilhelm and Bismark St. When closed try Charly's, the Hans Kriess Service Station, or the fuel stations in Walvis Bay.

The best **bottle stall** (or *drankwinkel*) is probably 'Harabobsky' on Kaiser Wilhelm near Breite St, though there are lots of others about.

WALVIS BAY

Until 1994 the port of Walvis Bay and the enclave which surrounds it had remained part of South Africa since Namibia became independent. However, at midnight on 28 February 1994 the South African flag was taken down, and five minutes later the Namibian flag was raised here – transferring the enclave to Namibian control and ending a point of contention between the two countries. Walvis Bay is strategically important as the coast's only deep-water port, and ceding control of it to Windhoek was a very significant step for South African politicians to make.

Where to stay
Category B
Casa Mia Hotel PO Box 1786. Tel: (0642)5975. Fax (0642) 5696. Found on 7th street, between roads 17 and 18, this seemed expensive to us with singles costing N$105 and doubles N$150, including breakfast. That said, the bars and restaurant lived up to expectations.

Atlantic Hotel PO Box 46. Tel: (0642)2811. Fax: (0642) 5036. On 7th street again, but between roads 10 and 12, this is comfortable and good value with singles at N$110 and doubles N$140, including breakfast.

Flamingo Hotel PO Box 30. Tel: (0642)3011 A reasonable hotel on the corner of 7th street and 10th road, though its restaurant is more like a cafe. Costs N$95 for singles, N$130 for doubles.

Category C
Mermaid Hotel PO Box 1763. Tel: (0642) 611/2/3. Fax: (0642) 6211. At 194 on 6th St. this is about the cheapest hotel in town. Singles cost N$55 and doubles N$82. Note that there's a handy Mermaid bottle store here!

Chalets. Located by the road running along the lagoon, the municipality has 26 very well-furnished bungalows. One to sleep five costs N$88, while one sleeping seven is N$121 per night – making it a good option for larger groups.

Camping. Opposite the yacht club, to the west of the harbour area, is the camping park. The ground is hard and the sites are small, if thankfully well sheltered, costing N$11 per site. There's a small kiosk for cool drinks and a swimming pool nearby.

Where to eat

Probst Bakery and Cafe, a German style coffee shop by the corner of 9th St and 12th Rd, is good for a mid-morning snack.

Georgie's Steakhouse, on 7th St, and **Bacher's Braai**, at 122 9th St, both serve steaks for around N$20 as well as lighter meals.

Lalainya's, on 7th St between roads 11 and 12, is very good and decidedly up-market. Their seafood platter for two, at N$75, has been recommended.

La Perla, in the Nictus Arcade on 8th St, and **La Tratoria**, again on 8th, both serve less expensive fare. La Perla's an informal spot for Spanish dishes, notably seafood, while the Italian La Tratoria concentrates more on pastas and pizzas.

What to see and do

The city is very much built for the harbour, with the numbered streets and roads forming an unexciting, if easily navigable, grid around it. There isn't Swakopmund's beautiful architecture or its holiday air and hence Walvis seemed to us to have little of interest during the day, although there are a few possible evening attractions.

There is, however, some excellent birdlife. Just take a walk on the southwest side of town, around the lagoon. The flock of feeding flamingos and pelicans which we found there allowed us to get much closer than any others which we came across in the area. Bird watchers might also look into the **bird sanctuary** at the end of 13 St, as well as stopping by at one of the guano platforms in the sea between Walvis and Swakopmund.

The **Namib Park Sports Club**, opposite the Flamingo Hotel on 7th St, allows visitors to use the squash courts and snooker tables for a weekly membership of N$5, while there are tennis courts available at the camping site.

Nightlife

The bar at the **Casa Mia** is popular, while at the weekends, **La Plaza** offers not only a cinema but also a bar with a lively dance floor. For the more adventurous, try **Le Palace** – a lively disco by the Desert Inn in the nearby township of Narraville, which is comparable to Windhoek's Namibia Nite club.

Getting organised

Generally it seemed easier to arrange excursions within Namibia from Swakopmund, though **Gloriosa Safaris**, based at 215 7th St, deserves a mention here. They offer similar long camping trips to those available in Swakopmund, though the day trips available are more limited.

THE NAMIB-NAUKLUFT PARK

2WD/4WD (see under relevant section). Entrance fees: N$5 per person and N$5 per vehicle (one-off charge).

People have different reactions when encountering a desert for the first time. A few find it threatening, too arid and empty, so they rush from city to city to avoid spending any time here at all. Some try hard to like it for those same reasons, but ultimately find little here which holds their attention, so they too come and go with scarcely a pause. Finally there are those who stop and give the place their time, delighting in the stillness, the strange beauty and the sheer uniqueness of the environment. To them the desert's ever-changing patterns and subtly adapted life forms are a constant fascination which will draw them back time after time.

Because of the park's size, we have split it into five sections which are ordered as follows: Sesriem and Sossusvlei; Naukluft; the northern section between the Kuiseb and Swakop Rivers; Welwitschia Drive; and Sandwich Harbour.

Getting organised

Permits to enter the park – which is probably the largest national park in Africa – are obtainable at any DNC office, as well as from Charly's Desert Tours or Hans Kreiss Service Station in Swakopmund, and from Troost Transport, Namib Ford or CWB service stations in Walvis Bay.

Camping fees for the sites in the northern section are N$10 per site and also available at these garages. However, the sites at Sesriem and Naukluft cost N$25 per site and must be booked in advance at the Windhoek DNC office.

Nara Bushes

Nara bushes (*Acanthosicyos horrida*) are perhaps the most striking of Namibia's endemic plants, occurring in the driest of areas and forming large tangles of green spiked stems - perhaps several metres across and a metre tall — but without a single leaf in sight. Not truly desert plants, their roots go down for many meters to reach underground reserves of water, without which they cannot survive. Thus their presence verifies the existence of water at Sossusvlei, while their demise warns us of a lowering of the water table in the Kuiseb river.

Sesriem and Sossusvlei
2WD/4WD.

Sesriem and Sossusvlei lie on the Tsauchab River – one of two large rivers (the other being the Tsondab, further north) which flow westward into the great dunefield of the central Namib but never reach the ocean. Both rivers end by forming flat white pans dotted with green trees, surrounded by spectacular dunes – islands of life within a sea of sand.

The National Park's camp at Sesriem, where the Tsauchab enters the great dunefield, makes an excellent base from which to see this area, and the only place to start on the 65km drive through the desert to Sossusvlei – the pan into which the river disappears. The classic desert scenery between Sesriem and Sossusvlei really is the stuff that postcards are made of – enormous apricot dunes with gracefully curving ridges, invariably pictured in the sharp light of dawn with a photogenic gemsbok or feathery acacia close by!

Getting there

Car – Sesriem presents no problems to drive to even in a 2WD, though getting there by hitching is a little more tricky. If you do manage to hitch to Sesriem then getting a lift for the trip along the valley should not be difficult – if you ask the warden when you arrive, he will probably help you to arrange one.

Driving from Sesriem to Sossusvlei itself does require a 4WD, but you can get right along the river valley, to within a kilometre or so of the pan, with a normal 2WD and then walk the rest. There's a petrol station (which is frequently closed), and basic shop at Solitaire – and not a lot more at Maltahöhe – with nothing else for miles, so take a week's food and a couple of days' water with you. When driving around the area make sure that you have read the rules on your permit – there are some strict regulations which you must comply with.

Hitching – Route 36 to the west of Maltahöhe is the closest place to hitch from, but route C24 which turns west off the B1 just south of Rehoboth is probably better. In either case, expect to spend several days getting there – and plan your reservations accordingly.

Where to stay

Sesriem campsite Of all Namibia's camp grounds, the one at Sesriem – with ten old sites and nine new ones – can be the most difficult in which to reserve space. It's always necessary to book ahead through Windhoek DNC, so do so as far in advance as possible, and try to allow yourself at least two nights here. The older sites are each surrounded by a low circular wall, which has a shady tree in the centre – with a tap positioned conveniently by its trunk. The ablution blocks only have electricity until 10pm. After that, take a torch.

Fuel, wood and even cold drinks are usually available from the warden, who will open the gates to Sossusvlei about an hour before sunrise. It's worth the effort to brave the cold (it can go below freezing here at night!) and get up well before sunrise so as to leave for Sossusvlei as soon as the warden opens the gates. That way, with luck, you should be there as the sun rises, preferably sitting high up on a dune.

NamibRand Game Ranch is just south of Sesriem, on the eastern boundary of the Namib-Naukluft park. It covers an area of over 110,000 hectares and is one of the subcontinent's biggest private game ranches. Amongst its facilities is **Mwisho Camp** – a small camp accommodating a maximum of 12 people in luxury tents. The activity here is ballooning, and this is Namibia's only venue for doing it. The costs are high: about N$200 per person for accommodation and food, plus another N$400-N$600 per person per *hour* for hire of the balloon. Apparently the balloons wear out quickly here because of the high ultra-violet light levels, which explains why the cost is so high.

Book ballooning at Mwisho through Namib Travel Shop, PO Box 9000, Windhoek, Tel: (061) 225178/226174. Fax: (061) 33332. For further details of NamibRand, Tel: (061) 36720.

What to see and do: Sesriem

It is tempting to regard Sesriem as just the DNC's campsite and office on the way to Sossusvlei, but it does have several attractions of its own nearby. Only about 4km from the camp is the narrow **Sesriem canyon**, so called because the early settlers drew water from it by knotting together six lengths of hide rope called *riems*. There's usually some blissfully cool water in here, especially following good rains, and after descending via the steps which have been cut into the rock you can take a swim if it's deep enough.

Nearly 5km from camp (in the opposite direction) is **Elim dune**. This is the nearest of the dunes and if you arrive towards dusk then, like us, you'll probably mistake it for a mountain. There's a parking spot at its base and it can be climbed, though it takes longer than you'd expect – allow at least an hour to get to the top. The views from there – over plains to distant mountains on the one side and dune crests on the other – are remarkable, especially at sunset, and well worth the long climb.

If you visit the area in the winter then it's difficult to imagine that the gravel plains surrounding the campsite will turn green with the summer showers, and carpets of small yellow flowers appear from nowhere.

The road from Sesriem to Sossusvlei

Beyond Sesriem, the road westwards is confined by huge dunes on either side to a narrow corridor, a few kilometres wide at most. This parting of the sand sea has probably been maintained by the seasonal action of the river and the wind over the millennia. About 24km after leaving Sesriem the present course of the Tsauchab River is crossed, and although it is seldom seen to flow note the green *Acacia erioloba* (camel thorn) which thrives here – a clear indication of underground water reserves.

Continuing westwards and parallel with the road, the present course of the river is easy to spot, but look around for the number of dead acacias which mark old courses of the river, now dried up. Some of these dead trees have been dated at over 500 years old. After a further 36km this road terminates in a shady parking area, with low sand dunes finally forming a barrier to the further progress of either the river or the road.

What to see and do: Sossusvlei

No more than 4km beyond the parking area, over a fairly low ridge of sand, lies the series of spectacular white clay pans – surrounded on all sides by apricot dunes and dotted with green camel thorns and *nara* bushes. You can either walk here from your car, or plough your way through the sand if you have a high-clearance 4WD. Either way, it's definitely worth the effort. Ideally, its best to be sitting high on one of the dunes overlooking the *vlei* for sunset or (better) sunrise, as then you'll catch the light at its best – casting sharp shadows on the ridges and bringing the dunes to life. Come with plenty of film as there's nowhere else quite like it – it is exceedingly photogenic.

On very rare occasions, during years when the rainfall on the eastern plateau has been exceptional, the Tsauchab will flow along the full length of its course and breach this sand barrier. When this happens Sossusvlei undergoes a complete transformation, with the pans becoming lakes and attracting water birds to the desert scene.

Naukluft
2WD

This area was created as a separate reserve in 1964, with the aim of preserving the unique ecosystem and saving the rare Hartmann's mountain zebra. More recently, it has been expanded by a narrow neck of land which now links it to the main Namib park, allowing a vital corridor for the migration of some of the park's larger herbivores.

The uniqueness of the area stems from its geology as well as its geographical position. Separated from the rest of the highlands by steep, spectacular cliffs, the Naukluft Mountains form a plateau – consisting mainly of limestone and dolomite. This is deeply incised with steep ravines – cut over the millennia as rainwater has dissolved the rock – and it covers a network of mainly subterranean water-courses and natural reservoirs. Where these waters surface, in the deeper valleys, there are crystal clear springs and pools – ideal for cooling dips – and they are often decorated by impressive displays of tufa (limestone which has been redeposited by the water as it has gone over a waterfall).

Scenically it is comparable in some ways to the Matopos Hills of Zimbabwe, though smaller and much less visited, with its mosaic of exposed rock areas, barren slopes and thickly vegetated ravines. The birdwatching here is excellent as Naukluft lies at the northern extreme of typical Namaqualand species, while also being just within the range of many species characteristic of northern Namibia. Where else will you hear the water-loving hamerkop one moment and see rockrunners the next?

Getting there

Car – Driving here, the entrance is on the D854 about 10km south-west of its junction with the C14 which links Solitaire and Maltahöhe. Alternatively, if you are coming from Sesriem, turn left after leaving the camp, right at the next junction onto route 36, and then after about 27km take a left onto the D854. The gate is about 66km along this very quiet road.

Hitching – Not advised! We have waited from morning until nightfall by the side of busier roads than these without being passed by a single vehicle.

Where to stay

There are four campsites here, but all are within a small area, and numbers at each are restricted to eight people – so book early through Windhoek DNC. Despite the water, firewood and basic ablutions that are available, these small sites still give the feeling of camping alone in the wilderness, miles from anywhere or anyone.

What to see and do

This is one of those increasingly rare corners of Africa where you can walk alone through a landscape that man has hardly affected, amongst game that is still not used to people – and so is often sensed, though rarely seen – without meeting another soul for days. Perhaps this is mostly due to the lack of roads through the area, for in this landscape you have no choice but to walk.

There are currently three trails mapped out, two of which are for day visitors, while one is for serious hikers only. The Olive trail takes about four and a half hours, while the Waterkloof trail (*kloof* means a steep valley or ravine, from the Afrikaans) is an hour or so longer. Ask for route plans as you book at the DNC in Windhoek.

A wilderness trail has recently been introduced here and is designed to last eight days – though it is possible to stop after the fourth. This trail, only available in the winter, from March 1 to October 31, can be started on the first and third Sundays and Wednesdays of the month. It needs to be booked through the DNC at Windhoek, and costs N$25 per person – with a minimum group size of three, and a maximum of 12. For such an extended hike you must carry all your food, as well as sleeping bags and mats. Your efforts will be rewarded as it is definitely the best way to really get a feel for any wild area such as this.

Because the area is mainly used for walking (which invariably involves an amount of scrambling) and is also fairly remote, the DNC have become concerned about the risks to visitors here, especially foreign tourists, and thus they now advise people to come as groups of at least three. Though this is only insisted upon if you plan to do the longest trail, it is good advice if you are new to the area and it is easy to find people in Windhoek who will share costs on a trip here.

The northern section between the Kuiseb and Swakop Rivers

2WD/4WD

The desert between these two important river-beds is largely one of rock and stone. Though the area has few classic desert scenes of shifting dunes etc., the landscapes are perhaps all the more unusual and certainly no less memorable. They range from the deeply incised canyons of the Swakop River valley to the open plains around Ganab, flat and featureless but for the occasional isolated *inselburgs* – islands of granite which jut up through the desert floor like giant worm casts on a well-kept lawn.

Key to map

Main road - no permit required	
Tourist road - permit required	
Four - wheel drive vehicles only	
▲ Official overnight camping sites	
Prohibited area	
✳ Watering places for game	
① Vegetation-lined lagoon with Pelicans, Flamingoes, Ducks	
② Salt-works at lagoon with Pelicans, Flamingoes, Waders	
③ Sewage disposal ponds with reeds & aquatic birds	
④ Guano platform - Cormorants, Pelicans	
⑤ Salt-works & guano platform with Cormorants, Flamingoes	
⑥ Old riverine farm in bed of Swakop River	
⑦ Moon Landscape - age old erosion	
⑧ Plain with fossil plants	
⑨ Desert Ecological Research Institute (NO VISITORS)	
⑩ View of Kuiseb Canyon	

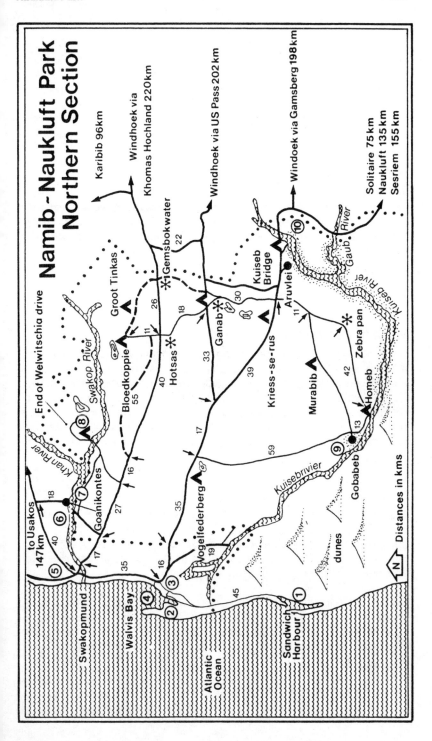

Namib ~ Naukluft Park
Northern Section

When to visit

The best time to visit this part of the park is just towards the end of the rains when the vegetation is at its best and, if you are lucky, there's the added attraction of herds of gemsbok, springbok or zebra. During this time the best sites to go to are the more open ones, like Ganab, on the plains. If, however, you visit during the dry season then perhaps it's better to visit Homeb or one of the *inselburgs*, as the flora and fauna there remain a little more constant than that on the plains – not shrivelling up so much in the dryness of winter.

Getting organised

Whenever you visit, you really need to spend at least a couple of nights camping here in order to do the area justice – though this requires you to be fully independent in terms of fuel, food and water. The permit to camp confers the freedom to use any of the sites in the area and as the map shows, most of the roads are navigable by 2WD, while only a few around Gemsbokwater and Groot Tinkas are classed as 4WD. Even these are probably negotiable with a high-clearance 2WD and a skilled driver, though you'd be waiting a very long time indeed for anyone to pass by if you became stuck.

What to see and do

Whist not famous for its game, the park is home to over 30 species of mammal including gemsbok, kudu, springbok, hartmann's mountain zebra, klipspringer, baboon, black-backed jackal, leopard, aardwolf, bat-eared fox, spotted hyena and even the rare brown hyena. One real delight that is not so difficult to spot is the sight of a group of meerkats foraging under the guard of a couple of 'sentries', members of the group that have been posted to stand watch by balancing on their hind legs – while their keen eyes scan the area around.

Where to stay – the campsites

Bloedkoppie. This large granite *inselburg* rises out of the Tinkas Flats and can provide some challenging scrambles if the heat's not drained your energies too much. *Be careful* not to approach any birds' nests, as some of the raptors in the park are very sensitive to disturbances. They may even abandon them if you go too close.

Ganab. Immediately next to a dry watercourse, which winds like a thin green snake through the middle of a large gravel plain, this open site has a wind-powered water pump nearby. Around March, if the rains have been good, then it can be an excellent spot for herds of springbok and gemsbok – and you can see for miles!

Groot Tinkas. Hidden away in a valley amidst an area of *kopjes* (small rocky hills), there's a small dam with sheer walls of rock here and some fairly rocky driving too!

Homeb. This excellent site is in the Kuiseb River valley which, with its perennial vegetation, forms the northern boundary of the great southern dune field. Its well placed location leaves you with the opportunity to cross the river-bed and climb amongst the dunes, as well as to explore the valley itself.

Kriess-se-Rus. Again found in a dry river-bed, Kriess-se-rus lies just below a bank of exposed schist – with the layers of rock clearly seen, providing an interesting contrast to the flat calcrete plains nearby.

Kuiseb bridge. Just off the main C14 route, west of the Gamsberg pass, the river is said to have less underground water stored here than further down its course, though it is more prone to flash floods. It can be very bare during the dry season, but is really pleasant after the rains.

Mirabib. Yet another great grey *inselburg*, but one that is even quieter than the others. It has great views from the top.

Swakop River. Being also beacon number 10 on the Welwitschia drive (see page 156) means that this beautiful dry river-bed can get rather busy at times.

Vogelfederberg. This rounded granite outcrop is the closest of the sites to the ocean, and as such it gets more moisture from the fog than the others. Its gentle shape helps form a number of fascinating temporary pools which contain a remarkable amount of life – including species of brine shrimp whose drought-resistant eggs can survive dry periods lasting many years, only to hatch within hours of the first rain. Polaroid glasses will help you to see past the reflections and into these pools, so if you've a pair, take them!

Welwitschia Drive
2WD

The Welwitschia Drive is situated in the most northerly part of the Namib-Naukluft park, a short drive from Swakopmund along the B2 towards Windhoek.

It's a route through the desert along which the DNC have set 13 numbered stone beacons at points of particular interest. It takes about four hours to drive, stopping at each place to get out and explore, and culminates at one of the country's largest, and hence oldest, Welwitschia plants.

An excellent, detailed little booklet – well worth getting – is available from the DNC to cover this route. However as it is often difficult to obtain here's a brief outline of the different points of interest at the beacons:

1. A lichen field   Look carefully at the ground to see these small 'plants', which are in fact the result of a symbiotic relationship (ie a mutually beneficial relationship between two organisms – each depending on the other for its survival) between an alga, producing food by photosynthesis, and a fungus, providing a physical structure. If you look closely, you'll see many different types of lichen. Some of these are thought to be hundreds of years old, and all are exceedingly fragile and vulnerable.

2. Drought-resistant bushes   Two types of bush found all over the Namib are the Dollar Bush, so called because its leaves are the size of a dollar coin, and the Ink Bush. Both can survive without rain for years.

3. Tracks of oxwagons made decades ago are still visible here, showing clearly the damage that can so easily be done to the lichen fields by driving over them.

4. This is the unusual and spectacular **moonscape** view, over a landscape formed by the valleys of the Swakop river.

5. More lichen fields   These remarkable plants can extract all their moisture requirements from the air. To simulate the dramatic effect that a morning fog can have, simply sprinkle a little water on one and watch carefully for a few minutes.

6. Here's another impressive view of the endless 'moonscape'.

7. This beacon marks the site of an old **South African camp**, occupied for only a few days during the First World War.

8. Now you must turn left to visit the next few beacons:

9. Here the road goes across a **dolerite dyke**. These dark strips of rock, which are a common feature of this part of the Namib, were formed when molten lava welled up through cracks in the existing grey granite. After cooling it formed dark, hard bands of rock which resisted erosion more than the granite – and thus has formed the spine of many ridges in the area.

10. The Swakop River valley   Picnicking in the river-bed, with a profusion of tall trees around, you might find it difficult to believe that you're really in a desert. It could be said that you're not – after all, this rich vegetation is not made up of desert adapted species. It includes *Tamarix usurious* (wild tamarisk) and *Acacia albida* (anaboom), better known for its occurrence in the humid Zambezi valley almost 1000 miles to the east. They are only sustained by the supply of underground water which percolates through the sand far beneath your feet.

11. Welwitschia Flats This open, supremely barren expanse of gravel and sand is home to the Namib's most celebrated endemic plant, *Welwitschia mirabilis*. These plants are only found in the Namib and even then only at a few locations which suit their highly adapted biology.

12. This beacon marks the end of the trail, and one of the largest *Welwitschia mirabilis* known — its age is estimated to be over 1,500 years old!
    On the way back, continue straight past beacon 8, without turning right, and where the road joins route C28 to Swakopmund there's one of the desert's many old mine workings — marked by the final beacon, number 13. In the 1950s iron ore was mined by hand here, but now it's yet another reminder of the park's chequered past.

Welwitschia Mirabilis

Welwitschia, perhaps Namibia's most famous species of plant, are usually found growing in groups on the harshest gravel plains of the central Namib desert. Each plant has only two long, shredded leaves and is separated from the other *welwitschia* plants by some distance. They appear as a tangle of foliage — some of which is green though most is a desiccated grey — which emerges from a stubby 'wooden' base.

They were first described in the west by Friedrich Welwitsch, an Austrian botanist who came across the plants as recently as 1859. Ever since then scientists have been fascinated by *welwitschia*, earning the plant the specific name *mirabilis* — Latin for marvellous!

Research suggests that *welwitschia* can live to over one thousand years of age, and are in fact members of the conifer family (though some sources class them with the succulents). Though their leaves can spread for several meters across, and their roots over a meter down, it is still a mystery exactly how moisture is obtained by the plants. One theory suggests that dew condenses on the leaves only to drip down where it is absorbed by the fine roots near the surface of the ground.

Another puzzle was how they reproduce. It's now thought that some of the specialist insects which live on the plants act as pollinators, the wind then distributing the seeds far and wide. Young *welwitschia* are rare indeed, only germinating when the conditions are right in years of exceptional rain. I was shown one on the skeleton coast that was known to be eight years old. It was minute, consisting of just two seedling leaves and no more than an inch tall.

Their ability to thrive in such a harsh environment is amazing, and their adaptations are still being studied. There has even been a recent suggestion that the older plants change the chemical composition of the soil around them, making it harder for young plants to germinate next to them and compete for space.

Sandwich Harbour
High-clearance 4WD only

This small area about 40km south of Walvis, contains a large saltwater lagoon, extensive tidal mudflats, and a band of reed-lined pools fed by freshwater springs – which together form one of the most important refuges for birdlife in southern Africa. It offers food and shelter to countless thousands of migrants every year, and some of the most spectacular scenery in the country for those visitors lucky enough to reach it. Where else can you walk alone along a pelican-covered beach while nearby pink flamingos glide photogenically above apricot-coloured sand dunes?

Getting there

Take the road by the lagoon south-west out of Walvis Bay and after about 4km ignore the sign to Paaltjies (where the road divides) and keep to your left. The tracks then split as you make your way across the **Kuiseb Delta**, but converge again near the shore about 16km later. At a gate in the fence, the checkpoint marks the boundary between South Africa and the Namib-Naukluft Park (Namibia). You'll be turned away if you don't have a permit.

From this checkpoint it's about 20km of sandy terrain to Sandwich Harbour. You can drive all the way on the beach if you wish, following in the footsteps of the fishermen, although the going is exceedingly rough. *Beware*: if the tide catches you, then you may face serious problems.

It's better to take an immediate left after passing the control post, and follow these tracks. After some 200m, they turn parallel to the sea and are considerably firmer than the ones on the beach. Note that leaving this set of tracks and trying to go across the apparently dry pans, where there are no tracks, is asking for trouble!

What to see and do

Once you reach the entry to the **bird sanctuary** of Sandwich, vehicles must be left though you can proceed on foot. The northern part consists of a number of almost enclosed reed-lined pools at the top of the beach, which back directly onto the huge desert dunes. These are fed partly by the sea via narrow channels which fill at high tide, and partly with freshwater which seeps from a subterranean watercourse under the dunes and enables reeds (albeit salt-tolerant ones) to grow. These in turn provide food and nesting sites for a number of the resident water birds to be found here.

On my last visit here I managed to spot dabchicks, moorhens, shelducks, common and marsh sandpipers, several species of tern (caspian, swift, white-winged and whiskered all visit) and even avocets and African spoonbills – as well as the pelicans and flamingos.

Continuing along the beach, the 'harbour' itself comes into view. During the early 18th Century it was used by whalers for its deep, sheltered anchorage and ready supply of fresh water, and subsequently a small station was established there to trade in seal pelts, fish and guano. Later, in the early part of this century, it was used as a major source of guano, but after difficulties with the mouth of the harbour silting up, this operation finally ground to a halt in 1947, leaving only a few bits of rusting machinery to be seen to this day.

It's worth climbing at least a little way up one of the enormous dunes. From such a vantage point you can see clearly the deep lagoon, protected from the ocean's pounding by a sand spit, and then to the south the extensive mudflats – which are covered from time to time by the high tide.

This is definitely a trip to make a whole day of, so when you start walking from your vehicle, bring some windproof clothes and a little to eat and drink, as well as your binoculars, camera and several spare films. Even if you're not an avid ornithologist, the scenery is so spectacular that you're bound to take endless photos!

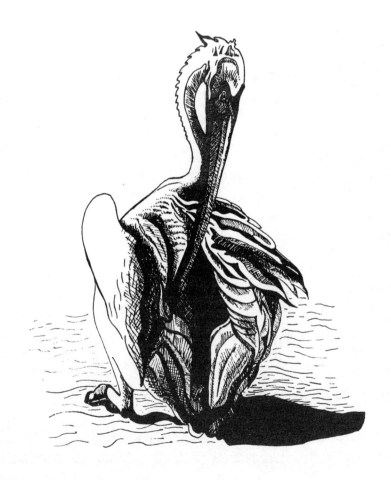

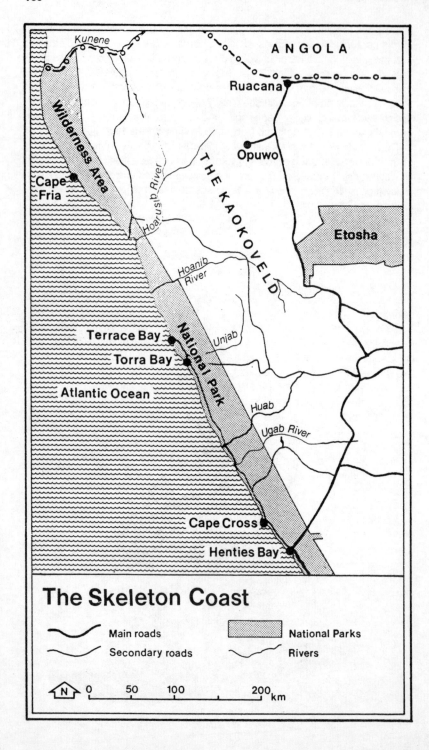

The Skeleton Coast

- ～ Main roads
- ～ Secondary roads
- ▦ National Parks
- ～ Rivers

N 0 50 100 200 km

Chapter 12

The Skeleton Coast

By the end of the 17th Century, the long stretch of coast north of Walvis Bay and Swakopmund had attracted the attention of the Dutch East India Company. They sent several exploratory missions, but after finding only barren desert shores, impenetrable fogs and dangerous seas, their journeys were curtailed. Later, in the 19th Century, English and American whalers operated out of Lüderitz to the south, but they gave the northern Kaokoveld coast a wide berth – it was gaining a formidable reputation.

Today, driving north from Swakopmund along the coast, you pass shipwreck after shipwreck stranded on the sand-banks by the shore. It's easy to see how this stretch of coast earned its names – 'The Coast of Skulls' and 'The Skeleton Coast'. Once a ship had fallen prey to the treacherous fogs and currents, the surviving sailors' problems had only just begun – the coast is but a thin barren line between the pounding ocean and the stark desert interior. Their only hope was to find one of the few 'linear oases', formed by the rivers that wind through the desert to reach the ocean.

These ribbons of green are few and far between, but each supports a surprising amount of life. Starting in the highlands of the Kaokoveld plateau, the water seldom flows above ground but instead filters through the sands of these apparently dry river-beds, allowing shrubs and trees to thrive, and creating narrow bands of vegetation. Occasionally, these rivers rise to the surface and trickle overland for a few hundred metres, perhaps avoiding an impervious rock barrier beneath, only to vanish into the sand again as suddenly as they appeared. Such watering places are few and far between, but of vital importance to all the inhabitants of the area. This scarce water supply has allowed isolated groups of the Himba people to stay in the area, whilst also sustaining the famous 'desert' populations of elephant and black rhino, and extending the ranges of giraffe, zebra, gemsbok, springbok, lion and even cheetah.

Outside the river valleys the scenery changes, with an astounding variety of colours and forms, from gravel plains to huge sand dunes – whilst farther inland, toward the Kaokoveld, jagged mountains rise up through the smooth sand to form strange, unearthly landscapes. Even here there is life. The gravel plains are covered by ancient lichens, whilst specially adapted bushes grow within the areas of sand – some species even forming their own small dunes as an aid to survival – and everywhere, if you search, you'll find small *tenebrionid* beetles.

North of the Hoarusib river, sandwiched between the dunefields and the wide sandy beaches, there are occasional reed-fringed pools of *fresh* water. These are well worth seeking out; we found one pool with a resident pair of moorhen, visiting plovers and avocets, and even fish!

The coast is divided into three separate regions: the **National West Coast Recreational Area**, the **Skeleton Coast National Park** and the **Skeleton Coast Wilderness Area**. For the Recreational Area no permits are needed, while access to the national park is controlled and a permit is required from the DNC (see below under *Skeleton Coast National Park*, page 164). The northern section of the Skeleton Coast – the wilderness area – is only accessible to tourists and visitors if you join an exclusive fly-in safari (see below under *The Wilderness Area*, page 167).

NATIONAL WEST COAST RECREATIONAL PARK

This stretch of coastline between Swakopmund and the Ugab River is mainly used for fishing. Driving north along the road you'll undoubtedly pass a succession of Toyota 4WD's parked on the sand every few kilometres. Nearby, three or four anglers will be casting their long lines out to sea, with a coolbox of cold beers close to hand. (The fishing is reputedly excellent and attracts anglers from all over the subcontinent.)

The scenery is barren in the extreme, with the flat beach becoming indistinguishable at times from the sand-and-gravel plains of the interior. The only real attraction is Cape Cross (the site where the first European set foot in Namibia in 1485), which is currently home to a large breeding colony of Cape fur seals. For those in search of total desolation, try driving along the C35 from just north of Henties Bay to Uis Mine – it's quite an experience.

Getting there

Car A normal 2WD car is fine for all of the main road along the coast, though 4WDs do come in useful for turning onto the beach. In either case, great care should be taken not to drive over the gravel plains on account of the permanent damage that tracks do to the flora and fauna (however lifeless the areas may appear – they'll be a lot more lifeless if you drive over them).

Hitching should be good (if you can put up with the strong sun and icy winds by the roadside), as there's only one coast road and lots of 4WD pick-ups cruising up and down with space in the back. Hitching is much better on the weekends and school holidays.

Where to stay

The small town of Henties Bay has a small hotel and a rest camp (see next page). Otherwise there are numerous campsites along the coast, although all are rather bare in appearance and have only the most basic facilities. The ones at Mile 14, Mile 72, Mile 108 and Jakkalsputz are all run by the DNC and a site costs N$10. Mile 72 and Mile 108 have filling stations, whilst all have hot showers for N$1 per turn and drinking water is for sale at 10c per litre.

If you want to fish, but haven't the gear, then your best bet would probably be to stay at a specialist lodge like **Sanpedi** (PO Box 1089. Tel: Edenvale 1610) where full board and all fishing trips will cost around N$200 per person per night.

The sea ponds

About 7km north of Swakopmund lie a number of large shallow ponds. Some are used for salt production – by filling them with seawater and leaving it to evaporate – while others are used for rearing young oysters. Sometimes you'll find one coloured bright red by algae, or pink with a flock of feeding flamingos!

Henties Bay

76km from Swakopmund, this windblown town is set astride the river Omaruru and immediately above the shore. There's little to do here (apart from fishing), though exploring the lower parts of the Omaruru on foot could provide a pleasant walk for a few hours. The town has a couple of garages, several shops, and a paint and hardware store that will rent out camping equipment.

Hotel De Duin This is the town's only hotel, and its busy bar and restaurant stands overlooking the sea. Singles are N$50-N$55 and doubles N$70-N$80, with breakfast for N$9. If you're just passing through and want a break then breakfast is served from 8am to 10am, lunch from 12.30pm to 2pm, and dinner from 7pm until 9pm.

The **Swaou-oord rest camp** has well-equipped bungalows for N$55-N$80, with N$10 for each extra bed.

Cape Cross

2WD. Entrance fees: N$5 per person and N$5 for a car.

Situated about 128km north of Swakopmund, Cape Cross was probably the site of the first landing by a European on the Namibian coast. Here, in 1485, the Portuguese captain, Diego Cão, landed and erected a stone cross on the headland to mark his visit. This remained in place until, in the 1890s, it was taken to Germany and replaced by the one that still stands there today. More recently, a replica of Diego's original cross – fashioned from local stone – has been erected on its original spot and the whole area has been carefully terraced with translations of the inscriptions on the terraces.

The animals here have been exploited by man for centuries. Firstly the seal colony was used by the early mariners as a supply of fresh meat, skins and oil; then later the offshore bird colonies were decimated by traders for the rich deposits of guano found there. Nowadays the area is a reserve where Cape fur seals congregate in their thousands to breed. The amazing sight of the ocean full of bobbing heads is matched only by the strong stench which strikes you as you approach the colony.

In October, the bulls come ashore to stake out their territories and compete for females, then about November/December the pups are born. Many of the pups die young, however, accidentally squashed by the huge bulls or preyed upon by the scavenging jackals – the mortality rate is high. After only a few months, the surviving pups are off into the surf on their own to feed in the ocean.

Park opening times   Every day from 10am until 5pm.

SKELETON COAST NATIONAL PARK

2WD. Entrance fees: N$8 per person and N$10 per vehicle. An entry permit is required from the DNC.

From the Ugab to the Kunene River, the border with Angola, the Skeleton Coast national park and wilderness area cover roughly one-third of Namibia's coastline and encompass the transition zone from the higher Kaokoveld interior to the foggy ocean shore. The landscapes become more interesting as you travel north, and the number of people that you see certainly become less.

The national park itself lies between the Ugab and Hoanib rivers and entry is carefully controlled. Visitors need a day permit to drive through the park, which is available from the DNC offices in Windhoek, Swakopmund, or Okaukuejo. This does not allow you to visit Torra or Terrace Bays though, the only camps in the area (see below). The description below imagines a route from south to north along the coast.

Note the entry gates – on the Ugab or inland at Springbokwasser – must be passed by 3pm.

Ugab River valley

The Ugab is one of the longest rivers to cross the Namib, its waters coming from as far east as Outjo and Otjiwarongo, and its valley forms an important corridor for animal movement between the interior and the coast. The dense vegetation found here is mostly wild tobacco (*Nicotiana glauca*) – a foreign import which has run riot – though various indigenous plants are also present. Some of the larger mammals do come right down to the sea, and

I've often heard the tale of a lion seen lounging around by the park's skull-and-crossbones gate!

Hiking trail   One of the best ways to learn about the river valley is to go on the three-day hiking trail, which has been set up by the DNC. It can be tough going in the harsh climate, but should leave you with a good appreciation of the complex ecosystem present in this specialised environment – and you may even spot an oryx or two.

For the trail, which is accompanied by a game ranger, you need to bring all your own equipment and supplies. As with the Fish River Canyon, the hike must be booked well in advance through the Windhoek DNC office. It costs N$75 per person, and groups should be six to eight people – all with medical certificates of fitness issued within the previous 40 days.

Huab River valley

About 38km north of the Ugab River, the coast road crosses the Huab River, and there's a small loop road off to the east which explores the valley further inland. It's worth getting out and wandering around on foot, among the **dollar bushes** (*Zygophyllum stapffii*) with their thick, fleshy leaves about the size of a US dollar coin. Notice how they collect a mound of sand on their leeward side, appearing to grow out of their own small dune. The dollar bush is a classic example of a plant which seems to alter its environment to suit itself. As sand collects in its lee, so does windblown detritus and on this feed a variety of beetles which live in the mounds and hence fertilise the bushes with their faeces. For moisture, the plants must survive on the morning fog, and the occasional shower, but it's noticeable that the higher mounds collect more dew than the lower ones – giving the older bushes (with larger mounds) yet another advantage in the survival stakes.

To the north of the river-bed, inland, are a few crescent-shaped *barchan* dunes (see Chapter 3, page 31), emerging from the river's sands and 'marching' northwards. Further north still, the wreck of the *Atlantic Pride* lies just off the shore.

Koigab River valley

This is one of the smaller rivers, and yet it still supports perennial vegetation and even flows occasionally. It's a good place to look for what are possibly the world's only **white beetles** – and the focus of much scientific study since their discovery. The unique coloration of these beetles, from the genus *Onymacris*, is thought to be an adaptation to reduce their absorption of heat, and hence allow them to forage above the sand's surface during the middle of the day. However, if this is the case then it remains to be explained why they only occur in the northern Namib, and why the vast majority of other desert beetles are black.

Torra Bay campsite
Open December 1 to January 31.

This seasonal camp-site, between the Koigab and the Uniab rivers, lies just south of the first dunes in the Namib's great northern dunefield. Here the first low *barchan* dunes start migrating north, eventually forming a sand sea stretching as far as the Curoca river in Angola.

You might notice that some of the dunes have purple tinges to their crests, contrasting with the lighter coloured sand below. This is caused by a high proportion of purple-brown garnet crystals in the sand – they collect on the surface, being less dense than the quartz sand grains. If you've a magnifying glass then look closely at a handful of the sand – you'll find a whole kaleidoscope of colours sparkling like jewels in your palm.

The camping site here is open only during the high season, December 1 to January 31, and it has a basic shop, a filling station and toilets. It costs N$10 per site, and must be booked in Windhoek or you won't be let past the gates.

Uniab River valley

Though fairly short, this is one of the most important rivers to cross the Namib as far as wildlife is concerned. Its headwaters come from around Palmwag, an area of relatively abundant game, and its lower reaches have formed an impressive, well vegetated delta. In between, there is a wide valley supporting rich flora and fauna, surrounded for some of its course by dunes on either side. The area by the road is a fascinating one to explore on foot for a few hours, so park the car and bring along your binoculars and a flask of water.

It seems that in the past the Uniab's mouth formed a large delta. This has subsequently been raised up above sea level, only to be cut into again by the river to form a series of five alternative routes to the sea. Only one of these has water flowing through it at present (and then only after good rains), though most have freshwater pools fed by underground seepage – forming small verdant oases dotted around the watercourses. These are a home for resident water birds and an important stop-over for migrants, including the delicate black and white avocets.

Currently, it is the second course from the north which hosts the flow, and if you walk downstream there is often an overground trickle through the canyon, which has been carved smooth by the water. Move quietly and you may see some of the springbok or gemsbok which often graze down here – or even catch a glimpse of the rare brown hyena, a harmless scavenger that's mainly nocturnal and known to inhabit the area.

Terrace Bay camp and chalets
Open all year

The camp   This is the most northerly public camp on the coast, with luxury chalets which are open throughout the year and must be booked in advance at Windhoek. It costs N$140 for a single, N$230 for a double, but includes a full three meals per day – and even space in the freezer! Fuel is available, and there is also a shop and a couple of bars – this camp is aimed primarily at anglers.

Dunes and beetles   Around Terrace Bay the dune belt widens to stretch down to the ocean. The crests of these dunes are good places to search for some of the highly unusual beetles which perform 'headstands' or dig trenches in order to drink, but you'll have to be up by sunrise to catch them at it.

The 'headstanding' beetles can be seen high on the dunes – with their backs to the wind and their heads down – 'fog basking' a little before sunrise. Water condenses out of the moist fog and onto their bodies, dripping down to hang in droplets below their mouths. By drinking this they obtain all the water that they need to survive.

The large round beetles of the *lepidochora* genus illustrate another way of collecting moisture from the fog. These dig small trenches (a couple of centimetres deep) near the dune crests, perpendicular to the prevailing wind and then collect the moisture which tends to condense on the trench walls!

SKELETON COAST WILDERNESS AREA

Covered by a patchwork of dunefields, and separated from the country's main populated areas by the arid regions of western Kaokoland, this most inaccessible area has remained largely unaffected by events further inland. In the distant past, perhaps when rains were better, bushmen moved here from the interior – leaving behind them only round stone circles as remnants of their shelters. More recently, earlier in this century, there was an attempt to mine amethysts at Sarusas – but that too proved impractical, and left only ruins remain.

Visitors approaching from the ocean fared little better. The countless wrecks, dating from as early as the American whalers of the 18th Century, earned the coast its name and formidable reputation. Driving along the shoreline you'll see endless piles of driftwood and scraps of metal which have been washed up from the wrecks. Old drums, winches, ropes – all lie exactly where they came ashore.

Perhaps it was this 'untouched' aspect of the northern coast which, together with the northern Namib's unique desert ecosystem, persuaded the government to proclaim it a 'wilderness area'. This important status allows for no permanent developments to take place at all – and forbids anything which would change the unspoilt character of the region. Consequently, entry to the area is prohibited unless you are booked on a professionally organised tour.

Getting there with 'Skeleton Coast Fly-in Safaris'

The Schoeman family – who were instrumental in persuading the government to protect the Skeleton Coast – conduct the area's only tours: Skeleton Coast Fly-in Safaris, PO Box 2195, Windhoek. Tel:(061)224248. Fax:(061)225713).

The tours are expensive, but operating in such a remote area is costly, and has many logistical problems – including the bringing of all the supplies almost 1,000km from Windhoek, and the removal of all rubbish. The safaris are typically between five and 10 days long, and at present there are five 'permanent camps' in the park, with visitors usually based at one for several days while they explore the surrounding area in 4WD vehicles.

Accommodation is in substantial two-person tents (complete with beds, lights, and a chemical toilet) which are about as comfortable as it's possible to be while not altering the area by erecting permanent buildings. The price, at around N$500 per person per day, includes everything (flights, 4WD excursions, all meals and drinks).

What to see and do

After visiting the area on an excellent five-day fly-in safari, the impression which I'm left with is of a number of incredibly beautiful landscapes – each with its own fragile ecosystem – existing side by side within a fairly small area. While out on safari, which took most of the day, we would frequently stop to study more closely the plants and animals, or try and capture the landscapes on film, and back at camp we relaxed by talking to the guides with a drink over dinner.

Some of the Fly-in safaris include a trip to an isolated settlement of Himba people – a fascinating and humbling experience – in which the cost of the trip includes an amount for the Himba whom you visit (see section on *Conservation and Development*, page 37).

There were also a number of specific 'sights' to see, but these seemed almost incidental when compared with simply experiencing the strange solitude and singular beauty in the area:

Sand temples of the Hoarusib Canyon   Here the sides of the Hoarusib's steep canyon are lined with tall structures which the wind has carved – implausibly – out of soft sand to resemble some of the ancient Egyptian temples. Watch out for the patch of quicksand on the river near here!

The beaches   Driving through the mist along these desolate beaches, fiddler crabs scuttle amongst the flotsam and jetsam of the centuries, while rare damara terns fly overhead. There is always something of interest here to take a closer look at or to photograph.

Cape Frio   Here there is a large colony of cape fur seals, and with care you can approach close enough to get a good portrait photograph.

Roaring dunes   Perhaps the strangest experience here, these large sand dunes make an amazing and unexpected loud 'roar' (reverberating all through the dune) if you slide down one of the steep lee sides. A truly weird sensation that really has to be felt to be believed! One current theory links the 'roar' with electrostatic discharges between the individual grains of sand when they are caused to rub against each other. Why some dunes 'roar' and others don't remains a mystery.

Rocky point   This rocky pinnacle, jutting out from a long, open stretch of sand, was an important landmark on the coast for passing ships in times gone by.

Bushmen rock circles   These occur further inland and are thought to be the remains of their shelters.

Lichen fields and Welwitschia plants are widespread throughout the gravel plains further inland. One Welwitschia plant, no more than a few centimetres high, is known by Louw and his guides to have germinated in 1982 – demonstrating just how slowly these plants do actually grow.

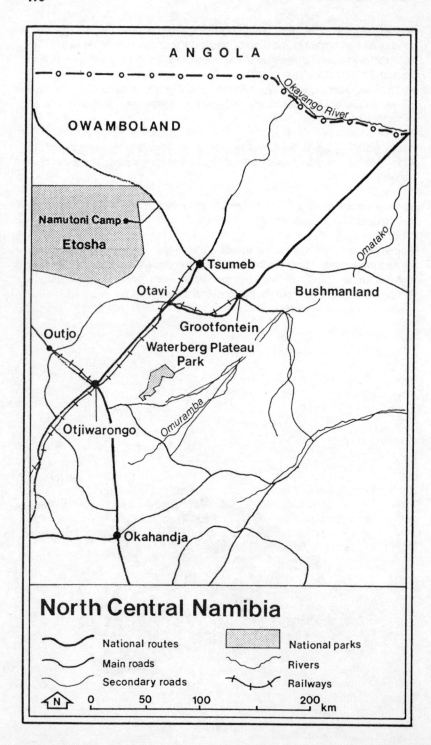

North Central Namibia

- National routes
- Main roads
- Secondary roads

- National parks
- Rivers
- Railways

N 0 50 100 200 km

Chapter 13

North Central Namibia

While Etosha is the main attraction in the north of the country, this region to its south and east should not be overlooked. There are interesting places here, so don't just dash through. The Waterberg Plateau is well worth a visit, especially if you're a hiker or want to try a walking safari. Geologists will find the area around Grootfontein, Otavi and Tsumeb particularly fascinating, with its interesting underground caverns and the famous Tsumeb mine.

To the west, Hereroland and Bushmanland extend from the agricultural plains of the central plateau into the Kalahari desert, adjacent to Botswana. Distinctly different in landscape and people from the Namib, these arid areas are sparsely populated and difficult to reach, but they offer a fascinating desert experience for the well-prepared,.

Otjiwarongo

Formed as a staging post on the railway from Tsumeb to Swakopmund, this small town is conveniently situated at a crossroads for both the railway and the road network, in an area used mainly for cattle ranching.

Apart from the accommodation detailed below, a new rest camp and possibly even a Kibbutz-style farm are being planned here. It remains to be seen if these will ever materialise, but talk to Johan Pretorius in the Photo Den on the main street for the latest information.

Where to stay

Category B
Hotel Hamburger Hof PO Box 8, Otjiwarongo. Tel: (0651) 3607. Fax: (0651) 3607. This has air-conditioned single rooms with telephones for N$120, and similar doubles from N$160, including breakfast.

Category C
Hotel Brumme PO Box 63, Otjiwarongo. Tel: (0651) 2420. This hotel was closed during 1993 for renovations, but is worth a telephone call to see if they have reopened yet.

Campsite There is a reasonable site with good, clean ablutions next to the Crocodile Farm (which opens 9am to 6pm daily). Camping here costs N$15.20 per site, plus N$2 .50 extra per person.

What to see and what to do

Dinosaur footprints About 25m of footprints, made almost 200 million years ago, have been preserved here in sandstone, on the Otjihaenamaparero farm. To get there take the C33 south for about 6km then turn left onto the D2414. The farm, with the unforgettable name, is 30km along this road.

Nearby Guest farms

Okonjima Guest Farm
P.O. Box 793. Tel: (0658) 18212. Fax: (0651) 3242. Run by Wayne and Lise Hanssen, this relaxed and unpretentious guest farm is rapidly gaining an excellent reputation for cats, and particularly cheetahs. Wayne is an ex-hunting guide turned conservationist (not an unfamiliar move in Africa), who is in the process of setting up a centre to rehabilitate cheetahs. The main problem faced in this area of large-scale farming is that ranchers trap and kill cheetahs on their land because they have a reputation for attacking young stock animals, especially calves.

Wayne is developing a treatment of aversion therapy at Okonjima. He aims to take cheetahs which have been trapped by farmers; teach them not to attack cattle; and then release them again back onto the ranches. Pessimists doubt that it will work, but this brave project is at least saving some cats while it adds to our knowledge of these beautiful animals.

As well as the wild cheetahs brought to the farm for rehabilitation, there are two relatively tame cheetahs who wander about casually. *Chinga* is a female who was found at the age of three months, and kept in a rabbit hutch before being rescued by Okonjima. Similarly *Caesar* was rescued from a local farm when he was about two. These amazing cats will miaow around your breakfast table, and *Chinga*, the tamer of the pair, will even purr if she's stroked. Having said that they are tame, for safety's sake the farm wisely maintains a policy of allowing **no children** to stay.

Getting there Okonjima means 'place of baboons' and the farmhouse is set in 60 square kilometres of rolling hills, complete with a troop of baboons who live on a nearby *kopje*. It is best reached from the B1. Take the D2515 turn-off about 124km north of Okahandja (50km south of Otjiwarongo) and follow the signs to the farm.

What to see and what to do Aside from the cats, attractions include a small water-hole for the local wildlife. Spend a relaxed evening here during the dry season, when there is a chance that, encouraged by edible offerings, aadvaaks and porcupines will appear.

Wayne and Lise also take visitors around an informative Bushman trail. This uses a variety of old Bushman artefacts, tools and traps to demonstrate how the Bushmen used their environment to survive. As a finale, Wayne will often demonstrate how to light a fire by rubbing two sticks together — a famous skill that few will even attempt.

Accommodation and Costs The farm has just eight solid brick double rooms which are built around a central lawn. All are in excellent condition and have en-suite facilities. The serve-yourself buffet meals are good, and the relaxed atmosphere is emphasised by the cheetahs who wander around the breakfast table. Okonjima is ideal for a gentle two-night stop towards the end of your trip to Namibia. Costs are from N$198 per person including meals and all activities, except for horse-riding which is an optional extra.

WATERBERG PLATEAU PARK

2WD. Entrance fees: N$5 per person and N$5 for a car.
Historically important during the war between the German forces and the Hereros, the plateau was first envisaged as a reserve for eland, Africa's largest species of antelope. In 1972 it was proclaimed a reserve and has since become a sanctuary for several rare animals, including eland and (introduced) white rhino. Now it is becoming equally renowned as a centre for walking safaris.

Geography

The park is centred around a plateau of compacted Etjo sandstone, some 250m high. This lump of rock, formed about 180 - 200 million years ago, is the remnant of a much larger plateau that once covered the whole area. This sandstone is highly permeable (surface water flows through it like a sieve), but the mudstones below it are impermeable. This results in the emergence of several springs at the base of the southern cliffs.

Flora and Fauna

For a fairly small park, there are a large number of different environments. The top of the plateau supports a patchwork of wooded areas (mostly broad-leafed deciduous) and open grasslands, while the foothills and flats at the base of the escarpment are dominated by acacia bush, but dotted with evergreen trees and lush undergrowth where the springs well up on the southern side. This diversity of vegetation gives the park its ability to support a large variety of animals. Recently, Waterberg has become an integral part of a number of conservation projects, seeing the relocation of several endangered species — including white rhino, roan and sable antelope — in an attempt to start viable breeding herds. These have added to the game already found here, which ranges from giraffe and kudu to leopard, brown hyena, cheetah, and wild dogs.

The birdlife is no less impressive, with more than 200 species on record. Most memorable are the spectacular black eagles, and Namibia's only breeding colony of Cape vultures. Numbers of these imposing raptors have sharply declined in recent years due to both the changing environment, and the increasing use of farm poisons (both intentional poisons, and the chemicals in fertilisers and pesticides). A recent innovation to encourage the vultures is the vulture restaurant (open once a week, on Wednesday morning) where carcasses are prepared and left out for them.

Getting there

This game park is well signposted, 91km to the east of Otjiwarongo — follow the B1, the C22 and finally the D2512.

Where to stay

The park was made for the animals, not the visitors, and the **Bernabe de la Bat rest camp** has only been operating since June 1989. Its accommodation and amenities are beautifully landscaped over the escarpment's wooded slopes, and include a restaurant, kiosk, pool and a range of accommodation.

Camping costs N$25 per site, and bungalows are N$120 for four people or N$80 for three. These can be booked in advance at the DNC in Windhoek, or at the park office between 8am and sunset (except lunch from 1pm to 2pm).

What to see and do

This park Is unusual in that you can't drive yourself around. Instead you must either hike around or hire a 4WD jeep with a driver, for N$220 per day, or take the scheduled half-day safaris up onto the plateau for N$25 per person. Consider taking a morning trip onto the plateau, getting off at one of the many hides, and just sitting and watching. You can then return to the camp with the afternoon safari. These restrictions on driving yourself around the park annoy some visitors, but they do result in very peaceful game viewing at the hides and viewing platforms.

The more energetic will book (in advance) a place on one of the excellent walking safaris (see hiking section below), or take some of the short trails around from the camp. Either way, the park is a good option for those who prefer not to see game through a windscreen.

Hiking

During the dry season, from April to November, there are two hikes available: an accompanied one in the west of the park, and an unguided one in the south. There are no better ways to experience a game park.

The three-day accompanied hiking trail begins on the second, third, and fourth weekends of every month. It starts at 4pm on the Thursday and continues until Sunday afternoon, taking between six and eight people for N$80 each. This starts at Onjoka, the wildlife administration centre, from where the group is driven up onto the plateau. There is no set trail to follow, the warden leading the trail will just guide you across the plateau and go wherever looks interesting. The distance covered will depend on the fitness and particular interests of the group, but 10-15km per day would be typical. This is not an endurance test, but an excellent way to get to know more about the environment with the help of an expert.

The four-day unguided trail starts during the same period, but it is on Wednesdays only, and groups must have between three and ten people. A short trail is taken from the rest camp to Mountain View, on the top of the escarpment, from where the trail proper begins. From here the trail is a relatively short 42km. The first night is spent at the Otjozongombe shelter, and the second and third nights are at the Otjomapenda shelter, allowing you to take a circular day-walk of about 8km.

Both these long trails must be booked well in advance (at Windhoek DNC) and you need to bring your own sleeping bag and food. All other equipment is supplied, and full details on the hikes are available at the DNC or the rest camp.

If you have not made advanced reservations then don't despair. Check with Windhoek DNC before you arrive, and they may be able to put you in touch with someone who has booked a trail who would allow you to join them.

Failing that, all year round there are nine short trails which you can take around the vicinity of the camp, described in booklets from the office. These are designed to give visitors a flavour of the park, and the panorama from the end of the trail up to Mountain View is definitely worth the effort that it takes to get there.

Outjo

This small ranching town of about 5,000 people lies in an area of grassland, dotted with cattle and sheep ranches, about 65km north-west of Otjiwarongo and 115km directly south of Etosha's Okaukuejo camp. In the centre of town is an open area, like a desolate village green, and adjacent is a good fuel station, a couple of poorly-stocked grocery shops, and a post office. The latter is memorable for its old-style public phone, which only accepts 10 or 20c pieces, and needs to be physically cranked into action.

Where to stay

Category B/C
Hotel Onduri PO Box 14, Outjo. Tel: (06542)14/165. Fax: (06542) 166. Singles from N$95 and doubles from N$140, with breakfast for N$15.

Hotel Etosha PO Box 31, Outjo. Tel: (06542) 26. Fax: (06542) 130. Costs N$95 for a single or N$170 for a double, excluding breakfast.

Municipal camp and campsite A basic four-person bungalow is N$60, complete with a fridge, a hot plate and bedding, while even simpler two-person bungalows with just bedding are only N$25. You can also camp here for N$10 per site plus N$1 for each person.

Otavi

Situated in a fertile farming area, near one of the country's biggest irrigation schemes, this small town has a 24-hour Total service station, a reasonable SENTRA store for groceries and a few take-aways. Nearby are several interesting cave systems, though visits to these need to be carefully organised in advance.

Where to stay

Category C
Otavi Hotel PO Box 11. Tel: (06742) 5/229. Fax: (06742) 73. This pleasant, though not luxurious hotel currently costs from N$55 for a single, N$90 a double. The rooms all have fans and telephones, and these rates include breakfast in the small restaurant.

Municipal camp and campsite This has half a dozen well-equipped, but not plush, bungalows for N$27.50 each plus N$1.11 per person. Thus, a full bungalow with four people costs a bargain N$31.90. Alternatively, you can camp here for N$11.50 per site plus N$1.11 per person.

Khorab memorial

This marks the spot where the German colonial troops surrendered to the South African forces on 9th July 1915. It is only a few kilometres out of town but exceedingly well signposted.

Gaub caves

Here, on the Gaub Farm, 35km north-east of Otavi, there some caves famous for their stalactites and Bushman paintings. Permits to visit must be obtained from the Windhoek DNC.

Aigamas caves

33km north-west of Otavi, on a tectonic fault line, this cave system is about 5km long. It has aroused particular interest recently as the home of *clarius cavernieola*, a species of fish which appears to be endemic to this cave system (ie it occurs nowhere else in the world). These fish, members of the catfish family, are a translucent light pink in colour and totally blind, having evolved for life in the perpetual darkness of these caves. Interestingly, their breeding habits are still unknown and no young fish have ever been found.

To visit the cave, you must make arrangements with Mr Boye at the municipal offices, just to the right of the rest camp, or phone him at home. Tel: (06742) 222. He has known the caves for years and, with a day or two of notice, will guide you to them.

Uiseb caves

More extensive than Gaub, these caves have several different chambers and passages containing some impressive stalactites and stalagmites. With no facilities at all, they are described as 'unspoilt' and arrangements to see them must be made at the municipal offices.

Tsumeb

The attractive town stands in the north of the central plateau, an area of rich farmland and great mineral wealth. Tsumeb's wide streets are lined with bougainvillaea and jacaranda trees, and in the centre of town is a large, green park — a favourite for the townspeople during their lunch.

Economically dominating the town is the Tsumeb Corporation, which mines a very rich ore pipe. This produces large amounts of copper, zinc, lead, silver, germanium, cadmium and the variety of unusual crystals for which Tsumeb is world famous. So far Tsumeb's one pipe has produced about 217 different minerals and gemstones, 40 of which have been found nowhere else on earth.

Where to stay and eat

Category B
Hotel Eckleben PO Box 27, Tsumeb. Tel: (0671) 3051. Fax: (0671)3575. The hotel, in the centre of town (see map), is a member of the Namib Sun group. Singles are N$110, while doubles are N$140, including breakfast. The restaurant has a reasonable menu, but is fairly expensive. It has reputedly good discos on Saturdays, which are lively in this young mining town.

Category C
Minen Hotel PO Box 244, Tsumeb. Tel: (0671) 3071/2. Fax: (0671) 3750. Just off Hospital St., opposite the park, the Minen is cheaper than the

Eckleben with singles from N$90 - 110 and doubles from N$120 - 150. Its rooms are basic but clean. They are individually priced and laid out around a pleasant courtyard, off which there is also a restaurant which opens during the week from 8pm to 9.30pm. At the front of the hotel is a bar which becomes busy at weekends.

The Campsite This is situated half way between the town and the main road intersection (about 1 km from each), which makes it feel a long way from the centre of things. The ablutions are good and staying here costs N$10 per site plus N$2 per person.

What to see and do

If you are passing through, there are several fuel stations around town (including a 24-hour BP), and Main St. has Standard and First National banks. This is a bustling shopping street, with Edgar's department store, various clothes shops, a couple of take-aways and even a curio shop.

Tsumeb's Air Namibia agent doubles as the Avis representative and also the main travel agent. Find them on the corner of the central park near the Minen hotel. Also nearby is a Model supermarket, the town's best.

If you are staying longer, then the information centre, in front of the museum, might be helpful, although most of its information is very dated.

Museum Facing the park, on Main St, this has an excellent section on the region's geology and exhibits many of the rare minerals collected from the mine. It also has displays on the German colonial forces, and a small section on the lifestyle of the Bushmen. The 'Khorab' room contains old German weaponry, recovered from Lake Otjikoto, which was dumped there by the retreating German forces in 1915 to prevent the rapidly advancing Union troops from capturing it.

Since that time, pieces have been recovered periodically, the most recent being the Sandfontein cannon on display here. The museum itself is located in the historic 1915 German School, and opens during the week from 9.00am - 12.00am and 3.00pm - 6.00pm, and from 3.00 - 6.00pm on Saturdays.

Lake Otjikoto

About 20km from Tsumeb, signposted west off the B1, this lake was formed when the roof of a huge subterranean cave collapsed, leaving an enormous sink hole with steep sides. Together with Lake Guinas, the lake is home to several endemic species of fish, including some mouth-brooding cichlids. These have attracted much scientific interest for changes in their colour and behaviour as a result of this restricted environment. There Is a kiosk here selling drinks and wood carvings from dawn until dusk, but no other facilities.

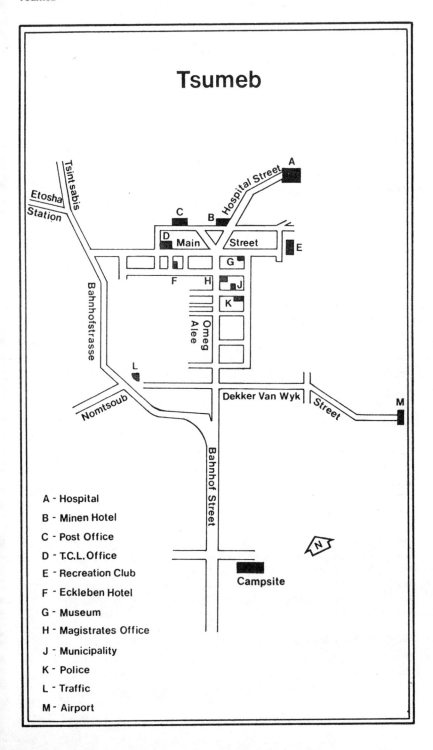

Tsumeb

A - Hospital

B - Minen Hotel

C - Post Office

D - T.C.L. Office

E - Recreation Club

F - Eckleben Hotel

G - Museum

H - Magistrates Office

J - Municipality

K - Police

L - Traffic

M - Airport

Lake Guinas

Reached 32km after Tsumeb by turning left off the B1 to Ondangwa, onto the D3043, and then left again after 19km onto the D3031. The lake is about 5km along, near the road. It is deeper and more attractive than Otjikoto, though there are no facilities at all here.

Grootfontein

This small, pleasant town is found at the northern end of the central plateau, amidst rich farmland. For the visitor, Grootfontein has few intrinsic attractions but is the gateway to both Bushmanland and the Caprivi Strip. If you are heading to either, then resting here for a night will allow you to tackle the long drive ahead in the cool of the morning.

Where to stay and eat

Category B

Meteor Hotel PO Box 346, Grootfontein. Tel: (06731) 2078/9/3071. Fax: (06731) 3072. Situated on the corner of Okavango Road and Kaiser Wilhelm Str, the Meteor has singles and doubles for N$80-N$110 per person, but it's often fully booked up. Their outdoor courtyard, complete with banana trees, is a great place for a light lunch or an early evening drink .

Nord Hotel PO Box 168, Grootfontein. Tel/Fax: (06731) 2049. Set back off the main road. The Nord is smaller than the Meteor and its rooms are not as pleasant. It is better for a late evening drink, and has a two bars with a good choice of wines and spirits — and a large collection of key rings. Rooms here are all N$55.50 per person, including breakfast.

Municipal rest camp and campsite PO Box 23, Grootfontein. Tel: (06731) 3100/1/2/3. Fax: (06731) 2930. This small, spruce camp has recently been upgraded by the addition of four new bungalows — one luxury and three standard. Entry to the site, including camping fees, is N$12.00 per vehicle plus N$3.00 per person. The luxury bungalow costs N$138 - N$220 per night, depending upon the number of occupants, while the standard ones are N$66 per night (plus N$11 each if bedding is required). The ablutions at this site are excellent, but the mosquitoes are bad in the rainy season.

What to see and do

Grootfontein makes a good stop for supplies with a Standard Bank, a First National Bank, several garages, a tyre centre, and a well-stocked Sentra supermarket all in the centre of town.

If you are staying here then the small, but up to date, tourist information centre inside the municipal offices is a good place to find out what is going on. It is just off the main Okavango road, two blocks east of Kaiser Wilhelm Str. During the summer (October to May) the **outdoor pool** by the caravan park is open every day until 6pm. On the same side of town is the **Old Fort Museum** (signposted as *Das Alte Fort*). This small, privately-run museum is a few kilometres from the centre of town, past the Total service station and opposite the rugby stadium, on your left *en route* to Rundu. It centres on the original forge of a local blacksmith, and opens on Tuesdays and Fridays 4pm - 6pm, and Wednesdays 9am - 11am.

Evening activities in Grootfontein are more limited. The bars at the Nord and Meteor hotels open all week, except Sundays, in contrast to the cinema which shows the current blockbusters only on Fridays and Saturdays.

Hoba Meteorite

The farm 'Hoba' is well-signposted about 20km west of Grootfontein. Here, in 1920, the farm's owner discovered the world's heaviest metallic meteorite. It weighs about 50 tonnes, which analysis suggests is mostly iron (about 80%) and nickel.

It was declared a national monument in 1955 and recently received the protection of a permanent tourist officer because it was suffering badly at the hands of souvenir hunters. The locals became particularly irate when even the UN's Transition Assistance Group (UNTAG) personnel were found to be chipping bits off as they supervised the country's transition to democracy. Now it is open full time, but with a guard on duty. There is a small kiosk selling sweets and soft drinks.

Dragon's Breath Cave and lake

This cave is claimed to contain the world's largest known underground lake. It's situated about 46km from Grootfontein, just off the Tsumeb road, on the farm Hariseb, owned by Mr Pretorius — identified by a roadside board with the head of a cow on it.

The lake has crystal clear, drinkable water with a surface area of almost two hectares, and lies beneath a dome-shaped roof of solid rock. The water is about 60m below ground level and to get to it currently requires the use of ropes and caving equipment, with a final vertical abseil descent of 25m from the roof down to the surface of the water. This perhaps explains why it is not, as yet, open to visitors, though it is quite likely to be developed in the near future, when an easier approach can be made to it.

BUSHMANLAND

To the east of Grootfontein lies the area known as Bushmanland. This almost rectangular region borders on Botswana and stretches 90km from north to south and about 200km from east to west. The land is flat and dry, with sparse low bushes and drought-resistant grasses growing on the Kalahari's sandy soil. It is very poor agricultural land, but home to a large number of **Bushmen settlements**.

To the east of the region, especially south of Tsumkwe, there is a network of **seasonal pans** dotted around, whilst straddling the border itself are the Aha Hills (see page 329).

One attraction here is the game, which gathers in small herds around the pans. The best time to see animals corresponds to the end of the dry season, around August to October, as then the area's game congregates around any remaining water, and driving along the tracks will not be too difficult. During and after the rains, from January to March, **beware**: this region can become an impassable flood plane. Whenever you come, don't expect to see vast herds comparable to Etosha's or you'll be disappointed.

Getting organised

To visit this area you must, as with Kaokoland, be totally self-sufficient and part of a two-vehicle party. The region's centre, Tsumkwe, has basic supplies and usually fuel, although if it's empty the nearest fuel stop will be Grootfontein or Mukwe (just before Bagani, as you enter Caprivi). It is *essential* to have supplies for your complete trip, with the exception of water which can usually be found (and purified if necessary) along the way.

Before embarking on such a trip, obtain maps from Windhoek and resolve to keep a close watch on the navigation. Travel in this sandy terrain can be very slow. You won't leave second gear for miles on end, and retracing your steps is a time-consuming business.

Getting there

The C44 road through to Tsumkwe is the main access route into the area. It is navigable by 2WD, but all the other roads in the area require a 4WD. One good way to visit is by combining it with a trip through Kaudum game reserve (see page 218), thus making a roundabout journey from Grootfontein to the Caprivi Strip. Alternatively, approaching the region from the south via Summerdown, Otjinene, and Hereroland would be an interesting and very unusual route, but expect the going to get tough.

Where to stay

Camping is possible anywhere, with no permits necessary, but obviously you must take great care not to offend local people by your behaviour or choice of campsite. Wherever possible, camp well away from other people or settlements, and ensure that you're not in a place that might block a game trail or keep any animals from a water-hole.

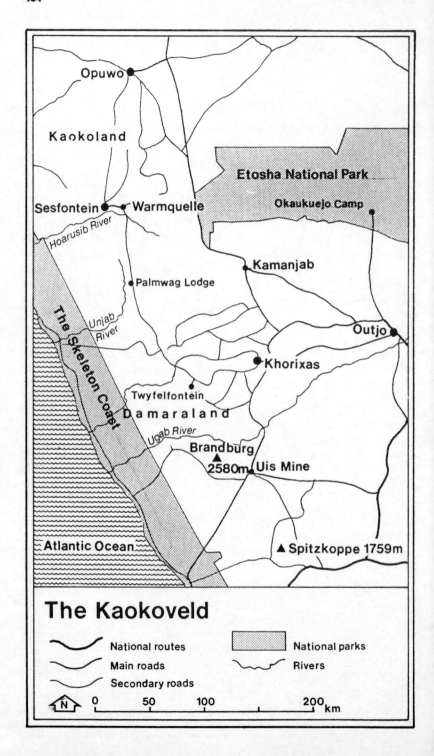

The Kaokoveld

National routes
Main roads
Secondary roads

National parks
Rivers

N   0   50   100   200 km

Chapter 14

The Kaokoveld

The Kaokoveld. Africa's last wilderness. This is Namibia's least inhabited area. It stretches from the coastal desert plain and rises slowly into a wild and rugged landscape. Here slow-growing trees cling to rocky mountains, whilst wild grass seeds wait dormant on the dust plains for showers of rain. This is the land of the Himba. Traditionally a pastoral people, relying upon herds of drought-resistant cattle for their livelihood, their villages are situated by springs which gush out from dry river beds.

Because of the low population in the northern parts of the Kaokoveld, there is some excellent game here, living beyond the boundaries of any reserve. This is one of the last refuges for wild black rhinos, which still survive by ranging wide, knowing where the season's plants grow, and when to move on. This is also home to the famous desert elephants. Some naturalists have cited their apparently long legs, and proven ability to withstand drought, as evidence that they are actually a subspecies of the African elephant. These rare animals are certainly adept at surviving in areas with virtually no surface water. Whether they are able to do this through physical adaptation, or by using some ancestral memory of the few water sources which do exist, is unknown.

Historically the Kaokoveld has been split into two areas: Damaraland in the south, and Kaokoland in the north. For visitors, Damaraland's most interesting places are accessible by 2WD — though a 4WD vehicle makes travel easier. Similarly, bringing your own food and camping equipment is a great help, but not strictly necessary as there are several basic camps in the area. Damaraland's main attractions are the mountains of Spitzkoppe and Brandberg, the wealth of Bushman rock art, and the three large private game reserves which border the Kaokoveld: Hobatere, Entendeka and Palmwag.

Kaokoland is different. Its remote 'roads' need high-clearance 4WD vehicles and are dangerous for the unprepared. The best way to visit is by air, or using one of the local operators. They know the area, understand the dangers, and run one or two spectacular camps.

To visit Kaokoland independently you would need your own expedition: two or more well-equipped 4WDs, with experienced drivers and enough fuel and supplies for a week or more. A daunting and expensive option.

DAMARALAND

Most of sites described here, such as Spitzkoppe, Brandberg, Twyfelfontein and the Burnt Mountain are cared for by the DNC, and are just being developed. As yet they have few regulations attached to them. However, the rest of Damaraland (with the exception of the farms in the east) is split into a number of concession areas — each of which is managed by a local operator who is responsible for maintaining the area and issuing permits for those who wish to enter it. So, before coming here, it's wise to ask the advice of Windhoek's DNC about current permit requirements.

Because of the region's sparse population, it's unwise to travel here without at least warm bedding and supplies of food and water. It is altogether better to be fully equipped to camp and fend for yourself, as then you can still use the facilities at the more basic camps without depending on them. There's usually no problem camping out by the roadside if you get stuck — but make sure you're not offending anyone by inadvertently camping on their land.

If you see local people hitching, bear in mind that there is no public transport here. In such a rural area, Namibians will stop to help if there is a hope of cramming a further person into their car. Seeing foreign tourists pass by with a half-empty vehicle will leave behind very negative feelings.

Spitzkoppe

At the far southern end of the Kaokoveld lies a small cluster of mountains which rise from the flat gravel plains that make up the desert floor. These include Spitzkoppe, Klein Spitzkoppe and Pondok Mountain. Of these the highest is Spitzkoppe which towers 600m above the surrounding plains: a demanding technical climb. Its resemblance to the famous Swiss mountain earned it the name of *The Matterhorn of Africa* while the extreme conditions found on its faces ensured that it remained unclimbed until 1946.

Getting there

Spitzkoppe is reached on the D3716. Approaching **from Henties Bay** take the D1918 westwards for 103km, then turn left onto the D3716. Coming **from Usakos**, take the Henties Bay turn-off after 23km on the B2 and follow it for about 18km before a right turn onto the D3716. **From Uis Mine**, leave on the C36 to Omaruru, but turn right onto the D1930 after only 1km. From there it's about 75km to the right turn onto the D3716

What to see and do

Currently there are no facilities here, though for the self-sufficient it's yet another spectacular place to camp — and its lower slopes provide some difficult scrambles. At the extreme eastern end of this group of hills is a verdant valley known as **Bushman's Paradise**, which you can reach with the help of a fixed steel cable. Sadly the rock paintings under the overhang have been vandalised (even here) and little is left of them, but the valley is still worth a visit. If you have an hour to spare, then an alternative descent is to continue to follow the gully out of the valley — though this route is not an easy option.

Because of their height and proximity to the ocean, these mountains receive more fog and precipitation than most, much of which runs off their smooth granite sides to form small pools. These are idea places to search for the shrimps and invertebrates which have adapted to the environment's extremes by laying drought-resistant eggs.

Uis Mine

As its name suggests, this small town is essentially an extension of the tin mine which dominates it. The fuel station opens from 7am to 7pm every day apart from Sunday, when it opens at 10.30am and closes at 4.30pm. There is a small supermarket, which opens from 8.30am to 2pm and 5pm to 7.30pm during the week and from 11am to 2pm and 5pm to 7.30pm on Sundays. Recently a **small rest camp** has opened here, with five four-bed bungalows, complete with their own bathroom and kitchen. Costs are N$100 per bungalow. To book contact PO Box 2, Uis Mine. Tel: (062262) 21.

Brandberg

Measuring about 30km by 23km at its base, and 2,573m at its highest point, this ravine-split massif of granite totally dominates the surrounding desert plains.

Getting there

Though you cannot miss seeing it whilst driving in the vicinity, getting to Brandberg without driving over the fragile lichen plains needs thought. Its eastern side, around the Tsisab Ravine, is easily reached using a 2WD car via the D2359, which turns west off the C35 about 14km after Uis Mine on the way to Khorixas. It is signposted to the White Lady (*Witvrou* in Afrikaans), the famous rock painting.

Those with 4WD vehicles can also use the extensive network of rough tracks which turn towards the massif from the north, west and south, off the D2342, startling some 14km south-west of Uis Mine on the Henties Bay road.

What to see and do

Two attractions are drawing increasing numbers of visitors here:

Climbing With the highest point in Namibia and some good technical routes in a very demanding environment, the massif attracts serious mountaineers as well as those in search of a few days' interesting scrambling. It's very important to remember to take adequate safety precautions though, as the temperatures can be extreme and the mountain is very isolated. Unless you are used to such conditions, stick to short trips in the early morning or late afternoon, and take a long siesta in the scorching midday heat. Serious climbers should seek advice from the Mountain Club of Namibia, in Windhoek, well before they arrive.

Paintings This area has been occupied by Bushmen for several thousands of years and still holds a wealth of their artefacts and rock paintings, of which only a fraction have been studied in detail, and some are undoubtedly still to be found. The richest section for art has so far been the **Tsisab Ravine**, on the north-eastern side of the massif. Here one painting in particular has been the subject of much scientific debate, ever since its discovery by the outside world in 1918: the famous *White Lady of Brandberg.*

The figure of the *white lady* stands about 40cm tall, and is central to a large frieze which apparently depicts some sort of procession — in which one or two of the figures have animal features. In her right hand is a flower, or perhaps an ostrich egg cup, whilst in her left she holds a bow and some arrows. Unlike the other figures, she has been painted white from below the chest. The coloration and form of the figure is very reminiscent of some early Mediterranean styles and, together with points gleaned from a more detailed analysis of the pictures, this led early scholars to credit the painters as having links with Europe. Among the site's first visitors was the Abbé Henri Breuil, a world authority on rock art who studied these paintings and others nearby in the late 1940s, and subsequently published four classic volumes entitled *The Rock Paintings of Southern Africa* (see *Bibliography*). He concluded that the *lady* had elements of ancient Mediterranean origin.

More recent scholars seem to think that the people represented are indigenous, with no European links, and they regard the *white lady* as being a boy, covered with white clay whilst undergoing an initiation ceremony. Whichever school of thought you prefer, the *white lady* is well signposted and worth the scramble needed to reach it.

Further up the Tsisab Ravine there are many other sites, including the friezes within the *Girl's School*, *Pyramid* and *Ostrich* shelters. If you wish to get more out of the rock art, then Breuil's books cannot be recommended too highly — though as classic antique books they are difficult to find, and expensive to buy.

Twyfelfontein rock art

Twyfelfontein means 'doubtful spring', a reference to failings of the perennial spring of water which wells up near the base of the valley. In the past, this spring, on the desert's margins, would have attracted huge herds of game from the sparse plains around, making this uninviting valley an excellent base for early hunters.

Perhaps this explains why the slopes of Twyfelfontein, amid flat-topped mountains typical of Damaraland, conceal one of the continent's greatest concentrations of rock art. This is not obvious when you first arrive. They seem like any other hillsides strewn with rocks. But the boulders which litter these slopes are dotted with thousands of paintings and ancient engravings, of which only a fraction have been recorded so far. Even with a knowledgeable local guide, you need several hours to start to discover the area's treasures. Begin early and beware of the midday heat.

Getting there

To reach the valley, which is well signposted, take the C39 for 73km west from Khorixas, then left onto the D3254 for 15km, then right for about 11km (ignoring a left fork after 6km) to the base of the valley.

Where to stay

Aba-Huab campsite Aba-Huab, c/o Elias Aro Xoagub, PO Box 131, Twyfelfontein via Khorixas. This is the first of several camps in Damaraland which have been set up with the help of Namibia's Save the Rhino Trust, and run by local people. Aba-Huab camp is managed by the very able Elias, and is well signposted a few kilometres from Twyfelfontein valley. It provides solar-heated showers, toilets, a communal fire pit, and shady campsites. As an alternative to camping there are simple A-frame shelters for sleeping which raise you off the ground, though you still need at least a sleeping bag and preferably a foam mattress.

Basic canned food and drinks are available here, and local meals can be arranged with notice. Elias and his staff also conduct tours around the rock's images, which are invaluable as many are difficult to find without guidance. Local walks and donkey-cart rides are also possible, but arrange these in advance.

Costs are N$10 per person for the sites, and a few dollars extra for the tours. A large proportion of this camp's profits are fed back into the local community.

Organ Pipes

Retracing your tracks from Twyfelfontein, turn right onto the left fork which you ignored earlier (see directions above). After about 3km there's a gorge to your left, followed by a flat area used for parking. Leave your vehicle and take one of the paths down into the gorge where you'll find hundreds of tall angular columns of dolerite in a most unusual formation.

Burnt Mountain

Continuing about 2km on the road past the Organ Pipes, you'll reach what is locally known locally as the 'Burnt Mountain'. Seen in the midday sun this can be a real disappointment, but when the red-brown shale catches the early morning or late afternoon light, the mountain side glows with a startling rainbow of colours, as if it's on fire.

Khorixas

Placed fairly centrally, Khorixas was Damaraland's administrative capital and is useful for supplies, but otherwise unremarkable. It does have a large **rest camp**, signposted as *ruskamp*, complete with a swimming pool and a small restaurant. Pleasant bungalows with towels, linen and en suite facilities cost from N$90 per person, whilst camping is N$25 per site plus N$5 per person. Fuel and supplies are available here. Contact PO Box 2, Tel: (0020) 196 or (0908) 3512.

Petrified Forest

Clearly signposted off the C39, west of Khorixas, lie a number of petrified trees on a bed of sandstone. Some are partially buried, while others lie completely exposed because the sandstone surrounding them has eroded away. It is thought that they were carried here as logs by a river, some 250 million years ago, and became stranded on a sand bank. Subsequently sand was deposited around them, creating ideal conditions for the cells of the wood to be replaced by silica, and thus become petrified.

Kamanjab

Just to the east of Damaraland, this town's sealed roads, a fuel station and well stocked supermarket will come as a relief to those driving south from Kaokoland. However, there are no major attractions here, and nowhere to stay, so most people just pass through after stocking up on fuel and cold drinks.

The road north from Kamanjab to Ruacana is about 291km of good gravel. Initially it passes through ranch country, and then between the game areas of Hobatere and Etosha (note the high game fences here).

About 8km north of the Hobatere entrance lies a checkpoint on the veterinary cordon fence, after which the land reverts to subsistence farms — remember to watch for domestic animals straying onto the road. From here the bush is bare and overgrazed: just low mopane bushes and acacia survive the goats' onslaught.

Hobatere

PO Box 110, Kamanjab. Tel: (06552) 2022. About 80km north of Kamanjab, on the road past Etosha's western fence, is the entrance to Hobatere. This **private game reserve**, one of Damaraland's wildlife concession areas, is run by Steve and Louise Braine, with a staff of professional safari guides.

The reserve covers a large area which becomes increasingly dry from its eastern side, by Etosha, to its western side, near Entendeka. In the north, the landscape is an undulating patchwork of mopane scrub and open plains, dotted with the occasional flat-topped acacia. A classic environment for big game animals, although rather too dry for buffalo, which prefer a more watery environment. Until very recently there were black rhino here, and it seems likely that they will soon return, when the reserve becomes a centre for rhino rescued from more vulnerable areas.

The southern areas of the reserve are mountainous, and here the guides will to stick to the dry river valleys in search of the large herds of springbok and Hartmann's mountain zebra. Interestingly, the area's predators use these steep, rocky valleys as places from which to ambush unsuspecting game.

Overall the animals are numerous, and quintessentially Namibian. The rare black-faced impala is well represented, as is the diminutive, endemic Damara dik-dik, whose first reaction to a disturbance is often to stop dead still — a photographer's dream. However, Hobatere's biggest attraction for the visitor is its air of luxurious tranquillity: a place with the space to relax.

Getting there Hobatere means 'find it here' or 'find here', and the lodge itself is easy to find on the banks of the Otjivasondu river. Just turn off west from the main road, through the imposing gate, and follow the clear track for about 16 km.

What to see and do The activities here revolve around game viewing in Hobatere's Land Rovers. The guides are all professional and — with nobody else in the area — there are good chances to get close to the bigger game. Options on request include the normal game drives; night drives, which are your best chance to look for the shy, smaller cats, bat-eared foxes and the like; and (for the energetic) walking with a guide. The lodge has a cool pool for those mid-afternoon dips — but keep your eyes open for thirsty elephants!

If you are staying for a while, then the guides have authorisation to visit the western area of Etosha, from which visitors are normally barred. This is only open to safari companies, so do take the chance to visit it if you stay a while.

Accommodation is mostly in separate twin-bedded, thatched brick cottages. These are comfortable and secluded with a shower and toilet en-suite, and plenty of space. In the lodge's main building there is a full bar and a separate dining area, which serves good food from the house menu. The cottages are quite spread out, which allows you a feeling of independence: to join in if you wish to, or to just relax if you don't.

The costs here are N$140 per person, with an extra N$15 each for breakfast and for lunch, and N$30 for dinner. Game drives are N$80 per vehicle per hour (6 people), while walks are only N$10 per guide per hour. Contact Hobatere directly using the address above, or by phoning Windhoek (061) 222281, or using one of Windhoek's major tour agencies.

Palmwag Area

The landscape is classic for the southern Kaokoveld: semi-desert scrub vegetation with sparse bushes and low, stunted trees. Water is scarce, often flowing underground in *omurambas* which rarely wet the surface sand. These mostly flow from east to west, heading for the Atlantic via the Skeleton Coast. Palmwag shares its western border with this park and, as you would expect, much of its wildlife is desert-adapted.

This means no large herds, but a good variety of interesting wildlife and usually very few visitors. The major attractions here are the desert elephant and black rhino — two of the continent's most endangered species, but as elusive as they are rare.

An enduring image from one visit here was the sight of a herd of giraffe, which we watched for almost an hour, skittishly grazing their way across a rocky hillside by the track. Their height seemed so out of place in the landscape of low trees.

Getting there

To reach it, take the C39 about 117km westwards from Khorixas before branching northwards onto the D2620. 40km later take a left onto the D3706 towards Sesfontein. This leads through a veterinary fence after 6km and the lodge is soon signposted on your left. Alternatively there is a good bush airstrip near the camp, so you can fly in. A half-hour game-spotting flight on your way out is the ideal way to end a trip here.

What to see and do

North of the veterinary fence, and south of Kaokoland, there are two camps, each with its own wildlife concession area to look after: Palmwag Lodge and Entendeka Mountain Camp. Palmwag's concession area, stretches east from the Skeleton Coast to the road, whilst Entendeka's extends eastwards from the road until Hobatere. Both have been set aside for game, and to explore either, you must stay at one of the camps.

Driving your own 4WD around either concession is not practical. It is remote, dangerous and the tracks are impossible to follow. People who don't know the area invariably get lost. Leave your car at one of the camps and hire a guide to show you around. The area's ecosystem is too fragile to withstand the impact of many vehicles and the animals are wary of people. They have enough problems without being frightened from water-holes by misguided tourists seeking the perfect picture.

Where to stay

Palmwag Lodge PO Box 339, Swakopmund. Tel: (0641) 4459. Fax: (0641) 4664. This is the base for visiting Palmwag's concession area, and the centre of operations for **DAS** (Desert Adventure Safaris). You can explore the area in one of their vehicles, which take a maximum of four people for N$100 per hour. Their guides know the area well, picking out the obscure tracks and going to areas frequented by game.

If you have the time, before you get here, consider booking a longer trip through the DAS offices in Swakopmund or Windhoek. They have operated in the Kaokoveld for several years, taking groups into Palmwag's area, and further north into Kaokoland, sleeping at both temporary and permanent tented camps.

Accommodation is in pleasant reed bungalows for N$140 per person full board (no half board or bed and breakfast options), whilst camping costs N$10 per person per night, plus a one-off charge of N$20 for the site. If camping you can eat in the restaurant, where a good evening meal costs around N$30, or simply sample the draught Hansa beer in the bar.

Palmwag has a poorly stocked shop, and fuel is available from 8am to 12.30pm, and 2.30pm to 6pm during the week and 8am until 12.30pm on Sundays. Outside these hours there is an extra N$2 charge from the reluctant attendant. To book contact DAS in Swakopmund (address above).

Entendeka Mountain Lodge PO Box 6850, Windhoek. Tel: (061) 226174/225178. Fax: (061) 239455. Entendeka is a new luxury tented camp situated a few kilometres from Palmwag's airstrip, on the Entendeka lave plains. It is run by Dennis and Barbera Liebenberg who aim to give guests a personal experience of the Kaokoveld's animals and ecosystem.

Numbers are limited to a maximum of 16 guests, accommodated in luxury tents complete with camp beds, wash basins, showers and bush toilets. The main dining and bar area is also under canvas, but meals are a social occasion and usually eaten together around the fire. The total cost, including food, all game drives, walks and activities is about N$250 per person per night.

The camp must be booked in advance (it is not even signposted from the road), and visitors who drive in can be picked up by 4WD from the veterinary fence, where there is covered parking available. To book contact the Namib Travel Shop in Windhoek, at the above address.

Warmquelle

About 87km north of Palmwag Lodge, on the way to Sesfontein lies Warmquelle, a small settlement situated on the site of a spring. In the early years of this century the spring was used in an irrigation project, for which an aqueduct was constructed. Now only a few parts of the old aqueduct remain, together with a small Damara settlement and quite a large school.

Sesfontein

Sesfontein, named after the 'six springs' which surface nearby, sits in the Hoanib valley and marks the northern edge of Damaraland. North of here, the going gets tougher. In the earlier part of this century, Sesfontein was an important control post and it remains the focal point of the area, complete with the remnants of an old German fort.

For most local people, who live by farming goats and the occasional field of maize, this is their main centre with a school and several shops. There are usually a few people about, so don't miss the chance to stop and watch village life go by. There's no better way than sitting with a cold drink on the concrete steps of one of the shops, though you may attract a crowd of playful children.

Where to stay

Like the Aba-Huab camp near Twyfelfontein, two new locally-run camps have started up in this area recently. Both have been set up with the help of the Rhino Trust or the Endangered Wildlife Society, and both aim to channel some of their income back into their local communities.

The turn-off for the **Khowarib campsite** is signposted about 75km north of Palmwag on the D7306. The track to the camp is suitable for 2WD vehicles and runs for about 3km from the main road along the Khowarib Gorge.

The Khowarib camp sits on the banks of the Khowarib river and consists of seven basic huts, built by the local villagers using local materials to a traditional design, and five different camp sites for pitching tents. Bucket showers and bush toilets are provided and with notice, basic local meals can be arranged. There are guides who conduct walks around the area.

The camp is run by Eliu Ganuseb, and charges are N$35 per night for one-bed huts, N$50 per night for two-bed huts and from N$25 to N$75 for a camp site. He can also arrange donkey cart rides, at N$35 per day, hiking trails at N$30 and even displays of 'traditional cultural singing and dancing.'

About 10km further north is the **Ongongo campsite**. To reach this, turn right at Warmquelle and follow the signs. You follow a water pipeline for about 6km before reaching the site's office hut. The main attraction is the Ongongo waterfall which has a a deep, clear pool beneath it, sheltered by an overhang of rock. In the past few have resisted the temptation to strip off and swim, which isn't surprising given the temperature.

Now there are two changing huts available and a donation is requested from visitors. You can also stay the night in one of three very basic, unfurnished huts (N$10 per person) or camp for N$10 per site, but you still need to have your own food and equipment as nothing is available.

KAOKOLAND

This vast tract of land is Namibia at its most enticing — and yet most inhospitable. Kaokoland appeals to the adventurer and explorer in us, keeping quiet about the dangers involved. On the eastern side, hilly tracks become mud-slides as they get washed away by the rains, whilst the baking desert in the west affords no comfort for those who get stranded. Even dry river-beds hide soft traps of deep sand, whilst the few which seem damp and hard may turn to quicksand within metres. Having struggled to free a Land Rover with just one wheel stuck in quicksand, it is easy to believe the tales of vehicles vanishing completely within an hour!

One road on the eastern side was particularly memorable — it started favourably as a good gravel track. After 20km, it had deteriorated into a series of rocky ruts, shaking us to our bones and forcing us to slow down to 10kph. After a while, when we'd come too far to think of returning, the track descended into a sandy river-bed. Strewn with boulders and enclosed by walls of rock, the only way was for passengers to walk and guide the driver, watching nervously as the tyres lurched from boulder to boulder.

Hours later we emerged — onto another difficult track. Gradually it flattened and the driving eased: we were happy to be travelling faster. Then the pace was interrupted. Streams, crossing the road. Someone would wade across to check the depth, and then the car would swiftly follow, its momentum carrying it across the muddy bed. The third stream stopped us in our tracks: more than thigh-high, fast-flowing — a river in flood. We slept dry in our tents, thankful that the floods hadn't reached that first rocky river-bed whilst we were there.

To come to Kaokoland independently, you need a two-vehicle 4WD expedition, all your supplies, a good navigator, detailed maps and good local advice on routes — and even then you'll probably get lost a few times. This is not a trip to undertake lightly: if things go wrong you will be hundreds of kilometres from the nearest help, let alone any hospitals.

If you can get an expedition together then, in contrast to Damaraland's concession areas, Kaokoland has yet to adopt any formal system of control. You are free to travel where you can.   That said, the drier areas have a very fragile ecosystem: simply driving a vehicle off the tracks and 'across country' can cause permanent damage — killing plants and animals, and leaving marks that last for centuries. Vehicle trails made 40 years ago can still be seen as the crushed plants and lichens haven't recovered yet. Here, more than anywhere, there is a need to be responsible and treat the environment with care. **Don't drive off the tracks**.

Where to stay

If you are planning an expedition then, realistically, you must camp. Another word of warning though: however inviting river valleys seem, never stay in one. Firstly, if it rains in the mountains you will be in for a flash flood: described by a witness as 'a wall of water thundering towards her'. Secondly, these dry river beds are vital for the increasingly scarce animals, as links between the region's scattered water-holes. If you camp in a river bed near one of these, then the animals will simply stop using it and have to take long detours to look for water elsewhere. They are more wary than their cousins in game parks, and far more easily scared.

The alternatives to camping are a couple of organised camps, but none of these welcome casual visitors. They cater for those on pre-arranged visits with operators.

Opuwo

This rough and ready, frontier town is the hub of Kaokoland. It has shops, a good bakery, several garages, a large school, and even a short stretch of tarred road in the centre of town, despite being over a hundred kilometres from the nearest other tar (south of Kamanjab, or east of Ruacana).

Getting there

Opuwo is 54km of mediocre gravel from the main Kamanjab-Ruacana road and greets you with large, irrigated maize fields on the right, and probably a couple of stray cattle in front. Soon the dry, dusty town appears, sprawling over a low hillside with no apparent centre: its buildings are functional rather than attractive, and the outskirts fade into groups of little round Himba huts.

Getting organised

Turn right for the town's main attraction — the fuel station. As recently as 1990 there were no proper fuel supplies: just a few private entrepreneurs who sold it from drums on the back of pick-up trucks for twice the normal price. Now it is available at the BP station, which helps with logistics, being the only fuel north of Palmwag and west of Ruacana. That said, beware of absolutely depending upon it, as this station can (and does) run out. It is usually open 8am - 7pm during the week, Saturdays: 8am -12 and 3pm - 7pm; Sundays 3pm - 6pm only.

Whilst waiting to fill up, or taking a stroll around, look around — there is a fascinating mix of people. The traditional rural Himba, who come into town to trade or buy supplies, with their decorated goatskin dress and ochre-stained skins. Strong, powerful faces speak clearly of people who have yet to trade their own culture for what little is being offered to them here. As with any trading post, the place abounds with shady local traders. These mix with occasional businessmen, and the eccentric characters who emerge from the bush to replenish supplies, and then disappear again with equal speed.

The bakery next to the BP garage is welcome for its fresh bread, rolls, and drinking yoghurt, whilst the garage sells essential cool drinks. For general supplies go to Groothandel Wholesale which has an excellent selection of hardware, tinned food and staples, and produces large blocks of ice for cool-boxes. If you need to change money, they may cash travellers cheques as a favour, but forget exchanging foreign notes or using credit cards. On the right of the BP station, the brightly painted curio shop sells postcards and Himba jewellery, and is closed on Sundays. Next to that is the new Opuwo Supermarket, but don't expect too much from it.

Next door there is a post office, and a couple of *drankwinkels*. There are few of these in Kaokoland, but they are multiplying rapidly.

Camps in Kaokoland

Because of the transport difficulties, camps are difficult to set up in Kaokoland, and hard to maintain. This makes them few in number, and expensive — but often they maintain a sense of uniqueness and a true feeling of wilderness.

Epupa Camp Reservations: Manfred Goldbeck, Top Travel, PO Box 80205, Windhoek. Tel/Fax: (061) 51975. About 145km west of Ruacana, the Kunene river spreads out as it starts to thread its way through the Baynes mountains, *en route* to the Atlantic. Lined by feathery green Makalani palms, and overlooked by barren hills, the river widens to accommodate a few small islands before plunging into a geological fault. These are the Epupa Falls.

There is only one permanent tented camp here, run by Ermo Fly-in Safaris, which takes a maximum of only eight guests. It is situated in the thin strip of permanent palm forest which flanks the river on either side, and is one of Namibia's most delightful camps.

Getting there A few kilometres from the camp is an airstrip, and flying is the only practical way to reach Epupa. Driving here along the hot rocky tracks would take days, much fuel and lots of spare tyres. Needless to say, these tracks become simply impassable during the rainy season.

What to see and do The falls are such a relaxing place that writing of activities completely misses the point. Epupa is remote and the camp's atmosphere makes you want to unwind. My favourite activity was lying under the palms, watching the colourful agama lizards race up and down in their quest for insects.

If you must do something, then the bird-life in the area is remarkable. The river attracts the inevitable fish eagles, and kingfishers range from the giant to the tiny malachite kingfisher. Their practice of spending an afternoon fishing is a good one — the camp has a few rods available.

Other birds seen around include purple, lilac breasted and European rollers, grey lowries, bulbuls, hornbills, scarlet-breasted sunbirds, golden and lesser masked weavers, the odd, lost, great white eagle and the very rare rufus-faced palm thrush. Visiting in May, a fearless pair of paradise flycatchers were nesting at eye-level by the tent.

Ornithologists will certainly want to visit the nearby valley where, amongst the trees, there is a breeding colony of rosy-faced lovebirds.

Others should go to the same valley, but keep their eyes on the ground for the rose quartz crystals which abound, or the chipped stone implements of past inhabitants. Until the late 1980s there were people living in the area who relied entirely on a hunter-gatherer existence, using only stone implements.

For the more energetic, there are a couple of Colorado-type inflatable rafts. These can be driven upriver and launched in order for you to float leisurely back to camp. There are crocodiles and hippos about, so restrain yourself from swimming until back at Epupa. Neither normally ventures near the falls, so there is a good, deep area that is safe for swimming. Check its precise location with the camp, and try not to stray from it.

Sunrise bathes the nearby hills in clear red light, and this is a good time to explore. The hills have an uneven surface of loose rock so wear a stout pair of shoes and watch out for snakes. Temperatures are cold at first, but it warms up very rapidly so take water, a sun-hat and sun-cream.

Situated in a traditional Himba area, there is sometimes the opportunity to visit a typical local family. With the aid of an interpreter, this gives you the chance to glimpse a little of their lifestyle. Of all the Namibians that you encounter, the Himba require the greatest cultural sensitivity. Their culture is in the process of adapting to centuries of changes within a matter of years.

Where to stay Accommodation at Epupa is in strong two-person tents, complete with folding beds and mosquito-netted windows. The camp has been professionally laid out to blend into the narrow band of palm forest which lines the river, and each tent is camouflaged by palms and secluded in its own alcove, with a basin and water for washing. Separately, for communal use, there is an efficient bucket shower and even a flush toilet.

The cost of visiting is high, due to the camp's remote position. Daily rates are about N$400 per day, including everything (flights, meals, drinks, excursions, etc.). A stay here must be arranged well in advance, and to book contact Manfred Goldbeck at Top Travel's address, given above.

Chapter 15

Etosha National Park

2WD. Entrance fees: N$8 per person plus N$10 per car.

Translated as the 'Place of Mirages', 'Land of Dry Water' or the 'Great White Place', Etosha is an apparently endless pan of silvery-white sand, upon which dust devils play and mirages blur the horizon. As a game park, it excels during the dry season when huge herds of animals can be seen amidst some of the most startling and photogenic scenery on the continent.

The roads are all navigable in a 2WD car, and the only advantage of a 4WD is that you are higher up when trying to spot game through the dense, low bushes. Each rest camp has a variety of accommodation, a restaurant, a bar, and even a pool, and yet the park is never busy in comparison with the crowded game reserves of East Africa.

BACKGROUND INFORMATION

History

Etosha first became known to Europeans in the early 1850s when it was visited by Francis Galton and Charles Andersson. They recorded their first impressions:

> '...we traversed an immense hollow, called Etosha, covered with saline encrustations, and having wooded and well-defined borders. Such places are in Africa designate 'salt pans'... In some rainy seasons, the Ovambo informed us, the locality was flooded and had all the appearance of a lake; but now it was quite dry, and the soil strongly impregnated with salt. Indeed, close in shore, the commodity was to be had of a very pure quality.'

They were the first in a line of explorers and traders who relentlessly hunted

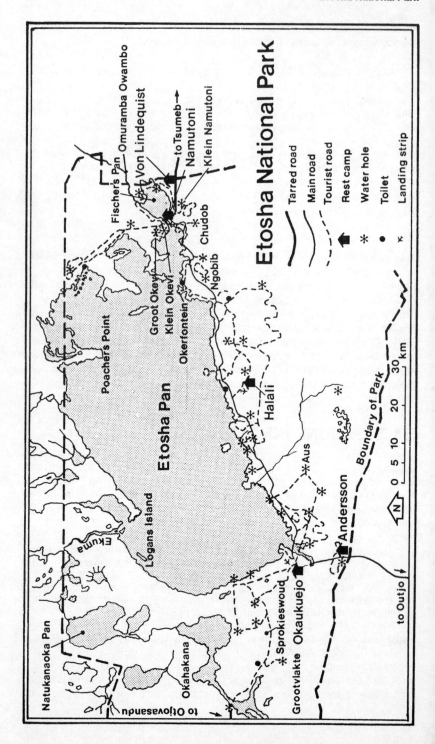

Etosha National Park

Tarred road
Main road
Tourist road
Rest camp
Water hole
Toilet
Landing strip

Boundary of Park

0 5 10   20   30 km

N

to Tsumeb →

Omuramba Owambo
Von Lindequist
Namutoni
Klein Namutoni
Fischers Pan
Chudob
Ngobib
Groot Okevi
Klein Okevi
Okerfontein
Poachers Point

Etosha Pan

Logans Island
Ekuma

Natukanaoka Pan

Okahakana

to Otjovasandu →

Halali

Aus

Andersson
Sprokieswoud Okaukuejo
Grootvlakte

to Outjo →

the area's huge herds of game. In 1876 an American trader, G.McKiernan, came through the area and wrote of a visit to Etosha:

> 'All the menageries in the world turned loose would not compare to the sight that I saw that day.'

The slaughter became worse as time progressed and more Europeans came until, in 1907, Dr. F. von Lindequist, the governor of German South West Africa (as Namibia was then), proclaimed three reserves. These covered all of the current park, and most of Kaokoland — between the Kunene to the Hoarusib rivers. The aim was to stem the rapid depletion of the animals in the area, and protect all of the land through which the seasonal migrations passed. It was an excellent plan for conserving the wildlife.

This protected area remained largely intact until the 1950s and 60s. Then, just as a nature conservation unit and several tourist camps were set up, the reserves were redefined, and Etosha shrank to its present size.

Geography, landscape and flora

The present pan appears to be the remnant of a large inland lake which was fed by rivers from the north and east. One of these was probably the Kunene, which flowed south-east from the Angolan highlands and into the pan. However, some 12 million years ago continental uplift changed the slope of the land and the course of these tributaries. The Kunene now flows west from the Ruacana Falls and into the Atlantic. Thus deprived, the lake slowly vanished in the scorching sun, leaving behind only a salty residue. Few plants can grow on this and so erosion by the wind is easy, allowing the pan to be gradually hollowed out.

The pan has probably changed very little in appearance over time. It is roughly 129km from east to west and 72km from north to south, covering an area of 6,133 square kilometres with flat, silvery sand and shimmering heat. If the rains to the north and east have been good, then the pan will hold some water for a few months at the start of the year, thanks mainly to the Ekuma River and Omuramba Owambo, but only very rarely does it fill completely.

In the rest of the park, beyond the pan's borders, the terrain is generally flat with a variety of habitats ranging from mopane woodland to wide open, virtually treeless, plains. In the east of the park, around Namutoni, the attractive **makalani palms** (*Hyphaene ventricosa*) are found — often in picturesque groups around water-holes. The small, round fruit of these palms, a favourite food of elephants, is sometimes called *vegetable ivory* because of its hard white kernel. In the west, one of the more unusual areas is the **Haunted Forest**, *Sprokieswoud* in Afrikaans, where the contorted forms of strange Moringa trees (*Moringa ovalifolia*) form a weird woodland scene.

Etosha is so special because of the concentration of water-holes which occur around the southern edges of the pan. These increasingly draw the game as the dry season progresses. In fact, the best way to watch animals here is often just to sit in your vehicle by a water-hole and wait. Three types of spring create these water-holes, which differ in both appearance and geology:

Contact springs occur in situations where two adjacent layers of rock have very different permeabilities. There are many to be seen just on the edge of the pan. Here the water-bearing calcrete comes to an end and the water flows out onto the surface because the underlying layers of clay are impermeable. **Okerfontein** is the best example of this type of spring, a type which is generally weak in terms of water supply.

Water-level springs. Found in hollows where the surface of the ground actually cuts below the level of the water table, often in large depressions in the limestone formations. These are inevitably dependant on the level of the water table, and hence vary greatly from year to year. Typical of this type are **Ngobib**, **Groot Okevi** and **Klein Okevi**.

Artesian springs. Formed when pressure from overlying rocks forces water up to the surface from deeper aquifers (water-bearing rocks). Here they normally occur on limestone hillocks, forming deep pools which will often have clumps of reeds in their centre. These springs are usually very reliable and include **Namutoni**, **Klein Namutoni**, **Chudob** and **Aus**.

Mammals

The game and birds found here are typical of the savannah plains of southern Africa, but include several species endemic to this western side of the continent, adjacent to the Namib desert.

The more common herbivores include elephant, giraffe, eland, blue wildebeest, kudu, gemsbok, springbok, impala, steenbok, and zebra. The most numerous of these are the springbok which can often be seen in herds numbering thousands, spread out over the most barren of plains. These finely marked antelope have a marvellous habit of pronking, either (it appears) for fun or to avoid predators. It has been suggested that pronking is intended to put predators off in the first place by showing the animal's strength and stamina; the weakest pronkers are the ones predators are seen to go for. Andersson, the early explorer, described these elegant leaps:

'This animal bounds without an effort to a height of 10 or 12 feet at one spring, clearing from 12 to 14 feet of ground. It appears to soar, to be suspended for a moment in the air, then, touching the ground, to make another dart, or another flight, aloft, without the aid of wings, by the elastic springiness of its legs.'

Elephant are common, though digging for water below the sand wears down their tusks and so big tuskers are very rare. Often large family groups are seen trooping down to water-holes to drink, wallow and bathe. The park's population has recently come under scientific scrutiny for the infrasonic noises which they make (below the range of human hearing). It is thought that groups communicate over long distances in this way.

Among the rare species, black rhino continue to thrive here, and the floodlit water-hole at Okaukuejo provides one of the continent's best chances to observe this aggressive and secretive species. On one visit here, I watched as a herd of 20 or so elephants, silently drinking in the cool of the night, were frightened away from the water, and kept at bay, by the arrival of a single black rhino. It returned several times in the space of an hour or so, each time causing the larger elephants to flee, before settling down to enjoy a leisurely drink from the pool on its own.

Black-faced impala are restricted to Namibia and southern Angola, occurring here as well as in Naukluft and parts of the Kaokoveld. With only these isolated populations, numbering under a thousand or so, they are one of the rarest animals in the region. The Damara dik-dik is the park's smallest antelope. Endemic to Namibia, it is quite common here in areas of dense bush.

Roan antelope and red hartebeest occur all over the subcontinent, though they are common nowhere. This is definitely one of the better parks in which to look for them.

All of the larger carnivores are found here, with good numbers of lion, leopard and cheetah. The lion tend to prey mainly upon zebra and wildebeest, whilst the cheetah rely largely upon springbok. The seldom-seen leopard take a more varied diet, including antelope, small mammals and even jackals.

Also found in the park are both spotted and brown hyenas, together with silver jackal (or cape fox), the red jackal (also known as the caracal), and the more common black-backed jackal — many of which can be seen in the late evening, skulking around the camps in search of scraps of food.

Birds

For the ornithologists, over 300 species of birds have been recorded including many uncommon members of the hawk and vulture families. The black vulture, largest of the vulture species, is often seen here, though elsewhere (like many vultures) its numbers are declining as farming increases.

The number of large birds stalking around the plains can strike visitors as unusual: invariably during the day you will see groups of ostriches or pairs of secretary birds. Equally, it is easy to drive within metres of many kori bustards and black korhaans which will just sit by the roadside and watch the vehicles pass.

PRACTICAL INFORMATION

To see Etosha you need to drive around the park as there is no way to either walk within it, or fly just above it. If you do not have your own vehicle then you must either hire one, or book an organised trip.

Hiring your own vehicle is best done in Windhoek — see Chapter 4, *Planning and Preparations*, on page 48. However, if you are just hiring a car for Etosha then you should consider doing so from Tsumeb. This is perhaps best organised through the head offices of the car hire companies in Windhoek, see page 105.

Organised trips centre around the three private game lodges: Mokuti, Ongava and (to the western end only) Hobatere. See the section on Private camps, page 208, for details of each. Other than these, there are several operators who organise all-inclusive trips into the park — usually using the National Park's accommodation, and their own transport. These operators are all based in Windhoek, so see page 106 for details.

When to visit

To decide when to visit, think about the weather, the number of other visitors around, and the best wildlife viewing.

Weather At the beginning of the year, it's hot and fairly damp with average temperatures around 27°C and cloud cover for some of the time. This gradually disperses until the rains cease, around April. The plants are bright and green during this time, but it seems to detract from the park's stark beauty: it isn't nearly as photogenic.

From May to July the land cools down and dries out. The nights become colder, accentuating the temperature difference between the bright, hot days and the cool, clear nights. From about August, the green plants gradually fade to grey as the heat builds. From a photographic point of view, Etosha is at its best when it is driest, so come between July and October.

From October the heat becomes more oppressive as the clouds grow darker and heavier. Even the game seems to await the coming of the rains in November, or perhaps December. When they do arrive, these tropical downpours last only for a few hours each afternoon, but they clear the air and swiftly revive the vegetation.

Other visitors Etosha could never be called crowded at any time of year and, compared to the hordes of tourists that fill the game parks of East Africa, Etosha always seems deserted. However, it does become busier around Easter time and in August, especially during the South African school holidays. At these times, advanced booking through Windhoek DNC is advised.

Game viewing Etosha's dry season is the best time to see game. Then, as the small bush pools dry up and the green vegetation shrivels, the

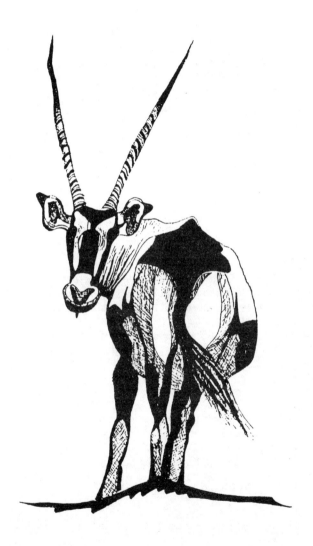

animals move closer to the springs on the pan's edge. Before the game fences were erected (these now surround the park completely) many of the larger animals would have migrated between Etosha and the Kaokoveld — returning here to the region's best permanent water-holes. Now most are forced to stay within the park and only bull elephants commonly break out of their confines to cause problems for the surrounding farmers.

Hence the months between July and late October are ideal for game, though the prospect of sitting in a car by a water-hole as the thermometer approaches 40°C can deter even the most enthusiastic. During and after the rains, you won't see much game, partly because the lush vegetation hides the animals, and partly because most of them will have moved away from the water-holes (where most of the roads are) and gone deeper into the bush.

Bird watching The start of the rainy season witnesses the arrival of many summer migrants and, if the rains have been good, the aquatic species which come for the water in the pan itself. If the rains are particularly good then thousands of flamingos may come to the pan to breed — an amazing spectacle, not to be missed (see box on flamingos, page 279). However, bear in mind that the ordinary feathered residents can be seen more easily in the dry season, when there is less vegetation around.

Getting there

You can enter the park via either the gate near Namutoni, which is 106km from Tsumeb, or the one south of Okaukuejo, 121 km from Outjo. There is a road through to the western border of the park, and a gate there, but until the planned fourth camp opens up, it is kept locked.

Entry permits to the park are issued at both gates, and then you must proceed to the nearest camp and pay a charge of N$8 per person and N$10 for the car. Your permit remains valid for the whole day, and then for as long as you stay in the park. However if you leave, and then wish to re-enter the park, you will have to pay again. This rule may be relaxed if you are just going to Mokuti Lodge for lunch, but you must tell the gatekeeper that you intend to return later in the day.

The gates open around sunrise and close about 20 minutes before sunset — for the precise times on any given day, see the notice just beyond the entry gates. Driving through the park in the dark is not allowed, and the gates invariably close on time. Note that neither hitch-hiking nor bicycles (push or motor) are allowed in the park

Where to stay — Public Camps

There are currently three National Parks camps, all of which are good value and well appointed. They each offer a full range of accommodation, including good campsites, and have a swimming pool, a shop, fuel and a restaurant. Expect the restaurants to cost about N$3-5 for a starter; N$10-

15 for salads and omelettes; up to N$30 for a full main course and N$5 for sweets.

Accommodation prices vary slightly between camps, though a campsite is always N$25, for up to eight people and two vehicles. This makes camping very cheap for large parties, but for two or three people it's often better to go for a small chalet.

Booking accommodation in advance at the DNC in Windhoek is advised, but of course you need to be very organised and stick to your itinerary. The alternative is to hope for spaces or cancellations, and ask at the camp office just before it closes at sunset. This is usually successful out of the main holiday times, but you will need a tent in case it is not.

Aim to spend a minimum of two nights at any camp you visit and don't miss out on Okaukuejo camp with its floodlit water-hole. Ideal would be two nights at Namutoni camp, two at Halali and three at Okaukuejo.

Namutoni camp

Situated on the eastern edge of the pan, Namutoni is based around a beautiful old *beau geste* type fort, in an area dotted with graceful Makalani palm trees. It originally dates back to a German police post, built here before the turn of the century, which was later used as an army base and then for English prisoners during the First World War, before being restored to its present state in 1957. Perhaps as a reminder of its military past, sunrise and sunset are heralded by a bugle call from the watch tower in the fort's north-eastern corner — onto which you too can climb for a better view of the surrounding country in the setting sun.

The rooms within the fort itself share facilities and are not air-conditioned. They cost from N$30 for two beds. The newer rooms, in the rectangular blocks, have en-suite facilities and air-con and, at N$80, cost considerably more. Four-bed tents, of a traditional canvas design, are available for N$25.

The restaurant here opens every day from 7am - 8.30pm for breakfast, 12 - 1.30pm for lunch and 6pm - 8.30pm for dinner. Meanwhile the shop sells tins, cold drinks, bread, meat, eggs, cheese and wine — as well as curios, print film, wildlife books and the ubiquitous postcards. During the week, it opens from 7.30am - 9am, 11.30am - 2pm and 5.30pm - 7.30pm. On a Sunday these times change to 8am - 9am, 12 - 2pm, and 6pm - 7pm, and it will not sell any alcohol.

Halali camp

The newest of the camps, Halali is in between the others, 75km from Namutoni, 70km from Okaukuejo and just to the north-west of the landmark *Tweekoppies*. Halali is the smallest, and usually the quietest, of the three camps.

Rooms start at N$46 for two people, using shared facilities but the more comfortable ones with en-suite facilities are N$80 for two beds, a kitchen and bathroom. Again four-bed tents are available for N$25.

Okaukuejo camp

This was the first camp to open to tourists and it currently functions as the administrative hub of the Park, and the centre of the Etosha Ecological Institute. It is situated at the western end of the pan, and about 120km north of Outjo.

The unique attraction of this camp is that it overlooks a permanent water-hole which is floodlit at night, giving you a chance to see some of the shy, nocturnal wildlife. The animals that come appear totally oblivious to the noises from the camp, not noticing the bright lights or the people sitting on benches just behind the low stone wall. The light doesn't penetrate into the dark surrounding bush, but it illuminates the water-hole like a stage — focusing all attention on the animals that come to drink.

During the dry season you would be unlucky not to spot something of interest by just sitting here for a few hours in the evening, so bring a couple of drinks, binoculars, and some warm clothes to settle down and watch. You are virtually guaranteed to see elephant and jackal, while lion and black rhino are also regular visitors during the dry season.

Okaukuejo's well-appointed bungalows start at N$58 for two beds and are probably the best of the park's three camps. Alternatively, you can camp or hire a four-bed tent for only N$25.

Where to stay — Private Camps

There are three private camps near Etosha. **Mokuti** is an established lodge near Namutoni; **Ongava** is a brand new, luxury camp just south of Okaukuejo; and **Hobatere** is a game ranch on the park's western side. Each is set in its own area, and each will arrange all your activities for you, including drives into Etosha. They cost more than the public camps, but their facilities are better and they have their own transport and guides for game viewing. Note that these guides are also subject to the park's strict opening and closing times.

Mokuti Lodge

PO Box 403, Tsumeb. Tel/Fax: (0671) 3084. Situated 25km from the B1 along the C38, Mokuti is set in its own small game reserve just outside the park's entrance gate. This is the flagship of the Namib Sun hotel group, with a number of awards for its excellent facilities. It feels like a rambling hotel — spread out, and yet modern.

The normal accommodation is in twin air-conditioned rooms with en-suite facilities, which are scattered in groups over quite a large area. There are also a few even more luxurious units, complete with double beds and separate lounges; several 'family units', which are cheaper if you are travelling with children; and two units for people with wheel chairs. Mokuti's costs start from a very reasonable N$210 for a single, or N$290 for a twin room.

The restaurant here is certainly one of the country's best. Starters are N$5-N$10; mains courses are N$20-30, specialising in game meats; and sweets for around N$5. The wine list is extensive, and it is worth the trip to eat here — even if it is only for the extensive buffet breakfast.

What to see and do Inside the Lodge there are lounges, a TV/video room, complete with a library of topical nature films (in English and German), and a comfortable bar. A gift shop has all the usual nature books, T-shirts, postcards and stamps; and the foyer even houses a couple of display tanks containing local scorpions.

Activities outside the Lodge centre on **game drives** into Etosha itself, either in your own vehicle or on one of the trips run by Namib Wilderness Safaris. These go for four hours in the morning, leaving at 7.30am, and for three hours in the evening, leaving at 3.30pm. They cost an extra N$125 and N$105 per person respectively.

Mokuti's own small game area has no big cats, elephant or buffalo. This means that it is fairly safe to wander about by yourself, and several short **hiking trails** have been marked out, although it is almost as easy to spot wandering buck from the side of the pool. (Look out for the Bontybok which are rare, although not indigenous: they originate from the Cape Area.) Alternatively **horse trails** are often available in Mokuti's own area: talk to reception for the details. These are an excellent way to view game as you can often just trot through herds of antelope without causing any disturbance at all.

Mokuti also boasts **Namibia's best collection of snakes**. These can be visited at any time and the enthusiastic warden, Wolfgang Ihmdor, conducts daily demonstration tours at 3.30pm, which are one of Etosha's highlights and not to be missed. He is adept at handling them and is a mine of information on their habits and ecology. All were caught locally, many by Wolfgang himself.

Ongava Lodge
PO Box 186, Outjo. Tel/Fax: (06542) 3413. Alternatively contact Ongava Europe, Worcs, UK. Tel: (0299) 405277. Fax: (0299) 404519. South of Okaukuejo, this is Namibia's newest luxury camp. It operates in its own private game reserve, abutting Etosha's southern side. The environment and wildlife are similar to Okaukuejo's, but there is a greater choice of activities than would be possible within a national park.

Getting there You can drive yourself, request a transfer from Windhoek (N$525 per person) or organise a private flight. The turn-off to Ongava is well signposted about 5km before the entry gate into Etosha, on the road to Okaukuejo.

Where to stay A range of accommodation is available, with three separate camps operating in Ongava's concession. The **Main Camp** is centred around a large, thatched *boma* which covers the lounge, bar and reception areas. Meals are served here, or on the veranda, around which there are 10 thatch-on-stone chalets. Each has full en-suite bathrooms, showers and toilets. These air-conditioned chalets are connected to 24-hour mains electricity and cost from N$600 per person per day, inclusive of game drives. Horseback trips or adventure trails will cost an extra N$120 per day.

There are two less opulent alternatives to this main camp. The **Himba Camp** has five basic twin-bed huts, built out of sticks and mud like Himba shelters. They are not luxurious, but have beds, insect screens, and bowls to wash in. Meals are cooked on an open fire, and this camp costs from N$250 per person per day, including walking or horseback trails. It is a good base for an adventure trail.

The **Tented Camp** has five twin-bedded igloo tents, erected on separate wooden platforms above ground level. These have insect nets and flashlights, so that you can find your way around in the dark. Meals are prepared outside, and the camp costs from N$250 per person per night, including walking trails.

What to see and do Activities include the normal options of **4WD safaris** across Ongava's concession area, and similar trips into the main park. Combining these drives with short, escorted walks is easy. After dinner, **night drives** are popular, giving an uncommon chance to spot the park's elusive night-life.

If you are staying for a few days, then **horseback trails** are available in the early morning or late afternoon. These are a good way to see antelope at close quarters, as animals don't seem to fear people on horseback.

Walking trails are available, while **adventure trails** can be arranged. These last one or two days, and aim to teach basic survival techniques. For the less energetic there is a **swimming pool** at the main lodge.

Booking in advance To stay at Ongava you must book in advance, either using the above numbers or via one of Windhoek's travel agencies. (eg Namib Travel Shop Tel: (061) 225178/226174. Fax: (061) 33332). Specify the activities which you would like.

Hobatere Lodge
PO Box 110, Kamanjab. Tel: (06552) 2022. This long-established game farm operates private safaris mainly in its own concession area within Damaraland. The game rangers here do have permission to enter the western part of Etosha, which is normally closed to visitors, although Hobatere is too far west to organise trips into the park's main area around the pan itself.

This western area has little, if any, permanent water but is interesting during the earlier parts of the year when the bush is wet enough for the animals to leave the vicinity of Etosha's permanent springs. See Chapter 14, *The Kaokoveld*, page 191, for full details.

Where to eat
If you are staying at one of the private lodges then you will normally eat there. If you opt for the public camps, then the restaurants there are very

reasonable, and the shops sell the basics for you to cook your own food. Check the opening times of the shop, as they are quite unusual. As with the rest of the country, the shops here will not sell any alcohol on a Sunday. Similarly, if you are planning on a drink in the bar then beware: it shuts remarkably early.

Game drives

The best times to go on game drives are in the early morning and late afternoon, when the animals are at their most active. So, if you have the energy, try to leave camp as the gates open at sunrise, for a few hours drive before breakfast. Use the middle of the day for either travelling between camps or just sitting in the car, parked by one of the more remote water-holes — though this can get very hot if you're not in the shade. That said, some visitors have reported excellent sightings at the water-holes between 10am and 2pm.

Before you leave camp, check the book of recent sightings in the park office — animals are creatures of habit, and this record should help you to choose the best times to visit specific water-holes. Also check the gate's closing time. Aim to spend the last few hours before sunset at one of the nearby springs, and leave in time for a leisurely drive back to camp.

The roads in Etosha are made of calcrete and gravel, which gives a good driving surface, without tar's unnatural appearance. That said, they can be slippery — be warned that most of the accidents in the park occur at sunset, when people leave water-holes late and try to dash back to camp before the gates close.

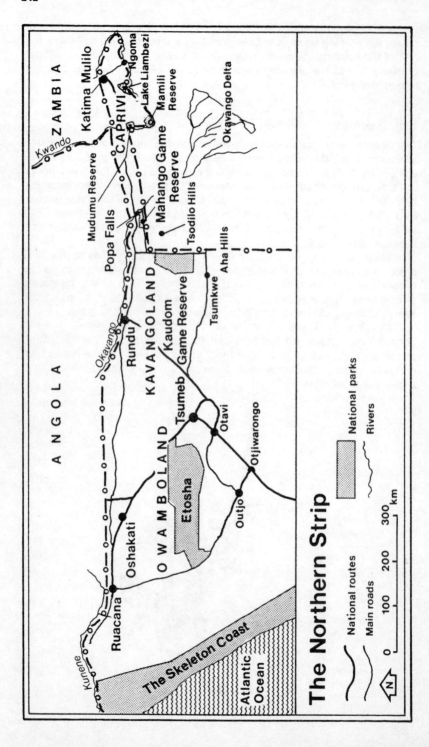

The Northern Strip

Chapter 16

The Northern Strip

Home to over half of the country's population, this verdant strip of land stretches eastward from the flat plains south of the Kunene River to the 'panhandle' of land between Angola, Zambia and Botswana. During the summer, it appears quite unlike the rest of Namibia, receiving over 500mm of rain and supporting a thick cover of vegetation and extensive arable farming.

Several of the continent's greatest rivers border the region. The Okavango, the Kwando, the Linyanti, the Chobe and the Zambezi all evoke powerful images of wild Africa. Here flows the lifeblood of the region, the waters which sustain the people and attract so much of its wildlife. Their river banks are invariably picturesque, and in the eastern areas most of the towns and the parks lie alongside them. Even away from the established parks, new camps are starting to open up on the rivers' banks which include canoeing and cruises among their attractions.

From west to east, the region consists of the three provinces of Owamboland, Kavangoland and Caprivi, which are described below in this order.

OWAMBOLAND

To the north of Etosha lies the province of Owamboland, a highly populated region adjacent to Angola where the people rely mainly upon subsistence farming of maize, sorghum and millet. Home of the Owambo ethnic group, this was the heartland of SWAPO's support during the struggle for independence, and hence something of a battleground before 1990.

Now the region is changing for the better. There are two tar roads, the B1 and the C46, lined by many small towns, like the trading posts along a Wild West railroad. Often there is a canal alongside the main road — a vital water supply during the heat of the dry season. Driving by, you pass women carrying water back to their fields, while others wash and children splash around to cool off. Occasionally there are groups meeting in the shade of the trees on the banks, and men fishing in the murky water. Some have just a string tied to the end of a long stick, but others use tall conical traps, almost a meter high, made of sticks. The successful will spend their afternoon by the roadside, selling fresh fish from the shade of small stalls.

Always you see people hitching between the rural towns, and the small, tightly packed combie vans which stop for them: their local bus service. If you are driving and have space, then do offer lifts to people — they will appreciate it. It's one of the best opportunities you will get to talk to the locals about their home area.

Owamboland has three major towns — Oshakati, Ondangwa and Ruacana — and many smaller ones. With the exception of Ruacana, which was built solely to service the big hydroelectric power station there, the others vary surprisingly little and have a very similar atmosphere.

There is usually a petrol station, a take-away or two, a few basic food shops, a couple of bottle stalls (alias bars) and maybe a beer hall. The fuel is cheaper at the larger 24-hour stations, in the bigger towns, and you can stock up on cold drinks there also. The take-aways and bars trade under some marvellous names: Freedom Square Snack Bar, Music Lovers Bar and the Come Together Bar, to name but a few. These can be lively, friendly places to share a beer, but a word of warning: they are not recommended for lone women visitors.

Away from the towns, the land seems to go on forever. There are no mountains or hills or even *kopjes* — only feathery clumps of makalani palms and the odd baobab tree break the even horizon. Visiting after a year of good rains, the wide flat fields are full of water, looking identical to Far Eastern rice paddies, complete with cattle wading like water buffalo.

Travelling eastwards and slightly south, towards Tsumeb, notice how, as the land becomes drier, the population density decreases, and maize becomes the more dominant crop. Where the land is not cultivated, *acacia* scrub starts gradually to replace the greener *mopane* bushes by the roadside. Keep your eyes open for raptors — especially the distinctive Bateleur eagles.

Towards the edge of Owamboland, at Oshivelo (about 150km from Ondangwa and 91km from Tsumeb) you must stop to pass through a veterinary cordon fence. This is just a kilometre north of the bed of the Omuramba Owambo, which feeds into the Etosha pan.

Oshakati

By Namibian standards, this is a large sprawling town and is typical of the region. There are no tourist attractions here, but the town acts as the centre for several government departments

Getting organised

Oshakati has all the major services that you might need. For the car there is a large California Auto-spares dealer and several small garages.

Towards the east of town, Phoenix Motors is the Nissan depot and there are lots of fuel stations, including Mobil and BP 24-hour stations.

The Eluwa supermarket has a fairly extensive range of supplies, and there's also a branch of Checkers — though it's more basic than most of their other branches.

For money, there are major branches of Standard Bank and the First National Bank, both with hole-in-the-wall automatic cash dispensers. (But don't expect credit cards from overseas to work.)

If you need medicine try one of the towns pharmacies which have good basic supplies. There is an emergency medical service on Tel: 20211, or the large Red Cross depot may be able to advise.

Where to stay

Category B
International Guest House PO Box 542. Tel: (06751) 20175/2142. Fax: (06751) 21001. This is just about the only hotel in the region, and it costs around N$90-N$130 per person. Currently it is used mostly by business people, aid-workers, and visiting government employees — so do not expect to meet many other tourists here. With air-conditioning, a swimming pool and even a tennis court, if you need a break this is the place to take one.

Where to eat

There is no shortage of place to eat, though all offer fairly simple fare. Jotty's Fish & Chips take-away is a favourite. For a drink, try out Club Fantasy (billed as 'Your Party Place'), the Let's Push Bar, the Moonlight Bar, or the small Country Club — but don't take these names too literally.

Ondangwa

This is the other main town of Owamboland, and in character it is very similar to Oshakati. There are Shell and Mobil 24-hour fuel stations, a couple of big supermarkets and even an outdoor market. Try the latter for fresh vegetables, and perhaps a cob of maize to snack on. As a last resort, there is always the aptly named 'Sorry Supermarket'.

As an alternative to Oshakati's International Guest House, Ondangwa boasts a dubious 'Private Bar with sleeping rooms' next to the Caltex garage.

Ruacana

This small town in the north of the country perches on the border with Angola, about 291km (mostly gravel) from Kamanjab and about 200km west of Oshakati. It owes its existence to the big hydroelectric dam here which is built at a narrow gorge in the river and supplies over half of the country's electric power. This is of major economic and strategic importance, so the road here from Tsumeb/Ondangwa is good tar all the way. There's a 24-hour BP petrol station, a general store and a large school, which make the town's nucleus feel quite modern. However, there are no other facilities, and few people either pass through or visit.

The Ruacana Falls used to be an attraction for visitors, but now the water only flows over them when it is not being diverted into the hydroelectric station. The falls are well signposted in no-man's land, so technically you have to exit the country to see them. However, at the large (and very under-used) border post you can do so temporarily, signing a book rather than going through the full emigration procedures. Be careful when taking photographs of anything apart from the falls, the area is still very sensitive.

KAVANGOLAND

East of Owamboland lies the region of Kavangoland, which has three excellent National Parks. Kaudum provides a wild, undeveloped wilderness, typical of the Kalahari. To visit you will need to have self-sufficient 4WDs, and a lot of patience for driving through the deep sand. Mahango is smaller and lies on the Okavango's banks, complete with expansive reedbeds and tall hardwood trees, typical of the lush, riverine parks further east. Popa Falls is basically a rest camp next to some of the Okavango's rapids. It has been enlarged to encompass a few islands amongst the rapids and its accommodation is conveniently close to Mahango.

The Road to Rundu

Grootfontein to Rundu is about 250km of good tar road. Initially the only variation in the tree and bush thorn-scrub is an occasional picnic site by the roadside, or band of makalani palms towering above the bush. About half-way to Rundu the land use changes from large ranches to subsistence farms, with more settlements and (beware) more animals on the road. Gradually shops and bottle stalls appear at intervals, and eventually stalls selling local wood-carvings (the biggest of these is called 'mile 30', about 42km from Rundu). Some specialise in large wooden heads, others sell unusual, tall, thin drums.

Closer to Rundu, especially during the wet season, kiosks appear piled high with neat pyramids of tomatoes and exotic fruit — evidence of the great agricultural potential in the rich alluvial soils and heavy rainfall.

Rundu

Situated 250km north-east of Grootfontein, and 500km west of Katima Mulilo, this town sits just above the beautiful Okavango flood plain and comes as a pleasant relief after the long, hot journey to reach it. Perhaps because of this distance, it can feel like an outpost with few specific attractions. But it remains a pleasant place to stay for the night and, being just over the river from Angola, there is a slight Portuguese flavour to the atmosphere here (try the Portuguese restaurant and take-away).

There are two 24-hour fuel stations — Shell and BP — a Kavango Toyota garage, a specialist 'Tyre World' centre, a well-stocked Kavango supermarket for supplies, an excellent bottle stall, a photolab, and a good number of other shops. If you have time to explore then Rundu's lively township area is immediately next to the centre of town, and Mbangura Woodcarvers Co-op (Development Centre, PO Box 86) is a few hundred metres towards the road to Grootfontein.

Rundu is also home to one of Namibia's very few zoos. Situated just 2km east of town, at Ekongoro, it might seem a little redundant when compared with the nearby game parks but this small zoo does have some beautiful gardens to relax in.

Where to stay and eat

Rundu's available accommodation seems to change every year. However, there are usually a few camps overlooking the Okavango river which are best reached by heading out of town and keeping to the old gravel road near the river, rather than the new tar highway slightly further inland. They are signposted off this, towards the river.

Kaisosi Safari Lodge is one such camp, on the banks of the Okavango, signposted off the gravel road to Katima - about 6km out of town. It has a variety of accommodation from basic bungalows for about N$110 for a single, N$165 for a double, to caravans at N$50 per day, tents at N$30 and camping at N$5. This does not include breakfast, but there is food available here (garlic steaks come highly recommended), and a swimming pool.

Sarasungu Lodge is signposted about 10km east of town, and its reed huts are quite a walk from the river. There is a set menu available here, and costs are relatively high at about N$120 for a single and N$180 for a double.

Kavango Guest Lodge Situated in a good spot on the western side of Rundu, overlooking the river, this camp is good value with a pleasant, helpful owner. Accommodation consists of fully-equipped bungalows, mostly for two people, which come with ceiling fans, en suite facilities, linen and even televisions. No cooked meals are available, but supplies of bacon, eggs, cereals, fruit juice, milk, coffee etc. are included in the price, which makes self-catering very straightforward. For dinner you can't beat your own *braai* overlooking the river, so simply pick up a few steaks and/or vegetables during the day, and get the fire going a little before sunset.

Costs, inclusive of supplies, are N$115 for a single, N$150 for a double, with extra children at N$30 each. To book, phone Mrs Hallie van Niekerk during the day on Rundu (067372) 13 (fax available on the same number) or call her after hours on (06732) 244.

Kaudum Game Reserve

Two or more 4WD vehicles. Entrance fees: N$5 per person and N$5 per vehicle
Situated next to Botswana and immediately north of Bushmanland, Kaudum is a wild, seldom-visited area of dry woodland savannah growing on old stabilised Kalahari sand dunes. These are interspersed with flat, clay pans and the whole area laced with a life-giving network of *omurambas*.

Omuramba is a Herero word meaning 'vague river bed', which is used to describe a drainage line that rarely, if ever, actually flows above ground but usually gives rise to a number of water-holes along its course. In Kaudum, the *omurambas* generally lie along east-west lines and ultimately link into the Okavango river system, flowing underground into the Delta when the rains come. However, during the dry season the flood in the Okavango Delta helps to raise the level of the water-table in these *omurambas* — ensuring that the water-holes don't dry up, and do attract game into Kaudum. The vegetation here can be quite thick in comparison with Namibia's drier parks to the west. Rhodesian teak and false mopane dominate the dunes, while acacias and leadwoods are found in the clay pans. The wildlife is definitely best observed in the dry season, and though seldom occurring in numbers to rival Etosha's vast herds, there's a much wilder feel about the place. Notable are populations of the uncommon tsessebe and roan antelope, as well as the usual big game species (interestingly excluding rhino and buffalo) and many smaller animals typical of the Kalahari.

Getting organised

Within the reserve, tracks either follow *omurambas*, or they link the dozen or so water-holes together. Even the distinct tracks are slow going, so a good detailed map of the area is invaluable. Try the Surveyor General's office in Windhoek before you arrive. Map number 1820 MUKWE is only a 1:250,000 scale, but it is the best available and worth having — especially when used in conjunction with the one on the previous page.

Water is available but nothing else, so come self-contained with fuel and supplies. Because of the reserve's remote nature, entry is limited to parties with two or more 4WD vehicles and each needs about 120 litres of fuel simply to get through the park from Tsumkwe to the fuel station at Mukwe, on the Rundu-Bagani road. This doesn't include any diversions while there. Bear in mind also that you'll need to use 4WD almost constantly, even in the dry season (and in the wet, wheel chains might even be useful), making travel slow and very heavy on fuel.

Getting there

From the north, turn off the main road about 115km east of Rundu at Katere, then Kaudum camp is about 75km of slow, soft sand away.

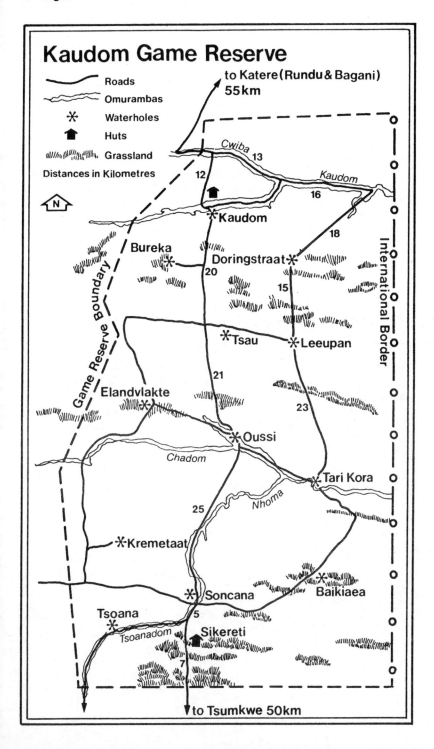

Kaudom Game Reserve

Roads
Omurambas
✳ Waterholes
🛖 Huts
Grassland
Distances in Kilometres

N

to Katere (Rundu & Bagani)
55km

Cwiba 13
12
Kaudom 16
✳Kaudom
18

Bureka
✳ Doringstraat✳
20
15

✳Tsau ✳Leeupan
21
23

Game Reserve Boundary
International Border

Elandvlakte
✳
✳Oussi
Chadom
✳Tari Kora
25 Nhoma

✳Kremetaat
✳Baikiaea

✳ Soncana
Tsoana 5
✳ Sikereti
Tsoanadom
7

to Tsumkwe 50km

From the south, the park is reached via Tsumkwe and Klein Dobe. Entering Tsumkwe, turn left at the crossroads just beyond the schoolhouse, then left again to go around the back of the school. Branch right just before the track bends back to rejoin the main road, and head north towards Klein Dobe. Sikereti camp is about 60km away from Tsumkwe and some 77km south of Kaudum camp.

Where to stay

Kaudum has two camps: **Sikereti** camp in the south, and **Kaudum** in the north. Each has basic wooden huts with outside facilities, and camp sites. The four-bed huts cost N$30 per hut, while the campsites are N$20. Advanced reservations, from Windhoek DNC, are essential here in order to be admitted — and you must arrive with an absolute minimum of 3 days food and water

Remember that neither camp is fenced, so leave nothing outside that can be picked up or eaten, and beware of things that go bump in the night.

Mahango Game Reserve

2WD/4WD. Entrance fees: N$5 per person and N$5 per vehicle, although if you're just going straight through on the main road into Botswana, there is no charge.

This small Reserve is tucked away in a corner of the Caprivi Strip, bounded by the upper Okavango River to its east and the Botswana border to its south, and bisected by one of the main roads between Namibia and Botswana. From this artery several game drives form loops to explore the area. Perhaps what makes Mahango stand out amongst Namibian parks is the presence of the mighty Okavango River, which starts to spreads out here, giving rise to extensive reed-beds at its edge, and lush vegetation all round. This brings water-loving species, like the rare **red lechwe** and **sitatunga**, into the park, and encourages good numbers of reedbuck, bushbuck, waterbuck and buffalo.

When to visit

The game varies greatly with the season. The best time to visit is August to October, during the dry season, as it is sometimes inundated with elephants. During the rains it can be disappointing. Visiting in early March can leave the highlights of a day's game spotting as the sighting of a distant kudu through dense vegetation, and snatched glimpses of a few fleeing sable.

Where to stay

There are no facilities or accommodation, so you must stay elsewhere and come in to Mahango for day trips. **Popa Falls rest camp** or **Suclabo Lodge** (see below) are the obvious choices.

What to see and do

Game drives There are two game drives to explore, both starting about 800m south of the main gate in the north of the park. The left road, which is good gravel, soon overlooks the flood plain, passing a picnic spot before returning to the main road farther south. The right course, suitable for high-clearance 4WDs only, follows a sandy *omuramba* away from the river, before splitting after about 10.7km. The right fork continues along the *omuramba*, terminating at a water-hole, while the left rejoins the main road again 19km later.

Bush walking One real bonus is that walking in the park is officially encouraged. However **beware** — the summer's lush growth is far too thick to walk safely in, so better to visit when the plants and shrubs have died down during the winter, and you are able to see for a good distance around you. Then you can get out of the car and go for it, but watch for the elephants, buffalo and occasional lion. (For comments on walking safely in the bush, see Chapter 6, *Driving and Camping in the Bush*, page 75.)

Popa Falls

2WD. Entrance fees: N$5 per person and N$5 per vehicle.
Popa Falls are really a set of gentle rapids where the Okavango River drops about 2.5m over a rocky section, before beginning its journey across the Kalahari's sands to become the famous inland delta. This park itself is small, and easily explored in a few hours, but the camp provides a convenient stop-over if you are driving across the strip, and an excellent base from which to explore Mahango Reserve.

Getting there

The rest camp and falls are right on the Okavango's western bank, south of the Bagani bridge. Coming from Rundu, take the right fork (signposted to Botswana) just before the Bagani bridge; the camp is on the left after 3.5km.

Where to stay

Popa Falls rest camp This is a neat, organised rest camp with a well-tended office, good campsites, and six excellent four-bed bungalows. The camp's office includes a small shop with a surprisingly wide range of foodstuffs, cool drinks (including some beer and wine) and postcards.

Camping sites cost N$20, while the bungalows are N$70 each, and both prices exclude the N$5 entry fees. The bungalows are well built of local wild teak and come with their own bedding, gas lamps, communal kitchens and ablutions. If you are camping then walk around before you pitch camp: there are secluded sites as well as the more obvious ones. Try taking the main track down to the river, and turning right along the bank.

Suclabo Lodge This private lodge is just a few kilometres down-river from Popa Falls and has a swimming pool, a restaurant, a bar, and slightly plusher bungalows than Popa's — though they cost N$60 *per person*, including breakfast. They'll organise river trips by motor boat with fishing tackle, and safaris into Mahango and Kaudum for you. That said, Suclabo is not recommended, except for perhaps a beer on the floating bar. The restaurant, like the accommodation, is expensive (N$30 per head) and not good value for money. Rumours suggest that it has changed ownership again recently, in which case it may have improved.

What to see and do

The camp area is thickly vegetated with tall riverine trees and lush green shrubs, which encourage **water-birds** and a variety of **small reptiles**. Footbridges have been built between some of the islands, and it's worth spending a morning **island-hopping** among the rushing channels, or **walking** upstream a little where there's a good view of the river before it plunges over the rapids. In a few hours you have a good chance of spotting a *leguvaan* (water monitor) or even a snake or two, and many different frogs. This is also a favourite area for cormorants, whose underwater fishing technique is truly captivating.

The bar at the nearby Suclabo Lodge makes an obvious excursion for the evenings, but Popa's gates are usually locked after sunset, so check with the warden about returning late.

Border crossing: Mohembo to Shakawe

4WD advised. Open from 8am to 6pm (check times if possible).

At the southern end of Mahango Game Reserve lies the Namibian border post, followed shortly by a well-camouflaged Botswana Defence Force (BDF) post. To complete immigration formalities and enter Botswana, you must take a left turn some 13km further south of this (just after an incongruous 'fasten your seat belt' road sign), and seek out Shakawe's police station by the river-side. The road on the Botswana side is for high-clearance 4WDs only in the wet season, though a good high-clearance 2WD would probably get through during the dry season.

CAPRIVI

The region's nerve-centre, **Katima Mulilo**, is closer to Lusaka, Harare or Gaborone than it is to Windhoek, and in many ways this region is more like the countries which surround it than like the rest of Namibia. For example, note the different designs of the *rondavels* and villages as you travel through. Some are identical to those in eastern Zimbabwe, while others resemble the fenced-in *kraals* in Botswana. Even the local language used in the schools, the Caprivi's Lingua Franca, is the Lozi language — as spoken by the Lozi people of Zambia.

Situated on the banks of the Zambezi, Katima Mulilo is a very lively, pleasant town with a bustling market and most of the facilities that you are likely to need. Away from the main town, the region has two new National Parks, Mamili and Mudumu. These are both lush, river-side reserves with increasing numbers of animals, and a very bright future.

Lianshulu Lodge, in Mudumu, is perhaps the area's most exciting development. This is not only the first private lodge to be built in a National Park, but it is also at the cutting edge of new strategies for conservation in Namibia. The camp is working with the local village people in a project to enable them to earn money directly from visitors.

History

Looking at the map, the Caprivi Strip appears to be a strange appendage of Namibia rather than a part of it. It forms a strategic corridor of land, linking Namibia to Zimbabwe and Zambia, but seems somehow detached from the rest of the country. The region's history explains why.

During the late 19th century the strip was part of the British protectorate of Bechuanaland (now Botswana). Geographically this made sense, even if the main reason for Britain's claim was to block Germany's expansion in the area. Meanwhile, off Africa's east coast, Germany laid claim to Zanzibar. This set the stage for the Berlin Conference of July 1900, when these two colonial powers sat down, in Europe, to reorganise their African colonies.

Britain agreed to sever this corridor of land from Bechuanaland and give control of it to Germany to add to their province of South West Africa (now Namibia). Germany hoped to use this to access the Zambezi's trade routes to the east, and named it after the German Chancellor of the time, Count von Caprivi. In return, Germany ceded control of Zanzibar to Britain, and agreed to redefine South West Africa's eastern border with Bechuanaland.

Driving across the Strip

The main B8 road from Rundu to Katima, always known as the **Golden Highway**, is currently gravel and fine for normal 2WD cars — although bad potholes cause many accidents. Remember that a high-clearance 4WD, driven in 2WD mode, is in as much danger of skidding and overturning as a normal 2WD car. In fact, a 4WD's high centre of gravity often means that, if it does skid, it will turn over more easily than a low-slung saloon car. The country's largest 4WD firm have several vehicles written off *each month* on this road. They comment that drivers tend to emerge from the slow sandy roads of Chobe or Kaudum and regard the gravel road as 'easy, fast driving' in comparison. The moral is always to drive slowly, and (if you have it) use the vehicle's 4WD setting to avoid skidding. That said, the tarred road is gradually being extended from Rundu towards Katima Mulilo, so these problems should end soon. Do not underestimate the distances here either, they are large.

Rundu to Bagani: 204km   This section of the road makes a pleasant drive, as it is often surrounded by green, irrigated fields, set against the backdrop of the Okavango River. This whole section should be tarred by 1994, but until then the gravel sections can be dangerously obscured by a haze of dust. **Take great care** driving to avoid the children and animals on this road, and the hazards of very slow-moving local traffic. 90km from Rundu, there is a useful BP fuel station (not 24-hours), and about 80km later the surface changes to one of pot-holed tar — different, but no easier to drive on. 10km before the Bagani checkpoint is Mukwe Service Station. This may not seem like a very important place, but it is, being the only reliable source of fuel for hundreds of kilometres.

A few hundred yards before the checkpoint the road forks: left for Katima Mulilo across the strip, and right to Botswana, via Mahango. The Bagani checkpoint puzzles many: why maintain it? Just a hut, by the bridge. But consider the importance of that one bridge over the Okavango, and you will realise why the checkpoint remains.

Bagani to Kongola: 191km: The Caprivi Strip Game Reserve   Looking at the map, a large chunk of the Caprivi Strip is taken up by this reserve. The Golden Highway bisects this undeveloped park, so watch for animals on the road. That said, while it is home to much wildlife, there are no facilities and no side roads suitable for exploring, so save your game-spotting energies for other parks, as the game seems to avoid the main road when it can. The most that you can usually spot is a few raptors aloft and the occasional elephant dropping on the road.

Because it borders on Angola, this area was very sensitive and controlled by the military for many years. Now only two control posts remain to remind you of Caprivi's past troubles: one at Bagani and another at Kongola. You do not need any permits to cross the strip and the people manning the control posts will usually just ask where you are going and wave you on with a smile.

There are only two larger settlements within this park: the Omega Shopping Centre, 70km from Bagani, and Babatwa (with a Baptist Mission Church), 23km further on. Neither township is large, and few visitors stop at either but they might be helpful in an emergency. Aside from these, this game reserve is very sparsely populated.

Kongola to Katima Mulilo: 110km   Kongola is very like Bagani, just a small hut by the bridge over the river Kwando. For those travelling eastwards it does mark the start of the tar road, which is a relief after the dust and potholes of the road from Rundu. About 5.5km from the bridge is small group of buildings, including a convenient bottle stall, and 1.5km later is the turn-off to the south, signposted Sanqwali and Lianshulu 40km. It also points out that the next fuel stop along this road is at Linyanti, 122km away.

Continuing towards Katima the road becomes busier, with more people around, on and off the road. 40km from Katima there are a collection of people selling wooden elephants, which are worth a stop if you have the time.

Katima Mulilo

Established originally by the British in 1935, Katima is the regional capital of the eastern Caprivi. It replaced the old German centre of Schuckmannsburg which now consists of just a police post, a clinic and a few huts. Interestingly the taking of Schuckmannsburg, on the 22 September 1914, was the first allied occupation of German territory during the first world war.

Katima is a large town with good facilities, beautifully placed on the banks of the Zambezi. There is an open central square, dotted with trees and lined with useful places like the Katima supermarket, the Ngwezi bottle stall, and the Ngwezi post office. The branch of Windhoek Bank here even has an auto teller, but don't expect foreign credit cards to work in it. The square also doubles as a stop for buses into Katima. For those driving, Katima Toyota is next to the Caltex Garage, just off the square.

A very short wander behind the square and you will find the Air Namib office, and the Butchy-butchy bakery, which sells good fresh bread. About 18km west of town is the airport, which has scheduled internal flights a couple of times a week.

Where to stay and eat

Zambezi Lodge PO Box 98. Tel / Fax: (067352) 203. This is the area's best hotel with a swimming pool, restaurant and even a bar which floats on the river — the ideal place to watch the sun go down. Zambezi Lodge is situated just off the main road, a few kilometres east of town (follow the signs). As you turn off the road, the drive which greets you is lined by flame trees and bougainvillaeas and surrounded by a nine-hole golf course. Inside, the hotel boasts a floodlit pool (surrounded by banana plants), full air-conditioning and even a sauna. Short boat trips can be organised on the river, though most people just relax here before moving on. Single rooms are N$160 and doubles N$184, excluding breakfast, and all rooms have en-suite facilities. (Note that there may no longer be an Avis office here).

As a separate venue, better suited to organised groups than casual individuals, the Zambezi Lodge runs a luxury riverboat called the *Zambezi*

Queen. This comes complete with 13 double air-conditioned cabins, on-board chefs and an extensive bar. Prices on application, but expect similar levels to the hotel prices.

Hippo Lodge PO Box 1120. Tel: (067352) 685. Situated 3 km out of town, Hippo Lodge opened in 1989 and remains very badly signposted, about 1km past Zambezi Lodge. Initially the visitor is met by a gaggle of aggressive geese on the lawn, which don't reflect the lodge's relaxed atmosphere at all. Basic meals are available, and there is a pool to swim in or lounge beside. If that seems too sedentary, then you can hire canoes for N$25 per day (free for residents) and explore the river, or go horse riding around the local area.

Hippo uses 15 solid thatched, brick bungalows for accommodation. These overlook the river bank and come fully equipped with en-suite facilities, linen, mosquito netting and fans. Costs are N$100 per day for a single, N$140 for double, including breakfast, and they make a pleasant change from the usual type of hotel accommodation.

Guinea fowl Inn Tel: (067352) 418. This new, small hotel is easily found by following the 'Guinea fowl' signs behind the back of the police station, off the main road from Katima to Ngoma. Though the buildings have a thin, prefabricated air about them, the Guinea fowl Inn is well kept, and set in lawns which slope off down to the Zambezi.

The rooms are small, but clean, and cost N$70 for singles, N$100 for doubles. Similarly the showers and baths are in good condition and mosquito nets and fans are provided. The restaurant serves breakfast, lunch, dinner, and even (unusually) real coffee. Typical costs are N$8 for burgers, N$16 for pizzas, and N$20-25 for steaks.

This is a good place to organise a boat trip, and the Inn's notice board usually has suggestions. Expect a small boat to cost N$150 per hour to hire. Try Dave Esterhuysen. Tel: (067352) 177.
N.B. Information in early '94 suggests that this may have closed in connection with some serious allegations.

What to see and do

Katima has few intrinsic attractions, although the lodges along the Zambezi are very pleasant places to stay. If you do have time here, then use it for trips onto the river, or as a base for longer expeditions into Mudumu, Mamili and Lake Liambezi.

Border crossing: Ngoma to Kasane

2WD. Open from 8am to 6pm.
This good gravel road from Katima to Ngoma is currently being tarred, and remains the only road link between Namibia and Botswana which is suitable for all vehicles. Namibia's border post is a smart office next to the bridge by the Chobe river and, 2km further on, Botswana's border post is an equally solid building perched high above the water, on the other side of the river.

EASTERN CAPRIVI'S WETLANDS

The southern border of eastern Caprivi is defined rather indistinctly along the line of the Kwando, the Linyanti and the Chobe Rivers. These are actually the same river in different stages. The Kwando comes south from Angola, meets the Kalahari's sands, and forms a swampy region of reedbeds and waterways — the Linyanti swamps. These form the core of Mamili Reserve. From here the river emerges, now known as the Linyanti, flowing to the north-east and into Lake Liambezi. It starts again from the eastern side of Lake Liambezi, renamed the Chobe. This beautiful river has a short course before it is swallowed into the mighty Zambezi, which continues over the Victoria Falls, through Lake Kariba, and eventually discharges into the Indian Ocean.

To explore any of these areas on your own, ensure that you have the relevant 1:250,000 maps from the Surveyor General (Nos.1723, 1724, 1823 and 1824), a compass and the normal tourist map of Namibia. Combine these with **local guidance** and you will find some interesting areas. The DNC does have two staff in Katima, who may be able to help you with specific information, Tel: Katima (067352) 27.

Lake Liambezi

This large, shallow lake is located between the Linyanti and Chobe rivers, about 60km south of Katima Mulilo. When full, it covers some 10,000 hectares, although it has been dry since 1985 and its bed is now populated by people and cattle.

Lake Liambezi's main source of water used to be the river Linyanti, but after this has filtered through the swamps it seems unable to fill the lake, even in recent years of good rain. However, next time the Zambezi is in flood it may be able fill the lake either via the Bukalo Channel, which runs south-west from the river to the lake, or even via the Chobe river — which can actually reverse its flow.

Mudumu Reserve

The more northerly of the region's two new reserves, Mudumu covers 850 square kilometres of riverine forest south of Kongola, either side of the D3511. Bordered by the Kwando River on the west, the reserve has a large variety of game, albeit in small numbers. Together with Mamili, it is notable for its buffalo (otherwise uncommon in Namibia), lechwe, puku, sitatunga and, occasionally, large numbers of elephants.

Mudumu can be explored on foot or by 4WD, though don't expect much organisation or many clearly marked game drives. To stay here, the choice is either an unfenced campsite with river water and basic sanitation, Nakatwa Nature Conservation Camp, or the luxurious Lianshulu Lodge. If you opt to camp, then follow the signs to the camp and note that the reserve, which is not fenced or clearly demarcated, borders onto hunting areas .... so ask the scouts where the boundaries are.

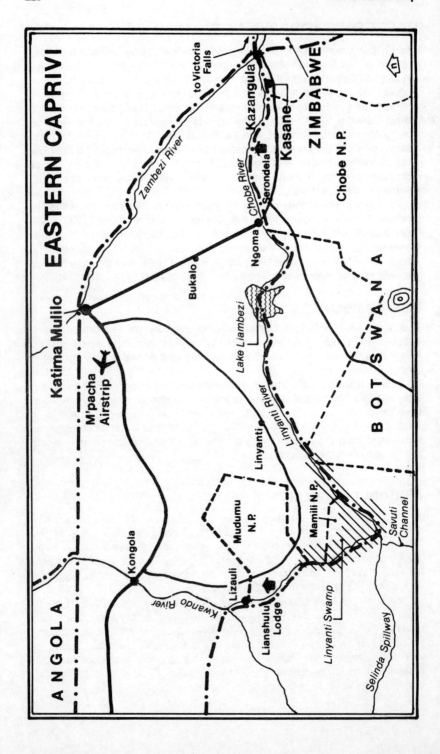

Where to stay

Lianshulu Lodge PO Box 142, Katima Mulilo. Fax: (067352) 486. Radio: Walvis Bay (0642) 3581 code277. Lianshulu has close links with Namib Wilderness Safaris and the Desert & Delta group (see pages 306 and 304). It is one of Namibia's best lodges, and the first to be built inside a National Park. Formerly there was an old hunting lodge here, started in the 1970's, but when Mudumu Reserve was created around it in 1990, this was taken over by Marie Holstenson and Grant Burton, who now run the lodge. Both gained experience running camps in Botswana's Okavango Delta, and this shows in Lianshulu's very professional style.

The camp is about 5km down a good bush track off the D3511, on the banks of the Kwando River. Accommodation is in one of eight beautiful, thatched A-frame bungalows, complete with en-suite facilities, a veranda overlooking the river, and lots of space. Meals are normally eaten together with Marie, Grant and the guides in the dining-room/bar area, and the food ranks amongst the best in the region.

Excursions vary from game walks and drives through Mudumu, to exploring the river's channels afloat. A day's visit to Mamili can also be organised if requested when you book. Because the guides have a detailed local knowledge, there is no better way to explore these reserves.

All meals and excursions are included in the lodge's tariff which ranges from N$300 per person per day (N$200 full board only). Lianshulu itself has no phone, but welcomes direct bookings. These can be made by using the above address, radio or fax, although it can be difficult to get a good telephone connection. It may be easier to book via the Namib Travel Shop on Windhoek Tel: (061) 225178/226174, Fax: (061) 239455, or as part of a Namib Wilderness Safari or a Desert & Delta Safari.

Lizauli Traditional Village

This small village is well signposted on the D3511, just to the north of Lianshulu, and is increasingly becoming an attraction for visitors. N$20 is charged as an entrance fee, and visitors are guided around the village where **traditional arts and crafts** are being practised. Aside from the fascination of the actual attractions, an iron forge, a grain store, and various carvers and basket weavers, a visit here gives a good opportunity to sit down and talk to some local people about their way of life.

This village is actually at the cutting edge of an important project initiated by Lianshulu Lodge which aims to involve the local community in conservation. The problem with many national parks in Africa has been that the surrounding local communities feel little benefit from the tourists. However, they are affected by the park's animals, which raid their crops and kill their livestock. Thus the game animals are regarded as pests, and killed for their meat and skins whenever possible.

Conservation projects The solution being tried here is simple: to link the success of the Lodge and the National Park with direct economic benefits for the local community, and thus to promote conservation of the local wildlife. In Mudumu this is being tried in three projects: the community game-guard scheme, the bed-night levy and the Lizauli Traditional Village.

The first employs local game-guards, recruited from the local villages, to stem poaching and educate about conservation. They are paid by grants from the US, WWF and Namibia's own Endangered Wildlife Trust. Secondly there is a nominal charge of N$5 per bed-night on the reserve's visitors (already included in Lianshulu's prices) which goes directly to the communities most affected by the park. This aims to compensate for any loss of crops or stock caused by wild animals.

Thirdly, Lizauli Traditional Village is an attraction by which the local people themselves can earn money from visitors. This inevitably depends upon the flow of visitors through the reserve. Thus more animals should mean more visitors and hence more income for the village — so the local people benefit directly if the area's wildlife is preserved.

Mamili Reserve

This unfenced swampland reserve of about 35,000 acres was created shortly before independence and consists largely of marshland, veined by a network of reed-lined channels. It includes two large islands: Nkasa and Lupala. Together with Mudumu Reserve, it has over 90% of Namibia's population of sitatunga and red lechwe antelope, and a handful of rare puku.

It is located in the south-west corner of the region, where the Kwando sharply changes direction to become the Linyanti, and as yet there are no facilities for visitors and few passable roads — even with a 4WD. The DNC will issue camping permits, so check with them for the latest information before you leave Windhoek or Katima Mulilo.

Nearby Camps

Between Mudumu and Mamili there are a couple of other safari camps, run by Touch Africa Safaris. These are new, and as yet disorganised. The most northerly is 4km from the D3511, 26km south of the Golden Highway.

Accommodation here is in A-frame huts with showers and toilets, for an all-inclusive rate of N$350 per person per day. Game drives, canoeing and fishing are offered, and those interested should contact Philip Nichol in Katima Mulilo, Tel: (067352) 446. This company also runs a tented camp further south, near Mamili, called Mvuba.

Part 3
Botswana

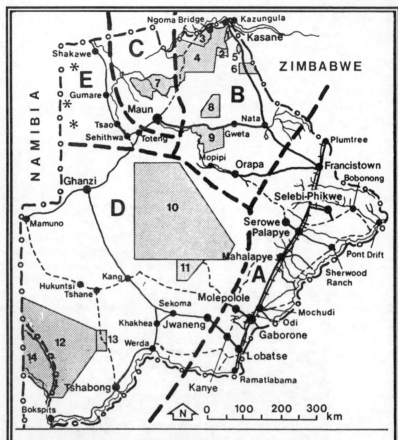

Botswana Regions

A **Eastern Corridor – Chapter 18**
B **Chobe & The Great Salt Pans of The North-East –**
   Chapter 19
C **Maun & The Okavango Delta – Chapter 20**
D **Central Kalahari – Chapter 21**
E **The Western Fringes – Chapter 22**

National Parks & Forest Reserves

1 Kasane F.R.	6 Sibuyu F.R.	11 Kutse
2 Maikaelelo F.R.	7 Moremi	12 Gemsbok
3 Chobe F.R.	8 Nxai Pan	13 Mabuasehube
4 Chobe	9 Makgadikgadi Pans	14 Kalahari
5 Kazuma F.R.	10 Central Kalahari	Gemsbok

Chapter 17

In Botswana

TOURISM IN BOTSWANA

'Low-density, high cost' tourism is the defined government policy. Whilst there has been a good deal of development of luxury lodges and exclusive safari operations in Botswana, the lower end of the market is barely catered for. From the government's point of view, and from the point of view of environmental conservation, this represents the best compromise – few people, maximum money. Alternatively, you can argue that it's not possible (or ultimately beneficial) to try to slow development in this way, and that a realistic and carefully planned budget tourist policy will be better than one that just chaotically springs up to the increasing demand.

Whatever view you take, it's undeniable that Botswana is one of the few countries in the world where the mark of the tourist is barely felt. A visitor to Botswana can look forward to uncrowded parks and reserves and a pristine landscape. Even the Okavango, which is probably the most visited part of the country, still offers an unspoilt water wilderness experience.

COST OF LIVING/TRAVELLING

Botswana is in many ways similar to Namibia but the absence of any budget accommodation or comprehensive public transport system does conspire to make Botswana difficult for budget travellers. This is then compounded by the very expensive national park and reserve entrance fees and the fact that much of Botswana's food and supplies are imported and therefore also expensive. However, there are still some fascinating places to visit that don't require you to pay park fees and there are few reasons to spend much time in the (expensive) large towns anyway. Alternatively, hitching to main tourist destinations, such as the Okavango, is easy and there are a few budget options available for those who look.

Currency

The unit of currency is the Pula (P), which is sub-divided into 100 Thebe. *Pula* means 'rain' in Setswana – water being one of Botswana's most precious commodities. The Pula only came into existence in 1976, displacing South Africa's Rand as the national currency. Even so, the financial and trading links between Botswana and South Africa remain very strong, and the Pula's strength varies with the Rand's. This means that the Pula is a 'hard' currency, and since it's freely convertible, there's no black market.

All people leaving Botswana are allowed to carry with them a maximum of P500 in cash, and the equivalent of P1,000 in foreign currency.

Exchange rates At the time of writing (March 1994) the exchange rates are £1=P3.80; and US$1=P2.53.

Banks

Currency can be exchanged at the commercial banks, hotels and at Gaborone International Airport. Normal banking hours are 0815-1245 weekdays and 0815-1045 Saturdays in the larger towns. Many smaller towns and settlements may have shorter hours or have an agent open for banking a few days a week. Having money sent in from abroad is not a problem in Gaborone, Francistown or Maun – and you can always use a credit card for a cash advance. Always make sure you have plenty of cash on hand – the main towns and banks are few and far between. Travellers cheques can be cashed at smaller places, and are the next best thing to straight cash.

Entrance fees to the national parks and game reserves

In July 1989, the Botswanan government increased ten-fold the national park and game reserve fees for visitors as part of its low-density, high cost tourist policy. Part of the policy was undoubtedly to milk something from the relatively large number of self-sufficient South African tourists driving their own vehicles into Botswana's parks, bringing their own supplies, and spending next to nothing in Botswana itself during their stay. The difference in rates between organising your own trip privately and being on an official tour or at one of the lodges, reflects this.

The prices quoted are for visitors to Botswana – residents and citizens pay very much less, as do children.

South African fees apply to Gemsbok National Park.

Don't forget that apart from the Moremi Wildlife Reserve, the great majority of the Okavango Delta has no entrance or camping fees and there are still huge tracts of the country that are wild, full of game, and outside the protected areas.

	Privately organised	Official tour/lodge
Park/reserve entry (per person, per day)	P50	P30
Camping fee (per person, per night)	P20	P10
Vehicle entrance (per day)	P10	P10

TRANSPORT

The little Shell road map is deceptively small and simple. Distances in Botswana are huge – as is the time it can take to get from one place to another away from the few tarred roads. If time is short, it makes sense to consider flying. Buses are much slower than driving and often even slower than hitching. Taking the train is more romantic than pragmatic, but you don't need to be a train buff to appreciate the steam trains which occasionally run along the eastern corridor.

Air

International flights   Scheduled Air Botswana flights link Sir Seretse Khama International Airport (15km NW of Gaborone) to Harare, Victoria Falls, Bulawayo, Windhoek, Lusaka, Luanda, Maputo, Manzini, Maseru, and Johannesburg. In addition, there are direct flights run by foreign carriers to Lilongwe (Air Malawi), Dar-es-Salaam (Air Tanzania), Nairobi (Kenya Airways), Paris (UTA) and London (British Airways).

Internal flights   There are frequent internal flights between Gaborone, Francistown, Selebi-Phikwe, Maun and Ghanzi. There's no public transport between the airport and Gaborone – you have to take a taxi, or convince a hotel 'courtesy' minibus to give you a lift. Bookings and reservations can be made at any of the Air Botswana offices in the main towns. The foreign airline offices are almost all in the main Mall, Gaborone.

Rail

The railway line that defines Botswana's Eastern Corridor is part of the route from Mafikeng (South Africa) to Bulawayo (Zimbabwe). The route used to be run by National Railways of Zimbabwe, but has now been taken over by Botswana Railways.

The trains are slow but comfortable and quite stylish in first or second class. They include private sleeper accommodation for the overnight services. Booking ahead of departure is recommended, particularly at month-end (government pay day), weekends and public holidays.

Passenger train timetable

South-bound trains	Daily	Daily	Thurs	Daily
Bulawayo	-	-	1030	1340
Plumtree	-	-	1335	1735
Francistown	0610	1410	1520	1955
Serule	0732	1531	1710	2150
Palapye	0839	1638	1830	2345
Mahalapye	1005	1805	2012	0145
Gaborone	1300a	2100a	0025	0720
Lobatse	-	-	0208	0910a
Mafeking	-	-	0430	-
Johannesburg	-	-	1035a	-

North-bound trains	Tues	Daily	Daily	Daily
Johannesburg	1300	-	-	-
Mafikeng	2100	-	-	-
Lobatse	2255	-	-	1710
Gaborone	0035	0610	1410	1900
Mahalapye	0440	0905	1705	0001
Palapye	0556	1027	1827	0133
Serule	0733	1133	1933	0318
Francistown	0930	1255a	2055a	0535
Plumtree	1150	-	-	0830
Bulawayo	1420a	-	-	1150a

Notes

1. All times are departure times unless indicated with an *a* for arrival time.
2. This timetable is not comprehensive – there are numerous small sidings and settlements at which the train may stop to pick up or put down – except for the overnight service between Lobatse and Bulawayo which stops at principal stations only and is faster.

Buses and minibuses

Buses do run fairly frequently between the main towns and it's possible to travel by 'express' bus as far as Johannesburg, Harare or Lusaka. Although guidelines to routes and times have been given under each of the main town headings in the regional chapters, it's always best to ask locally about the stopping places and times of the services. Fares are low. Minibuses – or *combis* as they're called locally – run over smaller distances, mainly around the capital, Gaborone.

Taxis

Taxis operate in the main towns and even some of the larger villages. Licensed vehicles have blue and white number plates. Metres are not used – bargain for a long journey or one outside normal routes.

Ferry

A ferry carries trucks and private cars across the Zambezi River at Kazungula, near Kasane – the border between Botswana and Zambia.

Driving

Only a small fraction of Botswana's roads are tarred and suitable for an ordinary vehicle. Whilst some of the dirt or gravel roads are passable in a high-clearance and tough 2WD, if you're exploring any of the national parks or game reserves you're bound to need – and know how to use – a 4WD vehicle. Full details on hiring a car, preparations and driving are in chapters 4 and 6.

Petrol costs are reasonable, but increase with remoteness. Supplies in many of the smaller villages are liable to run out, so away from the main centres it is always advisable to carry extra petrol.

Your can use an **international driving permit** for up to six months, after which you need to apply for a Botswanan licence. These are available from any AA office – take along your driving license, proof of identity and a couple of passport photographs.

Speed limits and safety belts On main roads, the upper speed limit is 110 km/h, whilst in towns and villages it is 60 km/h. National parks and game reserves have their own speed limits which are indicated at the entrance gates. Wearing safety belts (in all vehicles in which they are fitted) is compulsory.

Hitchhiking

If you don't have your own vehicle, hitching is probably the best way to travel. Although traffic can be very light, you're more than likely to get a lift from any vehicle that does pass. As there is so little public transport, people know why you're hitching, and regard it as a perfectly normal and acceptable thing to do. Apart from lifts from other travellers and expats, you should expect to pay for your transport – hitching is not so much a cheaper way to travel compared to the scanty public transport, but a more convenient way.

As with hitching anywhere in the world, a tidy appearance and easily identifiable 'image' (eg traveller with backpack) helps your prospects. Talking to drivers at fuel stations or other stops is better than just standing on the road, but if you are opting for the latter, make sure you walk sufficiently out of town so that it's obvious where you are going.

Hiking and cycling

The obvious problem with cycling or hiking in Botswana is the severe lack of water. Apart from the Okavango, there is very little surface water of any kind and wherever there are boreholes there are settlements or cattleposts. However, hiking or cycling from village to village can be a very interesting and challenging experience, and you're sure to be away from any other travellers! Cycling is perhaps the more rewarding, since with a strong bike you can carry water for several days and can reach places where no 4WD vehicle can go. The relatively large number of villages and the hilly landscape in parts of the Eastern Corridor and especially the Tuli area are recommended.

Maps

See page 47.

ACCOMMODATION

There is little budget accommodation in Botswana, few official campsites, and no youth hostels. 'Bush' camping, however, is easy, exciting, and free.

Hotels

Essentially Botswana's hotels cater for business people – those with expense accounts – and not for the medium to low budget visitor or tourist. They are mostly plush and upmarket, though rarely distinctive or particularly interesting. Prices drop as you move away from the main centres and can range from about P60 to P250 for a single room, and P80 to P300 for a double.

Tourist lodges and camps

Each lodge or camp – unlike most of Botswana's hotels – is distinctive and individual; many of the smaller ones are run by individuals or couples who impart their own hospitality on the place (they probably set it up in the first place). The vast majority are in the Chobe-Okavango region, with a few in the private game reserves of the Tuli Block.

Although the prices may seem very high – especially those camps in the Okavango or in Chobe National Park – they do often include sumptuous meals, and the full range of camp activities, including game drives and *mokoro*/canoe trips.

Camping

Combining camping with a 4WD vehicle is really the only way to see many of Botswana's most spectacular places. Though there are few official campsites – and these are frequently quite basic or run down – Botswana must be a camper's paradise. Most land is not privately owned (the main exception being the Tuli Block), and once away from the Eastern Corridor and main towns, people are very scarce. If you're well prepared with your own supplies and water, you can camp almost anywhere.

FOOD AND DRINK

Local food
The main staples in Botswana are sorghum and maize flour (mealie meal). These are both used to make a stiff savoury 'porridge', which is then eaten with a sauce or 'relish' made from meat and whatever vegetables are available. The mealie meal version is called *shadza*, and is a staple food throughout sub-Saharan Africa – albeit with a large variety of different names. Some travellers can't cope with the general stodginess of it all, but it's tasty, clean, nutritious and very cheap. You'll find local women selling *shadza* and stew for next to nothing in all the main population centres, usually around bus stations or markets.

Western food
Apart from the staples and beef, Botswana imports almost all its food – much of it from South Africa – and consequently prices are quite high by comparison with Zimbabwe, Zambia and East Africa with a take-away costing P7-P10 and an excellent restaurant meal in Gaborone costing P30.

The supermarkets are well stocked in the main towns, and you can easily find all the camping/travelling supplies you might need for your trip at reasonable prices. Vegetables are rare and expensive – make the most of the few markets in Gaborone and Francistown. Even the smallest settlements usually have a general store, with a small selection of essential supplies, and the occasional luxuries. Don't expect these dealers to be able to offer you the low prices of the cities.

Vegetarians
The local cuisine is not oriented toward the vegetarian – which is not entirely surprising in a country for which beef is the second largest export after diamonds. Equally, much of the Western food for sale in restaurants and take-aways is also meat biased. However, good vegetarian meals out can be found in Gaborone and Francistown, and there's bound to be something to eat in most of the take-aways, even if it's only an omelette or chip butty. If you're camping you'll be cooking your own food, and there are plenty of suitable camping supplies available in the main towns.

Alcohol

Bottle stores (off-licences) are spread throughout the country in even the smallest settlements – you'd be amazed where you can pick up a cold beer. The range is usually limited to a small selection of bottled beers, and a few soft drinks. Legally, alcohol is not sold before 10am, and bottle stores close at 7pm and on Sundays. The bars of the larger hotels usually have an excellent selection of wines and spirits imported from around the world.

Water

All piped and borehole water is on the whole safe to drink. Water from the Okavango or one of the few perennial rivers should be boiled or purified, though many do drink unpurified water from the Okavango and live to tell the tale.

Tipping

Tipping is not demanded in restaurants or hotels – many restaurants add a service charge. If you feel it is appropriate to tip, 10% is the usual practice.

HANDICRAFTS AND WHAT TO BUY

Botswana's crafts industry can be neatly divided into three regions. Most dominant and famous is the **basket weaving** of the Okavango Delta and areas to the north. The baskets are woven from a palm that grows in the swamps and come in an amazing variety of shapes, sizes and patterns. Each individual pattern is based on a number of basic design motifs that represent the many different practical and spiritual aspects of local life. The best range of baskets is in Maun, though as you travel around the Okavango you're sure to be offered them direct by the weavers.

Bushmen crafts – centred almost entirely around Ghanzi – are genuinely authentic and very unusual. If you're one of those people who shrinks at the sight of gifts and curios made specially for tourists around the world, then you might be surprised at these. The ostrich eggshell jewellery, and leather pouches, are exactly as the Bushmen have always made them – the mark of individual craftsmanship very evident.

A few small towns and villages in the Eastern Corridor have quite recently developed a new craft in Botswana, using imported **textiles** from Zimbabwe and South Africa. All sorts of very original wall-hangings and tapestries are being made by small community-based co-operatives, using new designs based on rural village life. The villages of Odi and Mochudi near Gaborone stand out.

For **general purchases**, the shops in the main towns are very well stocked with almost all basics and consumer items. Most goods are imported from South Africa and therefore cost more than in their country of origin.

ORGANISING AND BOOKING

Opening hours
Office hours are 8am to 1pm, and 2pm to 5pm weekdays only. Shop hours are roughly the same, though they are also open on Saturday morning. A few general stores stay open till the early evening for basic essentials.

Public holidays
January 1, 2
Good Friday, Saturday, Easter Sunday and Monday
Ascension Day (40 days after Easter Sunday)
President's Day (third Monday in July)
Day after President's Day
September 30 – Botswana Day
Day after Botswana Day (or if on a weekend, the following Monday)
Christmas Day & Boxing Day

The Botswana telephone directory
This relatively thin volume is an excellent source of all sorts of information and essential to locating a particular service you might want. Track it down in post offices, hotels and government departments. The single book which covers the whole of the country contains information and lists on the following: telephone, fax and telex numbers; international codes, and dialling direct from Botswana; PO box numbers and private bag numbers; lists of all government departments, region by region; comprehensive 'yellow pages' for all major services and businesses; street maps of Gaborone and Francistown, including the industrial areas; easy to find list of doctors, dentists and hospitals.

Tourism office
P. Bag 0047, Gaborone. Tel: 353024. (Located on the first floor of the BBS Building in Broadhurst Mall – it looks like an office block.) Good for a useful range of brochures etc. There's also an information office in town, in the main mall.

Visas
The Chief Immigration Officer, PO Box 942, Gaborone. Tel: 374545.

COMMUNICATIONS

Post

Incoming Post will be held for you by the central Gaborone Post Office –
labelled 'Post Restante'. If you have an American Express card or travellers
cheques, you can use the 'AMEX Customer's Mail Service' at the AMEX
agent: Manica Travel Services, Botsalano House, The Mall, PO Box 1188,
Gaborone. Tel: 352021.

International air mail is fast and reliable if sent from a main town – mail
posted in Gaborone is by far the fastest. Internal mail to post office box
numbers and private bags is reliable, but can be rather slow to the remoter
areas. There is an express letter delivery service and a registered letter
service. There's no door-to-door mail delivery in Botswana.

Telephone, fax and telex

Botswana has a good direct dialling system including international direct
dialling to anywhere in the world. There are public phones in Gaborone and
Francistown, and by the post office of many of the smaller towns. In
Gaborone, international calls can be made at Standard House from where
telegrams can also be sent. Major hotels offer telex and increasingly fax
facilities. Where there are no phones, there is usually some sort of radio
contact in case of an emergency.

There are no area codes in Botswana – to phone you just dial the number.

MISCELLANEOUS

Electricity

A 'European' 220/230V supply at 50Hz is standard and available in all the
main towns and settlements

Embassies and High Commissions in Botswana

British High Commission, Queen's Road, P. Bag 0023, Gaborone.
Tel: 352841.
Danish Consulate, 142 Mengwe Close, PO Box 367, Gaborone. Tel: 353770.
French Embassy, 761 Robinson Road, PO Box 1424, Gaborone. Tel: 353683.
German Embassy, 2nd Floor, IGI House, PO Box 315, Gaborone. Tel:
353143.
Netherlands Consulate, 6045 Haile Selassie Rd, PO Box 457, Gaborone Tel:
357335.
Nigerian High Commission, The Mall, PO Box 274, Gaborone. Tel: 313561.
Norwegian Consulate, Development House, The Mall, PO Box 879,

Gaborone. Tel: 351501.
Swedish Embassy, Development House, The Mall, P. Bag 0017, Gaborone.
Tel: 353912.
USA Embassy, Badiredi House, The Mall, PO Box 90, Gaborone. Tel: 353982.
USSR Embassy, 4711 Tawana Close, PO Box 81, Gaborone. Tel: 353389.
Zambian High Commission, The Mall, PO Box 362, Gaborone. Tel: 351951.
Zimbabwean High Commission, The Mall, PO Box 1232, Gaborone. Tel:
314495.

Hospitals, dentists and pharmacies

Although scantily distributed, Botswana's medical facilities are of a high
standard and comparable to anything you'll find in the West. The main danger
is the remoteness of much of the country – it is essential to carry full first aid
equipment if you intend spending much time exploring away from the main
towns. There are doctors and generally pharmacies in Francistown,
Gaborone, Kanye, Lobatse, Mahalapye, Maun, Mochudi, Molepolole, Palapye
and Selebi-Phikwe (full details in the Botswana telephone directory). The main
hospital and the most comprehensive facilities are at Gaborone. Dentists only
in Gaborone, Francistown and Lobatse.

Imports and exports

There are strict restrictions on taking into the country many agricultural
products, plants, skins and hides, and other animal products. If you do have
any of these, declare them to customs. Equally, if you must buy 'trophies',
game skins or ivory, and wish to take them out of the country, make sure that
you have the necessary documentation.

That said, remember that the recent CITES ban makes it an offence to
import or export ivory from any participating country. While there is a
legitimate case in favour of controlled ivory exports from Botswana – based
on the necessity of culling elephants to prevent over population of the game
parks – it's unlikely that you will be able to import ivory into your own
country. Our advice is, don't buy it.

Botswana is a member of the Southern African Customs Union (SACU),
along with South Africa, Namibia, Lesotho and Swaziland. This means that
there are no customs restrictions between any of these countries, except for
the specifically restricted items. Otherwise, if you are permanently importing
any new items into the country from outside the SACU, be warned that duties
are very high.

Newspapers, radio and TV

Whilst Botswana has a free press and no restrictions on broadcasting, it
nevertheless seems very conservative compared to Western media. The
government Department of Information and Broadcasting controls and runs
Radio Botswana which broadcasts daily in English and Setswana. It also

publishes the *Botswana Daily News* newspaper, which is printed Monday to Friday. Arguably one of the best newspapers, however, is the new and independent weekly *Newslink Africa*, published in English.

South African newspapers and journals are readily available in Gaborone and Francistown, and South African radio and TV can be received in most of the Eastern Corridor's main towns.

Theft

On the whole, Botswana is an extremely safe place to travel in. Violent crime is very rare, though don't tempt fate by walking through unlit and deserted parts of Gaborone at night. Petty theft from unattended vehicles and pickpockets in busy shopping areas and bus stations are as common as any other city and should be guarded against.

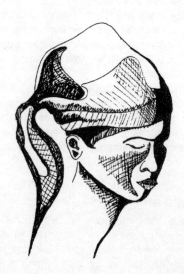

Botswana's Baskets

Basket weaving has been a tradition in Botswana for centuries. Although most of the baskets are being made in the Okavango Delta area of north-western Botswana, basket weaving is still carried on in many other areas of Botswana, each with its own particular style.

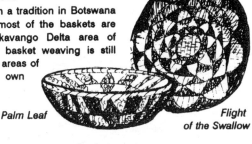

Palm Leaf

Flight of the Swallow

Construction The coil foundation of the basket is either made of bundled grass, split palm leaves or a single vine rod. The coils are then wrapped with a split palm leaf from the mokolane palm (*hyphoene ventricosa*). By drying and boiling the mokolane palm with the root of the mothakola tree (*euclea sp.*), the palm is dyed various shades of brown.

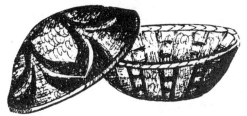

Forehead of the Zebra   *Forehead of the Kudu*

This brown and natural coloured palm is then used to weave designs into the baskets.

Traditional designs Designs on baskets have traditionally been used to commemorate an important aspect of the weaver's lives. For example, 'the flight of swallows' design is shown to mark the occasion of the first rain, whilst the 'urine trail of the bull' design symbolises the importance of cattle. Weavers often incorporate more than one design into their baskets as well as creating new designs with traditional meaning.

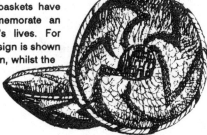

Urine trail of the bull

Knees of the Tortoise

Usage Each basket is made for a particular purpose. Round container-baskets, when made with a rod foundation, are used for storing grain — but if made with bundled grass or split palm leaves, the basket will hold liquids (such as traditional beer) due to the swelling of the weaving material. Open bowl shapes are commonly used for winnowing or for transport and storage of grains, vegetables or ground sorghum.

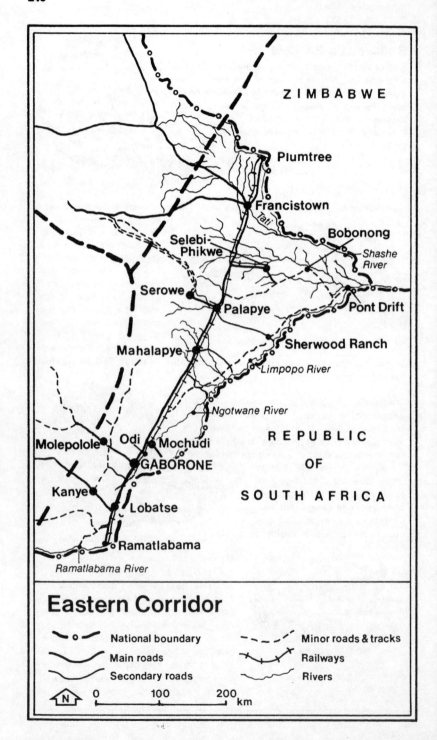

Eastern Corridor

National boundary	Minor roads & tracks
Main roads	Railways
Secondary roads	Rivers

N

0   100   200
km

Chapter 18

The Eastern Corridor

The eastern edge of Botswana is an area that lies outside the sands of the Kalahari Desert, and looks and feels more like neighbouring Zimbabwe than parts of the rest of the country. There are rivers and readily available ground water, giving a fertile environment which can support fair numbers of people. When Rhodes' British South Africa Company was looking for ways to get the rich mineral resources of the northern territories out to the sea, the railway was built through eastern Bechuanaland as Botswana was then called, connecting Zimbabwe with the Cape. Along this route, many small settlements sprung up, feeding off the meagre amount of wealth that was imparted by the rich railway corridor.

The region today contains the country's two main towns – the capital, Gaborone, and Francistown – and most of the population and infrastructure. The railway, good tarred roads linking Zimbabwe to South Africa, and the international airport at Gaborone, make the Eastern Corridor one of the main gateways into this part of the continent. In Gaborone or Francistown, you'll be able to pick up any supplies or spare parts that you might need for your trip, get yourself organised and prepare yourself for exploring the interior. At the gateway for travel north to Maun, the Okavango, Chobe and the spectacular salt pans of Nxai and Makgadikgadi, Francistown has become a main stopover for travellers and overlanders.

Most travellers see no more of the Eastern Corridor than endless vistas of bush and tarmac as they travel north or south. But for those with a 4WD or even without a car, the region offers the chance to explore many off-the-track places with relative ease, including the private game reserves of the Tuli Block. Tucked away in the east between the South African and Zimbabwean borders, the Tuli Block offers some of the most remarkable scenery in the country and excellent private game country.

GABORONE

Gaborone, was chosen as the site of the new capital in 1962 (in preparation for formal independence in 1966), because of its proximity to the railway line and the availability of water from the Ngotwane River. Prior to this it was just a small, traditional village named after chief Gaborone of the Batlokwa tribe. The initial projection of the city's population was a maximum of 20,000. However, the discovery of diamonds shortly after independence, led to a massive growth in the economy and now Gaborone is one of the fastest growing cities in the world, with a population of about 130,000. (Botswana as a whole has the fastest growing economy in black Africa.) This, needless to say, made much of the city's careful planning somewhat redundant and there is an acute shortage of housing, schools and other social amenities. Constant construction work is characteristic of the sprawling industrial areas.

The city is still looking for a heart, and most people find it frustrating in its anonymity. Gaborone is not so much a place to visit, as the place you may well fly into, or use to get things organised.

Getting there

Air   There are regular internal air services from Francistown, Maun, Ghanzi, and Selebi Phikwe – and international flights to and from all neighbouring countries (see page 235).

Train   Daily services link Gaborone with Lobatse in the south and Bulawayo in Zimbabwe, with one service a week continuing on to Johannesburg. See the train timetable on page 236.

Bus   Buses and minibuses leave at least once a day for Francistown in the morning, and more frequently for Lobatse and closer towns. There is also a bus link with Harare via Bulawayo which leaves from the African Mall on Tuesdays and Saturdays at 6.00am.

Where to stay

There is really no satisfactory budget accommodation in Gaborone. If you don't want to stay at one of the hotels listed below – or if they are all full – you should consider staying in Molepolole 50km away. There's a small cheap hotel there run by the Brigades and it's easy to get a lift or bus to Gaborone. Another possibility is to ask a taxi driver for 'private accommodation'. He's bound to know a friend of a friend who can give a traveller a place to sleep. Another possibility again, for those with a car, is just to head out of town and camp.

Category A
The **Sheraton** (Molepolole Road) is the most expensive at P220 (single),

whilst the **Cresta Lodge** (135 Independence Ave) is the cheapest at P99. The **Gaborone Sun**, the **Oasis** and the **President Hotel** are an intermediate price.

Category B
Cheaper hotels are generally all out of town. The **Morning Star Motel** is the closest, 5km east of Gaborone on the Zeerust road. This has single rooms for P80 and doubles for P125 with bathrooms en suite. Tel: 352301.

The **Mogotel** at Mogotishane on the road to Molepolole is more run down and cheaper. Tel: 372228.

There is one fairly central hotel – the new **Gaborone Hotel**. Tel: 375200 – just over the footbridge from the train station. Singles P100 and doubles P125.

There is also a **guest house** near the university (2km from the Mall along Notwane Road), run by R.K. Accountants, PO Box 2288. Tel: 372466. This has rooms for P75 each. They're often full, but it's worth ringing to check vacancies and to get directions.

Category C
The only relatively cheap place to stay is the **YWCA**, which has dormitory beds for women only for P30, though it's often booked out by university students. It's situated just opposite the Princes' Marina Hospital on Notwane Road.

Where to eat
Unlike its accommodation, Gaborone does have a good selection of places to eat that should suit most budgets. There are take-away chicken-and-chips and burger joints everywhere and street food (maize, peanuts and fruits) is cheap and clean. The cheapest hot meal must be the ubiquitous *shadza* and meat from the stalls around the bus station. The bars and restaurants of the central hotels are good for whiling away a few hours during the day – the **Pergola**, part of the President Hotel in the Mall, is a favourite meeting place for afternoon coffee, tea and cakes.

Other than the hotel restaurants which all serve the usual upmarket Botswanan fare of steaks and hamburgers, the best places to eat out are all located in the African Mall, a few minutes walk from the town centre. Here you'll find a choice of good Indian, Italian, French and Chinese food.

Park Restaurant and Pizzeria African Mall. The Park is very popular with visitors and residents alike and was voted best restaurant in town by a local newspaper. The food is good and the prices reasonable. Although it's often very busy – you may have a problem getting a seat – it has an excellent, relaxed atmosphere. It serves a good selection of pizzas, seafood, salads and crepes in addition to the more usual burgers and grills. The vegetarian selection is excellent. Expect to pay around P8 for a starter or salad, and P12-P15 for a main course – the seafood is not surprisingly more expensive.

Taj Restaurant Norman Centre, African Mall. Similarly priced and less crowded than the Park, The Taj serves good curries and Indian food.

Mandarin Restaurant African Mall. A new, very popular Chinese restaurant, with main courses from P10 to P20.

The Bourgainville African Mall. An excellent, but pricey, French restaurant.

Outside the African Mall, there are a number of places worth mentioning.

The Bull and Bush is modelled on an English pub, and serves steaks, salads and fish and chips for P15-20. On Old Francistown Road, opposite Red Square flats, **Mama's Kitchen** does pasta and pizzas for P15-20 in the New Broadhurst Mall some way north of the town centre, and was recently awarded a five star ('excellent – don't miss out') rating by the new *Newslink* newspaper. If you're waiting for a train or bus, the **Crazy Bull** near the station has good burgers and chips for P10.

Getting around

Finding your way around Gaborone is straightforward even if the distances are more that you're used to in a Botswanan town. The railway station, bus station and market all cluster together at the far end of Khama Crescent, about 15 minutes walk from the Mall and the centre of town. The Mall is a modern pedestrianised precinct with a good selection of shops, most of the embassies, and hundreds of offices. At the western end of this are the government offices, ministries and the national assembly – whilst at the eastern end is the library, museum and art gallery. One of the most interesting areas is the African Mall, five minutes from the conspicuous President Hotel in the main Mall, with a good variety of shops and restaurants.

Since the city is quite spread out, there's an efficient system of minibuses that operate up and down the main roads, and are useful to get to one of the suburbs or an out-of-town hotel. Though cheap, these are frequently crammed with people, and difficult if you're carrying a large backpack. Taxis can always be found outside the railway station and in the Mall. There's no public transport to the airport – take one of the hotel minibuses or a taxi.

What to see and do

The National Museum and Art Gallery   Open from 9am-6pm Tuesdays to Fridays and 9am-5pm on weekends and public holidays. Admission free. The museum has excellent exhibits on the history, geography and peoples of the country, with good displays of craftwork. This is complemented by the small but rich art gallery, with collections of paintings, crafts and sculptures from all of sub-Saharan Africa, as well as Batswanan artists.

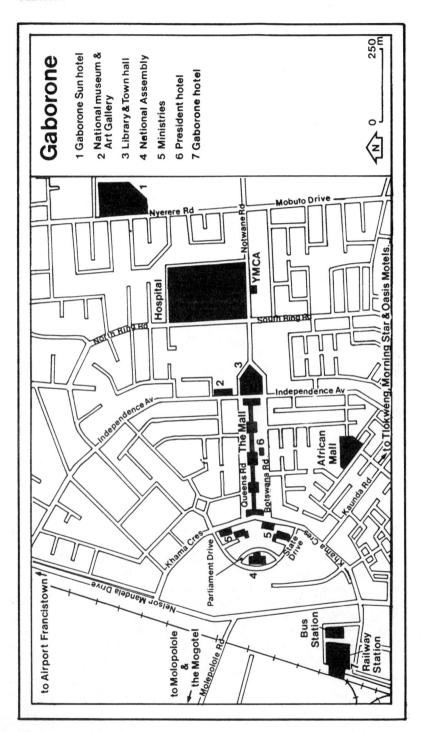

Gaborone

1 Gaborone Sun hotel
2 National museum & Art Gallery
3 Library & Town hall
4 National Assembly
5 Ministries
6 President hotel
7 Gaborone hotel

Nightlife

The Gaborone Sun hotel has probably the most lively of the hotel bars, with dancing to African and contemporary western sounds. The Oasis disco is reputedly also worth checking out. There are a number of nightclubs and the occasional live performances, but as these are constantly changing it's best to ask around, or check for advertisements in the local press and on roadside banners and posters. Weekends, particularly at month-end (pay day) are the best times, with performances by visiting artists from neighbouring states. The Capitol Cinema is right in the centre of town on the Mall, with the latest Hollywood releases.

Getting organised and shopping

All the airline offices, travel agents, the post office, main branches of the banks, and shops selling imported goods are situated around the central Mall. The Botswana Book Centre here has an excellent selection. For general food supplies, try the supermarkets in the Mall, or near the station.

Souvenirs   The African Mall has shops selling more traditional goods in addition to people selling carvings from Zimbabwe and Zambia in the Mall centre. There's one craft shop – Botswanacraft – in the central Mall, which has a good selection of crafts from around the country. However, prices are greater, and the selection poorer than the craft shops in Maun (baskets) or Ghanzi (Bushmen crafts and ostrich egg jewellery).

Kalahari Conservation Society   On the fifth floor of Botsalano House in the Mall. The Society has endless information on the interior, gives occasional lectures, and sells some excellent T-shirts. PO Box 859, Gaborone. Tel: 314259.

Excursions from Gaborone

Near town

Gaborone dam is just outside town and is a good place to relax and watch birds. The two traditional villages of **Odi** and **Mochudi** are 25km and 40km from Gaborone respectively, on the main road to Francistown. Both make worthwhile day trips from the capital, or are worth a slight detour if you're on your way driving north. At Odi, the **Lentswe-la-Odi weavers** co-operative makes distinctive tapestries based on mythological designs and rural scenes. Mochudi is another pretty village, and the capital of the Bakgatla tribe. On a hill above the village, in the buildings of an old school, is the **Phuthadikobo Museum** with an interesting historical and photographic collection on the settlement. There are some amazing textiles and wall-hangings for sale here, made by a local silkscreen workshop.

Further afield

Khutse game reserve is readily accessible from Gaborone with a 4WD, and is popular with city residents over the long-weekends. For full details of this reserve, see Chapter 21, *The Central Kalahari*, page 316.

Jwaneng and Orapa diamond mines can be visited, but you have to arrange this in advance with Debswana (De Beers Botswana Mining Company), Botsalano House, The Mall, Gaborone, PO Box 329. Tel: 351131. Mine tours are organised regularly.

FRANCISTOWN

Botswana's second largest town is one of the oldest settlements in the country. Traditionally it had close cultural and trading links with Bulawayo in Zimbabwe before the artificial international boundaries were drawn up. Today, a good tarred road and a railway line links Francistown and Bulawayo which are only three hours away by car. Francistown has a bit of a Zimbabwean feel to it, except for the very well-stocked shops and stores. It's a popular shopping destination for Zimbabweans looking for hard-to-get imported luxuries and spare parts – if they can get their hands on some foreign currency. Francistown's initial prosperity derived from acting as a service town to the gold, copper and nickel mining industry – now overshadowed by the diamond mine at Orapa and the soda ash plant being constructed on Sowa Pan.

Other main roads radiating from Francistown link it with Kasane and Maun in the north and the capital Gaborone in the south, making the town a pleasant and convenient stop-over and a good place to restock and resupply. It's also an excellent place for getting hold of vehicle spares.

Getting there

The town itself is very compact with the railway station at the northern end and the bus station at the southern end – both just a few minutes' walk from the centre. The airport is a few kilometres away, and you'll need to get a taxi – there's no public transport.

Air   Air Botswana has recently expanded and there are regular services to and from Gaborone, Maun, Harare, and Windhoek. The Air Botswana office is in the Thapama Lodge on Blue Jacket Street in the centre of town. Tel: 212393.

Train   These run daily between Lobatse and Gaborone in the south of the country and Bulawayo in Zimbabwe. (See the national rail timetable in Chapter 17, *In Botswana*, page 236.)

Bus   Most run in the morning and when they're full enough! It's best to get to the bus station by 9.00am or try and check the latest times, the day before departure.

Francistown to Gaborone: at least one each day. Francistown to Kasane: Mondays, Wednesdays and Fridays. Francistown to Maun: one each day.

There are also less regular services to Bulawayo and Harare.

Where to stay

Francistown has a good range of accommodation, with a choice of two budget hotels, an upmarket hotel, and the delightful Marang Motel just out of town. The campsite at the Marang is a major stop-over and meeting point, and highly recommended for its pleasant grounds and situation. Alternatively, as in any of the larger towns, asking a taxi driver for 'private accommodation' should find you a cheap and hospitable roof over your head. And if you have a car. you can drive a few kilometres out of town and camp in the bush.

Category B

Marang Motel   Situated 4km from the centre of town – head south from the town centre to the main roundabout and take a left turn, the motel is 4km further along past the golf course, on the right. Other than the campsite, the Marang has a number of attractive thatched chalets in amongst the acacia trees and mown lawns which offer good value for money. These cost from P200, and if you've a group of four you can get a chalet for a total of P225. The *á la carte* restaurant has kept its prices almost the same for three years, serving good food with generous portions. Breakfast is highly recommended at P15. PO Box 807, Francistown. Tel: 213991/2/3.

Marang Motel Campsite   The 'in place' for most travellers, it's not hard to see why at only P10 per person, inclusive of use of the swimming pool. The campsite has a beautiful setting near the banks of the Tati river and has a very clean shower/toilet block with hot water. This is a good place to meet other travellers and also look for lifts.

Thapame Lodge   Centrally located, near the southern end of town by the roundabout, Thapama Lodge is a business hotel, complete with air conditioning and TVs in the rooms. Expect to pay around P150 for a single and P225 for a double, inclusive of breakfast. The 'Sizzlers' cafe bar does good burgers. Private Bag 31, Francistown. Tel: 213872.

Category C

Grand Hotel   In the town centre, opposite the railway station, the Grand is much the same as its competitor, the Tati. It all depends on which rooms happen to be available – some can be a bit dark and run down, whilst others are perfectly reasonable. Singles from P65, doubles P90 with shower. There's a bar with set menu dining room which will serve a simple breakfast for P9. PO Box 30, Francistown. Tel: 212300.

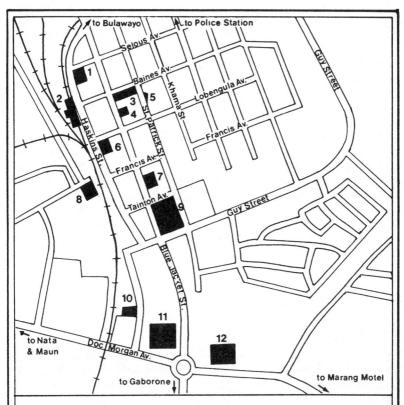

Francistown

1 Grand hotel

2 Railway station

3 Fruit & vegetable market

4 Post office

5 Swimming pool

6 Tati hotel

7 Fairways supermarket

8 BGI Craft shop

9 Mall shopping centre

10 Bus station

11 Thapame Lodge hotel

12 Hospital

N   0   250
                  m

Tati Hotel   Like the Grand, this is right in the town centre, on Haskins St. and Lobengula Ave. The Tati Hotel is similarly priced to the Grand and offers roughly the same standard of room. Camping is sometimes permitted in the back garden. PO Box 15, Francistown. Tel: 212321

Where to Eat

There are a number of take-aways in the shopping mall and around the bus station which are reasonable and fairly cheap. Alternatively, there are always women selling *shadza* (maize porridge) and meat, and cooked maize cobs around the vegetable market during the day. If you want to sit down there are a couple of small restaurants:

Ma Kim's   A block east of the Grand Hotel on Selous Drive. Ma Kim's serves Chinese and Korean dishes from P10 to P15 for a main course. Quiet and recommended.

Silver Spur Steak House   Near the shopping mall on Blue Jacket St. Main courses from P10 to P20.

Getting organised and shopping

Fairway's Supermarket in the centre of town carries a good range of most general foods, whilst more specialist camping and dried foods can be obtained in the Mall Shopping Centre. There's also a fruit and vegetable market on Baines Avenue up from the railway station.

Crafts   There's one craft shop with a fair selection of goods across the railway line from the Tati Hotel. If you're planning on visiting Maun or Ghanzi, save your money for the excellent craft markets there instead.

Selebi-Phikwe

This is Botswana's third largest town after Gaborone and Francistown – it was built after independence, to support one of the country's main mining centres. Other than being on one of the main routes into the private game reserves of the Tuli Block, there is little to attract the visitor here.

Where to stay

Category A
The one hotel here is the **Bosele** on the outskirts of town – plush and expensive at P140 for a single and P190 for a double. PO Box 177, Selebi-Phikwe. Tel: 810675

Serowe

Serowe is the largest of Botswana's traditional village settlements (as against purpose-built urban centres) with a population of over 100,000. Serowe has two main claims to fame: it was the birth place of the late Sir Seretse Khama, Botswana's first president; Bessie Head, Botswana's most prominent internationally known writer, made her home here and immortalised the village in her writings. The 'village' is an attractive place to visit for no particular reason other than to experience a traditional Botswanan town.

Where to stay

Category C
A basic and clean place to stay is the **Co op Hotel** run by the Brigades (a local cooperative organisation). It also serves reasonable meals.

TULI BLOCK & MASHATU GAME RESERVE

The Tuli Block and surrounding region in the far east of Botswana, adjacent to the Zimbabwean and South African borders, must be the most underrated part of the country. The landscape is quite different from elsewhere in Botswana, away from the sands of the Kalahari Desert and dominated by large rocky outcrops, hills and valleys. It's exciting game country – the hills and outcrops help viewing and make a change from Botswana's usual flat bush and plains – and is also good for walks and treks.

The Tuli Block itself is mostly white-owned land – a combination of game farms and private game reserves – which forms a long narrow strip next to the South African border. This was once land owned by Rhodes' British South Africa Company and was intended to be used for the building of the railway line. When the plans were changed, the land was sold off to white settlers instead. Outside this strip, there are a relatively large number of interesting and attractive traditional villages. These are worth exploring in their own right if you have your own vehicle or are thinking of some off-the-trail hiking and camping. Basic supplies are available in many of the villages, and the people are very friendly.

Despite being privately owned, some of the reserves have opened up for tourists, and offer the potential of good game viewing for a fraction of the cost of the government national parks and game reserves. Most of the private reserves include game drives in their entrance fee, and some also include guided walks.

Getting there

Car   In many ways, the reserves and lodges of the Tuli Block are designed more for South African visitors than those from Botswana. Road connections from South Africa are easier than from Botswana and the roads are tarred

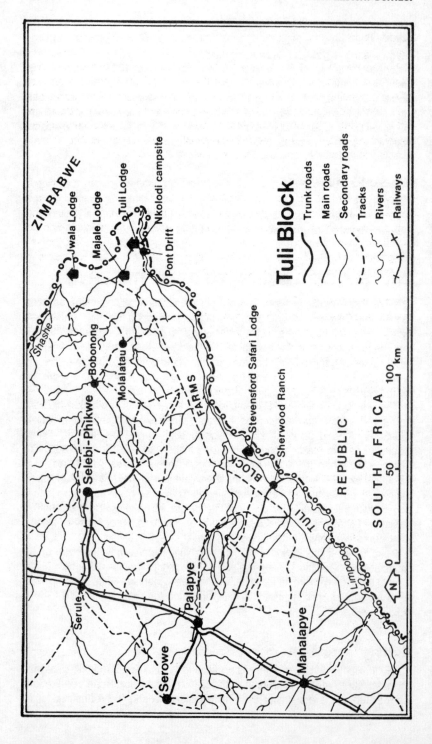

once across the border in South Africa. Many of the white residents do business and go shopping in South Africa – Johannesburg is only six hours away.

From Botswana, the main route to the Tuli Block follows the Gaborone – Francistown road, turning east on a smaller dirt road just before the town of Palapye, heading toward the border post at Martins Drift. 89km down this you'll reach the crossroads at Sherwood Ranch, at which you should turn left and head north – following the signs to Baines Drift. This will take you past Stevensford Safari Lodge, before eventually leading you to the border crossing at Pont Drift, and the Mashatu Game Reserve area.

Stevensford Game Reserve   Stevensford is the easiest of the game reserves to get to, being situated only about 20km north-east of the Sherwood Ranch turn-off on the road to Pont Drift. Here, on the banks of the Limpopo river, accommodation is in thatched self-catering chalets which go for about P80 per person per day. The price includes game drives, horse-riding and use of the bicycles. There are no predators or dangerous game in this reserve – the horse-riding and cycling is quite safe!

Jwala Game Lodge   Similar in cost to Stevensford, Jwala has self-catering chalets, and game drives and walks included in the price. The main difference is that Jwala has no boundary fences with the large Mashatu Game Reserve and you're bound to see plenty of big game in the area. The game lodge is some distance north of Pont Drift on the Zimbabwean border.

Majale Lodge and the **Mashatu Game Reserve**   This is the largest private 'conservation' area in southern Africa, with a great variety of landscapes and wildlife. It's especially known for its large elephant population. There is no access to the reserve unless you are staying at the lodge or on an organised trek, such as the **Ivory Trail**. This is a five-day organised trek through the Mashatu Game Reserve, strolling from one tented camp to the next. It's organised by Educational Wildlife Expeditions and costs over 750 Rand. Their address is: EWE, PO Box 645, Bedford View, R.S.A. 2008.

The only accommodation in the reserve is the very expensive Majale Lodge, complete with a thatched observation bar overlooking a floodlit water-hole. Access to the reserve and lodge is from Pont Drift.

Tuli Lodge   Adjacent to the Mashatu Game Reserve, only 7km west of the border at Pont Drift and near the Limpopo river. Tuli is another plush lodge like Majale, with very impressive gardens and grounds. Even if you can't afford to stay here, it's worth making the slight detour to its wonderful bar and swimming pool.

Nokolodi Campsite   This is a new development and the only cheap place to stay in the area. The campsite is situated in a beautiful setting on the banks of the Limpopo river, close to Pont Drift, and costs P20 per person per night. Ask for directions at the border post, or at Tuli Lodge.

Chobe & The Great Salt Pans

National Parks & Forest Reserves

1 Kasane F.R.
2 Maikaelelo F.R.
3 Chobe F.R.
4 Chobe
5 Kazuma F.R.
6 Sibuyu F.R.
7 Nxai Pan
8 Makgadikgadi Pans

- National border
- Trunk roads
- Main roads
- Secondary roads
- Tracks
- Rivers

N   0   100   200 km

Chapter 19

Chobe and the Great Salt Pans of the North East

South-east of the Okavango and north of the central Kalahari, Botswana's topography is dominated by great plains and huge shallow depressions or pans — remnants of the ancient lakes which once covered the region. There are two main parks here: Chobe and Nxai-Makgadikgadi. Outside these the country is almost equally wild and uninhabited, but in contrast to the central Kalahari it does have some permanent water. This draws huge herds of game from the desert's parched interior during the dry season, and these only return when the desert is flushed green again by the summer rains. This ancient annual migration rivals the more famous migration between the Serengeti and the Masai-Mara in East Africa and despite its decline in recent years, due to cattle fences and human pressure on the land, it still ensures that you are almost as likely to find game outside the reserves as in them.

Chobe, Botswana's premier park, is justly famed for its huge herds of game, especially elephant. Choose the right time of year, and with a little luck you will find the areas around the Chobe River, the Linyanti and the Savuti Marsh teeming with animals.

Just to the south, Nxai, Kudiakam and Makgadikgadi Pans have a stark beauty of their own and, during the first few months of the year, some good game viewing. By the side of Kudiakam Pan stand the famous Baines' Baobabs, a group of magnificent baobab trees which have made a spectacular backdrop for campers for a century or more.

Facilities for visitors in these National Parks are limited to either sparse public camp sites or, in Chobe, luxury private safari camps. The campsites are unfenced and primitive — expect just a cold tap, a simple toilet, and a shower. In contrast, several of the luxury camps are legendary: this is classic safari country. Chobe Game Lodge is renowned for its service, as well as its famous guests. Lloyd's Camp at Savuti maintains a reputation for top game guides.

Outside the parks there is a greater range of places to stay. Kasane and Maun are the main bases for trips into Chobe, and forays into Nxai and Makgadikgadi can be organised from Nata, or even Francistown. Kasane has a stunning situation on the banks of the Chobe River, but Maun remains the country's safari capital. All these towns have some mid-priced accommodation, but for cheap accommodation camping is the only option.

To explore the parks for yourself — in fact even to leave the main roads — you need a self-sufficient 4WD, lots of time and basic bush knowledge. The navigation is not particularly difficult because the tracks are usually clear (if slow and sandy), but the distances are large and there is nobody to help if you have problems.

A less demanding alternative is to take an organised safari. Your individual itinerary will probably fly you into two or three camps, for a few days each. Travel by light aircraft is practical here; almost everywhere has an airstrip and flying allows you to continue easily to visit the Okavango Delta.

Apart from Kasane, in the far north-east, there are few centres of population in this region. The small villages tend to be confined along the lines of the roads, and the people rely on passing trade and small scale cattle or subsistence farming on the dry sandy soil.

Kasane

Standing on the Chobe River in the north-east corner of the country, Kasane is a gateway to Namibia's Caprivi Strip, Zimbabwe and Zambia — and a springboard for trips into Chobe National Park. It has several places to stay, garages for vehicle repairs, a few shops for supplies and a very picturesque river front. Kasane is the best place to stay if you are arranging a day-trip into Chobe, or a budget mini-safari around the Serondela area.

Arriving from Nata, the road proceeds north-east to the Zimbabwean border-post at Kazungula, while the left turn at the Shell garage (where there is a good mechanic and useful car workshop) signals the start of the road through Chobe. Initially this leads through irrigated banana plantations, which give a clue about the proximity of one of the country's few permanent rivers.

On the right you pass the town's new commercial centre, an embryonic industrial area which lies between Kubu Lodge and the main road. Shortly afterwards, a clearly marked right turn points the way to Kasane, leaving the good tar road to degenerate into gravel as it continues to the Namibian border at Ngoma, some 65km away. If you want to speed your way to southern Chobe (avoiding Chobe's river-front) you could take this road, turning left before the border post at Ngoma, and reaching Kachikau after about 100km.

Taking the right turn, the first landmark is the country's newest, and probably most luxurious, hotel: the Mowana. Set back from the road, behind imposing gates, the Mowana's flagpoles do nothing to help it blend into a beautiful scene overlooking some of the Chobe's rapids.

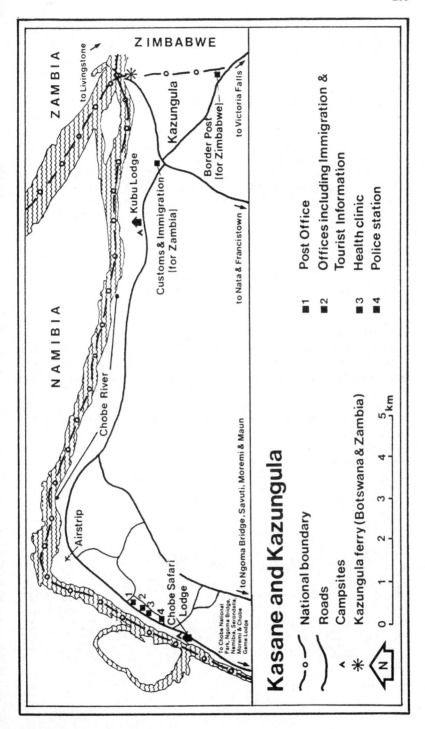

Kasane and Kazungula

◦‿◦ National boundary

⌒ Roads

⌃ Campsites

* Kazungula ferry (Botswana & Zambia)

✳ N

■1 Post Office
■2 Offices including Immigration & Tourist Information
■3 Health clinic
■4 Police station

0 1 2 3 4 5 km

In the town centre, a sharp, rectangular Barclays bank has replaced the delightfully thatched rondavel that used to serve as the area's financial hub, without making it any faster to withdraw cash. There is also a post office, basic grocery shops, a couple of gift shops, a police station, a fuel station, a hospital, and usually lots of activity.

The tourist information office is well stocked with brochures and has some excellent (if ancient) maps of Chobe, Nxai and the Okavango. This is one of the best places outside Gaborone for information on the National Parks. On the west side of the small centre, a new, wide tarred road leads up and away from the river to join the inland road to the Namibian border at Ngoma Bridge, whist the main road continues past the Kasane Filling Station and the Hertz office, into the bush and towards the park.

Getting there and away

From Francistown, Kasane is about 495km of variable tarred road away. Nata, the only fuel stop on the route, is 195km from Francistown. If you are hitching in either direction then this is an easy route with lots of traffic by Botswana's standards — make an early start from Francistown and you can expect to reach Kasane by nightfall.

From Zimbabwe there is an excellent tarred road to Kasane. This brings Africa's biggest waterfall, and a major centre for travellers, within a convenient day-trip from Kasane. Victoria Falls is only 75km away, so it is not difficult to reach by either hitching, or by hiring a car for a few days (see page 45). Alternatively there is a UTC minibus which shuttles between the two centres every day, though it is expensive (P90 each way). This calls at all Kasane's lodges and at UTC's office in Victoria Falls, so ask the lodge where you are staying for the latest details.

To Zambia there is a ferry over the river at Kazungula, 14kms away, but most visitors go via Victoria Falls in Zimbabwe, rather than directly across, since getting to Livingstone is much less difficult from there. If you want to hitch across, there are occasional lorries going. Try standing where the Zimbabwean and Zambian roads fork, hitching on both of them.

To Namibia there is a good road, suitable for all vehicles, which starts opposite Chobe Safari Lodge. Ngoma Bridge is a well signposted 65km away. The road passes a checkpoint after 5km and then cuts inland through Chobe, before heading north over the Chobe River, the border with Namibia. 2km before you reach the bridge, report into the border post to complete emigration and customs formalities. From the Namibian post in Ngoma, it's 60km to the Caprivi Strip's main town, Katima Mulilo, where most people stop for their first night (see Chapter 16, *The Northern Strip*, page 223).

Where to stay

Chobe Safari Lodge P.O. Box 10, Kasane. Tel: 250336. Overlooking the river, on the fringes of town as you head for Chobe, this is the oldest of Kasane's camps. Camping on the pleasant sites along the river costs P15 per person per night, and the lodge's accommodation ranges from basic chalets with shared ablutions at P65 for a single, P85 for a double, to those with private toilets and showers at P125 per single, P145 per double. Family rooms are available at P190.

Most of the independent backpackers stay here, so it's a good place to form a group if you are planning to hire a vehicle. The lodge's restaurant serves breakfast for P17, lunch for P20 and dinner for P35, but the bar's toasted sandwiches make a good alternative.

Daily river cruises (departing 3pm) give excellent game viewing, especially in the dry season, and cost P25 if you're staying here, P35 otherwise. Plus, of course, park fees of P30 per person. Alternatively you can hire your own motor boat (seating maximum of 4) for P40 per hour. You're bound to come across hippo and crocodiles on these, and the riverside is frequented by two of the region's rarer antelope, the puku and the Chobe bushbuck. The latter are very distinctive, but to the uninitiated, puku are similar to the more common impala. They are lighter in coloration (orange-yellow, paler underneath) and have stouter, more evenly curving horns.

Game drives lasting two and a quarter hours can also be arranged here, at about P35 each (plus the park fees) for a minimum of two people.

Kubu Lodge PO Box 43, Kasane. Tel: 650312. Fax: 650412. Situated about 10km east of Kasane and just a couple of kilometres from the border crossing at Kazungula, this is a beautiful camp set on lawns which stretch down to the river. With its proximity to the border posts, this makes a popular stop for overlanders with their own vehicles.

Most of the accommodation is in solid thatched chalets, built on stilts overlooking the river. These cost P125 single, P155 double and P180 for a triple, while there are also a few *rondavels* available which sleep two and cost P125. The chalets have double beds, rather than the usual twin beds, and come complete with overhead fans, flush toilets, showers and even have hair-dryers in the bathrooms. Alternatively there is camping for P20 per person per night, on riverside sites that slope steeply in places.

There's a bar, and comfortable seats, shaded by umbrellas, stretch down towards the river. The restaurant serves breakfast for P18 and dinner for P35. If you are camping then take a torch as the campsite is not well lit at night and the track back from the bar is very uneven.

Kubu does organise river cruises and game drives. The cruises start from Kasane and cost P40 per person, plus P20 if you need transport to get into town. The game drives last three hours and, similarly, cost P40 per person, and park fees (P30 per person) are extra.

Mowana Lodge PO Box 266, Kasane. Tel: 650300. Fax: 650301. Opened on April 30 1993 by the President of Botswana, Mowana Lodge is the flagship of the Cresta group of luxury hotels. This typically Botswanan hotel, conceived on a grand scale and built around a baobab tree, has 112 rooms, including 10 suites, 16 family rooms and two rooms suitable for paraplegics. All are spacious, indeed luxurious, with river views, remote control air-conditioning, fans, telephones and well appointed bathrooms.

Mowana's spectacular restaurant also overlooks the Chobe, and serves breakfast for P16, lunch for P20 and dinner (with a game bias) for about P35. Accommodation varies in price from P115-140 for a standard room for one/two persons, to suites for P145-P175.

Chobe Chilwero Run by Linyanti Explorations, this exclusive little lodge, on the banks of the Chobe near the Park's entrance, is run in a bush-camp style with professional guides giving guests individual attention. Guests are accommodated in eight thatched bungalows, each with a toilet and shower.

The price of about P500 per person per night, includes all meals, drinks, river boat trips and game drives into the park. To book contact Hartley Safaris — see under *Okavango Explorations* in *Booking Agencies and Operators*, page 305.

What to see and do

Kasane is essentially a base for excursions into Chobe National Park, and along the river. The town's only attraction is probably its **Reptile Park**. This is virtually next to Kubu Lodge, and holds guided tours around its collection of fauna at 9am, 11am, 2pm, and 4pm. Admission is good value at P10 for adults and P5 children, giving visitors a chance to see animals which they would rarely spot in the wild.

CHOBE NATIONAL PARK

4WD only, except northern strip by Chobe River, 2WD. Standard entrance fees.
Chobe is about 11,700 square km of Africa's wildest bush, teeming with game. It takes its name from the Chobe River, which forms its northern boundary, and since the first Europeans arrived in the 1850s, it has been a Mecca for the trophy hunters — so its proclamation as a National Park in 1968 was none too late.

Despite these first foreign visitors, the game has recovered exceedingly well, and still amazes people on their first trip. Simply driving the few kilometres from the park's entrance to Chobe Game Lodge or Serondela campsite can easily become an hour's drive when you are forced to halt by game wandering slowly across the road, or drinking from the river.

Perhaps more than any of Botswana's parks, Chobe has felt the impact of tourism. In the 1980s park fees were low and so the campsites were full. The rubbish left around was not a pretty sight, and the animals were becoming far too used to people. While Chobe has never been crowded, this was too many visitors for just three or four basic public campsites. However, in 1989 the government's policy of 'high cost, low density' tourism began, and the situation started to change. Now the campsites are empty and, if you can afford it, the park feels like a true wilderness again.

Chobe's areas of interest can be divided into three areas, each with a public camp site: the Chobe River-front (alias Serondela), Savuti Area, and the Ngwezumba Pans. These are described in order later in the chapter, but first a warning for those organising their own trip here.

Beware: none of Chobe's camps have fences. This means that, over the years, animals around the camps have become *very* used to humans, and very unafraid of them. Baboons, elephants, hyenas and lion cause major problems for campers. Do not leave anything outside at night, and never sleep even partly outside a tent. Make sure that your tent is fully zipped up and *never* use just a mosquito net to sleep out under the stars.

When to visit — the Great Migrations

Most of the Park's larger herbivores migrate with the seasons, to find water to drink and pastures new. These movements are, to a large extent, predictable, so plan your trip with them in mind to maximise your chances of good game viewing.

Like most of the continent's game migrations, the principle behind this one is simple: the animals move onto the open grasslands during and just after the rains, and return to permanent sources of water for the driest months. Then they head north and west, out of the interior's plains (including Makgadikgadi and Nxai) and towards the Chobe River, the Linyanti, and the Okavango. This gives the vegetation on the plains time to recover, so that when the rains come again the animals can return there for good grazing.

The finer details of this are more complex, and slightly different for each species. Zebra, for example, have recently been the focus of a research project which tracked them using radio transmitters and a micro-light aircraft, based in Savuti. This study suggested that they spend the rainy summer, from November to about February, in the Mababe depression — venturing south to Nxai, and even going further towards the central Kalahari. In March and April they pass through Savuti for a few months, where they foal. This makes a particularly good foaling ground as the rich alluvial deposits from the old Savuti Channel have left the area with mineral-rich soil supporting particularly nutritious grasses. A few months later, as dryness begins to bite around July, they move again towards the Linyanti for the dry season. Finally in late October and November, they return to Mababe as the rains begin and the grasses start to sprout.

For the visitor, this means that the game in the dry season is best in the river areas, whilst in the wet season, and just afterwards, the interior pans are definitely worth a visit. Savuti, remarkably, has good game all year, but is especially busy around April/May and November.

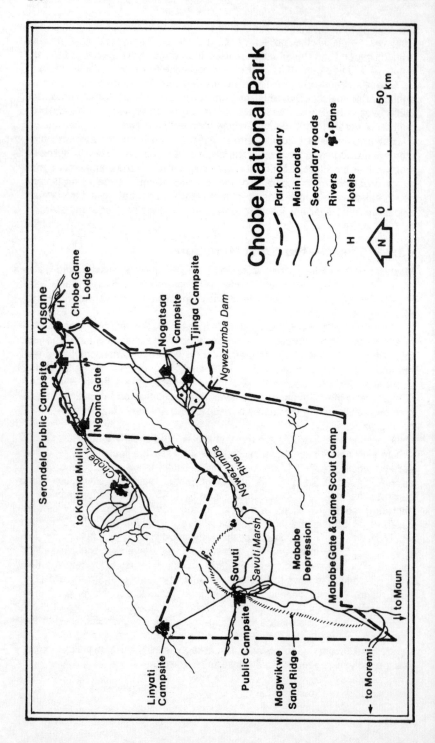

Chobe National Park

- – – Park boundary
-))))) Main roads
-))) Secondary roads
- ~~~ Rivers
- 🐾 Pans
- H Hotels

0   50 km

N

Kasane
Chobe Game Lodge
Serondela Public Campsite
to Katima Mulilo
Ngoma Gate
Chobe River
Nogatsaa Campsite
Tjinga Campsite
Ngwezumba Dam
Ngwezumba
Ngwezumba River
Mababe Gate & Game Scout Camp
Mababe Depression
Savuti
Savuti Marsh
Magwikwe Sand Ridge
Public Campsite
Linyati Campsite
to Maun
to Moremi

Getting there

To visit Chobe or the salt pans you have a number of options, depending on how you prefer to travel:

Car hire Having your own 4WD vehicle is the perfect option and allows you total flexibility to do what you want to, when you want. However, driving along Chobe's sandy tracks is tiring, time consuming, and requires confidence with a 4WD. Further, you must either book luxury camps in advance for each night, or organise all your own food, supplies and camping equipment for yourselves — like a small expedition.

If you decide to drive then the closest places to hire a 4WD from are Kasane and Maun. Charges are high, around P250-P300 per day, so this is not a cheap option. For a short one-way rental from Maun, consider a chauffeur-driven 4WD from the Island Safari Lodge (see page 296) as well as the major car hire companies. See Chapter 4, *Planning and Preparations*, for details of the best car hire deals

Organised mobile safaris Several good safari companies organise mobile camping safaris which take around six to twelve people in specially converted 4WD vehicles. These carry all the food and camping equipment, and the camp moves every few days. This option offers you flexibility with your itinerary, together with the relaxation of having someone else do all the planning and arranging. Some will require you to do occasional camp chores, like putting up the tents and cooking, but that's part of the fun anyhow.

The best of these are probably Okavango Wilderness Safaris and Afro ventures, both based in Maun. See the section on *Operators and Agents* (page 303) for more ideas, and note that several of the big international truck tours also pass through Chobe as part of their normal itineraries. Given the choice, go for the local operators who know the area: you'll get a much better feel for the country that way.

Day trips If you are on a tighter budget then shorter game drives into the park are probably your only option. All of the lodges and camps in Kasane organise short, circular game drives near Chobe's river-side which leave in the morning and evening for a few hours' drive. You will have to pay the normal park fees though so, for example, Kubu Lodge charges P40 per person (plus park fees of P30) for a three hour trip around the Serondela area. A better buy, in many ways, is a boat cruise along the Chobe, as there is the added excitement of hippos and the river's bird-life as well as the normal game. For Nxai and Makgadikgadi, the Lodge at Nata is closest and organises some of the least expensive trips — though if you only take a day trip to Sua Pan, you may end up seeing only the closest, least interesting corners of the pan.

Luxury camps There are four luxury camps in Chobe, three at Savuti and one — Chobe Game Lodge — at Serondela. All offer a high standard of comfort, and the expertise of experienced local guides. You just choose what you'd like to do and it will be organised. Game trips, meals and accommodation are normally included in the costs, so the only extras are alcohol, laundry and park fees. Transfers between the camps are usually by light aircraft, and often everything is lumped together in a 'package' price for time spent at several camps. You are expected to arrive with a few clothes, a camera and lots of sun-tan cream, and all will treat you like an important personal guest. Charges are high, expect about P250 - P700 per person per night (see page 271 and pages 275 - 6).

Hitching   Nowadays there are few independent visitors to Chobe, and fewer still with space for hitchhikers in their vehicles. This makes hitching through the park exceedingly difficult. Your only hope is to find a half-empty 4WD vehicle in Maun, Kasane or Victoria Falls, and offer to share costs for the trip through the park. Then buy a week's supply of food, and make sure your camping equipment is in working condition. In 1988, before the park fees increased, the authors first visited the park with the help of a lift like this, from Victoria Falls through Chobe, the Okavango, Nxai, Makgadikgadi and all the way to Francistown — but such lifts are few and far between now.

Chobe River-front and Serondela

Perhaps the park's greatest attraction is its northern boundary, the Chobe River. In the dry season animals converge on this stretch of water from the whole of northern Botswana, forming the huge herds for which the park is famous. In November 1853 David Livingstone passed through the area and described the river:

> '... though the river is from thirteen to fifteen feet in depth at its lowest ebb, and broad enough to allow a steamer to ply upon it, the suddenness of the bending would prevent navigation; but should the country ever become civilised, the Chobe would be a convenient natural canal.'

Fortunately the kind of civilisation that Livingstone envisaged can't have reached the Chobe yet as there are no canal boats to be seen. Today's traveller must make do with the small motor-boats which weave along the river, amongst channels which are still ruled by the hippos. These are a good place from which to spot the elephants for which the park is justly famous. In the afternoons, just before sunset, large family groups visit the river to drink and bathe, affording spectacular viewing and photography.

If you are not floating but driving then be cautious — the groups mainly consist of mothers with calves who are sensitive to any perceived threat or interference. Stay in your car, keep a respectful distance from the animals and when you move, do so *slowly*. If you find your car surrounded by a herd of elephants then relax. Don't panic or rev your engine, just sit there quiet, and still, until the animals have passed. Ideally switch off your engine, but this is not for the faint hearted.

From the main route, which shadows the river, there is a network of good (often 2WD) loop roads which allow you to explore both the river-bank and the surrounding *mopane* forest. All the big game is here in quantity, even herds of short-tempered buffalo, who find much of Namibia and Botswana too dry for their liking. The rarest of the big five, Rhino, occur too, though are seldom spotted now due to the scourge of poaching. Wildebeest, zebra, impala, giraffe and eland all arrive at the river, and the predators are never far behind. Lion are common and while leopard, cheetah and wild dog do occur, they are seen more rarely.

Perhaps the area's most unusual antelope is the Chobe bushbuck (a subspecies of *Tragelaphus scriptus*). These small antelope, endemic to this river-front, occur singly or in pairs and will first freeze if disturbed, before bolting for cover as the disturbance continues. Their coloration is red-brown, like the soil, with a covering of white spots which blend perfectly into the diffuse shadow patterns of the riverside's thick vegetation. Only the males have horns, which are short and spiralled.

Given that the animals are here for the water, one of the best ways to watch the game is from a boat. This can be organised from any of the lodges, allowing you to float along, scanning the bank for game, with a drink in one hand and a camera in the other, while the boat's driver avoids families of hippo and helps look out for the more unusual birds. There are a number of bird colonies along the sandy banks, their nests tunnelled into the banks for safety. Beautifully coloured pied and malachite kingfishers are often seen, while if you are very lucky you may sight the Cape clawless otters which also make homes in the river's banks

Where to stay

Many people visit the river-front whilst staying in Kasane, and may thus save a few days' park fees before visiting the park. Within Chobe, there are just two choices: Serondela's basic public campsite, about 10 km from the park gate, and the first class Chobe Game Lodge.

Serondela public campsite This is the only campsite in Chobe that can be reached by 2WD vehicle, but despite this, there are seldom more than a couple of groups here. You will find basic toilets and cold showers spread around a small area literally overlooking the river. Do try to pitch your camp away from the game trails and paths, though this is tricky when game seems to be everywhere. The camp's animal specialities are baboons, which will take anything that's not nailed down, and elephants who will tread gingerly over your tent's guy ropes to reach the river while you sleep.

Chobe Game Lodge PO Box 43, Kasane. Tel: 650340, Fax: 650280/650223. Reservations: PO Box 2602, Halfway House, Jo'burg 1685, S.Africa. Tel: (011) 315-1695/6/7/8, Fax: (011) 805.2882

Situated a few kilometres inside the national park, Chobe Game Lodge proclaims itself to be 'Botswana's most exclusive safari resort,' which seems a pretentious claim until you visit it. Visibly the Game Lodge is just another luxury hotel. Its design is unusual though, with tribal antiques in almost Moorish surroundings which, mysteriously, do not make them look out of place. However, its first class reputation is built on the staff's attention to detail, and their very personal service.

The rooms, all with en-suite facilities, are spread out along the river-bank, about 60m from the water's edge. Each is set slightly into the bank with a barrel-vaulted ceiling and one full wall of glass overlooking the river. Their design, and their *punkah-punkah* ceiling fans, keep them cool through the day, and secluded during the evening.

The food is excellent, and usually eaten outside on a covered veranda. Breakfast and lunch are buffet-style, while dinner is even more leisurely, à la carte by candle-light. During dinner you'll be asked which activities you would like to take part in the next day — the choice being a variety of game drives or river trips. If these become a little much, then the option of lounging by the swimming pool is one to remember, and the bar is probably Botswana's best.

Chobe Game Lodge's prices are high, about P580 per person sharing, (or P700 for a suite with its own private pool) but they do include all activities, meals, airport transfers and even park fees. Non-residents can savour the luxury of breakfast for P23, lunch for P34 and dinner for P40, or take an evening boat trip for about P35 per person. All considered, it's not surprising that Elizabeth Taylor and Richard Burton chose this as a romantic place in which to be re-married and spend their honeymoon.

Driving from Kasane to Savuti

There are two routes through the park between Kasane and Savuti. Certainly the shorter, and probably the more beautiful, is the **western route**. This takes about 172km to reach Savuti from Kasane, and it starts by following the banks of the Chobe River until Ngoma. The track then continues south-west, leaving the national park and entering village-owned and forest reserve land. About 24km from Ngoma gate the village of Kavimba is marked by two baobabs, with the road running between them. The second village on this route, Kachikau, makes a good stop for cold drinks.

About 80km from Ngoma the track leaves forest reserve land and re-enters the park just north of the Goha Hills. It then crosses the Magwikwe Sand Ridge before finally approaching Savuti from the north-east. Although this route is shorter and arguably more spectacular, it is probably more difficult and time consuming to drive.

For the **eastern route**, take the fast road from Kasane to Ngoma, away from the river. After about 32km a left turn leads, after a kilometre or two, through the Nantanga Pans area. About 35km later there is a left turn to the complex of roads around Nogatsaa airstrip, Ngwezumba campsite and Dam. Continue straight and after about 22km you'll pass another left, leading back to the same area. Shortly after this the road begins to follow the dry bed of the Ngwezumba River, and 60km later it takes a more southerly direction and leaves the river bed behind it. About 20km after leaving the river the road splits: both forks go to Savuti. The right leads almost directly to the camps, joining the western route just north of the channel, while the left continues south for a few kilometres before swinging west around Cotsoroga Pan. You then approach the south end of Savuti Marsh, from where you must bear north (and slightly west) to reach the camp area.

The total distance from Kasane to Savuti along the eastern route is about 207km, and it will take five or six hours to drive. An advantage is the possibility of a mid-way stop at the Ngwezumba Pans' campsites, although scenically the route lacks the beauty of the Chobe river.

Ngwezumba Pans

About 100km south of the Chobe River lies a complex of large pans surrounded by grassland plains and *mopane* woodlands. There are well over a dozen individual pans: Noghatsau, Gxlaigxlarara, Tutlha, Tambiko, Kabunga, Cwikamba and Poha, to name but a few, and all hold water after the rains. This makes them a natural focus during the first few months of the year, when the animals tend to stay away from the permanent waters of the Linyanti and Chobe Rivers.

This area is notable for its oribi antelope, perhaps the only place in Botswana where they occur naturally. These small, elegant grazing antelope are orange-red above, white underneath, have a dark circular scent gland under their ears and a short bush tail. Only the males have short, pointed horns which seem to curve slightly forward. They are usually seen in pairs, or small groups, feeding in the open grasslands during the morning or late afternoon. If startled they will often emit a shrill whistle before bounding off at a rapid rate with a very jerky motion.

Where to stay

There are just two places to stay here, the Tjinga (alias 'Tshinga' and 'Tchinga') and Nogatsaa campsites, and one or other is sometimes closed — ask the game scouts at either park entry gate for the latest information.

Nogatsaa, the more northerly site, is situated by a Nogatsaa Dam and has toilets and cold showers. The game viewing hide, which overlooks the dam, is invariably deserted so spend the late afternoon just sitting and watching the game coming to bathe and drink.

Tjinga is about 21km south of Nogatsaa, and has no facilities other than a water tank with a temperamental mechanical pump. However, it is another site where you are unlikely to be disturbed by anything except the animals, so relax and enjoy the solitude.

Savuti

Savuti, in the heart of Chobe National Park, is one Africa's most famous big game areas. At times it has amazing concentrations of game, whilst always remaining a beautiful place with an atmosphere all of its own. The key to its attraction is the mysterious Savuti Channel, which is often dry but sometimes, inexplicably, flows. Then it spills out from the southern end of the Linyanti swamps and, after passing through a gap in the Magwikwe Sand Ridge, starts to spread out across the Mababe Depression, forming the Savuti Marsh.

The Mababe Depression itself is, in fact, the bed of an ancient lake that used to cover a large area of northern Botswana. The Magwikwe Sand Ridge is thought to mark this lake's north-western edge. Oft-quoted evidence for the lake's existence is the steep, wave-washed cliffs and intriguing, rounded pebbles to be found at the Gubatsaa Hills near Savuti's camps.

Savuti Marsh, even at its peak, only covered a relatively small area in the north-western corner of this flat, bush-covered plain — and even that was enough to attract huge quantities of game. Now the channel is dry, and its sandy bed is littered with the shells of freshwater mussels. The marsh is a flat, open grassland, and the eerie, leafless camelthorn trees which punctuate it — drowned in the late 1950s when the marsh flooded — are simply perches for resident eagles.

In the early 1850s when Livingstone arrived here, there was a 'dismal swamp' some 16km long, fed by both the Mababe (now called Khwai) River, which spilled over from the Okavango system, and also by the 'strongly flowing' Savuti Channel. However, when Selous came in 1879, the swamp and the channel were dry. They remained like this until 1957 when the channel began to flow strongly once again.

This water in the desert seemed permanent and enhanced the area's reputation until, once again, the channel ceased to flow in 1982. Nobody really knows why it stopped, as nobody understood why it started again after 80 years of dryness. Explanations range from tectonic shifts to changes in the paths used by the Linyanti's hippos. But even with the channel dry, the rich soil here ensures that Savuti remains a classic area for game with a reputation for lone elephant bulls, lion, and hyena.

Where to stay

The camps are all close to each other, and linked by a maze of game viewing tracks which criss-cross the channel and reach south-east into the marsh area. Being a day's drive from either Kasane or Maun, most guests fly in to Savuti's airstrip (which can take plane's as large as a DC3), but it's also quite possible to drive here yourself.

Savuti public campsite This camp used to be busy with visitors, but now it has the air of a place once besieged, where people tried resist the animals, failed, and left. There are a number of simple toilet blocks, some taps ingeniously encased in concrete to prevent elephants from drinking, and lots of spaces in the bush which were once flattened by cars and tents. There is even an electric elephant fence — now broken and trampled.

That said, it is deep in the bush and it remains a wonderful place to stay. The camp's animal specialities are spotted hyenas and, of course, elephants. Like Savuti's private camps, the campsite has nightly visits from spotted hyenas which, we discovered, could carry away a full rucksack at high speed — despite being pursued. With a powerful torch and a little patience you can pick out their ghostly green eyes beyond the circle of your fire-light at night. They will steal and eat anything from a camera lens to a bar of soap, so leave *nothing* outside. Remember that hyenas will push their luck, but are essentially cowardly animals: chase them and they will always run, sometimes dropping their spoils.

Remember One of Savuti's golden rules is *never* to arrive with any citrus fruit, as elephants find this particularly irresistible. Recently there was a case of campers, sleeping in the back compartment of their 4WD, who were woken at 5am by an elephant. It had shattered both the windscreen and their nerves by using one of its tusks as a 'can-opener' to get into the vehicle's front cab. Foolishly, they had left some oranges in there, not knowing that one of Savuti's bulls — Baby Huey — had developed a fondness for citrus fruit. Two days later, the game scouts shot Huey. He had too much of a taste for these forbidden fruits and was becoming a danger. This wouldn't have occurred if he hadn't been fed oranges in the first place by well meaning tourists.

Lloyd's Camp PO Box 37, Maun — contact by radio, via Merlin Services, Maun. Alternatively make a reservation with Educational Wildlife Expeditions, 11 Glendower Place, Linksfield Road, Edenvale, 1610 Johannesburg, S.Africa. Tel: (011) 453-7645/6/7, Fax: (011) 453-7649.

Run by the legendary Lloyd Wilmot, Lloyd's camp has become something of an institution in Chobe. Run as the best of safari camps used to be, with an independent and individual style, it caters for a maximum of 12 guests who come to watch the animals with the experts.

The food is excellent, the bar well stocked, and the tents very comfortable, but the real draw of Lloyd's camp is its guides: Lloyd, Lionel and Kaiser. Their enthusiasm encourages the dedicated to be up as the sun rises for coffee and rusks, before driving out in an open Land Rover. Then they will actually track the game by following its spoor from the vehicle, an impressive feat which gives them the very best chance of spectacular game viewing. This is a camp that wildlife enthusiasts should not miss

When the sun's high, and the game's mostly under cover, you'll return for a more extensive brunch, after which time is your own, to sleep or watch from the hide, until the afternoon drive. This is approached with equal enthusiasm, and may last three or four hours if the game is good. This leaves day to be concluded on the dark side of dusk with drinks over dinner, and stories around the fire.

Note that Lloyd's does not accept any credit cards, so traveller's cheques or cash are needed. It costs from P250 per person per night, including all meals and activities.

Allan's Camp Run by Gametrackers — see page 304. With Lloyd's and Savuti South, its sister camp, Allan's camp stands on the south side of the Savuti channel. Accommodation is in one of eight comfortable A-frame bungalows, constructed solidly from local thatch on a wood and brick base. Each hut is protected with mosquito netting and has en-suite toilet and shower facilities, and even a 12V power system to provide lights during the night.

The bungalows, which look out onto the dry channel, are positioned around the large dining room/bar area. Activities here revolve around game drives, which complement perfectly the waterborne activities at Gametrackers' other camps in the Okavango Delta. Ideally, spend a few days here, or at Savuti South, as part of a longer trip encompassing one or two camps within the Delta area.

Savuti South Run by Gametrackers — see page 304 — in a similar style to Allan's, Savuti South's accommodation is large East-African style, Meru tents set in an open aspect under some imposing *acacia erioloba* trees, overlooking the channel. Perhaps because the elephants love the trees' ear-lobe shaped seed pods, the camp is constantly visited by elephants. They come to stand at the base of the trees, shaking steadily, before sucking up the fallen pods with their trunks. Occasionally one visits the camp's open dining area, but always care is needed when walking around. At least you are guaranteed some close-up views of elephant here.

Driving from Savuti to Maun

About 4km south of the campsite, just before the hill known as Leopard Rock, the track splits two ways. The left, signposted Savuti Marsh, is more scenic but leads into a very rutted track across the marsh itself. This is fine (if bumpy) during the dry season, but a bad route during the rainy season as you will get stuck. The right fork is signposted Sand Ridge and heads more directly towards Maun, skirting along the edge of the marsh.

Taking the right fork you cut across the Magwikwe Sand Ridge about 26km south of Savuti. Don't expect this to be too obvious, as the ridge is little more than a wide, vegetated sand-dune which you will climb slightly to get on to, and drop slightly to come off. That said, you will notice that driving across it is more difficult than normal as the vehicle's tyres will sink deeper into the sand. These two roads join up about 38km later, and in a further 10km you will reach the park exit point, some 52km south of Savuti. The sign here reads: Khwai 45km, North Gate 54km and Maun 133km.

South from the gate the road becomes difficult during the rains. In contrast to Savuti's relatively lush vegetation, there is little ground cover here, and only low stunted *mopane* trees to protect the soil from the extremes of the elements. The road's fine earth is hard-baked when dry, and very slippery when wet.

A little over 10km past the gate the road forks, without a signpost in sight. Left leads directly to Maun while right takes 3 kilometres to cross the Magwikwe Sand Ridge (from 16km to 19km after Chobe's exit gate) before entering Moremi National Park via its North Gate, about 20km beyond the sand ridge (see section on *Moremi*, page 307). The right route, through Moremi, finally joins up with the left again about 68km north of Maun.

If your destination is Maun then don't underestimate the time that a detour through Moremi will take. Going directly from Chobe's gate to Maun is about 133km, around a five-hour drive. However, driving via Moremi is 193km, which will take nearer nine hours, including some slow, heavy driving across the sand ridge. Also remember that you will have to pay an extra set of park fees for Moremi, even if you have just left Chobe. So if you can spend a night or more in Moremi, don't miss the chance to stop off, but if you only have one day to get from Savuti to Maun then go direct.

This approach to Moremi's North Gate from Chobe follows the northern bank of the Khwai River, which is truly stunning scenery. After the unrelenting dryness of southern Chobe, the Khwai's lily-covered waterways and shady forest glades are completely magical.

The Linyanti

4WD. No entrance fees.
The Linyanti river, as it passes through the Linyanti Swamps, acts as a magnet for game during the dry season. However, reaching this area can be difficult for the visitor. Botswana's side is remote, and rarely visited, being the preserve of a couple of small hunting camps working within their own concession areas. If you wish to visit, then it is much more practical to approach the Linyanti Swamps from Namibia, either staying at **Lianshulu Lodge** (see page 229) or camping in **Mamili Reserve** (page 230).

The intrepid and well-prepared, who do want to try their luck from the southern side should ask directions from the National Park's game scouts in Savuti, as the best track to the Linyanti branches off from the main cross-park road around there.

THE GREAT SALT PANS

To the west of the Delta, Botswana is dominated by the great salt pans. Seen from the air, Makgadikgadi is a vast sea of grey salt, bordered in places by low cliffs of sand which marks the start of the endless grasslands. These strange areas are fascinating places to explore, offering a real wilderness for those with their own vehicle.

Once submerged beneath warm shallow water, these salt pans are all that's left of one of the world's greatest lakes. Several million years ago, the whole of the northern Kalahari formed the bed of a huge expanse of fresh water, perhaps stretching as far as the present Okavango Delta and the

Magwikwe Sand Ridge. Why it dried out isn't known, but the most popular theory suggests that the rivers which fed the lake changed course as the continent gradually tilted. Whatever the cause, the water's mineral salts were concentrated in the pools which remained where the lake was deepest.

When finally dry, these salts inhibited plant growth on the lake's old bed and so allowed the wind to scour the dusty pans, making them still deeper and exposing great expanses of salty grey clay. Adjacent to the pans themselves are large expanses of grassland, in which small depressions have accumulated deposits of wind-blown detritus. These 'islands' of richer soil support trees and other plants and make a fascinating place just to sit and relax, in what always seems like the middle of nowhere.

The end of the wet season is the best time to visit either Makgadikgadi or Nxai, as during the dry season some of the animals migrate northwards to the areas of permanent water. Other than this the choice of which area to visit will probably depend on your available time. Nxai and Kudiakam are smaller and more self-contained than Makgadikgadi, but without the same feeling of an immense wilderness. Bear in mind that only the eastern side of the Makgadikgadi Pans has less game, but there are no park fees here.

Makgadikgadi Pans

The Sowa and Ntwetwe Pans that comprise Makgadikgadi cover 12,000 square kilometres to the south of the Nata-Maun road. The western side is protected within a National Park, while the east is either wilderness or cattle ranching land.

There are few landmarks, and so you're left to use the flat, distant horizon as your only line of reference — and even that dissolves into a haze of shimmering mirages in the heat of the afternoon sun. It is only during the rains that the area comes to life, with huge migrating herds of zebra, wildebeest, and occasionally (if the pans fill with water) millions of flamingos. Occasional outcrops of isolated rock in and around the pans add to their sense of mystery, as well as providing excellent vantage points from which to view the endless expanse of silver, grey and blue.

If you're exploring the area in a 4WD, you are recommended to get hold of a copy of *Visitor's Guide to Botswana* by Main and Fowkes (see *Bibliography*), which has excellent sections on the various tracks.

Kubu 'Island' (Sowa Pan)

This protected National Monument, in the south-west corner of Sowa Pan, is the best known of Makgadikgadi's isolated rock outcrops. Although the rocks only rise about 10m above the pan floor, the view and general atmosphere is breath-taking — don't miss out on the sunset. The island is host to a number of ancient and extremely picturesque baobabs, as well as the remains of a human settlement, dating back to between 500 and 1600 AD. Kubu Island is a magical place to visit and highly recommended.

Flamingos

Of the world's half-dozen or so species of flamingo, two are found within southern Africa: the Greater, *phoenicopterus ruber*, and the Lesser, *phoenicopterus minor*. Both species have wide distributions — from southern Africa north into East Africa and the Red Sea — and are highly nomadic in their habits.

Flamingos are usually found wading in large areas of shallow saline water where they filter feed by holding their specially adapted beaks upside down in the water. The Lesser Flamingo will walk or swim whilst swinging its head from side to side, mainly taking blue-green algae from the surface of the water. The larger Greater Flamingo will hold its head submerged while filtering out small organisms (detritus and algae), even stirring the mud with its feet to help the process. Both species are very gregarious and flocks can have millions of birds, though a few hundred is more common.

Only occasionally do flamingos breed in southern Africa, choosing Etosha pan, the Makgadikgadi pans or even Lake Ngami. When the conditions are right (usually March to June, following the rains) both species build low mud cones in the water and lay one (or rarely two) eggs in a small hollow on the top. These are then incubated by both parents for about a month until they hatch, and after a further week the young birds flock together and start to forage with their parents. Some ten weeks later the young can fly and fend for themselves.

During this time the young are very susceptible to the shallow water in the pans drying out. In 1969, a rescue operation was mounted when the main pan at Etosha dried out, necessitating the moving of thousands of chicks to nearby Fisher's pan which was still covered in water!

The best way to tell the two species apart is by their beaks: that of the Greater Flamingo is almost white with a black tip, whilst the Lesser Flamingo has a uniformly dark beak. If you are further away then the body of the Greater will appear white, whilst that of the Lesser looks smaller and more pink.

The best place to see them is probably around Walvis Bay or Sandwich Harbour — unless you hear specific news that they are breeding on one of the great pans.

Getting there To get to Kubu Island take the track south from the Nata-Maun road, 16km west of Nata and follow this south for about 100km between Sowa Pan and Ntwetwe Pan. An alternative route is to head north from the Francistown-Orapa road at the turn-off next to Mmatshumo village. **Warning:** Avoid driving on the pan surfaces. These are deceptive as they may look solid and hard, but treacherous mud is often lurking just below the surface.

Where to stay Your choice is either to find a sheltered position, if you can, and camp rough, or to book ahead and stay at the only luxury camp in the area: Jack's Camp. If you choose to camp rough, then be scrupulous about removing all traces of your camp when you leave as these open pans will be easily spoiled by unsightly litter and traces of old camp fires. Jack's Camp can be booked via Hartley Safaris — see under *Okavango Explorations* in *Booking Agencies and Operators*, page 305.

Makgadikgadi-Nxai Game Reserve

4WD advised. High-clearance 2WD is OK for the southern part, away from pans, in dry season. Standard entrance fees.
The north-western corner of the Makgadikgadi Pans, to the east of the Boteti River and south of the road, has been a Game Reserve for some time, giving it some protection from the cattle which now graze most of Sowa Pan. Similarly Nxai has been protected for many years, but recently the area of land between the two pans was also declared a National Park, thus safeguarding a vital corridor much used by the game.

The area still has no facilities, and only a few game scouts — but it does have a network of readily distinguishable tracks. Those south of the road, on the Makgadikgadi Pans, can mostly be negotiated by a high-clearance 2WD vehicle during the dry season. Needless to say, a good map and compass are essential for exploring the area, and you must be totally self-sufficient in everything, including water and firewood.

Getting there

Since few of the tracks in the reserve are signposted, entry into the area is a bit arbitrary. However a major north-south route through the Reserve starts in the north, about 150km from Nata (154km from Maun) on the Nata-Maun road, and ends in the south 105km later, roughly 17km west of Mopipi, near a small group of huts and a cairn of whitewashed stones. The turn off point from the Nata-Maun road is indicated by a fairly new, thatched lodge manned by game scouts. (Note that the main Nata-Maun road is being tarred at the time of writing, so these directions are necessarily imprecise. Hopefully a signpost to the reserve will be erected.)

Kudiakam Pan and Baines' Baobabs

4WD advised. Standard entrance fees.

Sandwiched between Nxai Pan and the main road, Kudiakam is the largest of an interesting complex of pans lying in sparse bush that appears to continue for ever. The game here doesn't usually match Nxai's (see below), but the main attraction is an extraordinary beautiful group of trees known as Baines' Baobabs, which stand at a spectacular site on the eastern edge of the pan. They were immortalised in a painting by Thomas Baines who came here in May 1862 with James Chapman and wrote:

> 'A lone circuit brought me, with empty pouch, to the clump of baobabs we had seen yesterday from the wagon; five full-sized trees, and two or three younger ones were standing, so that when in leaf their foliage must form one magnificent shade. One gigantic trunk had fallen and lay prostrate but still, losing none of its vitality, bent forth branches and young leaves like the rest... The general colour or the immense stems was grey and rough: but where the old bark had peeled and curled off, the new (of that peculiar metallic coppery-looking red and yellow which Dr Livingstone was wont so strenuously to object in my pictures) shone through over large portions, giving them, according to light or shade, a red or yellow, grey or a deep purple tone.'

The baobabs themselves have changed very little since they were painted by Baines: the one lying prostrate is still thriving, having lost none of its vitality. The night sky here is phenomenally clear.

In the last few years, there has been an increasing numbers of visitors here, and the trees have now been included in the National Park. Camping is discouraged under the trees, but there are several sites nearby.

Getting there

To reach Baines' Baobabs, take the Nxai turn-off on the main road and follow the track for about 17km before turning right at a cross-roads. In under a kilometre the road forks. The right leads directly through the pans to the great baobabs, 11km, though during the wet months of the year this route is impassable and shouldn't be attempted. The left route is longer, skirting around the north of the pans. It follows the Old Maun Road, so after about 13km take a right turn, from where the trees are about 4km.

Nxai Pan

4WD only. Standard entrance fees.

About 30km north of the Nata-Maun road lies Nxai Pan. This is typical northern Kalahari wilderness and the game is based around three pans, two of which usually flood after good rains. Visiting once just after the wet season, the game was spectacular with large numbers of giraffe, springbok, gemsbok and zebra. These wide open grasslands, dotted with groups of trees, are said to be ideal for cheetah, though we have never seen any. From November to April, while the grasslands are lush, game congregates here, though it tends to leave and the area becomes increasingly lifeless as the dry months wear on.

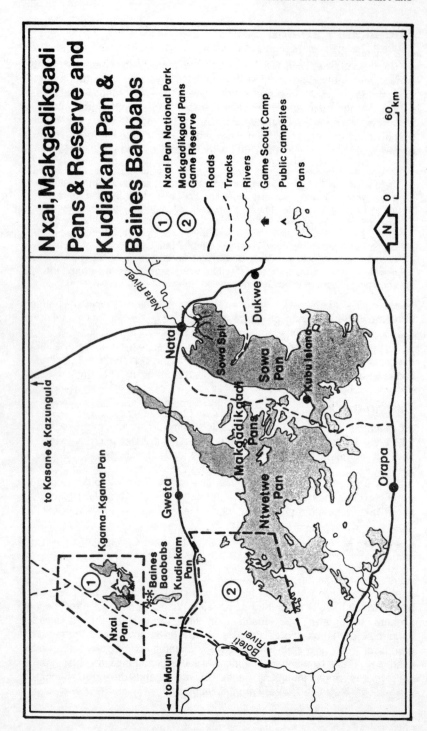

Nxai, Makgadikgadi Pans & Reserve and Kudiakam Pan & Baines Baobabs

① Nxai Pan National Park
② Makgadikgadi Pans Game Reserve

Roads
Tracks
Rivers
Game Scout Camp
Public campsites
Pans

N

0   60 km

Getting there

Turn off the main Nata-Maun road about 171km from Nata (134km from Maun) and head north along the sandy track to the game scouts' camp. From here it's only a few kilometres to either of the campsites — the one to the pan's south has a more pleasant situation, and hence is slightly busier.

The only obvious tracks lead around and across Nxai, Kgama-Kgama and the central (unnamed) pan. Thus most of the park is a wilderness, through which the only route is the Old Cattle Trek to Pandamatenga. This comes from north-east on a bearing of about 30° and passes 2km from Nxai's western edge. However, it disappears in places so beware.

Nata

Nata has grown up around the turn-off for Maun on the main Francistown-Kasane tar road. Initially it was little more than a filling stop for most people, with an important garage (complete with hand-operated pumps), a basic hotel and the well-stocked 'Sowa Pan Bottle Store' for cool drinks.

It now makes a natural place at which to refuel, which most vehicles take advantage of, and has a couple of places to stay.

Where to stay

Nata Hotel This hotel is very basic, but clean and friendly. Prices are around P100 for a double or you can camp there for P15.

Nata Lodge Private Bag 10, Francistown. Tel: 611210. About 10km south of Nata, just off the road, lies Nata Lodge. This makes a good overnight stop, with a simple *a la carte* menu for dinner and a cooked breakfast for P14. The large three-bed chalets are P115, and best booked in advance, though there is always space to camp at P15 per person.

For small groups, the manager will organise a trip to Sowa Pan for P200 per vehicle. This is the cheapest way to get to see the pans if you do not have your own 4WD. Afterwards you can cool off in the lodge's pool.

Gweta

Gweta village is situated 103 km from Nata, in a small grove of palm trees on the road between Nata and Maun. The village retains a traditional, rural atmosphere, whilst at the same time being on a main road. It is well situated for those exploring the Makgadikgadi and Nxai Pans, with a couple of good basic stores and even a vehicle workshop for minor repairs. There is usually (but not always) fuel available here.

Where to stay

Gweta Rest Camp This small camp has simple accommodation in thatched rondavels costing P100 for bed and breakfast. Alternatively, camping is P15 per person. There is a basic restaurant, and a lively bar, and game drives into the surrounding region can be organised from here.

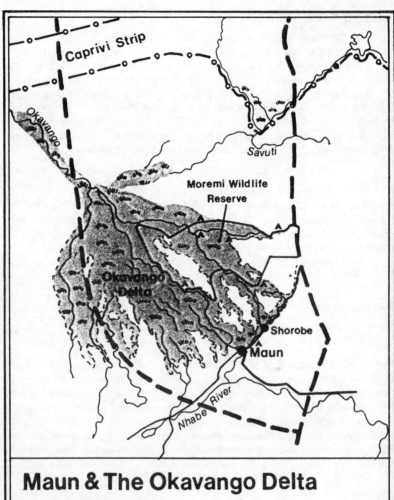

Maun & The Okavango Delta

∼○—	National border
∼∼	Main roads
∼∼	Secondary roads
—-—-	Tracks
∼∼∼	Rivers
ʌ	Camps

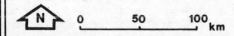

N   0   50   100 km

Chapter 20

Maun and the Okavango Delta

From its source in the Angolan highlands, the Okavango River flows south-west across Namibia's Caprivi Strip and into the sands of the northern Kalahari. Here it spreads out, forming a unique inland delta — 16,000 square kilometres of water wilderness, dotted with islands and laced with a network of channels.

It's an unusual and relaxing environment, where you can glide silently along in a *mokoro* (dugout canoe, made from a single tree trunk) through a maze of reeds, watching the wildlife at eye level and soaking up the sun. Beneath you, the crystal clear water reveals a myriad of fishes and aquatic animals and plants. It's like floating across a huge fish tank — complete with terrapins and the occasional crocodile or hippo.

Some of the larger islands within the Delta are rich with game, so stalking around these with an guide is fascinating. However, you'll be disappointed if you come here for a big game safari. Just take your time, savour the tranquillity, and enjoy the white and yellow lilies and the deep blue sky. The Delta is simply a very special environment to experience.

Centuries ago, the Delta was home to a group of Bushmen, the Banoka, who were displaced by Hambukushu, Bayei and later Batswana tribes people. At present, most of the scattered villages are inhabited by Batswana, who keep cattle. There are still some Hambukushu left who live deeper within the Delta and rely more on fishing. Many families, however, now seek extra income, by working outside the Delta or basket weaving.

In response to growing environmental threats, part of the Delta has been safeguarded by the creation of Moremi Wildlife Reserve — a fully protected area adjoining Chobe National Park's south-western boundary.

How to visit the Delta

The Okavango Delta is by far the most popular destination for visitors in Botswana, and the range of accommodation and other facilities reflects this. Because of its size, it isn't practical to take day-trips there unless you just want to fly over it. To do the Delta justice, you can either organise your own canoe expedition through the swamps, stopping on different small islands to sleep and camp, or you can stay at one of the camps within the Delta and make trips into the surrounding swamps. Neither option is cheap.

Your own expedition will take several days and a lot of effort to organise, and over a week in the swamps to complete. Your costs will soon mount up, but will probably still be less (on a per-day basis) than staying at one of the camps in the Delta. If you aim to visit this way, then you need at least a week or two, and such a trip would be best organised whilst staying at one of the camps near Maun.

Staying at a camp in the Delta will give you a more concentrated view of the environment, and will probably feel more like a luxury holiday. Someone else will cook for you and organise all your activities for the next day while you sit back and relax. However, the logistics of supplying these remote bush camps by small aircraft (and their sheer exclusivity) ensure that they remain expensive. Some rank amongst the most expensive safaris available in Africa today. All should be booked in advance, so study the *Camps in the Delta* section below, get the latest details and prices from your chosen travel agent, and book before you arrive. You can then fly straight to your camp when you arrive in Maun.

Whichever option you choose, you may need to add the expense of flying into the Delta, and also park fees of up to P40 per person per day, if you visit Moremi. But if you are only going to see the Delta once, it is worth paying to see it properly.

When considering your options remember that the swamps are not all the same. Where the Okavango really starts to spread widely, around the base of the panhandle, there are permanent lagoons of deep water, and islands fringed by papyrus reeds. This is hippo and crocodile territory and a great destination for fishing trips by motor boat, though the rivers are too deep here to be ideal for canoes or *mokoros*.

Further from the panhandle, the rivers and lagoons spread out. Now they are separated by expansive reedbeds which are themselves criss-crossed by narrow hippo trails, which make ideal paths for canoes to follow. Towards the edges of the swamps, these trails of water through the reedbeds become fewer. Here many of the lagoons and channels are temporary, drying up completely during the dry season. From the air, many of these outer swamps appear to consist of just small, tree-encrusted islands in a sea of green reedbeds.

Bear these different regions in mind when you are organising your visit.

Draining the Okavango

Edited from an article by Damien Lewis

The Okavango Delta, the last unspoilt wetland in southern Africa, has long been the subject of numerous World Heritage proposals to give it international recognition and protection, but to no avail. Within the Delta there is only one small protected area — the Moremi Game Reserve — which, like much of the Delta, has recently become the subject of 'general management and development plans to raise increased tourist revenue', says Alison Ross, of Greenpeace UK. But the numerous plans to harness the waters of the Delta for industrial and agricultural purposes pose a much more serious threat to the Delta ecosystem. The most recent — the *Southern Okavango Integrated Water Development Project* (SOIWD) — may signal the beginning of the end for the Okavango Delta.

SOIWD was launched in 1985 as part of Botswana's new drive towards food self-sufficiency. It called for the harnessing of the Okavango Delta's waters to irrigate 10,000 square kilometres of land and supply water to the nearby town of Maun, the regional capital and a major tourist centre. This involved raising the outflow of the Delta by dredging 42 kilometres of the Boro River — the main channel through the Delta — and building a series of dams along the its southern fringe. The other main (but understated) aim of SOIWD was to increase the water supply to the Orapa diamond mine — one of the World's richest — 250 kilometres south-east of Maun in the central Kalahari Desert. The Orapa mine — run as a joint venture between the South African mining giant De Beers and the Botswanan government — produces the majority of Botswana's diamonds which account for three-quarters of the country's Gross National Product. By the year 2,000, the Orapa mine is projected to require over twice as much water as it does today for diamond production.

SOIWD has received a mixed reception. Its most enthusiastic exponent — after the Botswanan government — is the Australian-based Snowy Mountain Engineering Corporation (SMEC), the project consultants. But in light of the controversy SOIWD has provoked, even they admit to their limited understanding of the Okavango Delta and their inability fully to predict the effects of draining the Delta. Others — anticipating the storm of protest SOIWD has caused — have divorced themselves from the project. The German aid agency KFW, which funds various water projects in Botswana, have withdrawn funding on environmental, social and developmental grounds.

Although SOIWD would nominally only affect 250 square kilometres directly, or 1% of Okavango's area, critics such as Greenpeace believe it may have much wider effects on the complex Delta ecosystem, which they argue is very vulnerable to outside interference. The 'inherent unpredictability of the Delta...lack of knowledge and shortage of data' are all aspects which the SOIWD scheme fails to take into consideration. Greenpeace have accused SMEC of using inaccurate and insufficient data in their planing of the project. They believe that the SOIWD project threatens the integrity of 'the whole fragile and exceptional delta ecosystem'. As a result of the dredging of the Boro River — the most serious of the proposed works — they predict a general drying of the delta and reduced permanent water levels as the floodplain is disrupted and flooding severely limited.

The proposed benefits of SOIWD have also been questioned by Greenpeace. Local water demand could be met by reservoirs which would not require dredging of the Boro or draining the Delta. Recent studies show that the irrigation potential originally put at 10,000 hectares by SOIWD, is in fact less than 1,300 hectares and will need to be a high-technology, high-input affair. The soils in the region are very poor and require large inputs of fertilisers and pesticides. Mechanised irrigation.

using high levels of chemicals in the immediate vicinity of a fragile delta, is an ecologically reckless and impractical way to increase food production, especially when low-tech, sustainable methods have not been considered. Alternative sources of water for the Orapa mine — ground-water or 'dry-processing' — have been identified but are not being considered due to the costs involved.

There is another, contributing factor pushing SOIWD towards completion. Beef represents the second largest export earner after diamonds, and the cattle owners are also a powerful lobby in Botswana. Draining Okavango would release large amounts of land for ranching and boost the profits made by beef exports to the European Community. As inconceivable as an 'Okavango cattle ranch' may seem, other factors — such as the pesticide spraying programme in the Okavango Delta against the tsetse fly (the carrier of sleeping sickness and a major threat to cattle) — reflect the priority already given to cattle over wildlife and the environment in Botswana.

Opposition amongst the local people to SOIWD is strong; most feel it is wrong to interfere with a complex living system that no-one understands. Okavango residents fear that SOIWD will devastate their livelihood — presently based on small-scale agriculture and a world-famous tourist industry. Their concerns are echoed by tour operators, who bring over 30,000 tourists to the Okavango each year to view its unique wildlife and ecology. At a recent meeting with the Minister of Water in Maun, they asked 'What will happen to us if the water dies?' These people have added their voices to the wave of international protest, headed by Greenpeace's threatened campaign — 'Diamonds are for Death'.

All this has won a stay of execution for Okavango. But for how long? Shortly after Greenpeace's February 1990 visit to the region, the Botswanan Government pledged to review SOIWD. Yet, 'rather than being a total review of the project', says Alison Ross, 'this simply means re-consulting the people on the ground, not examining environment-friendly options. Okavango is still not being seen as sacrosanct'. Bearing in mind the efficacy of attacks on the ivory and fur trade, Botswana would have much more to lose from a successful 'Diamonds are for Death' campaign than the Orapa mine would gain by exploiting the Okavango Delta's waters.

The Botswanan government also risks losing one of its greatest potential income earners. Responsible tourist development in the Okavango, coupled with sensitive protection measures, could both preserve Botswana's precious natural heritage and boost foreign exchange earnings. At present, Greenpeace is calling for World Heritage nomination for the Okavango Delta; with the Government's help they could succeed and the Okavango Delta remain the Jewel of The Kalahari for all humankind.

MAUN

This dusty, sprawling town has been the start of expeditions into the wilds since the turn of the century, and it is now the safari capital of the country. Maun's elongated centre is dotted with modern shops and offices, while its suburbs are mainly traditionally built, thatched rondavels. A few years ago, everywhere and everything seemed geared towards the tourism bonanza. Now government departments are moving in, as Maun is becoming the administrative centre for the northern and western parts of Botswana.

That said, a little of its rough-and-ready frontier feel remains — contemporary cowboys still ride into town for their supplies in battered 4WDs, even if the main roads are now sealed tar rather than potholed, dusty gravel tracks. For the visitor, this is the base for trips into the Delta, Moremi Reserve and Chobe. There are banks, including a Barclays and Standard Chartered, garages, well-stocked supermarkets and a number of travel agents and operators. Maun is important as a communications centre for all the camps, so it is the best place from which to organise a last-minute trip.

Getting there

Air Maun is 3,100 feet above sea level, and well connected by scheduled Air Botswana flights. These connect with Gaborone and Victoria Falls on Wednesdays, Fridays and Sundays; Johannesburg on Wednesdays and Sundays; Francistown on Wednesdays and Saturdays; Ghanzi on Mondays, Wednesdays and Sundays; and Windhoek on Sundays only. For more detail contact Air Botswana at their stylish office near the airport (Tel: 660391). Maun also has several air-charter companies, where you can hire light aircraft for private flights and transfers — see page 293.

Car The Nata to Maun road is now almost completely tarred, but the other roads to Maun are not so swift. The road from Ghanzi is being tarred slowly, and a lot of tenacity is needed if you don't have a high-clearance 4WD. The route from Kasane through Chobe National Park is strictly for those with time and a 4WD.

Bus Daily buses run from Francistown to Maun via Nata in the mornings.

Hitching Hitchhiking to Maun via Nata from Kasane or Francistown is not difficult in a day, and is usually faster than the bus. Hitching to or from Ghanzi is rather more tricky, and will require quite a wait. Hitching to or from Kasane through Chobe is something of misnomer as it is only practical if you have a pre-arranged lift. Try putting up notices at the Duck Inn and Maun Fresh Produce, or asking around at Island Safari's campsite.

Where to stay

Nowadays most visitors to the Delta just pass through Maun's airport, arriving from scheduled air services and simply connecting to small six-seater planes for a flight to one of the camps. Thus several of the lodges near Maun have been forced to close — Kubu and Thamalakane to name but two. This leaves two hotels, Riley's in town and the other a little further north, and a couple of nearby camps.

If you arrive with no trip organised, and are travelling on a tight budget, then stay at Island Safari Lodge or Crocodile Camp and use your first few days to ask around and compare the options. Both these camps organise their own trips into the Delta, and the booking agents in town will tell you what else is available. Shopping around can be disappointing, as some safari operators are not enthusiastic about helping. Don't give up, just find out what they offer and compare it against your other options. All will charge you dearly for just a couple of days, so don't be afraid to ask exactly what you get for your money.

Riley's Hotel PO Box 1, Maun. Tel: 660204. Fax: 660580. Riley's is more of an institution than a hotel. It was founded when Harry Riley arrived in Maun, in 1910. Initially he simply built an extra rondavel next to his own, suitable for one person. It had no bed, just reed matting on the floor. A few years later he joined the two rondavels together, building a simple dining room between them, and soon he was running Maun's first hotel. In his book *The Lost World of the Kalahari,* Laurens Van Der Post described Riley's in the 1950s as a

'... remarkable little hotel which he [Harry Riley] had founded for the odd, intrepid traveller who had been determined enough to cross the desert, as well as for the score or so of Europeans patient and courageous enough to make Maun the unique outpost of life that it is today.'

Now those first buildings form part of the manager's house, and Riley's is a luxury hotel owned by Cresta — a group who run excellent hotels and lodges across the subcontinent.

For the visitor, Riley's has a very central location, on the eastern side of the main street, and is probably the only accommodation in the region which has air-conditioning. Its added benefits include a good restaurant, bar, well-appointed rooms, and — for business-people — excellent communications. Costs are P220 per night for a single, P365 for a double, including breakfast, Advanced reservations are essential as the hotel is usually full, and often booked for weeks ahead.

Sedi Motel PO Box 29, Maun. Tel: 660177. The Sedi Motel is about 800m off the main road, on the left, a few kilometres north of Maun. It is used by few tourists, most of its rooms being occupied by people staying in town for several months. Guests entering the Sedi are greeted by a Grecian-style foyer, complete with indoor fountain. The basic rooms do have en-suite facilities and are laid out around a concrete quadrangle. They cost P105 for a single, P145 for a double.

Note that breakfast (P14) is organised by separate caterers rather than the hotel staff, and must be booked in advance. There is a handy bottle-stall next door, but beware of rowdy customers around the end of the month (local pay day).

Island Safari Lodge PO Box 116, Maun. Tel/Fax: 660300. The Lodge sits on the northern bank of the Thamalakane, overlooking a picturesque bend in the river. To get there, take the signposted turn-off about 7km north of Maun, and follow the well-used track a further 3km to the camp. If you don't have your own transport, then hitching to this turn-off is easy. Failing that, ask one of the agents in Maun to ring the camp and they will collect you, for a transfer fee of P25 (per person).

The camp itself is very well established, with good value bungalows for P120 single, P140 double and P195 for four people. These are brick-built and provided with towels and linen, but as they are all of the same size, those with four beds are quite cramped. However, for P10 the majority of independent travellers choose to stay on the rambling campsite by the river

There is a restaurant here, which needs booking, where breakfast is about P15 and a three course dinner P25. The lively bar makes a good meeting place, and serves burgers for P6, chips for P5 and pies for P4.

For those without a 4WD, Island Safari offers a chauffeur-driven vehicle service which is about as cheap as you will find. The vehicle and driver cost P280 per day, excluding fuel. The first 100km is free, but thereafter it costs P1.15 per kilometre, plus fuel.

Finally they do operate their own trips into the Delta, aimed at those with limited budgets. See the section *Expeditions from the Delta's Edge*, on page 296, for full details.

Crocodile Camp PO Box 46, Maun. Tel/Fax: 660265. More intimate (and upmarket) than Island Safari Lodge, and known for serving some of the best food in the region, 'Croc Camp' is small and well organised. The turn-off to Croc it is about 3km further north of that for Island Safari, and if you've no transport there then a lift from town will cost P35 for four people.

Most of Croc Camp's eight reed-walled chalets have en suite facilities. They cost P125 single, P140 double. A few have shared facilities for P30 less, and all are simple, but clean and adequate. Camping, at P10 per person, must be arranged in advance and allows you the use of the camp's spotless floodlit pool.

The thatched dining area, with bar, is small but beautiful, and a full breakfast is served there for P13, a light lunch for P18 and an excellent dinner for P37. Note that all meals need to be arranged in advance, so telephone from Maun in the morning if you plan to come for dinner.

To mess about on the river by the camp, a self-paddle canoe is P22 per day, or P3 per hour. Alternatively you can hire canoes and *mokoros* to go into the Delta from here for P40 per day.

Croc Camp acts as nerve-centre for **Crocodile Camp Safaris,** who organise tailor-made safaris. For further details see the sections on *Operators and Agents*, page 303, and also *Expeditions from the Delta's Edge*, page 296.

Sitatunga Camp Private Bag 47, Maun. Tel/Fax: 660570. This camp is something of an 'outsider' being 12km south of town — all Maun's other camps lie to the north. However, situated next to the crocodile farm, it remains a good place for campers with vehicles who want a peaceful spot to stay for a few days. There are no bars or restaurants here, only a small shop and bottle-store which opens from 10am until 8pm.

Accommodation is either in one of two basic chalets, which have a double and a single bed in each and cost P130 per night, or on the campsite for P10 per person per night. Campers have reed-walled toilets and memorable bucket showers, from which you can watch the stars.

In addition to the campsite, Sitatunga operate a small mobile safari operation. P450 per day will hire for you a 4WD vehicle (taking a maximum of six people) with a driver and unlimited mileage included. Tents and camping equipment are provided, but you will need your own sleeping bags, food and drink.

Where to eat

Even if you're not staying at **Riley's Hotel** you can still eat there, and the food is good. Breakfast costs P20, and dinner about P35 — whilst the bar by the pool is a cool place to escape when the heat gets too much. This is really for residents only, but if the hotel's not too busy then non-residents are usually tolerated.

The best alternative, the **Duck Inn**, is opposite the entrance to the airport. This is the closest that Botswana ever gets to the atmosphere of an English pub, so find a seat under the corrugated iron veranda and relax. The Duck's typical pub fare includes soup for P6, cheeseburgers and hamburgers for P12, salads P8 and snitzels and steaks P18 - 25. Chips are P4 extra, and sweets about P5 - 7.

The Duck opens on Monday to Friday from 8.30am to 11pm, on Saturday from 10am to 5pm and on Sunday from 8.30am to 5pm. It acts as a permanent watering hole for most of the professional safari guides, and has the town's best notice board. Failing that, there are a few take-aways in the centre of town, of which **Le Bistroti** and **Chicago Fried Chicken** are the more memorable.

If you have transport, then eating at **Croc Camp** is worth the trip — but remember to book your table by 4pm the same afternoon.

Getting organised

Supplies
Of the two supermarkets, Maun Fresh Produce, on the south side of the main street, is by far the better. If something is edible (and available in Maun) then you will find it here. This normally includes a selection of canned goods, dairy produce, fresh fruit and vegetables — though some of these look worse for wear by the time they reach Maun. Their second useful feature is a notice board just inside the doors, so if you want to buy

or sell a car, or offer someone a lift, then use this as well as the board outside the Duck Inn.

Maun's other supermarket is opposite the Standard Chartered Bank, set back in the shopping mall behind Barclays Bank, two short blocks to the east of the 'Ice Man', which supplies ice for cool-boxes.

Camping Equipment

Kalahari Kanvas PO Box 689, Maun. Tel: 660568. Fax: 660035. are in town, by the airport, and they manufacture and hire out an amazing range of tents and safari equipment. For the forgetful backpacker there are camping kits available (for a minimum of five days), costing about P30 per day, including a backpack, sleeping bag, tent, cooking pots and cutlery. For larger expeditions, Kalahari Kanvas offers a tent repair service, and will make to measure any specialist equipment.

Alternatively, to buy smaller items, try Delta Sports, next to Maun Fresh Produce. They stock a few basic tents, sleeping bags, torches, penknives, sunglasses and other essentials for a trip into the Delta.

Souvenirs and Books

The best places for souvenirs and curios are the General Trading Company, to the left of Delta Sports, and BGI, Botswana Game Industries, which is behind Le Bistroti take-away. Both have some excellent T-shirts, typically P40-P50 each, a large selection of baskets, postcards, coffee-table books, and wildlife guides.

Maun Book Centre Tel: 660853. Fax: 660854. is about 500m off the main road, in the streets behind Barclays Bank. This has good Africa and travel sections. It's just the place if you have forgotten to pack a novel.

Maps

Maps are useful if you are driving your own 4WD into the parks, and essential if you are planning to explore at all. In Maun, the Surveyor General's Office is cunningly disguised as an unused building, just to the left of the stylish Air Botswana office near the airport. Despite its appearance, at the back of this building is an office where you can buy excellent maps for about P7.50 each. Otherwise, these are only available in Gaborone, so make the most of this convenient office. Even if you're not exploring yourself, then the map of Moremi and the Delta makes a great souvenir, and will help you to recall the areas which you visit.

Aircraft charter

In an area where roads are poor or non-existent, travel by light aircraft makes a lot of sense. In fact, if you are visiting one of the camps in the Delta, then you will usually have no choice but to fly there. Flying is not cheap, but it is fast and fun, and will give you a unique overview of the country. The Delta, especially, is difficult to appreciate from the ground. If you want to visit the **Tsodilo Hills** (see page 327) then think seriously about flying, as they are just a short hop away by plane, but a day by 4WD.

Maun has several air charter companies; all are based around the airport and charges similar prices. The main one is:

Air Kavango PO Box 169, Maun. Tel: 660393. Fax: 660623. Situated next to the Tourist Information Office, a few yards from the Duck Inn, Air Kavango normally charges about P600 per hour (or P2.80 per kilometre), for a standard Cessna 206 which seats five plus the pilot. Alternatively, there is a faster high-wing Cessna which also seats five for P650 per hour or P2.95 per kilometre. The minimum charge for either is P465 for anything up to 20 minutes.

If you have a large group, then a twin-engined Islander seats nine and costs P895 per hour, or P4.30 per km, with a minimum charge of P665 for 20 minutes. Air Kavango also have a nine-seater Cessna for the same price which is faster than the Islander.

Another alternative is **Elgon Air** PO Box 448, Maun. Tel: 660654. Fax: 660037, whilst those unconcerned about cost should consider **Wildlife Helicopters** Private Bag 161, Maun. Tel/Fax: 660664 who aim to provide the ultimate in game-viewing flights.

Merlin Services
Private Bag 13, Maun. Tel: 660351. Fax: 660571. No guide to Maun would be quite complete without a mention of Merlin Services. Housed in a small building on the corner by the airport, opposite the Duck Inn, Merlin has always acted as a communications and booking centre for some of the area's older, independent camps, and it is now expanding to encompass Botswana's first agency for Kessler 4WD Hire (see Chapter 8, *Windhoek*, page 105).

Like the wizard, Merlin can arrange anything from the unusual to the very obscure. They open during the week from 8am to 1pm, 2.30pm to 5pm, and on Saturdays from 8pm to 12.30pm.

Tourist Information Office
This office, next to the Duck Inn, is small but provides some useful up-to-date information and a few good maps. This is the place to check the latest information about the National Park's campsites, and it opens during the week from 7.30am to 12.30pm, 1.45pm to 4.30pm.

THE DELTA

When to visit

There isn't an ideal time to visit the Delta, it depends upon which part you're going to, what you want to see, and how tolerant you are of the heat. Because of its immense size, the flood water resulting from the rainy season in the Angolan Highlands usually takes about six months to get through the Delta. It enters the northern panhandle, by Shakawe, between

February and April, and then accumulates in the lower delta, near Maun, during the height of the dry season, around September.

When the water levels are low, the fishing tends to be better, but higher water levels do mean less land area and so the game becomes more concentrated, and easier to find. These game concentrations are notoriously variable, but the best time to see the migrating animals escaping from the parched lands to the east is from September until the start of December.

The climate is most pleasant around April/May and August/September. June and July can be quite cold, whilst October and November are very hot. December to March brings the rains, and some of the camps shut down during January and February. This makes accommodation more difficult to find within the Delta, but fewer tourists sometimes means bargain rates at the camps which do stay open. For the ornithologists, the migrants from the northern hemisphere visit from October to January, adding extra interest to an area already rich in birdlife.

Expeditions from the Delta's Edge

A swamp covering 12,000 square kilometres is too large to paddle into on your own — you will get dangerously lost. To make an expedition into the swamps you need to find canoes (or *mokoros,* their dug-out equivalents) accompanied by polers, who will also act as guides.

Staying on small islands by night, and relaxing in a *mokoro* by day, may leave you feeling in closer harmony with nature — or simply in need of a comfortable bed. Not everybody enjoys this lack of comfort: camping and cooking isn't everybody's idea of a holiday. However, for those who want to leave civilisation behind, this is one way to do it.

Hiring a canoe or *mokoro*

The problem with poling from the very edge of the swamps is that the outer reedbeds can be very boring indeed, especially when viewed from a canoe. Thus starting at, say, Croc Camp, will probably mean about four days' poling (and three back) before the reedbeds thin out and the scenery gets interesting. That said, the cheapest *mokoros* are found here (P40 per day), and if you plan on an expedition lasting a few weeks then you will need extra canoes to carry your supplies, so why not start from here.

Another alternative is to drive or take a motorboat through the least interesting areas, and then start poling from the buffalo fence (the cordon which divides the wild swamps from the surrounding cattle lands). This will save you about four days in the canoes (two out and two back), but cost perhaps P110 per person in 'transfer fees'. Maun's Island Safari Lodge specialises in such a deal, with *mokoros* for P50 per day, and similar deals are offered by others.

Regardless of where you want to start from, do ask around for the best deals and consider forming a group with others, as this can make transport cheaper and give you more bargaining power. Also ask about the polers. If you are not fluent in Setswana, it may be worth asking if English-speaking polers available. Quite apart from being able to talk to, and learn from, your guide, visitors complain that without a common language they are at the mercy of the poler, with little choice over when, or for how long they stop, where they go, or what they do.

Check the kind of boats used. This is usually a choice between wooden dug-outs (true *mokoros*) or fibreglass Canadian canoes. *Mokoros* are undoubtedly more photogenic and fine for shorter trips, but Canadian-style canoes are more practical for longer trips, being comfortable, stable and with more room for storing food and kit.

The obvious places to arrange this type of trip include:

Island Safari Lodge PO Box 116, Maun. Tel/Fax: 660300. For those on limited budgets, Island Safari does employ its own polers, whose canoes are stationed at the edge of the Delta, by the buffalo fence on Dixie's Island (see '*Kunoga Maxanasasunds*' on the survey maps). Although their polers rarely speak much English, these *mokoros* are cheap, at P50 per day for a two-seater, but you must supply all your own food and equipment. Return transport to the canoes, by 4WD and/or motorboat, is about P105 per person.

Visiting the Delta this way, it will take you two or three days to reach the more interesting areas of permanent swamp, so this type of trip is really only suitable for long trips into the Delta, say of eight days or more. If you can plan well in advance, then it is better to arrange a one-way canoe trip to, say, Shakawe. This avoids you retracing your route through the reedbeds of the outer Delta to return to Dixie's Island.

Crocodile Camp PO Box 46, Maun. Tel/Fax: 660265. Aside from its upmarket **Crocodile Camp Safaris,** (see page 303), Croc Camp does offer an option for those on more limited budgets. It is possible to hire canoes and *mokoros* from the camp itself for P40 per day, including the poler. Croc Camp is about two days' pole (plus two to return) from the buffalo fence though, so don't be tempted to take a canoe out for just three or four days, as you'll see nothing but reeds. That said, this is a good base for a very long expedition and there are some English-speaking guides available if you ask for them well in advance.

For those in a hurry just to take a glance at the Delta and return, there is also a motorboat available from the camp, with driver, for P195 per day excluding fuel.

Camps within the Delta and Moremi

If your time is restricted, or your finances are not, then the easiest option is probably to book in advance into any one of the Delta's camps and take day-trips on the waterways around your camp. Virtually all of these will arrange your flights, meals and activities, and they will normally accommodate you in comfortable two-person bungalows or tents.

All these camps offer good standards of accommodation, but they do differ. Some supply electricity from generators, some have solar cells, others have none at all. Some serve truly excellent food, while at others it is less memorable. However, the biggest distinction is in the location of the camps, and hence the activities which are available. Those in drier regions concentrate on 4WD game safaris; those in the outer reedbeds conduct more *mokoro* trips; and those in areas of deeper water tend to use motorboats more than *mokoros*.

Ideally, split your time between a couple of different camps in areas which offer different attractions. This will be easiest (and most economical) to book if they all belong to the same operator, eg Ker & Downey, Okavango Wilderness or Gametrackers. Contact your own local travel agent to investigate, or talk to a branch of the operators concerned. See *Booking Agencies and Operators*, page 303, for specific details.

Finally two of the camps listed in the next section, notably **Oddballs** and **Gunn's**, are slightly different in that they specialise in acting as a base for independent *mokoro* trips through the Delta lasting several days. The costs for these two camps appears low, but note that the *mokoros* hired from them tend to be more expensive than those hired near the edge, at P75-P80 per day. Moreover, these two do not charge on the all-inclusive basis that most camps do, and may insist on you spending a minimum time there, or they may limit the luggage you bring into the camp by weight, thus ensuring that you buy your supplies there. Do not assume that a trip from these is automatically your best option; add up all the costs carefully before deciding.

Finally, if you fly into any of these camps, it will probably be in a small six-seater plane so consider paying a little more for an extra half hour game flight on the way back. Transfer flights are very different from game flights, despite what some will claim, and a slow, low-level trip back to Maun, looking for game, is a great way to round off a visit. Listed alphabetically, the camps in the Delta and Moremi include:

Abu Camp Run by Ker & Downey. Set up near Pom Pom, as a base for unique elephant-back safaris, this is probably the Okavango's most exclusive camp. The three elephants which visitors ride — Abu, Kathy and Bennie — are African elephants, not their easily-tamed Indian cousins. They were returned to Africa from a circus in the United States by their trainer, Randall Jay Moore, and now plod through the bush accompanied by six or seven smaller, orphaned two-year old elephants.

Accommodation at the camp itself is in five twin-bedded tents, each with a basic (but en-suite) bucket shower and a long-drop toilet. The food is good, the bar extensive, and everything (transfer flights, bar, etc.) is included in the price of US$3,625 per person for a stay of five nights and six days. This is the only elephant-back safari available in Africa today.

Chobe Chilwero Run by Linyanti Explorations. Whilst far to the north-east of the Delta, on the banks of the Chobe River near Kasane, this camp is often mentioned in the context of safaris to the region. It can be booked via any of Maun's agents.

Camp Okavango Run by Desert & Delta Safaris. Camp Okavango is a large camp, set in the permanent swamps just to the north of Moremi Reserve. Accommodation is in one of 11 large Meru tents, complete with en-suite flush toilets and hot showers, set among the trees on one of the islands.

Activities are water-based, with small motor boats and Canadian canoes available for trips along the rivers and smaller waterways nearby. Fishing is also available, and the deeper rivers are ideal for bream and the famous fighting tigerfish.

Camp Okuti Private Bag 11, Maun. Tel: 660307. One of the Delta's more independent camps, Okuti is situated in the centre of Moremi on the edge of the Mopane Tongue on Xakanaka Lagoon. It concentrates on 4WD trips around Moremi, and so makes a good camp for the game spotter. The accommodation is in thatched brick chalets, but few other details are available as the camp has been closed recently.

Camp Moremi Run by Desert & Delta Safaris. This tented camp, situated on the tip of Moremi's Mopane Tongue, is set under giant tropical ebony trees by the side of the Xakanaxa Lagoon. Its large communal lounge, dining area and bar are solidly constructed from thatch on timber, and overlook the lagoon, whilst the guest's accommodation is in one of 11 large Meru tents. All have en-suite hot showers and flush toilets.

The camp has a good reference library of wildlife books and a knowledgeable staff, allowing guests either to take 4WD trips in search of big game, or small river boats onto the lagoon for fishing and bird watching.

Delta Camp Run by Okavango Tours and Safaris. The costlier sibling of Oddball's, Delta Camp was established in 1976 at the southern end of Chief's Island. This is a good area for birds, but do not go expecting much big game here or you may be disappointed. Excursions from camp are on short *mokoro* trips, sometimes combined with walks, and guests normally return to the camp for their meals.

Accommodation is in one of eight rustic reed chalets, complete with en-suite facilities including hot showers, flush toilets and lighting powered by solar batteries. There is a larger family suite available, and also a more secluded honeymoon suite. Food, drinks, laundry etc. are included in the price of P480 per person per night. Only park fees and the transfer flights (at P250 per person, return) are extra. Note that in the low season there is sometimes a discount available for residents of southern Africa (defined as 'south of Malawi').

Drotsky's Cabins Book via Merlin Services. South of Shakawe, on the western side of the panhandle, see page 326 for more on this this river-side camp.

Gunn's Camp Book via Trans Okavango. Private Bag 33, Maun. Tel: 260351. Fax: 660040. Situated in Moremi on the Boro River, near the western edge of Chief's Island, and run by the brusque Mike Gunn, this camp has changed its emphasis in the last few years. Initially it concentrated on offering long fitness in the wilderness courses, which aimed to get participants fit, teach them to punt a *mokoro*, and instil in them some understanding of the bush. However, this has now been superseded by four different options, all less energetic.

Basing yourself in the camp's luxury Meru tents, you can take *mokoro* day-trips before returning to three-course meals and a few drinks around the fire. This costs P290 per person per day, all inclusive.

For more adventure, Gunn's will organise long *mokoro* expeditions finishing either back at Gunn's or at some other point in the Delta. These include meals, equipment and a guide for P250 per person per day, but require at least four people and lots of notice. You may also need an air charter to collect you from your destination.

If you have no time to get organised for a normal *mokoro* expedition, then Gunn's will provide a *mokoro*, poler, all your equipment and food (to be cooked by yourself) for P175 per day.

For fully equipped budget travellers who have all their own food and equipment, the campsite at Gunn's costs P17.50 per day and *mokoros* are available from the camp at P75 each (seating two people).

Whatever you choose to do, Gunn's is reached by either motor boat or plane costing P110 one-way. A minimum of three passengers is needed, but this can include those needing transport in the opposite direction.

Jedibe Island Camp Run by Okavango Wilderness Safaris. In the centre of the permanent Delta, in the Jao concession area (as is Mombo Camp), Jedibe is surrounded by clear lagoons and fast-flowing rivers. This camp is not for big game safaris, but it makes an excellent base for gentle *mokoro* trips through the backwaters, or motor boat trips onto the Boro River, one of the Okavango's main arteries, which flows nearby.

There are eight large walk-in tents here, each with its own flush toilet and hot shower, all set under palm trees and tropical hardwoods on the small island of Jedibe. For 1994 there is new dining-room and swimming pool under construction, and a floating jetty will give access to the camp's own houseboat. This has en-suite shower and flush toilet as well as a bar, a fridge, and a stove for extended stays away from the camp. Staying at Jedibe costs P600 per person from July to September, and P450 during the rest of the year. A flight from Maun to Jedibe is about P220 per person, one way.

Khwai River Lodge Run by Gametrackers. Overlooking the wide Khwai River, just outside Moremi's North Gate, this is one of Moremi's oldest camps. The game here is excellent, and most of it will come and see you if you sit under the covered veranda of your reassuringly solid brick bungalow for long enough. The lodge's main activities are 4WD trips around Moremi, but accompanied game walks can be organised on request — and there is a swimming pool for cooling down afterwards.

Each of the 12 roomy, twin-bedded bungalows have en-suite flush toilets and showers, as well as 24-hour electricity. The dining-room and bar are large, and the meals good, but note that drinks and park fees are not included in the price of P370 per person per night.

Machaba Camp Run by Ker & Downey. Machaba is set in 3,200 square kilometres of prime wilderness, its own private game reserve, north-east of the Mopane Tongue. The Khwai River acts as a boundary between the Machaba concession area and the Moremi Game Reserve, affording wildlife viewing which is second to none.

Accommodation is plush, with en-suite facilities, and the camp even has a specially-built viewing platform in a tree nearby. A three night, four day stay here costs US$1,055, including all transfers, meals and activities.

Mombo camp Run by Okavango Wilderness Safaris. Mombo Camp lies just off the north-western tip of Chief's Island, in the Jao Safaris concession area adjacent to the Moremi Reserve. This gives Mombo's guests sole use of the area around camp and total privacy. Though there are permanent waters all around, Mombo is used as a base for 4WD safaris because the game found here is so impressive. Night drives are also possible in the concession, and for game walks, you are accompanied by Joseph Tekanyetso — one of the camp's managers who is regarded as an excellent tracker.

Behind the camp's reed walls, accommodation is in nine large tents, and one reed chalet, all of which have en-suite toilets and showers. There is solar-powered electricity and solar-heated water, ensuring that the hum of generators never disturbs the quiet of the camp. As with Jediba, Mombo costs P600 per night from July to October, and P450 for the rest of the year. A flight between here and Maun costs P220 per person, one way, and park fees of P30 per day are extra.

Nxamaseri Fishing camp Book via Merlin Services. South of Shakawe, on the western side of the panhandle, see page 326 for more details on this fishing camp.

Oddballs Run by Okavango Tours and Safaris. Situated just off the western edge of Chief's Island, and technically just outside Moremi, Oddballs was established in 1984 to provide a cheap alternative to the luxury all-inclusive camps. While no longer cheap, it remains very popular as one of the less expensive ways to see the Delta.

The only way to get there is to fly, for P250 return, and the minimum stay here is five days. The maximum baggage allowed is 10kg (enforced in the high season), and budget travellers should think about how to take the maximum amount of food and equipment, whilst not exceeding this limit. Start by taking a mosquito net rather than a tent, during the dry season, and keep your camera equipment with you during the flight.

Once at Oddball's, you can buy supplies at the small shop, Molly's Pantry, but you'll pay a premium. Similarly, you may need to hire camping equipment unless your own is very light, but prices are high. A comfy seat for your *mokoro*, as opposed to the boat's wet, rough-hewn floor, or even a knife/fork/spoon set, will cost P1.50 per day to hire. Meals are available at P8.50 for breakfast and P25 for dinner, and you can always drown your sorrows at the Skull Bar.

You must camp for at least your first and last nights, which costs P20 per person per night, unless you want to use the tree-house 'bridal suite' (at an expensive P200 for two). Most people spend their time on a *mokoro*, camping and cooking on islands at nightfall. A *mokoro* for two costs P80 per day, and you must supply all your own food and equipment. Park fees will add an extra P40 per person per day, unless you request that your poler avoids entering the Reserve.

Pom Pom Camp Run by Ker & Downey. Pom Pom, one of the Okavango's most luxurious camps, is situated in its own concession area, outside the Moremi Reserve and to the west of most of the other camps This remote situation allows for the excitement of night drives as well as the more usual mix of 4WD daylight excursions, *mokoro* trips and guided walks. The guides at Pom Pom are good, and their ability with English is a major plus point.

Set overlooking a small lagoon, fringed by reedbeds, the camp comprises a large, open-thatched dining, lounge and bar area, with seven large walk-through tents around it. Each tent overlooks the lagoon, and each has its own en-suite facilities (including gas-heated shower and flush toilet), surrounded by reed walls. There is continuous hot/cold water, and a 32V electricity system.

Four excellent meals will be arranged around your activities each day, and typically a light breakfast will set you on your way. After an early game drive, there is normally a substantial brunch, taken at leisure. Time in the middle of the day is your own, to take a siesta, or watch the resident eagles fishing from a tree conveniently placed in front of the dining area. A light afternoon tea precedes the afternoon's *mokoro* trip, which leaves time enough to shower before dinner. Everybody eats together, and gathers around the fire afterwards to sample the camp's extensive bar.

The staff at Pom Pom will pander to your every wish, from the provision of cushioned *mokoro* seats to towels by the swimming pool, and a daily laundry service. The price for this level of comfort is high, at about US$1,055 per person for three nights, but it includes everything (even flights).

San-Ta-Wani Safari Lodge Run by Gametrackers. Just outside Moremi's South Gate, San-Ta-Wani Lodge consists of eight African-style huts (thatched, brick bungalows) spread out under a canopy of trees. All have en-suite flush toilets and showers, electricity and electric lights. Meals are eaten together under a large, open-sided thatched *boma*, and there is a well-stocked bar and a swimming pool.

Visitors usually go out for two 4WD trips per day around the Moremi Tongue area, one in the evening and one in the morning, but walks and boat trips are also possible. The latter obviously depend upon water levels.

Semetsi Camp Run by Crocodile Camp Safaris. This small tented camp, close to Xaxaba, is used only by Crocodile Camp Safaris. Accommodation is in large tents with shared facilities, and the camp can be reached by motor boat or plane. Activities here are either *mokoro* or motor boat outings, and costs (including boat transfer, meals etc.) are about P300 per person per day, for a group of four people.

Shakawe Fishing Camp Book via Merlin Services. South of Shakawe, on the western side of the panhandle, see page 327 for more details on this fishing camp.

Shinde Camp Run by Ker & Downey. Located in the far north of the Delta, well away from Chief's Island, Shinde offers a very high standard of accommodation and daily trips using either motor boats or *mokoros*. This is a good camp for fishing, and there are also some fascinating colonies of storks, egrets and herons on the nearby Gadikwe Island. The costs of a three night stay here is US$1,055, including all transfers, activities and meals.

Tsaro Lodge Run by Okavango Explorations. On the northern bank of the Khwai River, on the edge of the Delta, Tsaro Lodge consists of eight thatched, brick bungalows spread out under a grove of knobthorn and fig trees. Morning and evening game drives are the main attractions, whilst back at the camp the covered dining and lounge areas overlook a water-hole. For the intrepid, escorted game walks are an attraction, after which you can cool off in the swimming pool.

Xakanaxa Camp Book via Okavango Tours and Safaris. Located on the Moremi Tongue, by the edge of the large Xakanaxa Lagoon, Xakanaxa is a small but well appointed tented camp for a maximum of 16 guests. The game and the bird watching are both good here, with big game coming to drink, and Xakanaxa's heronries nearby, in the tall trees surrounding the lagoon.

Accommodation is in large Meru tents, but the toilets and showers are separate, enclosed by reed walls and shared between several tents. Excursions are either into Moremi by 4WD, or onto the lagoon by motor boat (*mokoros* are not very suitable here). Costs are about P400 per person per night, including meals and drinks.

Xaxaba Camp Run by Gametrackers. On a small island to the west of Chief's Island, Xaxaba is a delightful camp with 12 twin-bedded reed chalets built under tall trees. Each chalet overlooks the surrounding waters and has an en-suite flush toilet and shower, as well as a simple system of electric lights. The food is good, as is the bar, and the activities are arranged around the meals, which are usually eaten together.

The surrounding waters are, in fact, quite shallow for most of the year and thus ideal for *mokoro* trips, although a deep waterway nearby allows for some spectacular motor boat trips. There is often a relaxing sunset cruise as well. The camp's staff are good and flexible, so brave the morning chill and request an early *mokoro* trip to watch the sun rise from one of the small islands nearby. Take your camera: you won't regret rising so early.

Xaxanica Camp Book via Merlin Services. This is a small tented camp, complete with a large thatched dining-room on stilts.

Xugana Lodge Run by Okavango Explorations. In the middle of the northern side of the Delta, Xugana is a small lodge offering thatched accommodation and outings by either *mokoro* or motor boat.

Booking Agencies and Operators

There are many tour agencies in Maun, most of whom have affiliations to different camps. Some will act solely for 'their' camps, while others will also function as independent travel agents and will book you into any of the other camps.

Although Maun is the centre for most of Botswana's safari operators, some do insist that you book elsewhere, through an outside travel agent, rather than contact them directly. Don't count on an automatically friendly reception from all of these, especially if you are travelling on a tight budget and looking to cut costs. In alphabetical order:

Bonadventure
PO Box 201, Maun. Tel: 660502/3. Fax: 660502. This is an established independent travel agent who is able to book most of the camps in the Delta. Having no strong links to any of the camps, it is a good place to seek advice if you have arrived in Maun without making any prior arrangements.

Bush Camp Safaris
PO Box 487, Maun. Tel: 660847. Fax: 660307. This new, shoestring operator aims at budget travellers and offers return transfers to the north of Chief's Island, for P100 per person and, from there, *mokoros* with polers for P60 per day.

Crocodile Camp Safaris
PO Box 46, Maun. Tel/Fax: 660265. Croc Camp, near Maun, acts as the nerve-centre for **Crocodile Camp Safaris,** who organise tailor-made safaris with multi-lingual guides. Trips into the Delta are usually based at Croc's own tented camp in Moremi, Semetsi. Alternatively, they will take

you into Botswana's other Parks in fully-equipped 4WD vehicles, including a driver/guide and all equipment and food. Prices depend on precise itineraries, but P300 per person per day for a private four-person safari would be typical.

For those on lower budgets they do have the option of hiring *mokoros* from the camp, see page 296, *Expeditions from the Delta's Edge*, for more details. Finally, Croc Camp also acts as a staging post for **Into Africa Safaris**, a safari company with branches in Zimbabwe, Malawi and Namibia.

Desert & Delta Safaris

PO Box 32, Kasane. Tel: 650340. Fax: 650280 or Johannesburg Tel: (27.11) 886-01524. Fax: (27.11) 886-2349. This well-established group has two camps in the Delta region, **Camp Okavango** and **Camp Moremi**. Both are relatively large, accommodating a maximum 22 guests in comfort and one of their strengths lies in close links with two excellent centres for safaris: **Chobe Game Lodge** and **Lianshulu Lodge** in Namibia's Mudumu National Park. If you want a three-centre safari, then Lianshulu, Chobe Game Lodge and Camp Okavango (in that order) would make an excellent combination.

Gametrackers

PO Box 100, Maun. Tel: 660302.
Booked via any Orient Express Hotel or office, eg
Johannesburg, S.Africa: Tel: (27.11) 884-2504. Fax: (27.11) 884-3159
London, England: Tel: (44.71) 620-0003. Fax: (44.71) 620-1210
Paris, France: Tel: (1) 42.60-3663. Fax: (1) 42.56-2354
Dusseldorf, Germany: Tel: (40)35-1951. Fax: (89) 29-7632
Rome, Italy: Tel: (2) 653-563. Fax: (2) 657-2344
CA 91205, USA: Tel: (818) 507-8401. Fax: (818) 507-5802
Owned by the world-wide luxury hotel group, Orient Express Hotels, Gametrackers have Botswana's largest range of permanent camps. Around Moremi's Mopane Tongue they run the old established **Khwai River Lodge** and **San-Ta-Wani Lodge**, while deeper into the Delta they operate **Xaxaba Camp**. Further east still, they run two of the three camps in Chobe's Savuti: **Savuti South** and **Allan's Camp**. As you would expect, Gametrackers' aim is to provide camps at the hotels' luxury standard.

If you are booking from overseas and want one integrated package staying at several different safari camps then Gametrackers could be for you. Generally all your food and activities are included in a price of about P370 per day. To this add P175 for each transfer flight, and P30 per day park fees for each night you spend at a camp within Moremi or Chobe.

Ker & Downey

PO Box 40, Maun. Tel: 660211. Fax: 660379. Alternatively contact:
14, Old Bond St., London: Tel: (44.71) 629.2044. Fax: (44.71) 491.9177
Houston, Texas, USA: Tel: (713) 744.5222. Fax: (713) 895.8753
(See also *Safari South* for hunting safaris.)
This upmarket safari operator runs probably the Okavango's best camps, linked to its other safari concerns in Tanzania and Nepal. In Botswana, Ker & Downey have **Shinde**, **Machaba** and **Pom Pom** camps, as well as Pom Pom's offshoot camp which specialises in elephant-back safaris: **Abu Camp**. All their camps offer the highest standards of comfort, complete with crystal glasses and silver service, for prices of around US$350 per person per night.

Most visitors book whole safari packages, including flights. Some divide their time between these camps, and temporary, private tented camps, which are set up on request and cost around US$450 per person per night.

Merlin Services

Private Bag 13, Maun. Tel: 660351. Fax: 660571. Merlin, also described above, acts as direct booking agent for some of the independent camps, including Chobe's **Lloyd's Camp**, the panhandle's **Nxamaseri Fishing Camp, Drotsky's Cabins** and **Shakawe Fishing Camp**. Equally, if you want to visit several camps run by different companies then Merlin will organise this for you, complete with the flights to link them together. That said, Merlin is probably not the place to ask advice if you have no idea of where you want to go, what you want to do, or if you are on a very limited budget.

Okavango Explorations

Private Bag 48, Maun. Tel/Fax: 660528. This is an offshoot of Hartley's Safaris. Contact via:
Johannesburg: Tel: (27.11) 708.1893. Fax: (27.11) 708.1569
London: Tel: (44.71) 584.5005. Fax: (44.71) 584.5054
Sydney: Tel: (2) 264.5710. Fax: (2) 267.3047
Okavango Explorations operate two camps in the Delta: **Xugana Lodge** and **Tsaro Lodge**. In addition, they operate Xugana Mokoro Trails, offering fully serviced and arranged *mokoro* trips, and Tsaro Walking Trails, which are three-day accompanied walks along the Khwai River on the northern edge of Moremi. They also have close links to *Linyanti Explorations*, *Jack's Camp* in Makgadikgadi, and *Kalahari Kavango* — who offer tailor-made safaris around the region.

Their Maun office is really just a supply post, marked with a small Xugana Air sign (their own offshoot air charter company) above the entrance, and bearing no signs for Okavango Explorations at all. It is pointless to enquire here as the staff cannot book any trips; they will just refer you to their offices overseas.

Okavango Tours and Safaris
PO Box 39, Maun. Tel: 260220/339. Fax: 660589. Alternatively contact:
Johannesburg: Tel: (27.11)788.5549. Fax: (27.11) 788.6575
London: Tel: (44.81) 341.9442. Fax: (44.81) 348.9983
Montreal: Tel: (15.14) 287.1813. Fax: (15.14) 287.7605
OTS is perhaps the most aggressively promoted operator in Maun, and its
main booking office is on the main street, just to the left of the Maun Fresh
Produce supermarket. Offshoot offices act as travel agents in South Africa,
Canada and England.

Obviously they do concentrate on filling up their own camps, **Oddball's**
and **Delta Camp**, but they will also act as a normal agents for other camps
and activities. Among the more interesting options that they actively
promote are **Xakanaxa Camp** and the Okavango Horse Trails. The latter
operate from a tented camp in the north of the Delta, and offers five to six
hours of horse-back safari per day. For riders with some experience, this is
an excellent way to see the Delta because wildlife does not flee from a
mounted rider as it does from a canoe or people on foot.

Okavango Wilderness Safaris
Private Bag 14, Maun. Tel: 660086. Fax: 660632. Alternatively contact
Johannesburg: Tel: (27.11) 884.1458/4633. Fax: (27.11) 883.6255.
Okavango Wilderness Safaris has not only two permanent camps in the
Delta, **Jedibe Island Camp** and **Mombo Camp**, but it also organises a
wide variety of interesting and unusual safaris. These integrate with trips
into neighbouring countries through sister-companies in Namibia, **Namib
Wilderness Safaris**, and Zimbabwe, **Zambezi Wilderness Safaris**.

All these 'Wilderness' companies stress three vital aspects of their
projects: firstly, conservation of the environment; secondly, the integral role
that development for the local people must play; and thirdly, their goal of
introducing visitors to a real wilderness experience — typified by the siting
of their camps on a private concession area.

Amongst their other trips are new safaris to the remote Central Kalahari
Game Reserve, and Botswana's section of the Kalahari Gemsbok National
Park. Finally, Okavango Wilderness are developing several projects which
aim to help San/Bushmen settlements to protect their traditional hunting
lands by using revenue from visitors, whilst enabling visitors to get a real
glimpse of traditional San/Bushmen life.

Penstone Safaris
Private Bag 13, Maun. Tel: 660351. Fax: 660571 (Also known as **Skatul
Safaris**). This small independent safari company maintains no permanent
camps, but offers mobile safaris across all of Botswana which are tailored
specifically to visitor's requirements. This could be ideal if you have a small
group and want a lot of flexibility in your trip. Costs will be about P600 per
person per day, including everything except park fees.

Safari South
PO Box 40, Maun. Tel: 660211. Fax: 660379. Or contact via
14, Old Bond St., London: Tel. (44.71) 629.2044. Fax: (44.71) 491.9177
Houston, Texas, USA: Tel: (713) 744.5222. Fax: (713) 895.8753
Safari South is the sister-company of Ker & Downey, and specialises in big
game-hunting safaris. These are run on some of Safari South's extensive
concession areas, usually from temporary tented camps.

The Swamp Thing
Billing itself as the cheapest of budget options, the Swamp Thing claims to
have a pretty camp on the Santandibe river from which it offers cut-price
accommodation for backpackers. They have no address or contact
number, but ask for Dave Sandenburg or Brett Hedley at the Duck Inn.

Trans Okavango
Private Bag 33, Maun. Tel: 660023. Fax: 660040. This travel agent behind
Barclays Bank, in the middle of Maun, is the centre of operations for
Gunn's Camp. They will also act as a general travel agent, but seem to be
less well connected than some of the other agents.

MOREMI WILDLIFE RESERVE
4WD. Standard park fees
Gazetted as a game reserve by the Batawana people (a sub-group of the
Batswana 'tribe') in 1962 in order to combat the rapid depletion of the
area's game, Moremi is certainly one of the most beautiful and interesting
reserves in southern Africa. It includes regions of permanent swamp, flood
plain, islands and two large areas of dry land: Chief's Island and the
Mopane Tongue. Both have excellent populations of big game, including all
of the 'big five': elephant, buffalo, rhino, lion and leopard. **Remember** that
despite its beauty, the density of game makes the reserve very dangerous.
Never relax your vigilance for animals when walking or camping here.

Chief's Island is the largest island in the Okavango Delta, and usually
cut off from the mainland by water. It's easily big enough to support
populations of resident game, which are augmented by animals from the
surrounding flood plains which concentrate here when the annual
floodwaters rise. The western side of Chief's Island is especially popular for
camps, which then have access to the permanent swamps, as well as good
game viewing on the island.

The **Mopane Tongue** is a large, triangular spit of sand covered
(mostly) in Mopane trees. This juts into the Delta from the east, between
the Khwai and Mogogelo rivers, and provides Chobe's game with access to
water during the dry season. Being accessible from the Maun-Chobe track,
the Mopane Tongue is where visitors usually go for land-based 4WD
safaris in Moremi Reserve. The game viewing here is invariably
spectacular, especially during the dry season months (April/May to
October).

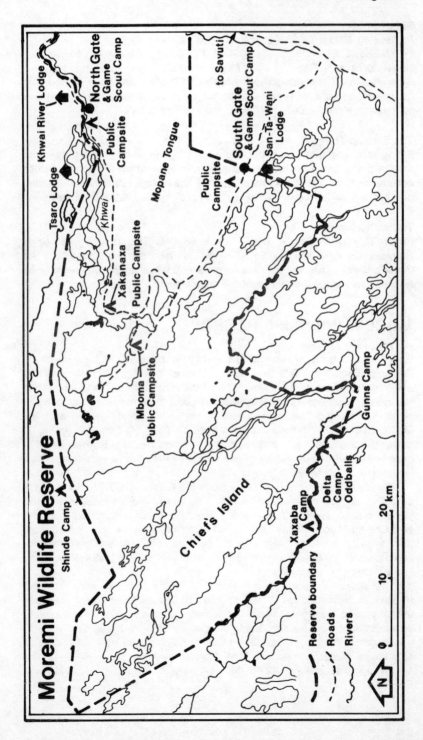

The diverse range of habitats found within this small area, where dry scrub rooted on Kalahari sand gives way to reedbeds and lagoons, results in a wide variety of animals being found. The game doesn't stop at the Reserve's boundaries either — most of the land, and the swamps, around Moremi are safari concession areas. These territories are run by various safari companies as private game reserves and this significantly increases the area available to the wildlife.

In May 1993, we left the reserve and drove south from Moremi towards Maun. After about 14km the road was blocked by a large pack of lazy wild dogs wandering about the road, but showing little interest in our vehicle. These ruthless predators were once shot as vermin, and hence virtually exterminated, so the sight of this relaxed group well outside the National Park was a very good sign.

Getting there

If you are not flying in, or arriving by boat, then there are two ways to drive into the Reserve:

From Maun The road is tar all the way to Shorobe, a small village on the Thamalakane where basic supplies and quite good baskets are sold. After that, it's about 27km to the veterinary fence and a further 3km to the signposted left turn for Moremi's South Gate. A left turn about 10km after Shorobe (just beyond the Tsetse Camp) also leads to the South Gate, but this road is difficult to find and not in good condition.

It's not unknown for 2WD saloon cars to make the trip this far — but it is highly unlikely they will get any further. If you want to chance your luck, try with a high clearance pick-up and a spade in the back.

From Chobe About 20km after Chobe's exit at Mahabe Gate, is a right turn which crosses the Magwikwe Sand Ridge almost perpendicularly. This leads to Moremi's North Gate some 38km after leaving the main Chobe-Maun track. But a **warning**, if you haven't a high clearance 4WD, don't even consider trying to cross the sand ridge.

Where to stay

There are numerous private camps in Moremi, and just outside it, which offer their guests tours of the Reserve by 4WD, motor boat or *mokoro* (see *Camps within the Delta and Moremi*, page 296). Understandably, these seldom welcome independent visitors without bookings, except in dire emergencies.

The alternative to these, for those with their own vehicles, equipment and supplies are Moremi's four public campsites. There is one each at the North and South Gates, with scout camps adjacent, and there are two near the tip of the Mopane Tongue. The facilities at all of these camps are basic, with natural river water to drink and basic showers and toilets. Camping in such a wild area, with all the dangers that this entails, is unsuitable for reckless or nervous campers.

Third Bridge is perhaps the most attractive of the campsites, situated some 48km from South Gate (allow five hours driving for this). The site itself actually consists of about five separate camping areas, each a short distance from the main track to the bridge.

Warning: This area has earned a reputation for fearless, aggressive lions and several attacks have recently been reported. Further, this river crossing is used by animals as well as people, so treat it like any game trail. **Do not camp anywhere near the wooden bridge**, despite the 'campsite' sign and the convenient water taps. Instead, back-track half a kilometre away from the bridge, going towards South Gate, take one of the small tracks to the right, and camp there.

Xakanaka Lagoon (Lediba) is the beautiful site for not only another luxury camp, but also the second of the public campsites on the Mopane Tongue. It is interesting to spend time exploring the numerous tracks at the tip of the Tongue itself. The open water here is a classic spot for hippos which lull campers to sleep with their grunting sessions in the early evening. (**Warning:** most campers are unaware that hippos probably claim more lives than any other animal in Africa, so see *Animal Encounters*, pages 75-77 for advice.)

North Gate doesn't compare scenically with the other camps, but it is regularly visited by lion, elephant and hippo, and some thieving monkeys. We were lucky enough to see both leopard and lion whilst sitting beside our camp fire here. Try to find time to take the Khwai River Loop, west from North Gate, and also to follow the river to the east, past the airstrip and the Safari lodge. It is exceptionally beautiful.

South Gate is the busiest of the camps, being the usual entry and exit point for visitors. If you want to make an early start into the Park, to make the most of your park fees, you might consider camping a few kilometres outside the gate itself. However, we have encountered lion in this area so remember that there is as much game outside the Park as in it.

North of the Delta

Between the Okavango and the Chobe/Linyanti river systems lies a rarely visited, sparsely populated, corner of the country. Some of this land is private hunting land and safari concession areas though, so go carefully.

A minimum of two vehicles are needed, and it could prove fascinating for the well-prepared who just want to explore. The major feature here is the Magwegquana river, which links the Okavango's Selinda Spillway with the Linyanti swamps and may, unpredictably, form a total barrier at times.

Getting there

In the eastern part of the area, there's a track which runs along the margins of the swamps to Xugana Safari Lodge. It starts by turning west, just to the north of the bridge over the River Khwai and appears to cut across the Spillway, near its base. From there it reaches Seronga fairly swiftly, though it becomes impassable if there's much water in the spillway and local advice should be sought before it's attempted.

The alternative way into the region is to take the track which starts in Chobe, south of Savuti, and meets the Magwikwe Sand Ridge squarely before crossing the Magwegquana just south of the Linyanti swamps. This is the better, more reliable, track and to find it ask for directions from the game scouts at Savuti.

Seronga

Situated at the panhandle's base, in the centre of 'area five', Seronga has an airstrip and, reportedly, a *mokoro* ferry on which you can cross the river, though obviously not with a vehicle. Do not expect to be able to buy fuel here.

The only good track here goes north-west until the border and then, according to some maps, crosses it into the Caprivi Strip. In an emergency you could probably cross this border, and reach the Caprivi Strip's main road, but this is not recommended and you would have to keep police on both sides of the border very well informed to avoid getting into a lot of trouble.

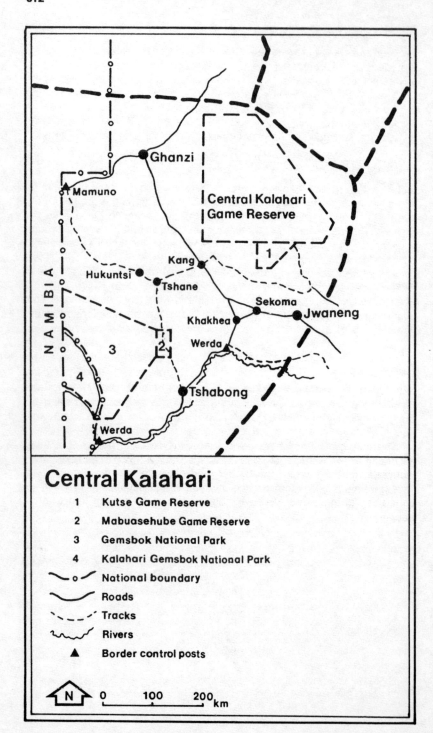

Central Kalahari

1	Kutse Game Reserve
2	Mabuasehube Game Reserve
3	Gemsbok National Park
4	Kalahari Gemsbok National Park

- National boundary
- Roads
- Tracks
- Rivers
- ▲ Border control posts

0 100 200 km
N

Chapter 21

The Central Kalahari

To many people, the Kalahari Desert is synonymous with Botswana and, indeed, it covers over two-thirds of the surface of the country. Geologically, the Kalahari is a huge sand-filled basin in the centre of southern Africa. Kalahari sands, under the surface of the topsoil, cover an extraordinary 2,500km from the Orange River of South Africa to the equatorial rainforests of Zaire – the largest continuous stretch of sand in the world. The Kalahari Desert today is defined not by sand but according to its very low rainfall. Rain is most scarce in the south (the north-westernmost edge of South Africa) where the Kalahari represents a classic desert environment of extensive sandy plains and ochre-red dunes. As one moves north, rainfall increases, and the Kalahari becomes scrub and bush land through central Botswana, which in turn gradually merges with the woodlands and swamps of the Caprivi Strip region.

The Botswanan central Kalahari is predominantly an area of acacia grasslands and sandy scrub – encompassing most of the area south-west of the Okavango Delta and Makgadikgadi Pans, and north of Botswana's southern border. Only in the extreme south-west of Botswana – around Tshabong and Mabuasehube Game Reserve – does it revert to sand and red dunes.

For the visitor, the wonder of the central Kalahari lies not so much in the large concentrations of game found in the more well-watered areas, but in the unique environment and the fascinating adaptations made to it by its animal, plant and human populations. Some Bushmen (San) still live hunter-gatherer lifestyles in the desert interior – particularly in the Central Kalahari Game Reserve – in ways that haven't changed much for millennia.

Practically, the area is difficult to visit and a 4WD vehicle is essential. Ghanzi, the only town in the region, is hundreds of kilometres from anywhere, and generally regarded as the capital of the Kalahari. With San, Tswana, Herero, Afrikaner and English speaking inhabitants, it's a fascinating place to stay for a few days.

Khutse Game Reserve is the most accessible part, and easily reached by 4WD from Gaborone. For the well prepared and self-sufficient, Mabuasehube

Game Reserve and the fascinating desert settlements around Tshane offer a focus for some adventurous exploration. The Central Kalahari Game Reserve is closed to the public, and requires a special permit for access. Gemsbok National Park is only accessible from South Africa, but has especially beautiful desert sand-dune scenery. Everywhere in the region, there is a great sense of remoteness – and you're unlikely to see many other visitors.

GHANZI – 'CAPITAL OF THE KALAHARI'

Ghanzi must be one of Botswana's most intriguing towns – situated in the middle of nowhere and separated from the rest of the world by hundreds of kilometres of rough dirt track. The town owes its existence to the limestone ridge on which it is situated which supplies it, and the surrounding 200 farms, with a plentiful year-round supply of ground water.

Today it is the centre of a thriving Afrikaner cattle ranching industry, but Ghanzi was once a major centre for several Bushmen hunter-gatherer groups. The town began to grow when at the end of the nineteenth century, Rhodes encouraged bands of Boer trekkers who were already heading north to move to Ghanzi instead, promising excellent ranching land and a wonderful climate. Rhodes's intention was probably to annex this western corner of British Bechuanaland in the name of his own British South Africa Company, so enhancing his own territorial interests in this part of the continent. To do this, Rhodes had to fill the area with white people. However, when the Boer trekkers arrived, many found that much of the good land had already been taken by the few previous settlers and that Rhodes's claims were at the most fanciful. Within ten years or so, most of the original trekkers had left. A few remained, and their descendants – and those of the handful of white settlers that arrived shortly after Rhodes under encouragement from the British government – now form the strong Afrikaner and English speaking communities.

Once the road from Ghanzi to Lobatse was completed – allowing relatively easy access to the country's main abattoirs – land prices improved dramatically and Ghanzi established itself firmly on the map. The farming community is now one of the most prosperous in the country.

Getting there and away

Air   The quickest way is to fly. There are two flights a week to Ghanzi from Gaborone via Maun. Check details with an Air Botswana office or, if in Ghanzi, at the Kalahari Arms Hotel.

Car   Ghanzi lies at the intersection of three main roads through the interior of the country.

Maun to Ghanzi   A 4WD is not essential for this route, though as the road can become fairly badly corrugated a high clearance 2WD vehicle really is necessary. The 280km, which should take only about five hours, has no particular points of interest except for the veterinary cordon fence at Kuke. The gate here is manned throughout the day and night, and divides the Okavango region from the Ghanzi farming area.

Ghanzi to Lobatse   This epic journey of 644km involves the longest stretch of demanding 4WD in the country and will take at least 12 hours of difficult bone-shaking driving. It is used by the farmers of Ghanzi to take their cattle – driving them on horseback or by truck – to the great slaughterhouses in Lobatse. The boreholes sunk along this route to water the cattle have resulted in a series of tiny settlements on the way which will usually have a small store and bar. Kang, the largest of these, also has petrol usually, though as you would expect it's expensive.

From Lobatse, the tar ends at the diamond mining town of Jwaneng, and turns into a fair gravel road to Sekoma. From here to Ghanzi, the road becomes very poor with very little sign of habitation (the numerous small settlements along the chain of boreholes are often off the road).

Ghanzi to Windhoek (Namibia) via Mamuno   The road is in poor condition to the border, but once inside Namibia it improves enormously. The scenery is typical of the Kalahari, consisting of rolling plains and low dunes of bright orange sand. Everything is covered by a sparse undergrowth of grasses and low bushes, above which the occasional tree rises. The sides of the road are sometimes fenced, and often marked by hedge-like mounds of sand where the tracks are lower than the surrounding dunes.

For mile after mile your tyres will try to follow one of the sets of ruts, while you guide the steering wheel and wonder how the undercarriage is avoiding the sand piled between the tracks. A good high-clearance 2WD vehicle should be considered as the bare minimum requirement for this route. The border post at Mamuno (200km from Ghanzi) is just less than half way and will take up to five hours. From here to Windhoek should take another five hours. The road is surfaced from the main town of Gobabis in Namibia.

Where to stay and eat

The heart of the town is undoubtedly the **Kalahari Arms Hotel** PO Box 29, Ghanzi. Tel: 296311 (*Category B*). This old and well-known establishment is the only place to stay and eat in Ghanzi. Rooms are not cheap at P140 for a single and P190 for a double, but it's possible to camp at the back for P20 with the use of hot showers etc.

The restaurant round the back serves a surprisingly extensive and interesting menu. Breakfast is P15, and avoid the coffee. The hotel will also organise laundry – hand in your clothes before 10am and collect after 4pm.

Getting organised

Apart from the hotel, Ghanzi has all the basic necessities, including a hospital, post office, telephone exchange (with somewhat incongruous call boxes outside), a collection of government offices, and a new Barclays bank.. Check out the Oasis bottle store, the Oasis self-service supermarket, the Oasis garage...

Bushmen crafts

Whilst in Ghanzi you must make a point of visiting the **Ghantsicraft shop** between the hotel and the post office. This is one of southern Africa's finest craft centres, with an extensive and authentic collection of Bushmen crafts. It was started in 1983 by several Danish volunteers, with the specific intention of returning as much money as possible from the sale of the crafts back to the Bushmen producers themselves. The prices are considerably lower than you'll find elsewhere and at least 80% goes back to the craftsman or craftswoman. The staff make regular visits to remote Bushmen settlements in the Ghanzi district, including the Central Kalahari Game Reserve, to collect crafts. These are then individually tagged and the name of the maker is recorded.

The ostrich eggshell bracelets and necklaces are particularly attractive – and take weeks of labour to make. The ostrich eggshells are hatched chick shells, collected from within the game reserves and national parks. If you can't see what you want in the shop, ask about it – they keep more stock than is on display. The shop is open from 9.00am-12.00pm Mondays to Fridays.

Khutse Game Reserve
4WD. Standard entrance fees.

Khutse is the closest of Botswana's game reserves and parks to the capital Gaborone, and being easily reached in a day from the capital it is a popular long weekend destination for city dwellers. It adjoins the southern boundary of the Central Kalahari Game Reserve, and has classic bush, acacia and pan scenery typical of this part of the Kalahari Desert.

Whilst the reserve has small herds of gemsbok, springbok, hartebeest and wildebeest together with the more common predators, the game is limited by the amount of water available and in times of drought may be very scarce – even around the pans. Nevertheless there are many species of fascinating smaller mammals (ground and bush squirrels, hares, foxes, porcupine, pangolin, aardwolf, aardvark, African and black-footed cats) and a huge variety of birds, especially around the pan margins. Khutse should be treated as much a Kalahari wilderness experience as an opportunity for game viewing.

Getting there

From Gaborone   The 240km journey typically takes around five hours in a 4WD. From Gaborone, head north-west along the tarred road to Letlhakeng

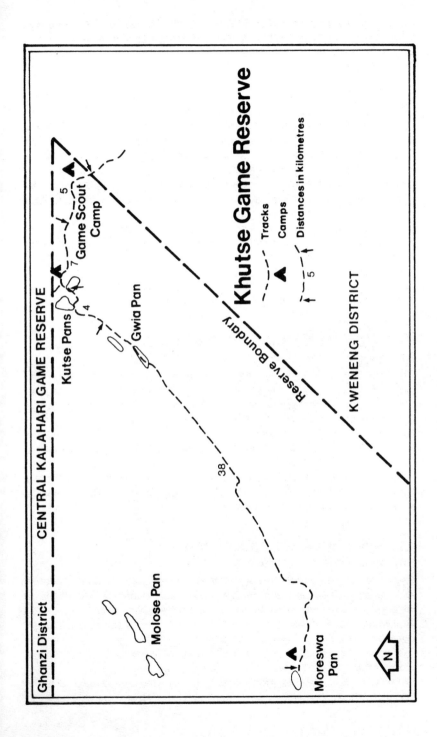

via Molepolole (last petrol stop). From Letlhakeng, the road is sandy with poor signposting through the villages of Khudumelapye and Salajwe – if in any doubt stop and ask directions to the Khutse gate.

In the Reserve

At the gate you should pay your entry and camping fees and stock up on water. Since the water is from a borehole it can be a bit mineralised and salty, so bring your own supplies if possible. You'll also have the option of hiring a guide, though this shouldn't be viewed as essential as there's only one main track through the reserve and it's difficult to get lost. A guide will of course be able to show you the best areas for game viewing, spot hard-to-see animals, as well as help you understand some of the innumerable facets of this unique environment.

From the gate at Galalabodimo Pan, it is a single track to Kutse II Pan 13km away where there is a pleasant campsite, and the track forks. The right fork (more northerly) heads off into the Central Kalahari Game Reserve and should be ignored. The left-hand track heads to Moreswa Pan, 41km further on, into the heart of the Reserve and you will reach a quiet, rarely-used campsite at the edge of the pan by a couple of trees.

The Central Kalahari Game Reserve
No access except with a permit

This massive Reserve is reputedly the second largest in the world and dominates the centre of the country. There are no facilities, roads or even water and the Reserve is closed to the public unless you have a permit. These are obtainable in principle to groups who can satisfy the authorities of their expedition competence and good intentions. Try the District Commissioner in Ghanzi, or the Department of Wildlife and National Parks in Gaborone.

Other than the dwindling small groups of Bushmen people that still share the land with the animals, the reserve is traversed by exploration geologists for ever in search of minerals and oil.

Mabuasehube Game Reserve
4WD only. Standard entrance fees.

Remote and rarely visited, this is true desert country of the southern Kalahari with dunes, grasslands and plentiful salt and grassy pans. The reserve lies on a huge strip of slightly higher ground, forming a watershed that crosses Botswana from east to west. Some of the pans scattered across this area will even hold water for a few months of each year following the rainy season, and they have played an important role in the understanding of the Kalahari – part of the reason for establishing the reserve in the first place.

The best time of year for game viewing is during the rainy season when the usual Kalahari game (springbok, gemsbok and eland) gather at the six

The last Bushmen
The situation in 1989

Survival International has issued an 'Urgent Action Bulletin' and written to the President of Botswana protesting at plans to force some of the last Bushmen in southern Africa out of the Central Kalahari Game Reserve. This would evict the very people whose lands the Reserve was set up to safeguard.

Though ostensibly to protect the wildlife from overhunting by the Bushmen, the true reason behind the expulsion of the 1000 or so Bushmen, and of the 300 Bakgalagadi who also live there, may be to create a scapegoat for the real danger to the wild animals — the extensive growth of cattle ranching in the area. The cattle owners — having over-grazed most of their present land — want the government to allow cattle grazing in the Central Kalahari Game Reserve.

The most serious problem for the Bushmen is that alternative lands still do not exist. Previous attempts to re-settle Bushmen in Botswana have been tragic failures. One anthropologist who worked for several years trying to make re-settlement sites work, admits that 'in almost every case' the Bushmen suffer sickness, malnutrition and unemployment — becoming 'dependent, alcoholic and apathetic'.

At the same time as the Bushmen are being obliged to move out, the government is also granting leases to mining companies to prospect in the Reserve. Among the companies involved are De Beers Botswana (a subsidiary of the South African mining giant), Selection Trust/British Petroleum, and Falconbridge Botswana. It is these activities, not the Bushmen and Bakgalagadi who have lived in equilibrium with their environment for millennia, who pose the real threat to the Reserve.

The situation in late 1990

Survival International's campaign met with some success. The Botswanan government assured Survival that it did not intend to move the Bushmen and the Bakgalagadi out of the Reserve by force, and that they were free to continue to live there in peace. Their long-term future however, is far from secure — so long as the government or mining companies covet the Reserve's potential mineral and grazing wealth, the Bushmen's traditional lands will remain under pressure.

Survival International is a worldwide movement to support tribal peoples. It stands for their right to decide their own future and helps them protect their lands, environment and way of life. If you would like to join Survival and take part in their campaigns for tribal people in Africa and worldwide, you can contact them at: Survival International, 310 Edgware Rd, London W2 1DY. Tel: 071-723 5535.

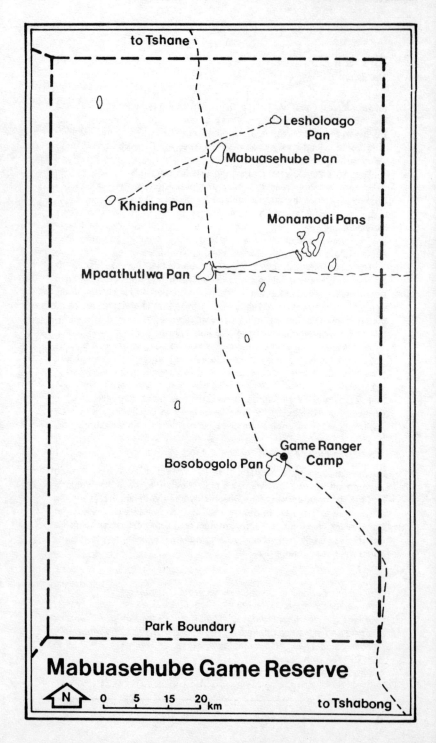

to Tshane

Lesholoago Pan

Mabuasehube Pan

Khiding Pan

Monamodi Pans

Mpaathutlwa Pan

Game Ranger Camp

Bosobogolo Pan

Park Boundary

Mabuasehube Game Reserve

N   0   5   15   20 km

to Tshabong

principal pans. Like Khutse, the smaller mammals and birds (including ostrich) can offer endless entertainment even if the larger game is scarce. The small mammals (Cape fox, aardwolf, meerkat and black-footed cat are most common) are best seen around the edges of the pans in the evening (most are nocturnal). The spectacular large dunes to the south of the pans provide an unusual habitat for many of the birds, including Kori bustard, secretary bird and a variety of eagles and vultures.

The reserve has no facilities and you must be fully self-sufficient, with food, water, petrol and spares. In an emergency, you might be able to obtain bore-hole water from the sporadically resident game ranger at Bosobogolo Pan in the south of the reserve – it's the only pan you actually drive across. Many of the roads are in bad condition, and since you may not see another vehicle for days on end, a visit to the reserve should not be undertaken casually.

Getting there

The main road through the reserve is a poor, very sandy track from Tshabong in the south of the country, to Kang on the main Ghanzi-Gaborone road to the north. This long route (described below) can be incorporated into a larger 4WD circuit of the region, and has the added attraction of passing through the interesting group of villages of Tshane, Hukuntsi, Lokgwabe and Lehututu. The easiest, most direct route to Mabuasehube however, uses a track that enters the reserve from the east joining the main north-south road at Mpaathutlwa Pan.

From Gaborone Head to the end of the tarred road at Jwaneng (last petrol stop) and thence onto Khakhea, taking the left fork at the village of Sekoma. From Khakhea, the road is sandy, and continues like this as you head south towards Werda. The landmark to look out for is the dry river-bed of the Moselebe, about 49km from Khakhea and 20km from Werda. About 1km to the north of the river is an unmarked turn-off to the west, which will take you along a good and almost completely straight track to Mabuasehube. It's about 145km to the junction with the Tshane-Tshabong road.

Through the Reserve from Tshabong to Kang Unlike the route into the Reserve from the east, this road can be very difficult, rutted and sandy. To travel the 240km from Tshabong to Tshane in one stretch would take around eight to nine hours. The four villages of Tshane, Hukuntsi, Lokgwabe and Lehututu are all within about 10km of one another, and each is worth a visit if you have the time. Beyond this it's another 104km of sandy road to the junction at Kang where you join the more frequented Ghanzi-Gaborone road – three or four hours driving, which take you through a couple of Bushmen settlements.

Tshane, Hukuntsi, Lokgwabe and Lehututu villages

By about 1750, the Kgalagadi people had begun to settle on the eastern and southern edges of the Kalahari, using the pans to provide seasonal water for themselves and their cattle herds. The village of **Lehututu** was the first to be settled, followed within the next 50 years by other villages nearby. Today, Lehututu is very small and a far cry from the once busy commercial centre it was. **Tshane** has an attractive setting by Tshane Pan and an interesting old police station. **Lokgwabe** is notable for having the Hottentot descendants of Simon Cooper who led an unsuccessful rebellion against the German administration of South West Africa in 1904. In a curious deal between the British and German governments, Cooper and his rebel group were given 'protection' by the British administration in Lokgwabe, whilst being indirectly paid by the Germans to stay at home! **Hukuntsi** village is the administrative headquarters of the area and it's possible to pick up basic supplies here.

Gemsbok National Park

Entry only from South Africa, 2WD, South African entrance fees

This massive area is effectively shared between South Africa and Botswana – the South African portion being called the Kalahari Gemsbok National Park, and separated from the Botswanan Gemsbok National Park by only the dry bed of the Nosop River. The Botswanan side has no roads or facilities, remaining purposefully undeveloped so as to provide a game reservoir and retreat from poachers. The southern Kalahari has always suffered from a poaching problem, which is presently getting worse as the game outside the protected area of Kalahari Gemsbok disappears. The scenery is characteristic of the drier areas of the Kalahari with fossil river-beds and high sand dunes.

The best time of year to visit is probably following the rains from March to May, when you can expect to see large herds of gemsbok, springbok, hartebeest, wildebeest and eland – along with lion, hyena and cheetah.

Getting there

The (dirt) roads on the South African side are good and suitable for ordinary 2WD saloon cars, though if you approach the South African entrance from within Botswana you'll need 4WD. Entry to the park is through Twee Rivieren Camp (South Africa) in the south. Entry also used to be possible at Mata Mata Camp from Namibia in the west. However due to an unprecedented amount of traffic using the park as a fast through-route between Namibia and South Africa – and so causing disturbance – the gate has unfortunately been closed. It would nevertheless be worth checking with the authorities on the current situation.

From Botswana to Twee Rivieren   You must first make your way to Bokspits at the extreme southwest corner of the country via the town of Tshabong (see *Getting there* section, *Mabuasehube Game Reserve*, page 269). From Tshabong, there are two possible routes to Bokspits, one staying in Botswana, and the other going through South Africa. The former road follows the (mostly dry) Molopo River, and although used regularly is slow and rough, taking nine or ten hours. Alternatively, you can cross the border post at McCarthy's Rust and travel to Bokspits via Vanzylsrust on good gravel roads. Although about 80km further, it should take you an hour or two less. The park entrance at Twee Rivieren is 55km north of Bokspits.

Where to stay

There are three excellent camps in the Kalahari Gemsbok National Park – Twee Rivieren, Mata Mata and Nosop – all offering chalets, camping sites and basic supplies, including beer and wine! The three main sand roads in the park essentially connect the camps together in a triangle. Do note though that the road from Nosop Camp – north-west along the Nosop River to Unions End, at the Namibian border – is a dead end. You cannot (currently) cross the Namibian border here.

It is advisable to book accommodation in advance during holiday periods from the Chief Director, PO Box 787, Pretoria 1000, South Africa.

Mother of Goats

by Phil Deutschle

In the village of Mapoka, there lived an old woman. She had two goats which she took out each day.

One day, as she was taking her goats out, two young men of the village shouted to her, 'Hello, Mother of Goats!'

The old woman smiled and called back to them, 'Hello, my sons!'

324

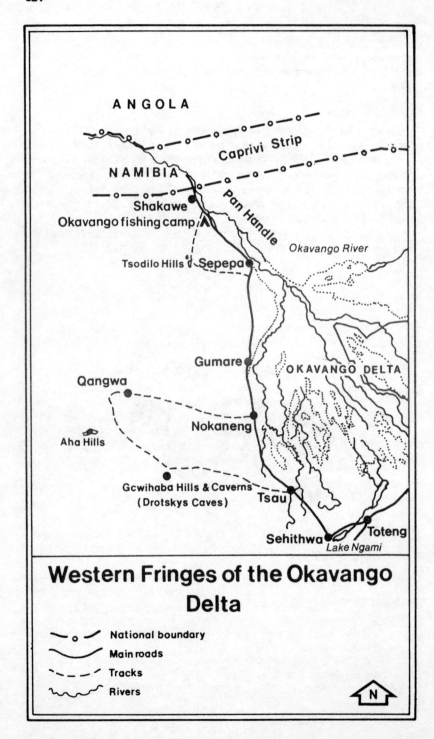

Western Fringes of the Okavango Delta

—o—	National boundary
——	Main roads
- - -	Tracks
∿∿	Rivers

Chapter 22

The Western Fringes

On the western fringes of the Okavango Delta lie some of Botswana's most mysterious and ancient destinations. The main attraction is undoubtedly the Tsodilo Hills (immortalised by Laurens van der Post in his book *The Lost World of the Kalahari*). Lake Ngami, to the south, is fairly easily accessible, yet untouched and rarely visited. For those with two 4WDs in their group, there's a circular route from Tsao to Nokaneng via Qangwa, allowing access to the Gcwihaba Hills (with Drotsky's Caves) and the ancient Aha Hills. This is a fascinating and remote journey through the Kalahari – though it's not an easy route and takes several days.

Access to the region is made easy by the road from Toteng (68km from Maun on the Maun-Ghanzi route) which skirts the edge of the Delta as it heads up to the Caprivi Strip. The road from Sehithwa to Shakawe is mostly tar now, but you still need a high-clearance 4WD to cope with the sand and, in the rainy season, the mud if you drive off this one road. None of these destinations is in national parks or reserves – so no entrance fees.

Lake Ngami
4WD

The existence of a great lake within the Kalahari was known to Europeans from early reports of Bekwena and Batawana tribespeople, though it wasn't reached by them until the mid 19th Century. Livingstone arrived in 1849, with Cotton Oswell and Murray, narrowly beating Andersson, who set out specifically to reach it from present-day Namibia. He described it as 'an immense sheet of water bounded only by the Horizon,' and wrote that it was 'the object of my ambition for years, and for which I have abandoned home and friends and risked my life'.

When to visit
The scene here varies greatly, depending upon whether the Delta's flood –

Ngami's main source of water – has been high enough to overflow into the Nhabe river which feeds the lake. Talk to the operators in Maun, and especially the pilots, because if the lake's empty it's better to save yourself a trip – often it's just a wide expanse of clay.

When flooded, Lake Ngami comes alive with birdlife. From October, the ducks, geese, waders and other northern migrants arrive, lining the muddy shores until the weather cools towards the end of April. The flamingos, both greater and lesser, don't choose their times so carefully – being found here in their thousands whenever the conditions are right for the algae on which they feed. They appear from the shore as a pink haze settled on the water's surface.

Where to stay

There's nowhere specific to stay here, but the land's open enough to camp rough – we asked the local villagers, who suggested going a few kilometres away from the lake itself to avoid the mosquitoes. A wise move. You'll need to be self-sufficient, of course, and don't rely upon any drinkable water here.

Shakawe

This large fishing village stands on the northern banks of the panhandle of the Delta, some 279km from Sehithwa and 13km south of the Mohembo border post on the Caprivi Strip. Driving into the village feels like entering a maze of reed walls, with each surrounding a small kraal, as the track split countless ways between the houses.

It's large enough to make finding the police station (where you must complete border formalities if you're crossing to Caprivi) quite a puzzle: you must head through town towards the river and look for several large, white buildings surrounded by wire fences and probably having 4WDs dotted nearby. The officials can be very relaxed though you'll be sent back here by the border post if you try to miss out this stop.

If you've the time, take a walk along the river which is immediately behind the police station. Sometimes there's a *mokoro* ferry shuttling local people to and from the eastern side of the river, full with their wares to sell or recent buys to take back home.

Where to stay

Driving further downstream, within the next 30km or so, there are several safari camps on the river which cater mainly for fishing and birdwatching – and are more casual than the expensive ones further into the delta. 12km south of Shakawe is **Drotsky's Cabins** (not to be confused with caves!), further still is the **Fishing Camp** and finally **Nxamaseri**, the most expensive of the lot at about P250 per person per night.

Shakawe Fishing Camp   Going south about 17km from Shakawe you come to a crossroads: to the left is the Shakawe Fishing Camp; to the right a sign reading 'Tsodilo Hills' which points, confusingly, to a track that immediately forks into two.

Tsodilo Hills
4WD only

Rising to 400m above the monotony of the Kalahari's thick bush, archaeologists say that the hills have been sporadically inhabited for about 30,000 years – making this one of the world's oldest historical sites. For only about the last millennia has this included Bantu people: previously, for thousands of years, Bushmen (San people) had settled here, hunting, using springs in the hills for water and painting animals (over 2,000 of them) on the rocks. For both Bushmen and Bantu it was a mystical place, 'home of very old and very great spirits' who demanded respect from visitors and as told in *The Lost World of the Kalahari* created so much trouble for some of the first Europeans to visit.

Long ago it must have been, in van der Post's words, '... a great fortress of living bushman culture, a Louvre of the desert filled with treasure'. Though now only a shadow of its former glory, it's well worth a visit if you've the tenacity to reach it and the patience to spend several days there. Some of the individual paintings have been among the most impressive that I've seen on the subcontinent.

Getting there

Air   For flights, inquire at Shakawe Fishing Camp, Drotsky's Cabins or at Shakawe's airstrip, or alternatively talk to the air charter firms in Maun. From the air you'll appreciate the hills' uniqueness within the desert, though miss the excitement as they're first sighted over the tree tops.

Car With a 4WD, there are two tracks to the hills, both of which are through dense bush across vegetated dunes (so fold in your wing mirrors). This difficult driving is made all the worse by corrugations in the sand which, when driven over at anything greater than walking pace, cause the whole vehicle to bounce up and down violently with everybody hitting their heads on the ceiling. You physically can't drive at more than 10kph sometimes.

From the north, turn right at Shakawe Fishing Camp and then fork immediately left onto a small track, no wider than a vehicle. (Do not make the mistake of following the clearer, broader track which forks right.) After about 13km of difficult sandy driving you'll reach a dune crest from where you can see the hills. From here it's a further 30km.

From Sehithwa, take the road northwards to Gumare, and continue past the '1st Restaurant' on the left and the Okavango Bottle Stall, before heading by two large steel storage tanks and out of town. Follow this road for about 56km north, before taking an obvious left turn – which may still have a Botswana museum sign, complete with zebra logo, pointing the way. This is a firm track for about 28km until, shortly after two livestock ponds, it deteriorates into sand for the remaining 24km to the hills.

Of the two approaches, the southern track from Sehithwa is slightly faster and easier, even though longer. Either will take two and a half hours at the minimum.

Apart from the car hire firms in Maun or Katima Mulilo (in Namibia), the Shakawe Fishing Camp or Drotsky's Cabins will sometimes organise trips out to the hills – expect to pay about P350 for a five-seater vehicle with a guide for a day trip to the hills.

Where to stay
Once there, you can camp anywhere in the bush which surrounds the hills – there are good spots between the two main hills, about a kilometre from the Museum's board – though there are no facilities here at all so you must carry in everything that you need and take it away when you go.

What to see and do
The hills form a group of four called, from south to north (and in descending order of size), male, female, and child – with the last remaining nameless. The road from the south approaches with the male hill on the right and passes close to the Bantu settlement (where you must stop and sign the visitors book), before going past the Bushman village on the left and splitting: the left fork goes around the female hill, the right between it and the male hill.

To find your way around to any of the paintings, you'll need a guide – Benjamin speaks good English, and will probably find you before you find him. Several of the Bushmen act as excellent guides, sharing their knowledge of both the bush and the paintings, though as few visitors speak !Kung, communication may be difficult. Consider taking both a Bushman guide and Benjamin to act as a translator.

For those with images of proud, defiant bushmen stalking game on the open plains, the Bushman village at the hills is a sad place, a poignant reminder of the Western world's extermination of an ancient and wiser culture. The few remaining Bushmen people there rely heavily upon passing tourists, selling bows and arrows, ostrich eggshell necklaces, bracelets, and other curios, for money or food. Before bargaining for goods, consider carefully just how long they have taken to make, and how little they're being sold for.

Gcwihaba (Kwihabe) Hills
4WD only
This isolated range of hills, some 150km west of Tsao, houses a rarely visited and spectacular system or caves known as the Gcwihaba Caverns, or

Drotsky's Caves – after Martinus Drotsky, a Ghanzi farmer who was shown the caves by *!Kung* bushmen in 1934.

Getting there

Less than 2km north of Tsao, there's a turning to the west, signposted with one of the Museum's zebra signs and reading 'Drotsky's Cave'. Follow this track over the sandy desert, past a number of pans and through several dry river valleys for about 150km, before taking a signposted left turn onto an even smaller track. This finally reaches the caves after about 26km. You can expect this to take about seven hours of rough, tiring driving – and bringing two 4WDs would be a sensible precaution.

Drotsky's Caves/Gcwihaba Caverns

There are two known entrances to the cave system. The track leads to the main one, with an information board outside it, while the smaller entrance is about 200m from the first, further away from the (dry) river.

Going underground at the main entrance, you'll first enter an outer chamber and then – under a hanging curtain of rock – an inner chamber decorated with huge stalactites, some many metres long. The passage leads on from here through further impressive caverns until it starts to descend more steeply. The route from the other entrance leads through several small caverns to a larger one deep below the surface. Thence a narrow passage does eventually link up with the caves reached from the main entrance. The route is not at all easy as there are many dead-ends.

Warning   Because there's no light at all in the caves, and no one to help in an emergency, you must carry with you several torches, spare batteries and bulbs, emergency matches, and some food and water – just in case you encounter problems.

It's worth spending a few days here: you probably won't visit a more serene, natural part of the desert. The best plan is perhaps to climb the hills in the cool of morning, and venture underground as it starts to get hotter. Camp anywhere, though there's no water at all (even in the caves) so you must be totally self-sufficient.

Aha Hills
4WD only

Split by the Namibian border and, like the Gcwihaba Hills, composed largely of dolomite and limestone, these isolated hills form a plateau of about 250 square kilometres and afford impressive views of the Kalahari all around. They're largely unexplored and it would be surprising not to find Bushman paintings there and possibly cave systems – though there are no reports of any, except for two sink holes, both of which are described as vertical and dangerous, so stay well clear of steep chasms in the rock.

Getting there

Take the turn-off to Drotsky's Caves, north of Tsao, and then continue past the left turn, 26km from the Caves. After about 40km, the track passes the village of Xai Xai and then heads straight for the hills – some 15km to the north. Camp anywhere convenient.

There is an alternative route to return to the main road. Continue northwards from Aha, and after about 60km you'll meet a track of deep sand going east-west, following an old *omuramba* (vague river bed). If you go east, then it's a difficult 170km to Nokaneng, while west leads, after 20km or so, to Dobe – the border village where much of the research into Bushman culture was originally done.

Don't expect to average more than 30kph for any of this driving, and remember how heavy it is on fuel – the nearest reliable supplies being at Maun or in the Caprivi Strip (though Shakawe Fishing Camp, Gumare or Sehithwa are worth checking in an emergency). There is traffic along here, though it's very infrequent, so come in a two vehicle party – and be fully equipped with fuel, food and water for your whole trip, plus some to spare.

Further information

Maps of Drotsky's Caves and information on Aha's sink holes can be found in *Botswana Notes and Records*, volume 6, 1974. It's the journal of the Botswana Society, of which the National Archives, in Gaborone, have a copy.

Quoted in *The Okavango River* by C J Andersson:

'There's an island that lies on West Africa's shore,
Where the penguins have lived since the flood or before,
And raised up a hill there, a mile high or more.
This hill is all guano, and lately 'tis shown,
That finer potatoes and turnips are grown,
By means of this compost, than ever were known;
And the peach and the nectarine, the apple, the pear,
Attain such a size that the gardeners stare,
And cry, 'Well! I never saw fruit like that 'ere!'
One cabbage thus reared, as a paper maintains,
Weighed twenty-one stone, thirteen pounds and six grains,
So no wonder Guano celebrity gains.'

Cattle, Wildlife and the Veterinary Cordon Fences
Edited from an article by Damien Lewis

Cattle ranching is having as disastrous an effect on Botswana's wildlife as it has had on the Amazon rainforests. Thousands of miles of cattle fences, strung out across the savannah and bushlands of Botswana, have caused the death of countless wild animals and overgrazing has led to the desertification of huge areas of land. Now, a new fencing programme in the north of the country heralds the expansion of cattle ranching into Botswana's last isolated wilderness – the Okavango Delta.

The explosion of ranching (fuelled partly by World Bank livestock loans and by highly subsidised beef prices paid by the EU) has had catastrophic ecological consequences, according to a recent Greenpeace report, 'causing serious overgrazing, environmental degradation and the decline of wildlife'. Yet the most serious impact of the ranching business has been the *Veterinary Cordon Fencing* (VCF) policy, launched in 1954 by the Botswanan Department of Animal Health.

The fences are designed to keep Botswana's cattle and natural wildlife separate from each other, in the belief that the dreaded *foot-and-mouth disease* is spread from wildlife (especially buffalo) to cattle and that it can be controlled by segregation. Like the beef industry itself, the fencing programme is driven by the EU, whose disease regulations dictate which animals may be imported to the Community. More than 3,000 kilometres of fencing have been built across huge areas of the country. Yet there is little evidence of the effectiveness of this fencing policy in preventing the spread of disease. The fences criss-cross the country with no relation to regional ecology and block off the wildlife from their traditional migration routes, often with devastating effects. Mark and Delia Owens – zoologists who lived in the Kalahari for seven years between 1974 and 1981, studying the predators – claim that the fences are destroying game populations. They also assert that no one knows for certain that wild animals are a source of infection, or that foot-and-mouth disease can be held in check by the fences.

The most seriously affected area is the central Kalahari – now almost entirely enclosed by the fences. In 1964, at the Kuke fence, 80,000 wildebeest perished, piled up against the wire. Again in 1983, 50,000 wildebeest met their death on the Kuke. Wildlife has died entangled in the wire, or searching for water and grazing in the parched lands left behind them. Bushmen say that elephant, rhino, buffalo, roan, sable and tsessebe, which once regularly roamed the northern Kalahari, are now absent from the area. A recent study funded by the EU found that the central Kalahari has lost 99% of its wildebeest and 95% of its hartebeest over the last decade. Despite this record of wildlife fatalities, the Government of Botswana has taken few steps to review its fencing policy. Indeed, the new fencing programme in northern Botswana indicates the Government's continuing commitment to the VCFs. The first of the new fences will be 100 kilometres long, stretching across the north of the Okavango Delta. It will extend the 250 kilometre long fence that already runs along Okavango's western and southern flanks and is the first step in a plan to fence in all of northern Ngamiland. The fence – over five feet high and strung with wire and thick steel cable – will be impenetrable to all but the most determined of adult elephants or agile antelope. Zebra and wildebeest are already reported dying along new fences built in 1990, in the Nata region of north-east Ngamiland.

Despite the deadly effects of fences across Botswana and the proximity of the wildlife-rich Okavango Delta, no environmental impact assessment has been carried out for the new fencing scheme. Many animal species migrate to and from the Delta, to take advantage of the availability of grazing and water during the wet and dry seasons. Local people, with in-depth knowledge of the delta and its wildlife, claim the Government has seriously underestimated the size and movements of animal herds, and the impact the fence will have on them. Although Botswana's Department of Wildlife admits that some animals will die on the fences, this is an 'acceptable level of mortality'. Overcrowding of wildlife within the fenced-off areas will be dealt with by 'active management', or culling.

Construction of the fence is well under way. Yet while its justification in terms of disease control is questionable, its effect on wildlife may be disastrous. Greenpeace says 'it heralds the expansion of cattle into northern Botswana...[which] threatens the stability of the region and jeopardises the most ecologically sensitive part of the Okavango Delta, its source'.

While the scientific evidence against the cattle-ranching is very strong, some scientists question the allegations of the anti-fence lobby. The authors felt that the following summary of a paper by Alec Campbell, a Botswanan naturalist, would be of interest.

Wildlife disasters are nothing new. During the early 1930s, after a prolonged drought, wildebeest came out of the central Kalahari only to die in their thousands at Sebele, Mosomane, and around Francistown and Maun. This was before the advent of the new cordon fences and a major cause of death then was the lack of suitable, or any, food during the previous drought years. The contention is that the pressure of expanding human and livestock (especially cattle) populations has progressively squeezed the desert's ecosystem over this last century. The competition for water and food with the cattle has upset the natural game species in the desert and this encroachment has been the major factor in the relatively recent loss of zebra, rhino, giraffe and buffalo from the central Kalahari. However, wildebeest have a population structure which is better suited than most species to recover after herds have been wiped out by famine or drought. Thus, although not truly adapted to the desert, they have come to dominate the central Kalahari this century. Their numbers are naturally subject to large fluctuations, growing bigger and bigger until over-population and drought cause the population to collapse.

During recent years the fences have received much of the blame for these crashes in the wildebeest population, and also the apparent decline in Kalahari species in general. It would appear from the evidence that these changes precede the fences which have really only affected the wildebeest and, even then, not to any permanent extent. So long as the fences are used as a scapegoat, the real problems affecting wildlife in the Kalahari will remain unsolved.

Summary from *A Comment on Kalahari Wildlife and the Khukhe Fence, Botswana Notes and Records* (Volume 13), by Alec Campbell (currently Senior Curator at the National Museum and Art Gallery, Gaborone, Botswana).

Bibliography

Reference books

Lake Ngami and *The River Okavango* by Charles John Andersson. Published 1856-61 in London. Fascinating records of one of the region's first white explorers.

Travels and Researches in Southern Africa by David Livingstone. Published 1857 in London. A record of the travels of the continent's most famous missionary and explorer.

Explorations in South-West Africa by Thomas Baines. Published 1864 in London. The travels of the artist who gave his name to the clump of baobab trees south of Nxai National Park, Botswana.

The Rock Paintings of Southern Africa by the Abbé Henri Breuil. Published by Trianon Press Ltd, from 1955-60 in four volumes and distributed through Faber and Faber.

The Skeleton Coast by Amy Schoeman covers the area in detail with stunning photographs. A classic coffee-table book.

The Namib by Dr Mary Seely. Published 1987 in Windhoek, by Shell Oil. A detailed work on the desert's origins, with descriptions of many sites and the animals and plants that live there. This paperback is well worth getting when you arrive in Namibia.

Namib by David Coulson. Published 1991 by Sidgwick and Jackson. Another coffee-table book of breathtaking pictures covering the whole of the desert.

Namibia – Africa's Harsh Paradise by Anthony Bannister and Peter Johnson. Published 1990 by New Holland Ltd, London. Yet another for the coffee-table, this covers the whole country and concentrates on the Bushmen and Himba people.

Namibia – The Facts. Published by IDAF Publications Ltd, London in 1989. Concentrates mainly on the liberation struggle over the last ten years. Highly emotive text and pictures!

History of Resistance in Namibia by Peter H Katjavivi. Co-published by: James Currey, London; OAU in Addis Ababa; Unesco Press, Paris. Rather more 'scholarly' than *Namibia – The Facts*, it's impressive in its detail.

Okavango: Jewel of the Kalahari by Karen Ross. published 1987 by BBC Publications, London. Another one for the coffee-table, with snippets of excellent background information.

Okavango: Sea of Land, Land of Water, P. Johnson and A.Bannister. New Holland. £17.95. A beautiful book of photos.

Botswana: a Brush with the Wild, Paul Augustinus. £43.75. Illustrated by colour paintings, sketches, and photos; records the author's experiences after living in Botswana several years.

Pamphlet entitled *The History of Rehoboth* by Robert Camby is very useful for understanding Rehoboth's history.

Elephant Talk article: National Geographic, Vol 176, No 2, August 1989, pp 264-277. On infrasound communication in elephants, with some interesting comments about desert elephants in the Hoarusib river.

Etosha: Namibia's kingdom of animals article: National Geographic, Vol 163, No.3, March 1983. A general article about managing the park – with discussion of the problems of waterholes, anthrax, and too many lions!

Travelogue

Cry of the Kalahari by Mark and Delia Owens. Published 1985 by William Collins, subsequently in paperback by Fontana (1986-1989). A recent book about the experiences of two American scientists who spent seven years in the wilds of the Central Kalahari Game Reserve studying the wildlife.

The Lost World of the Kalahari by Laurens van der Post. First published in 1958, many subsequent reprints by Penguin. Laurens van der Post's classic account of how he journeyed into the heart of the Kalahari Desert in search of a 'pure' Bushmen group – eventually found at the Tsodilo Hills. His almost mystical description of the Bushmen is fascinating, so long as you can cope with the rather dated turgid prose.

Serowe: Village of the Rain Wind by Bessie Head. Published by Heinemann 1981, last reprinted 1988. By one of Botswana's leading writers, it evokes the history of Serowe through the eyes of some of its inhabitants and contrasts this to the village at present.

The Sheltering Desert by two German geologists (Henno Martin and Hermann Korn) who lived out the war hiding in the Kuiseb canyon promises to be interesting.

Guide books

Rough Guide to Zimbabwe and Botswana by Barbara McCrea and Tony Pinchuck (published 1993). Contains good information on both countries, especially Zimbabwe.

No Frills Guide to Zimbabwe and Botswana by David Else, Bradt Publications. This slim volume gives conveniently brief, up-to-date information if you are travelling into Zimbabwe also.

Visitors Guide to Botswana by Mike Main and John and Sandra Fowkes. Published by Southern Books, Johannesburg (1991). Written primarily for the visitor with a 4WD vehicle, the book has excellent route descriptions on hard-to-get-to places and is recommended for these. Some route descriptions are now very outdated though.

For a complete bibliography on Namibia (Botswana is still in preparation) see *Namibia* by Stanley and Elna Shoeman, published by Clio Press, Oxford.
    Also the *African Travel Resource Guide and Bibliography* by Louis Taussig, published by Hans Zell Associates, Oxford. (Split into two volumes, the *Eastern and Southern Africa* volume will cover this region.)

South Africa Guide by John Platter. Published by John and Erica Platter, Somerset West, South Africa. An excellent pocket guide which visitng wine-buffs will find indispensable.

INDEX

Come lose yourself in a land as vast and big as the sky.

A place where the mountains are made of sand

and the plains stretch to an endless horizon.

Where the quiver tree speaks of the dawn of creation

and the wild roams free from the intrusion of man.

Come to Namibia and find a land of never-ending discovery.

Perhaps it's from living in the land of wide open spaces that we appreciate how space can make a world of a difference to your journey. So on all our flights across Namibia into Africa, and across Africa to Europe, we removed seats from our cabins so that you can stretch out in spacious comfort.

Come fly in the care and comfort of the airline that has been carrying passengers across the wide open spaces of Southern Africa for more than 40 years.

For further information contact your local travel agent or phone Air Namibia in London: 081 543 2122. Fax. 081 543 3398.

Air Namibia